INTERNATIONAL ASSOCIATION OF EGYPTOLOGISTS
ASSOCIATION INTERNATIONALE DES ÉGYPTOLOGUES

ANNUAL EGYPTOLOGICAL BIBLIOGRAPHY

BIBLIOGRAPHIE ÉGYPTOLOGIQUE ANNUELLE

1979

Compiled by / Composée par

L. M. J. ZONHOVEN

with the collaboration of / avec la collaboration de

INGE HOFMANN

and / et

JAC. J. JANSSEN

ARIS & PHILLIPS LTD

British Library Cataloguing in Publication Data

Annual Egyptological bibliography. - 1979
1. Egyptology Bibliography Periodicals
016.932.007.2   DT60

ISBN 0 85668 220 9

Volume 33 (1979)

© International Association of Egyptologists 1983. All rights reserved. No part of this publication may be reproduced or transmitted in any form or by any means, electronic or mechanical including photocopying, without the permission in writing of the publisher.

Published by Aris & Phillips Ltd for the International Association of Egyptologists.
Printed in England by Aris & Phillips Ltd, Teddington House, Warminster BA12 8PQ.

CONTENTS

Systematic Classification	iv
Acknowledgements	vi
Foreword	vii
Abbreviations	viii
List of Authors and Titles	1 - 295
Index of Authors	297 - 305

SYSTEMATIC CLASSIFICATION

I GENERAL   entry number 79...
   a. History of Egyptology; obituaries   1-25
   b. Present-day Egyptology: progress reports,
      methodology, prefaces, etc.   26-82
   c. Research tools: bibliographies, indexes,
      encyclopaedic works   83-105
   d. Egypt's legacy and aftermath; Hellenistic
      world; classical authors   106-138
   e. Varia   139-150

II SCRIPT AND LANGUAGE
   a. Scripts   151-164
   b. Grammar   165-200
   c. Lexicography, expressions, proper names, epithets   201-233

III TEXTS AND PHILOLOGY
   a. Epigraphy   234-266
   b. Literary, historical, autobiographical   267-320
   c. Religious, magical   321-346
   d. Socio-economic, juridical, administrative   347-361
   e. Demotic and related material   362-390
   f. Coptic   391-410
   g. Relations between Egyptian and Biblical literature 411-421
   h. General and varia   422-424

IV HISTORY
   a. Up to the New Kingdom   425-434
   b. From the New Kingdom   435-458
   c. International affairs   459-493

V ART AND ARCHAEOLOGY
   a. Methodology of archaeology and museology;
      technological research   494-505
   b. Excavation reports
      1. Lower Egypt and Memphis and surroundings   506-532
      2. Upper Egypt   533-559
      3. Surrounding areas and countries   560-574
   c. Museum collections and exhibitions   575-623
   d. Monuments   624-640
      CEDAE   641-648
   e. Architecture   649-658
   f. Sculpture   659-686
   g. Relief and painting   687-711
   h. Tomb equipment, furniture and cult objects   712-730
   i. Minor arts, small objects, utensils, pottery, dress 731-770
   j. Scarabs and seals   771-785
   k. General and varia   786-800

VI RELIGION
    a. Gods, mythology, cosmology, syncretism, symbolism   801-822
    b. Theology, religious attitude, ethics and world view   823-835
    c. Funerary belief and funerary cult   836-838
    d. Temple, priests, cult and ritual   839-849
    e. Kingship   850-854
    f. Magic and popular religion   855-858
    g. General and varia   859-862

VII SOCIETY AND CULTURE
    a. Civil organisation, titles and functions, military organisation   863-881
    b. Economy and law; economic activities   882-899
    c. Prosopography, genealogies   900-908
    d. Cultural interrelations   909-926
    e. General and varia   927-932

VII SCIENCE AND TECHNOLOGY
    a. Science and medicine   933-939
    b. Technology   940-947

IX THE COUNTRY AND NEIGHBOURING AREAS
    a. Natural environment   948-957
    b. Topography, toponymy, maps   958-989
    c. Physical anthropology and mummies   990-1011

X NUBIAN STUDIES   1012-1088

ACKNOWLEDGEMENTS

The editor acknowledges the financial assistance of UNESCO (subvention CA.2/9 in 1980, under the auspices of the International Council for Philosophy and Humanic Studies, ICPHS) in collecting the material for this volume.

Other grateful acknowledgements must be made for the permission from Leiden State University to the editor to work on the AEB project, and for the financial contributions kindly given by the following institutions in 1980:

Ægyptologisk Institut, København Universitet,
Centre d'Études Orientales, Genève,
Deutsches Archäologisches Institut, Berlin-Cairo,
Durham University, Durham,
Egypt Exploration Society, London,
The Griffith Institute, Oxford,
Heidelberger Akademie der Wissenschaften, Heidelberg,
The Metropolitan Museum of Art, New York,
Museum of Fine Arts, Boston, Mass.,
Oosters Genootschap in Nederland, Leiden,
The Oriental Institute, The University of Chicago, Chicago, Ill.,
Royal Ontario Museum, Toronto,
Schweizerisches Institut für Ägyptische Bauforschung und Altertumskunde, Kairo,
Société Française d'Égyptologie, Paris,
University of Liverpool, Liverpool,
The University Museum, The University of Pennsylvania, Philadelphia, Pa.,
Kon. Vitterhets-, Historie- och Antikvitetsakademien, Stockholm.

Adres van de redacteur/Editor's address
Adresse du rédacteur/Anschrift des Schriftleiters:

L.M.J. Zonhoven, Editor,
Annual Egyptological Bibliography,
Instituut voor Egyptologie,
P.B. 9515,
2300 RA LEIDEN.

FOREWORD

This volume is one with significant changes. Professor Janssen has retired from the position of responsible editor from this edition onwards, owing to the demands of the professorship at Leiden University. I feel certain that I speak in the name of all Egyptologists when I thank him for his exacting contribution to the cause of Egyptology by his undertaking of the editorship of the Bibliography from AEB 1966, published in 1971, to AEB 1978, published in 1982.

From this volume onwards the AEB will be published in a systematic arrangement, with an authors' register added, which was compiled for the present edition by Mrs Jana Loose. I am very indebted to Mr H.O. Willems, the assistant of the AEB, who has taken care of the scheme of classification and of the distribution of the entries over the subject headings, some 50 in total. He was also responsible for the cross-references, which for convenience are placed immediately below the subject headings. That some of these comprise a considerable number of entries, while others have only few, turned out to be unavoidable. That on the other hand, some major subjects have only relatively few entries but many cross-references, lies in the nature of the subjects, which, as in the case of religion, pervade the Egyptian culture and, in consequence, the Egyptological literature. As a last remark on the systematic arrangement, it depended on the overall approach of a book or an article, subject-oriented or text-oriented, as to where the entry was here included.

Finally, the indication that an entry is a monograph, formerly the book-scroll sign above the number, is now the printing of the number in italic type.

L.M.J.Z.

LIST OF ABBREVIATIONS

1. *Periodicals*, Festschriften, *and Serials*:

Acts 1st ICE: Acts. First International Congress of Egyptology – Actes. Premier Congrès International d'Égyptologie – Akten. Erster Internationaler Ägyptologenkongress – وثائق ۰ المــؤتـمـر الــدولى الأول للــمـصـريـات ۰ Cairo-Le Caire-Kairo- القاهرة, October 2-10, 1976. Edited by Walter F. Reineke, Berlin, Akademie-Verlag, 1979 (17 x 24.5 cm; 704 p., fig., maps, plans, 93 pl.) = Schriften zur Geschichte und Kultur des Alten Orients, 14; at head of title: Akademie der Wissenschaften der DDR. Zentralinstitut für alte Geschichte und Archäologie; rev. *BiOr* 38 (1981), 28 (Hans Goedicke).

Aegyptus: Aegyptus. Rivista Italiana di Egittologia e di Papirologia, Milano 59 (1979).
Address: Università Cattolica (Scuola di Papirologia), Largo A. Gemelli 1, 20123 Milano, Italia.

AfO: Archiv für Orientforschung, Horn 26 (1978/1979).
Address: Verlag Ferdinand Berger & Söhne OHG, Wiener Strasse 21, A-3850 Horn, NÖ., Österreich.

Africa in Antiquity: Africa in Antiquity. The Arts of Ancient Nubia and the Sudan. Proceedings of the Symposium Held in Conjunction with the Exhibition, Brooklyn, September 29 - October 1, 1978. Edited by Fritz Hintze, Berlin, Akademie-Verlag, 1979 (17.2 x 24 cm; 199 p., 118 fig., 28 pl.) = Meroitica. Schriften zur altsudanesischen Geschichte und Archäologie, Herausgegeben von Fritz Hintze, 5; at head of title: Humboldt-Universität zu Berlin. Bereich Ägyptologie und Sudanarchäologie.   Pr. M 40

AJA: American Journal of Archaeology, [New York] 83 (1979).
Address: General Secretary, Archaeological Institute of America, 260 West Broadway, New York, N.Y. 10012, U.S.A.

Antiquity: Antiquity. A Quarterly Review of Archaeology, [Cambridge] 53 (1979).
Address: Heffers Printers Ltd, 104 Hills Road, Cambridge CB2 1LW, G.B.

Archaeology: Archaeology. A Magazine Dealing with the Antiquity of the World, [New York] 32 (1979).
Address: Archaeology, 260 West Broadway, New York, N.Y. 10013, U.S.A.

ASAE: Annales du Service des Antiquités de l'Égypte, Le Caire 63 (1979) = Mélanges Selim Hassan II.
   Address: Service des Antiquités de l'Égypte, Le Caire, Égypte (R.A.U.)

Aspekte der spätägyptischen Religion: Aspekte der spätägyptischen Religion, herausgegeben von Wolfhart Westendorf, Wiesbaden, Otto Harrassowitz, 1979 (17 x 24 cm; 115 p., 1 fig.) = Göttinger Orientforschungen. Veröffentlichungen des Sonderforschungsbereiches Orientalistik an der Georg-August-Universität Göttingen. IV. Reihe: Ägypten, 9; rev. ZDMG 131 (1981), 202 (J. v. B[eckerath]).

BASOR: Bulletin of the American Schools of Oriental Research Number 233 (February, 1979), 234 (April 1979), 235 (October 1979) and 236 (Fall 1979).
   Address: American Schools of Oriental Research, Publications Office, 126 Inman Str., Cambridge, Massachusetts 02139, U.S.A.

Beiträge zur meroitischen Grammatik: Fritz Hintze, Beiträge zur meroitischen Grammatik, mit Kommentaren von M. Bierwisch, N.B. Millet, K.-H. Priese, R. Ružička, W. Schenkel, B.G. Trigger, Abdelgadir M. Abdalla, Berlin, Akademie-Verlag, 1979 (17.2 x 24 cm; 214 p.) = Meroitica. Schriften zur altsudanesischen Geschichte und Archäologie. Herausgegeben von Fritz Hintze, 3; at head of title: Humboldt-Universität zu Berlin. Bereich Ägyptologie und Sudanarchäologie; rev. *BiOr* 38 (1981), 57-64 (Inge Hofmann).   Pr. M 38

BES: Bulletin of the Egyptological Seminar, New York 1 (1979).
   Address: Scholars Press, 101 Salem Str., P.O. Box 2268, Chico, CA 95927, U.S.A.

BIFAO: Bulletin de l'Institut français d'Archéologie orientale, Le Caire 79 (1979) = Volume dédié à la mémoire de Charles Kuentz, with portrait.
   Address: Imprimerie de l'Institut français d'Archéologie orientale, 37 Rue el Cheikh Aly Youssef (ex-rue Mounira), Le Caire, Egypte (R.A.U.).

BiOr: Bibliotheca Orientalis, Leiden 36 (1979).
   Address: P.B. 9515, 23oo RA, Leiden, Nederland.

BMMA: Bulletin. The Metropolitan Museum of Art 36 (1978-1979).
   Address: The Metropolitan Museum of Art, Fifth Avenue at 82nd St., New York, N.Y. 10028, U.S.A.

BSFE: Bulletin de la Société française d'Égyptologie. Réunions trimestrielles. Communications archéologiques No. 84 (mars 1979); No. 85 (juin 1979); No. 86 (octobre 1979).
   Address: Mme. F. Le Corsu, Cabinet d'Égyptologie, Collège de France, 11 Place Marcelin-Berthelot, Paris 5e, France.

Bulletin. Société d'Égyptologie: Bulletin. Société d'Égyptologie, Genève, Genève 1 (Mai 1979); 2 (Novembre 1979).
   Address: Secrétariat de la Société d'Égyptologie, 86, St. Jean, 1201 Genève, Suisse; rev. *AfO* 27 (1980), 185-186 (Günther Vittmann); *GM* Heft 39 (1980), 41-44 (Friedrich Junge).

CdE: Chronique d'Égypte. Bulletin périodique de la Fondation égyptologique Reine Elisabeth. Bruxelles LIV, Nos 107-108 (1979).
Address: Fondation égyptologique "Reine Elisabeth". Musées Royaux d'Art et d'Histoire, Parc du Cinquantenaire, B 1040-Bruxelles, Belgique.

CRIPEL: Cahier de Recherches de l'Institut de Papyrologie et d'Égyptologie de Lille, 5 [1979] = Études sur l'Égypte et le Soudan anciens.
Address: Presses Universitaires de Lille, 9 Rue Auguste Angellier, 59000 Lille, France.

Egitto e Vicino Oriente: Egitto e Vicino Oriente. Rivista della sezione orientalistica dell'Istituto di Storia Antica Università degli Studi di Pisa, Pisa 2 (1979).
Address: Giardini editori e stampatori de Pisa, Via Santa Bibbiana 28, 56100 Pisa, Italia.

Egyptology and the Social Sciences: Egyptology and the Social Sciences. Five Studies. Edited by Kent R. Weeks. With Contributions by Manfred Bietak, Gerhard Haeny, Donald B. Redford, Bruce G. Trigger, Kent R. Weeks, Cairo, The American University in Cairo Press, 1979 (15 x 23 cm; X + 144 p., 2 maps, 8 plans, 2 fig., 1 table); rev. *JSSEA* 11 (1981), 111-114 (Edmund S. Meltzer).

Enchoria: Enchoria. Zeitschrift für Demotistik und Koptologie. Herausgegeben von E. Lüddeckens, H.-J. Thissen, K.-Th. Zauzich, in Kommission bei Otto Harrassowitz, Wiesbaden 9 (1979).
Address: Otto Harrassowitz, Taunusstrasse 5, Postfach 349, 6200 Wiesbaden, Bundesrepublik Deutschland.

Études et Travaux: Études et Travaux, Warszawa 11 (1979).
Address: PWN-Éditions Scientifiques de Pologne, Warszawa, Pologne.

Festschrift Elmar Edel: Festschrift Elmar Edel. 12. März 1979. Unter Mitwirkung von Agnes Wuckelt und Karl-Joachim Seyfried herausgegeben von Manfred Görg und Edgar Pusch, Bamberg, 1979 (21 x 29.8 cm; XII + 499 p., 7 pl., 1 map, 17 plans, 9 tables, 30 fig., frontispiece); series: Ägypten und Altes Testament. Studien zu Geschichte, Kultur und Religion Ägyptens und des Alten Testaments, 1.   Pr. DM 105

Glimpses of Ancient Egypt: Orbis Aegyptiorum Speculum. Glimpses of Ancient Egypt. Studies in Honour of H.W. Fairman. Edited by John Ruffle, G.A. Gaballa and Kenneth A. Kitchen, Warminster, Aris & Phillips Ltd, 1979 (20.8 x 29.7 cm; X + 201 p., frontispiece = portrait, 5 plans, 3 tables, 1 chart, 24 fig., 62 ill.); rev. *Acta Archaeologica Academiae Scientiarum Hungaricae* 32 (1980), 475-476 (L. Castiglione).
                                                                Pr. £12.50

GM: Göttinger Miszellen. Beiträge zur ägyptologischen Diskussion, Göttingen Hefte 31-36 (1979).
Address: Seminar für Ägyptologie der Universität, 34 Göttingen, Prinzenstrasse 21, Bundesrepublik Deutschland.

Hommages Sauneron I-II: Hommages à la mémoire de Serge Sauneron 1927-1976. I: Égypte pharaonique. II: Égypte post-pharaonique, Le Caire, Institut français d'archéologie orientale, 1979 (20 x 27 cm; I: VI + 500 p., fig., plans, maps, 54 pl., frontispiece = portrait; II: 496 p., fig., plans, maps, 40 pl., frontispiece = portrait) = Bibliothèque d'Étude, 81-82.

JAOS: Journal of the American Oriental Society, New Haven, Connecticut 99 (1979).
Address: American Oriental Society, 329 Sterling Memorial Library, Yale Station, New Haven, Connecticut 06250, U.S.A.

JARCE: Journal of the American Research Center in Egypt, Princeton, New Jersey 16 (1979).
Address: J.J. Augustin Publisher, Locust Valley, New York 11560, U.S.A.

JEA: The Journal of Egyptian Archaeology, London 65 (1979).
Address: Honorary Treasurer of the Egypt Exploration Society, 2-3 Doughty Mews, London WC1N 2PG, Great Britain.

JNES: Journal of Near Eastern Studies, Chicago, Illinois 38 (1979).
Address: University of Chicago Press, 5801 Ellis Avenue, Chicago, Illinois 60637, U.S.A.

JSSEA: The SSEA Journal, Toronto 9 (1978-1979).
Address: The Society for the Study of Egyptian Antiquities, 30 Chestnut Park, Toronto, Ontario, M4W 1W6, Canada.

MDAIK: Mitteilungen des Deutschen Archäologischen Instituts Abteilung Kairo, Wiesbaden 35 (1979).
Address: Verlag Philipp von Zabern, P.O.B. 4065, Mainz/Rhein, Bundesrepublik Deutschland.

Mundus: Mundus. A Quarterly Review of German Research Contributions on Asia, Africa and Latin America. Arts and Science, Stuttgart.
Address: Wissenschaftliche Verlagsgesellschaft mbH, Postfach 40, 7000 Stuttgart 1, Bundesrepublik Deutschland.

Newsletter ARCE: Newsletter of the American Research Center in Egypt, Princeton, N.J. Nos 107 (Winter 1978/1979); 108 (Spring 1979); 109 (Summer 1979); 110 (Fall 1979).
Address: 20 Nassau Street, Princeton, N.J. 08540, U.S.A.

OLZ: Orientalistische Literaturzeitung, Berlin 74 (1979).
Address: Akademie-Verlag GmbH, Leipzigerstrasse 3-4, 108 Berlin.

OMRO: Oudheidkundige Mededelingen uit het Rijksmuseum van Oudheden te Leiden (Nuntii ex museo antiquario Leidensi), Leiden 59-60 (1978-1979).
Address: Rijksmuseum van Oudheden, Rapenburg 28, Leiden, Nederland.

Oriens Antiquus: Oriens Antiquus. Rivista del Centro per le Antichità e la Storia dell' Arte del Vicino Oriente, Roma 18 (1979).
   Address: Centro per le Antichità e la Storia dell' Arte del Vicino Oriente, Via Caroncini 27, 00197 Roma, Italia.

Orientalia: Orientalia. Commentarii trimestres a facultate studiorum orientis antiqui pontificii instituti biblici in lucem editi in urbe, [Roma] Nova Series 48 (1979).
   Address: Pontificium Institutum Biblicum, Piazza della Pilotta 35, I-00187 Roma, Italia.

RdE: Revue d'Égyptologie, Paris 31 (1979).
   Address: Librarie C. Klincksiek, 11 rue de Lille, Paris 7ᵉ, France.

Le rêve égyptien: Le rêve égyptien = Silex No 13, 1979 (16 x 24 cm; 144 p., 53 ill., 4 fig.).   Pr. FF 30
   Address: Silex, BP 812 RP, 38035 Grenoble Cedex, France.

Rivista: Rivista degli Studi Orientali, Roma.
   Address: Dott. Giovanni Bardi editore, Salita de crescenzi 16, Roma, Italia.

SAK: Studien zur Altägyptischen Kultur, Hamburg 7 (1979).
   Address: Helmut Buske Verlag, Hamburg, Bundesrepublik Deutschland.

Sarapis: Sarapis. The American Journal of Egyptology, Chicago 5, No. 1 (1979).
   Address: Sarapis, 1155 E. 58th Street, Chicago, Ill. 60637, U.S.A.

State and Temple Economy in the Ancient Near East: State and Temple Economy in the Ancient Near East. I-II. Proceedings of the International Conference Organized by the Katholieke Universiteit Leuven from the 10th to the 14th of April 1978. Edited by Edward Lipinski, Leuven, Departement Oriëntalistiek, 1979 (15.6 x 23.8 cm; 2 vols, XVI + 780 p., 1 map, 4 charts [3 folding], 2 pl.) = Orientalia Lovaniensia Analecta, 5-6.

Studien zu altägyptischen Lebenslehren: Studien zu altägyptischen Lebenslehren. Herausgegeben von Erik Hornung und Othmar Keel, Freiburg Schweiz, Universitätsverlag/Göttingen, Vandenhoeck & Ruprecht, 1979 (15.5 x 23.5 cm; 392 p.) = Orbis Biblicus et Orientalis, 28; rev. *Liber Annuus*. *Studium Biblicum Franciscanum* 30 (1980), 428-430 (A. Niccacci).

Шампольон и дешифровка: Ж.Ф. Шампольон и дешифровка египетских иероглифов, Москва, Издательство "Наука". Главная редакция восточной литературы, 1979 (14.2 x 21.6 cm; 137 p., 7 fig., 13 ill.); at head of title: Академия Наук СССР. Институт Востоковедения.   Pr. 95 коп.

Ugarit-Forschungen: Ugarit-Forschungen, Kevelaer/Neukirchen-Vluyn 11 (1979) = Festschrift für Claude F.A. Schaeffer zum 80. Geburtstag am 6. März 1979.

ВДИ: Вестник Древней Истории, Москва 1 (147)-4(150), 1979.
   Address: Москва В-36, ул. Дмитрия Ульнова. Д. 19, Комн. 237, Институт всеобщей Истории, АН СССР.

WZKM: Wiener Zeitschrift für die Kunde des Morgenlandes, Wien 71 (1979).
   Address: Selbstverlag der Wiener Zeitschrift für die Kunde des Morgenlandes, Universitätsstrasse 7 V, A-1010 Wien 1, Österreich.

ZÄS: Zeitschrift für ägyptische Sprache und Altertumskunde, Berlin 106 (1979).
   Address: Akademie-Verlag GmbH, Leipzigerstrasse 3-4, 108 Berlin.

ZDMG: Zeitschrift der Deutschen Morgenländischen Gesellschaft, Wiesbaden.
   Address: Franz Steiner Verlag GmbH, Bahnhofstrasse 39, Postfach 743, 62 Wiesbaden, Bundesrepublik Deutschland.

2. *Other Abbreviations*:

AEB:	*Annual Egyptological Bibliography/Bibliographie égyptologique annuelle*	M.K.:	Middle Kingdom
		N.K.:	New Kingdom
		O.Eg.:	Old Egyptian
B.D.:	Book of the Dead	O.K.:	Old Kingdom
cfr:	*confer*, compare	O.T.:	Old Testament
cm:	centimetre(s)	p.:	page(s)
col.:	column	pl.:	plate(s)
C.T.:	Coffin Texts	pr.:	price
etc.:	*et cetera*	P.T.:	Pyramid Texts
fig.:	figure(s)	publ.:	publication(s)
F.I.P.:	First Intermediate Period	rev.:	review *or* summary
ill.:	illustration(s)	S.I.P.	Second Intermediate Period
J.J.J.:	J.J. Janssen	T.I.P.	Third Intermediate Period
km:	kilometre(s)	Urk.:	Urkunden
L. Eg.:	Late Egyptian		
m:	metre(s)		
M. Eg.:	Middle Egyptian		

LIST OF AUTHORS AND TITLES

I. GENERAL

a. History of Egyptology; obituaries

See also our numbers 79115; 79538; 79598; 79611; 79612; 79617; 79623; 79788 and 791022.

79001   Anonymous, Eckley Brinton Coxe, Jr., *Expedition*, Philadelphia, Penn. 21, No. 2 (Winter 1979), 44, with 1 ill.

   Biographical note on one of the benefactors of the University Museum, Philadelphia.
   Compare our numbers 79021, 79026, 79527, 79535, 79547, 79548 and 79550.

79002   Anonymous, Professor Sami Gabra, *Newsletter ARCE* No. 108 (Spring 1979), 7.

   Obituary notice.

79003   BLUMENTHAL, Elke, Ägyptologie in Leipzig bis zum zweiten Weltkrieg, *Wissenschaftliche Zeitschrift der Karl-Marx-Universität. Gesellschafts- und Sprachwissenschaftliche Reihe*, Leipzig 28 (1979), 119-129, with 2 pl.

   Survey of the history of egyptology in Leipzig, with particular attention to Seyffarth, Ebers and Steindorff.   J.J.J.

79004   BRESCIANI, Edda, In memoria di Michela Schiff Giorgini, *Studi classici e orientali*, Pisa 29 (1979), 13-14.

   Obituary notice. See our number 78900.

79005   BURRINI, Gabriele, Profilo storico degli studi sul camito-semitico.- II, *Annali. Istituto Orientale di Napoli*, Napoli 39, N.S. 29 (1979), 351-384.

   Sequel to our number 78145.
   In this general historical survey of Hamito-Semitic studies section 5 (p. 357-364) is devoted to the contribution of Egyptologists in the field.

79006   CLAYTON, Peter, Samson in Egypt, *The British Museum Society Bulletin*, London No. 29 (November 1978), 27-29, with 6 ill.

Biographical note on Belzoni. See also the same periodical No. 28 (July 1978), 15.

79007   CURTO, Silvio, Giovanni Battista Belzoni, antesignano dell'archeologia, *Oriens Antiquus* 18 (1979), 353-355, with 1 pl.

Biographical note on Belzoni.

79008   Early Photography in Egypt (30 p.) = *Creative Camera*, London No. 186 (December 1979), 400-429, with numerous ill.

After an introduction on the mid 19th century photographers in Egypt, by Gerry Badger, the prints of various photographers, all having ancient Egypt as its subject, are presented. Biographical notes of the photographers are added at the end of the article.

79009   ENGEL, Helmut, Die Vorfahren Israels in Ägypten. Forschungsgeschichtlicher Überblick über die Darstellungen seit Richard Lepsius (1849), Frankfurt am Main, Josef Knecht, 1979 (15.7 x 22.7 cm; 253 p.) = Frankfurter Theologische Studien, 27; rev. *Ugarit-Forschungen* 12 (1980), 478-479 (O. Loretz).   Pr. DM 58

The author thoroughly surveys the studies devoted to the question of the Israelite sojourn in Egypt by the early Egyptologists who are dealt with in the 1st chapter. In the 2nd chapter he discusses the period about 1900: i.a. Naville and Petrie and their excavations, and the conceptions of Eduard Meyer. Then follow in chapter 3 the ideas as expressed in the first half of the 20th century by e.g. Gardiner and Montet. The 4th chapter is devoted to i.a. the contribution of Palestinian archaeology and the hypotheses of Noth and Alt, and various attempts at synthesis. Of the excursuses we mention those on the ꜥprw and the Hyksos problem. After a very extensive bibliography follow the indexes, among which one on Egyptian names.

79010   GAFUROV, B.G., Гениальное открытие Франсуа Шампольона, *in*: Шампольон и Дешифровка, 4-5.

"The Brilliant Discovery of François Champollion."
The author stresses the inspiring influence of Champollion's deciphering of the hieroglyphs, also on Russian scholars. *J.J.J.*

79011   GEORGE, Beate & Bengt PETERSON, Die Karnak-Zeichnungen von Baltzar Cronstrand 1836-1839, Stockholm, [Medelhavsmuseet], 1979 (19.2 x 25.6 cm; 80 p., 36 fig., 5 ill., frontispiece = portrait) = Medelhavsmuseet Memoir, 3.

From May 1836 to September 1837 the Swedish officer Baltzar Cronstrand (cfr our number 67442) stayed in Thebes, making drawings and water-colours of the monuments which largely exceed the accurancy of those of Champollion and Rosellini. They are at present preserved in the National Museum at Stockholm, and have never been published. Thirty-three of them are here reproduced and discussed.

After an introduction presenting a survey of Cronstrand's life and work and a list of his Karnak drawings with their museum numbers the catalogue itself occupies p. 14-80. For it the most important pieces have been chosen, representing elements of the Forecourt (1-2), the Hypostyle Hall (3-19), the rooms N. of the Granite Sanctuary (20), the Vestibule of Tuthmosis III (21), his Festival Temple (22-27), the Heb-sed Temple of Amenophis II (28) and the temple of Khons (29-33). Each drawing is accompanied by a minute description in which the texts are translated and references to the pages in Porter-Moss II^2 are given.

The drawings have been shown in 1980 on an exhibition in the Medelhavsmuseet, to which the authors wrote a catalogue entitled: Baltzar Cronstrand i Egypten 1836-1837. En svensk officer bland faraoniska tempel och gravar, [Stockholm], Nationalmuseum - Medelhavsmuseet, [1980] (17.5 x 21 cm; 32 p., 1 plan, 39 ill., fig. on cover).   J.J.J.

79012   HABACHI, Labib, Zaki Iskander Hanna: November 16, 1916 - July 16, 1979, *Newsletter ARCE* No. 109 (Summer 1979), 2.

Obituary notice.

79013   HAMON, Paul, Champollion et l'égyptologie en Dauphiné du XVIIIe siècle à nos jours. Exposition. Bibliothèque municipale de Grenoble,1979 (14.5 x 21 cm; 40 p., 6 ill., 1 colour ill. on cover).

This small catalogue of an exhibition held in September-December 1979 in the Library of Grenoble contains documents from institutions, viz. the Abbey de Saint-Antoine en Viennois and the Municipal Library of Grenoble, as well as on persons: Dolomieu, Dubois-Aymé,Fourier, Champollion le Jeune, Champollion-Figeac, Saint-Ferriol, Chabas, Camille Lagier, Manteyer and Abbé Tresson concerning Egyptology in the province of the Dauphiné from the 17th to the 20th century.

79014   HEERMA van VOSS, M., Henri Asselberghs, *Phoenix*, Leiden 25 (1979), 60-62, with 1 ill.

Obituary notice.

79015   KATSNELSON, I.S., Франсуа Шампольон и Россия, *in*: Шампольон и Дешифровка, 18-28.

"François Champollion and Russia."
The author presents a survey of the Russians who in the time of

Champollion collected Egyptian antiquities and studied Egyptian texts.
                                                                J.J.J.

79016   KATSNELSON, I.S., Три запнски Ф. Шампольона из собрания автографов Акад. Н.П. Лихачева, *in*: Шампольон и Дешифровка, 129-136, with 5 ill.

"Three Short Letters of F. Champollion from the Collection of Autographs of the Academian N.P. Likhatsev."
Publication of three short letters of Champollion, to Jumath, Cherubini and Tyron respectively, which are now preserved in the Institute of History of the USSR in Leningrad. They deal with unimportant social matters. The letters are presented in photograph, with the printed French text and a Russian translation.
                                                                J.J.J.

79017   KOROSTOVTSEV, M.A., Пятьдесят лет Египтологии в СССР, *in*: Шампольон и Дешифровка, 6-10.

"Fifty Years Egyptology in the USSR."
Survey of the Russian Egyptologists and their work, from 1922 to 1972.   J.J.J.

79018   KUENY, Gabrielle, Extraits du Journal du Comte de St-Ferriol rédigé pendant la durée de son voyage en Égypte en 1841-42, *in: Le rêve égyptien*, 70-75, with 1 ill. and 1 fig.

The author presents some parts of the journal of the Comte de St-Ferriol written during his stay in Egypt, 1841-1842.

79019   LECLANT, Jean, Kuentz (Charles), né à New York (U.S.A.) le 19 juin 1895, décédé au Caire (Égypte) le 24 mai 1978 - Promotion de 1914, *Annuaire. Association amicale des anciens élèves de l'École Normale Supérieure*, Paris, 1979, 81-82.

Obituary notice. See our number 78896.

79020   LECLANT, Jean, Sauneron (Serge), né à Paris le 3 janvier 1927, décédé en Égypte le 3 juin 1976 - Promotion de 1947, *Annuaire. Association amicale des anciens élèves de l'École Normale Supérieure,* Paris, 1979, 119-121.

Obituary notice. See our number 76869.

79021   O'CONNOR, David and David SILVERMAN, [The University Museum in Egypt] The Past, *Expedition*, Philadelphia, Penn. 21, No. 2 (Winter 1979), 4-43, with 5 ill., 4 maps, 3 plans and 3 fig.

This article on the history of the University Museum in Philadelphia as regards Egypt consists of an introduction dealing with the initial period at the end of the last century and the first curator of the Museum's Egyptian section, Sara Yorke Stevenson. In the second section, "The University, The Museum and the study

of ancient Egypt" the general background of early Egyptology is
sketched. In the third section, "The museum in the field", the
authors stress the enormous activity of the Museum in Egypt, and
the lack of adequate publication thereof, and let pass in review
those names involved in Museum's excavations: Sara Yorke Stevenson, David Randall MacIver (Nubia), Clarence Stanley Fisher, who
was very skilled, but hardly published results (Memphis, Dendera),
Alan Rowe (Meidum) and Rudolf Anthes (Memphis). In the section
on the Egyptian collection the authors point out that due to the
Museum's enormous activity in the field the collection is very
vast and rich, and deal next with its curators who were normally
connected with the University: W. Max Müller, B. Gunn, H. Ranke
and R. Anthes.
For other subjects relating to the museum's past see our numbers
79001 and 79026. For the modern activities see our numbers 79527,
79535, 79547, 79548 and 79550.

79022 PETERSON, Bengt, Ein Besucher in Tell el Amarna 1837, *Orientalia Suecana*, Uppsala 27-28 (1978-1979), 31-33.

Extract (in a German translation) from Baltzar Cronstrand's diary
(see for him our number 79011) where he gives a description of
his visit to "El Tell", where obviously more was visible than
today of el-ʿAmarna. The extract is followed by a bibliography.
J.J.J.

79023 PICKAVANCE, K.M., Robert Huntington, Bishop of Raphoe (1673-1701) *in: Glimpses of Ancient Egypt*, 196-201.

The author deals with the life of the Reverend Robert Huntington
from Oxford who visited Egypt in A.D. 1678 and in 1681-'82, and
presents extracts from his letters in an English translation.
J.J.J.

79024 POSENER, G., Ф. Шампольон н расшифровка иератического письма, *in*: Шампольон и Дешифровка, 11-17.

"F. Champollion and the Deciphering of the Hieratic Script."
Survey of Champollion's work in the deciphering of the hieratic
script. The author argues that Champollion was not only brilliant
but that he also possessed a logical mind and great perseverance.
J.J.J.

79025 SMITSKAMP, Rijk, Typografia hieroglyphica, *Quaerendo*. A Quarterly Journal from the Low Countries Devoted to Manuscripts and Printed Books, 9 (1979), 309-336, with 1 table.

The article is devoted to the typography of hieroglyphs. After
introductory remarks the author gives much information, often
very detailed, about the various types which are named after the
persons engaged in them, and which are dealt with in chronological order.

b. **Present-day Egyptology: progress reports, methodology, prefaces, etc.**

79026   Anonymous, The Egyptian Antiquities Organisation, *Expedition*, Philadelphia, Penn. 21, No. 2 (Winter 1979), 45.

A note on the Service des antiquités d'Egypte, in connection with the field activities of the University Museum, Philadelphia, in Egypt.
Compare our numbers 79001, 79021, 79527, 79535, 79547, 79548, and 79550.

79027   Anonymous, Jahresbericht 1977 des Deutschen Archäologischen Instituts. Abteilung Kairo, *Archäologischer Anzeiger*, Berlin, 1979, 589-593.

Yearly report of the activities of the German Archaeological Insstitute, with short sections on the excavations at Elephantine, Thebes-West, el-Tarif, Abydos, Dashûr, Saqqâra and Merimde-Benisalama.

79028   BIETAK, M., The Present State of Egyptian Archaeology, *in*: *Acts 1st ICE*, 103-110.

The author indicates the relative position of archaeology within the field of Egyptology, arguing that philology and archaeology may produce quite different results. He also stresses the need of cooperation with the natural sciences. The paper particularly makes an appeal to integrate archaeology into the University training programs, pointing out the pressing need of salvage work centering around the threatened tell areas.   *J.J.J.*

79029   BIETAK, M., The Present State of Egyptian Archaeology, *JEA* 65 (1979), 156-160.

The text of a paper read during the first International Congress of Egyptology, in which the writer seeks to expand on the meaning of the term archaeology, going beyond the mere matter of actual excavation. The objectivity of archaeological method is stressed and the need for its increased use to fill many of the lacunae of Egyptian and Nubian history.   *E.P. Uphill*

79030   BINGEN, Jean, Rapport des directeurs, *CdE* LIV, No. 107 (1979), VI-IX.

79031   BJÖRKMAN, Gun, Nachforschung, *GM* Heft 31 (1979), 7.

Verfasser bittet Mitteilung darüber, wo sich noch eine Statue befindet, die einen offenen Mund hat.   *Inge Hofmann*

79032 BLUMENTHAL, Elke, Ingeborg MÜLLER, Adelheid BURKHARDT, Walter F. REINEKE, Übersetzung der Hefte 5-16 der Urkunden IV, *ZÄS* 106 (1979), 88.

Announcement of the preparation of a translation of Urk.IV, Hefte 5-16.
M. Heerma v. Voss

79033 BOGOSLOWSKY, E.S., Egyptology in the USSR, *GM* Heft 35 (1979), 7-12.

Das Zentrum der Ägyptologie in Russland ist das Institut für orientalistische Studien der Akademie der Wissenschaften der UDSSR mit dem Hauptsitz in Moskau, während sich in Leningrad ein Department befindet. Die Wissenschaftler der Institution, ihre Forschungsprojekte und Publikationen werden vorgestellt. Der Sibirische Zweig der Akademie der Wissenschaften befindet sich in Novosibirsk, an der Universität von Chernovtsy (Ukraine) befasste sich ein Wissenschaftler mit der Geschichte der Ackerbau-Techniken im alten Ägypten.
Weiterhin werden die Museen und Sammlungen mit ägyptischen Objekten vorgestellt. Publikationsorgane sind "Vestnik Drevney Istorii" und "Palestinskiy Sbornik".
Inge Hofmann

79034 BOURRIAU, J., The Manual of Ancient Egyptian Pottery, *in*: *Acts 1st ICE*, 117-120.

Report on the preparations for the composition of a manual of Egyptian pottery.
J.J.J.

79035 [BURRI, Carla M.], Bollettino d'informazioni. Sezione archeologica. Istituto Italiano di Cultura per la R.A.E., No. 49 (Gennaio-Febbraio-Marzo-Aprile 1979), 22 p.

Sequel to our number 78144.
The issue contains reports on the Italian activities in the Sudan, at Luxor, and on the Philae temples; the French excavations at Balat (Dâkhla) and Douch; the Polish Mission at Kadero (Sudan) and their work in the temples of Hatshepsut and Tuthmosis III at Deir el-Bahri and the tomb of Ramses III in the Valley of the Kings; and the Anglo-Dutch excavations in the Saqqâra tomb of Horemheb.

79036 [BURRI, Carla M.], Bollettino d'informazioni. Sezione archeologica. Istituto Italiano di Cultura per la R.A.E., No. 50 (Maggio-Agosto 1979), 20 p.

Sequel to our preceding number.
The issue contains reports on the Italian activities in the Sudan (Prehistoric Mission); short remarks on the work of the American Research Center in Egypt at several places; the German researches in the temple of Seti I at Gurna, at Dashûr and at Minshat Abu Omar (Tell es-Sabaa Banat); and the Austrian excavations at Tell ed-Dabʿa.

79037   [BURRI, M.], Bollettino di informazioni. Sezione archeologica. Istituto Italiano di Cultura per la R.A.E., No. 51 (Settembre-Dicembre 1979), 26 p.

Sequel to our preceding number.
The issue contains reports on the Italian activities at Sheikh Abada (Antinoe), in the tomb of Sheshonq at Asâsîf, in the Late Period tombs at Saqqâra, and a mission to photograph some Theban tombs; on the study of the tomb of Ta-nedjemy (No. 33) in the Valley of the Queens by the Centre de Documentation; on the Franco-Egyptian researches at Karnak; and brief notes on the Swiss and German activities. At the end a note on a resolution of the Congress of Egyptologists at Grenoble, 1979, concerning archaeology in Egypt and the Sudan.

79038   DAUMAS, François, Un corpus de traduction de tous les textes dans la collection *Littératures anciennes du Proche Orient*, in: Acts 1st ICE, 141-143.

After pointing out the isolation in which egyptologists usually work the author stresses the importance of publishing translations, as has appeared in the series *LAPO* (see Barguet, our number 67052, and Goyon, our number 72270). Several others are ready and will be published in the future.
See now A. Barucq et F. Daumas, Hymnes et prières de l'Égypte ancienne, Paris, Les Éditions du Cerf, 1980 = LAPO, 10 (F.F.244).
                                                                                        J.J.J.

79039   DAUMAS, François, Projet d'un dictionnaire égyptien ptolémaique, in: Acts 1st ICE, 145-147, with 1 fig.

The author argues that we need a dictionary to the Graeco-Roman texts and indicates how he imagines its organization.
                                                                                        J.J.J.

79040   DREISINE, M., Le Bulletin Signalétique, in: Acts 1st ICE, 187-188.

Presents information on the issues of the *Bulletin Signalétique* that may be of importance for Egyptologists.   J.J.J.

79041   EGGEBRECHT, A., Bericht über des Projekt des "Corpus Antiquitatum Aegyptiacarum (CAA), in: Acts 1st ICE, 199-201.

Report on the CAA project.

79042   ERTMAN, E.L., Documentation of Minor Collections in the United States, in: Acts 1st ICE, 209-213.

Announcement of the author's project to publish objects from minor collections in the U.S.A. in the form of the CAA. As examples the author discusses two pieces from the Albright-Knox

Art Gallery in Buffalo, New York. The first is a limestone relief of a king (Inv. No. 27:13), on stylistic grounds ascribed to the XIth Dynasty and probably representing Mentuhotep Seankhkare; the other a fragmentary limestone female figure (Inv. No. 45:5.1) offering her breast to a lost child, from the M.K. and possibly a votive figure. J.J.J.

79043 GÖRG, M., Bericht über die Arbeit an einem Wörterbuch der Semitischen Fremdwörter im Ägyptischen, *in*: Acts 1st ICE, 237-241.

The author explains aims, material and system of a planned dictionary of Semitic foreign words in Egyptian, illustrating his argument with two examples, *brk* and *brt*.

79044 GRAEFE, E., Bericht über die Arbeit an einem Korpus der Funktionäre und Priester der thebanischen Gottesgemahlinnen, *in*: Acts 1st ICE, 243-247.

The author explains his project of a corpus of functionaries and priests of the Divine Consorts and its organization, with an example (p. 245-246).
See now E. Graefe, Untersuchungen zur Verwaltung und Geschichte der Institution der Gottesgemahlin des Amun vom Beginn des Neuen Reiches bis zur Spätzeit, 2 Bde, Wiesbaden, 1981 = Ägyptologische Abhandlungen, 37. J.J.J.

79045 HABACHI, Labib, Damages and Robberies of Egyptian Monuments in the Last Half Century, *in*: Acts 1st ICE, 271-275.

The author presents examples of recent robberies and damages in temples, tombs, storehouses and museums, and on sites, and he proposes recommendations to assure the safety of the monuments.

79046 HEERMA VAN VOSS, M., Methodology and the Egyptian *Book of the Dead*, *in*: *Science of Religion. Studies in Methodology*. Proceedings of the Study Conference of the International Association for the History of Religions, held in Turku, Finland, August 27-31, 1973. Edited by Lauri Honko (= Religion and Reason, 13), 11-15, with a portrait.

The author points out three essentials in the exploration of the *Book of the Dead*. Sources other than papyri, "vignettes" and other pictures, and hieroglyphic mss. of Dynasty XXI should be examined no less than the current texts.
An analysis of *spell* 161 is offered as a model.
A commentary by Jan Bergman follows: see p. 18-21 in particular.
M. Heerma van Voss

79047 HINTZE, Fritz, Statistische Methoden in der Ägyptologie ?, *in*: Acts 1st ICE, 289-295.

Discussion of some basic aspects of mathematical statistics in view of their possible application to egyptological problems.

79048 HODJASH, S.I., Отдел востока государственного музея изобразительных искусств им. А.С. Пушкина, Народи Азии и Африки, Москва No. 6, 1979, 143-147.

"Oriental Department of the A.S. Pushkin Museum of Fine Arts."

79049 HOLTHOER, R., Egyptology in Finland, *in*: Acts 1st ICE, 307-311, with 3 pl.

Survey of the history and present position of egyptology in Finland and of recent Finnish fieldwork in Egypt. The author particularly mentions the presence of the coffin of Ankhefenamun, Overseer of the Works of the Estate of Amon, from the cache of Deir el-Bahri (XXIst Dynasty). *J.J.J.*

79050 International Association of Egyptologists. Articles of Association, *in*: Acts 1st ICE, 51-58.

The articles are followed by a list of the members of the committees and the resolutions accepted by the congress. *J.J.J.*

79051 JANSSEN, J.J., Annual Egyptological Bibliography, *in*: Acts 1st ICE, 333-336.

Report on the activities of the AEB.

79052 KLEMM, Rosemarie, Altägypten im deutschen Schulbuch, *GM* Heft 34 (1979), 13-102, with 6 fig.

Bei dem Beitrag handelt es sich um die Magisterarbeit der Verfasserin, München 1976, der deutlich zeigt, dass die Ergebnisse der wissenschaftlichen Erforschung Altägyptens im Bereich der allgemeinbildenden Schulen nur ein schwaches und verzerrtes Echo fanden. Untersucht wird besonders die Darstellung der gesellschaftlichen Gliederung, der Pyramiden, von Religion und Totenkult, der Geschichte, der Wissenschaften, des Handwerks und der Kunst. *Inge Hofmann*

79053 KLENGEL, Horst, Staats- und Tempelwirtschaft im alten Nahen Osten. Internationale Konferenz, Leuven (Belgien) 1978, *Ethnographisch-Archäologische Zeitschrift*, Berlin 20 (1979), 157-159.

For the publication of the papers of the conference, see the preliminary pages under: *State and Temple Economy*.

79054 KURTH, Dieter, Zur Einleitung, *GM* Heft 34 (1979), 7-11.

Introduction to our numbers 79052 and 79070.

79055 LECLANT, Jean, Bilan du IIe Congrès International des Égyptologues. Grenoble, 10-15 septembre 1979, *BSFE* No. 86 (Octobre 1979), 8-15.

Evaluation of the Second International Congress of Egyptologists, held at Grenoble, 1979.

79056 LECLANT, Jean, Histoire de la diffusion des cultes égyptiens, *Annuaire. École Pratique des Hautes Études.* V^e section - sciences religieuses, Paris 87 (1978-1979), 183-188.

Fortsetzung unserer Nr. 78476.
Der Verfasser berichtet über die Weiterführung der Untersuchungen zur Ausbreitung des Isis-Kultes, über die Tätigkeiten seines Seminars hinsichtlich des Meroitischen und stellt eine Liste seiner Tätigkeiten und Publikationen zusammen.   *Inge Hofmann*

79057 LLAGOSTERA, Esteban, The International Association of Egyptologists. El Segundo Congreso Internacional de Egiptologia, *Boletin de la Asociacion Española de Orientalistas*, Madrid 15 (1979), 226.

Brief note.

79058 LLOYD, Alan B., Editorial Foreword, *JEA* 65 (1979), 1-4.

Included are short reports from:
H.S. Smith, The Anubieion at North Saqqâra, 1978-9 season;
G.T. Martin, The Memphite tomb of Ḥoremḥeb;
ʿAli el-Khouli, The Saqqâra Epigraphic Survey, 1978;
Barry J. Kemp, Recent work at el-Amarna;
Ricardo Caminos, The Epigraphic Survey at Gebel es Silsilah.

79059 MAJEWSKA, Aleksandra, Ancient Egyptian Collections in Poland, *in*: *Acts 1st ICE*, 443-447.

The author briefly reports on the Polish ancient Egyptian collections, their collectors and the more recent fieldwork activities.

79060 MICHAŁOWSKI, Kazimierz, Conclusion, *in*: *Acts 1st ICE*, 49-50.

Concluding speech of the honorary vice president of the International Association of Egyptologists.   *J.J.J.*

79061 MOKHTAR, Gamal, Opening Speech, *in*: *Acts 1st ICE*, 37-43.

79062 NIBBI, Alessandra, Some Rapidly Disappearing and Unrecorded Sites in the Eastern Delta, *GM* Heft 35 (1979), 41-46.

Aufruf zu Survey-Arbeiten im Ostdelta, das in zunehmendem Masse hinsichtlich der antiken Stätten dem Untergang geweiht ist. Folgende Gebiete sind besonders gefährdet: 1. Die Wüste im Ostdelta, 2. das Wadi Tumilat und der Suez - Kanal, 3. Attāka und die Berge in der Suez-Region, 4. Bilbeis, 5. Suwa, 6. Sheik Gebail. Die Verfasserin beschliesst ihren dringenden Appell mit den Worten: "It would be a great gift from this generation of scholars to the next if 1979 - 1980 could be designated as the "year of the surveys."

Inge Hofmann

79063 NIBBI, A., The Urgent Scientific Investigation of the Eastern Delta and the Eastern Desert, *in*: Acts 1st ICE, 493-497.

The author stresses the importance of profound environmental studies as regards the Eastern Delta and the Eastern Desert. In this connection she discusses the representations of the Two-Dogs palette from Hierakonpolis, now in the Ashmolean Museum, Oxford.

79064 OERTER, Wolf B., Koptologie - dějiny a předmět nového vědního oboru, *Nový Orient*, Praha 34, No. 9 (1979), 279-281.

"Die Koptologie - Geschichte und Gegenstand einer neuen Disziplin".
Verfasser macht kurz mit Geschichte und Aufgaben der Koptologie bekannt und unterstreicht insbesondere die mannigfaltigen Aurgaben einer tschechoslowakischen Koptologie, in deren Vordergrund zur Zeit u.a. die Bearbeitung der 1978/79 durch die Grabungen des tschechoslowakischen ägyptologischen Instituts auf dem Südfeld von Abusir zutage geforderten koptischen Funde steht.

B. Vachala

79065 The Oriental Institute Annual Report 1978/1979, [Chicago, 1979] (14.8 x 22.8 cm; 162 p., 1 map, 3 plans, 9 fig., 43 ill.).

The present volume contains i.a. reports on the Epigraphic Survey at Luxor, by Lanny Bell, which i.a. mentions the discovery of some stone fragments bearing approximately one fifth of the original version of the Bentresh stela; on the Nubian Project, by Bruce Williams; on the Quseir el-Qadîm Project, by Janet H. Johnson and Donald S. Whitcomb; on the Demotic Dictionary Project, by Janet H. Johnson; and on individual researches by the staff members.

J.J.J.

79066 POSENER, G., Tâche prioritaire, *in*: Acts 1st ICE, 519-522.

The author makes a strong appeal to devote more Egyptological attention to the publication of texts.

79067 REDFORD, Donald B., The Historiography of Ancient Egypt, *in*: *Egyptology and the Social Sciences*, 3-20.

Critical remarks on the present state of the historiography of ancient Egypt. The author points out that its major failure is that is too much object-orientated and that Egyptologists shrink from writing history since they set the minimum level re-

quired to do so much too high. They are in the happy position
as against, for instance, historians of the classical world,
that their source material has not been subject to a long process of selection; they are directly dependent on what field
archaeology brings to light. Demonstrating that the historian
of Egypt, like every historian, is influenced by his own time,
the author warns against being biased. He points out that Egyptology has suffered from extensive insularity, particularly
field archaeology, and insists on choosing sites for excavation
for their possibilities to solve historical problems and to
study the material with a combination of techniques. It is also
necessary that the large numbers of texts preserved in museums
are published. After pointing out the arrears in form-critical
evaluation of the sources, he pleads the application of more
adequate designations for the periods in Egyptian history.
J.J.J.

79068 ROBINSON, James M., Introduction, *Biblical Archaeologist*, Cambridge, MA 42 (1979), 201-205, with 2 maps, 8 ill. (7 in colour)
and 1 table.

Introduction to our numbers 79408, 79542, and 79556.

79069 SCHENKEL, Wolfgang, Probleme der Ägyptologie, *GM* Heft 35 (1979),
59-75.

Die Antrittsvorlesung des Verfassers (2.5.79 in Tübingen) befasst sich zunächst mit der Wissenschaft der Ägyptologie und
ihrem Untersuchungsgegenstand, der altägyptischen Hochkultur,
wobei die Notwendigkeit einer Detailarbeit betont wird. Zu einer
Gewinnung weiterer Beobachtungsdaten muss eine schärfere Analyse
der Beobachtungsdaten treten, wie nach einer Darlegung der Daten-
basis an vier Beispielen demonstriert wird: Bedeutung und frühes-
tes Auftreten von künstlichen Bewässerungstechniken, Entwicklung
im Totenglauben, Verschiebung in der Gottesvorstellung, Entwicklung der altägyptischen Sprache.   *Inge Hofmann*

79070 SCHENKEL, Wolfgang, Übergang zur Hochkultur. Ägypten und Ägyptologie aus der Sicht zweier Schulmänner, *GM* Heft 34 (1979), 103-
118.

Der Verfasser setzt sich mit einer umfangreichen Arbeit auseinander, die Armin Helm und Dieter Sippel als Beitrag zur Curricu-
lum-Entwicklung verfassten, indem sie innerhalb ihres Faches Ge-
sellschaftslehre am Beispiel Ägyptens den "Übergang zur Hochkultur" als eine Unterrichtseinheit für die 5./6. Klasse erarbeite-
ten. Das Problem der interdisziplinären Verständigung kommt
intensiv zur Sprache.
Inge Hofmann

79071   TRIGGER, Bruce G., Egypt and the Comparative Study of Early Civilizations, *in*: *Egyptology and the Social Sciences*, 23-56.

The author examines the relationship between Egyptology and anthropology, first presenting a historical survey and then an example.
After an introduction the anthropological studies on Egyptian material and the Egyptological studies influenced by anthropological theories and methods pass the review, from Fraser's "The Golden Bough" to Lévi-Strauss, which enables the author to touch upon a large number of problems and to demonstrate the possibilities of a confrontation between the two sciences.
In the second part, intended as an illustration to the topic, the author deals with the nature of kingship in Mesopotamia and Mexico as compared with kingship in Egypt. The parallels between the two former civilizations (see p. 41) contrast with the Egyptian evidence (see p. 51).

J.J.J.

79072   VERCOUTTER, J., Préface, *in*: *Hommages Sauneron* I, V-VI, with portrait = frontispiece.

79073   VERCOUTTER, Jean, Les travaux de l'Institut français d'Archéologie du Caire à Douch et à Balât, *Comptes rendus de l'Académie des Inscriptions et des Belles-Lettres*, Paris, 1979, 241-251, with 6 ill.

The author, first presenting a rapid general survey of the activities of the IFAO at Balat, Dâkhla and Douch, Khârga, is mainly concerned with the rather intact burial of a VIth Dynasty governor of the Oasis found in a mastaba at Balât.

79074   VERCOUTTER, Jean, Les travaux de l'Institut français d'Archéologie orientale en 1978-1979, *BIFAO* 79 (1979), 451-477, with 1 folding fig., 1 folding plan and 16 pl.

Sequel to our number 78808.
Among the activities of the IFAO that are here recorded those in the Oases el-Khârga (Dûsh) and el-Dâkhla (Balât) take most space, while others are only briefly mentioned.

J.J.J.

79075   WEEKS, Kent R., Art, Word, and the Egyptian World View, *in*: *Egyptology and the Social Sciences*, 59-81.

It is generally accepted that wall pictures in O.K. tombs were intended to supply the deceased with the necessities of life, but what were the criteria on which the scenes and their attributes were chosen? This problem is connected with the way in which the Egyptians viewed and categorized their world. From the words accompanying the scenes we determine their meaning, supposing that the principles of classification were the same as ours, which, as Weeks demonstrates, is not correct. He then discusses in detail three points: the words for colours; the way in which artists removed from their representations all that was unique and transitory (e.g. avoidance of portraiture); the tendency to associate physical attributes (e.g., baldness) with certain social roles. At the end some subjects requiring special attention are mentioned, e.g. the rules for placing scenes on the tomb walls and the regularity of labelling or non-labelling particular plants or animals, and the need of an attribute list and a motif-index of O.K. relief.

J.J.J.

79076 WESSETZKY, V., Archivarbeit in der ägyptologischen Forschung, in: Acts 1st ICE, 679-682.

The author reports on his attempts to recover as many data as possible through research in archives etc. about an expedition organized in 1907 by Philip Beck to excavate in Sharuna and Gamhud.

79077 WESSETZKY, Vilmos, Egyptológiai konferencia Ljubljanában 1978-ban, Archaeologiai Értesitő, Budapest 106 (1979), 135.

Brief report on the Egyptological symposium in Ljubljana, 1978. See our number 78542.

79078 WILDUNG, D., Results, Effects and Perspectives of the 1st ICE, in: Acts 1st ICE, 45-48.

Survey of the congress by its secretary.

79079 [YOYOTTE, Jean], Sujets de thèses V, BSFE No. 85 (Juin 1979), 32.

Suite de notre no. 78882, concernant quelques thèses de l'École du Louvre.

79080 YOYOTTE, J., Sujets de thèses VI, BSFE No. 86 (Octobre 1979), 39-44.

Sequel to our preceding number. Lists defended and announced theses, and some modifications.

79081 ZAUZICH, K.-Th., Forschung in der Papyrussammlung. I. Demotische Papyri, Berichte aus den Staatlichen Museen Preussischen Kulturbesitz, 3. Folge, Beiheft Forschungen 1979, 1-2.

Bericht über die Arbeit an demotischen Papyri; gute Abbildung des Berliner Achikar-Romanfragmentes (P 23729). H.Thissen

Not seen; see Demotische Literaturübersicht 10 (1980), no, 56 in Enchoria 10 (1980), p. 150.

79082   ZONHOVEN, L.M.J., A Proposal for a Classification of the Annual Egyptological Bibliography (AEB), *in*: *Acts 1st ICE*, 699-704.

After having explained the need for a new systematization of the AEB the author presents the proposed classification scheme in some detail.

c. Research tools: bibliographies, indexes, encyclopaedic works

See also our numbers 79039; 79043; 79065 and 791026.

79083   Anonymous, Bibliographie Elmar Edel, *in*: *Festschrift Elmar Edel*, 1-12.

131 numbers are listed in a chronological order, going from 1939 to 1979.

79084   BASTA, Mounir, Historic Monuments of the Gizeh Pyramid Zone, Cairo, Anglo-Egyptian Bookshop, [1979] (14 x 20 cm; 112 p., 35 fig. and ill.).

After a historical introduction on the pyramids and remarks on the methods of their construction the author briefly deals with i.a.: the Great Pyramid; the tomb of queen Hetepheres, the Cheops solar boat, the Chefren pyramid complex, the sphinx and its temple, the tomb of queen Mersyankh III, the Mycerinus pyramid complex, the tombs of Qar and Idu, Khafu-Khaf, Yasen, Nefernesu and Kaemankh.

79085   DAVIS, Whitney M., Sources for the Study of Rock Art in the Nile Valley, *GM* Heft 32 (1979), 59-74.

Es handelt sich um eine Bibliographie zu unseren Nummern 78197 und 78198. Besonders bedeutsam bei der Arbeit mit Felsbildern ist ihre Datierung die vom Mesolithikum bis in die heutige Zeit reicht und kurz besprochen wird. Der Zweck der Bibliographie ist es, denen die das Material noch nicht studiert haben, einen Zugang zu ihm zu verschaffen. Nach einer Übersicht über die allgemeinen Arbeiten folgen, geordnet nach der Zeit ihrer Erscheinung die Arbeiten einzelner Wissenschaftler und grösserer Expeditionen. Ein 2. Teil bringt Studien über die Sahara-Felskunst, ein 3. Teil die wichtigsten Arbeiten über die Niltal-Felskunst einzelner Regionen.

Inge Hofmann

79086   DECKER, Wolfgang, Bibliographie zum Sport im alten Ägypten für die Jahre 1978 und 1979 nebst Nachträgen aus früheren Jahren, *Stadion*, Leiden 5 (1979), 161-192.

Complement to our number 78201. Besides additions from earlier years, the article contains the bibliography to sport in ancient Egypt for the years 1978 and 1979. The systemization is the same but less detailed. A new heading "Pictorial documentation" is introduced, while additional reviews are mentioned separately at the end. The bibliography is concluded by an author's index.

79087 FISCHER, Henry G., Index of Personal Names to Abdel-Moneim Abu-Bakr, *Excavations at Gîza* 1949-1950, [New York, The Metropolitan Museum of Art], 1979 (21.5 x 28 cm; 7 p.).

This index belongs to our number 3155 and refers to the nine Gîza tombs containing inscriptions there published, in which 83 names occur, many of which are rare. Copies are available to Egyptologists and Institutions on request to the author.

J.J.J.

79088 GRENIER, Jean-Claude, Temples ptolémaïques et romains. Répertoire bibliographique. Index des citations 1955-1974. Incluant l'index des citations de 1939 à 1954 réunis par N. Sauneron, [Le Caire], Institut français d'Archéologie orientale du Caire, 1979 (20.3 x 27.4 cm; XIV + 468 p.) = Bibliothèque d'Étude, 75.

New edition of the repertory published by Nadia Sauneron in 1956 (our number 4838), including one part of that earlier work and bringing it up-to-date to 1974. Parts 1, 3 and 4 of the earlier edition are omitted, only part 2 being extended to 1974, so that the volume contains an index to the texts quoted in the literature between 1939 and 1974.
The temples of which the texts are arranged as follows: first the major ones, Edfu, Dendera, Esna, Kôm Ombo, Philae, and the Graeco-Roman buildings at Karnak (particularly quotations referring to Urk. VIII and to the Opet temple); then in the last chapter the smaller temples in an alphabetical order, from Athribis to Tôd, including Nubian ones such as those of el-Dakka, Debôd, Dendûr and Kalâbsha. For each sanctuary the major publications are listed, older ones (e.g. Champollion, Monuments; Lepsius, Denkmäler; etc.) and, particularly, the most recent (e.g. Sauneron's publication of Esna). To each page and line the relevant references occurring in the literature are mentioned. Indications of translations, which had been marked by an asterisk in the first edition, are omitted as being too arbitrary.

J.J.J.

79089 Index du Bulletin de l'Institut français d'Archéologie orientale (Tomes 1 à 79), Le Caire, 1979 (20 x 27.5 cm; IV + 49 p.) = Supplément au *BIFAO* 79.

List of the articles that have been published in the 79 volumes of the BIFAO (since 1901), arranged in an alphabetical order after the authors' names.

J.J.J.

79090 Index Multiplex ad Zeitschrift für ägyptische Sprache und Altertumskunde 1863-1943. Herausgegeben von J.-P. Lobies unter Mitarbeit von Isabelle Brandière, Osnabrück, Biblio Verlag, 1975 (19.5 x 25.5 cm; V + 351 p.) = Index Multiplex ad periodica scientifica, 10.

Very extensive indexes to the *ZÄS* 1-78 (1863-1943). The indexes are divided into an authors' register listing also the title of the article and the pertinent volume of the *ZÄS*, in which each entry bears a number (almost 2000), and a series of subject indexes also giving the title and the pertinent volume referring to the entry numbers in the authors' register.
We mention: geography, chronology, ethnology; Pharaohs (names, titularies, jubilees); religion (cults and gods); personal names; grammar (detailed); lexicon and script (detailed); papyri (places and museums, finders, the texts); science and technology; Greek index; Coptic index (detailed); and Demotica.

79091 KARIG, Joachim Selim, International Directory of Egyptology. 1979, Mainz am Rhein, Verlag Philipp von Zabern, [1979] (21 x 30 cm; 37 p.).

This international directory of Egyptology contains two lists: one of Egyptological institutions each having their own code and arranged after countries and places, to which the names of their collaborators are added; and a list of Egyptologists with usually their private addresses, but also provided with references to the codes of the first list.

79092 LECLANT, Jean, Fouilles et travaux en Égypte et au Soudan, 1977-1978, *Orientalia* 48 (1979), 340-412, with 1 plan, 2 fig. and 35 ill. on 26 pl.

Sequel to our number 78474.
The invaluable chronicle of the archaeology of Ancient Egypt from this year deals with 69 sites in Egypt, including Egyptian Nubia, 21 in the Sudan, and with discoveries of objects outside Egypt (12 numbers). Apart from the usual sites such as Gîza, Saqqâra and Thebes the article pays ample attention to excavations in Alexandria, the Kellia, Kôm Giʿeif (Naucratis), Merimde-Beni Salame, Tell el-Rubʿ (Mendes), Tell ed-Dabʿa, Tanis and Tell el-Maskhûta (Pithom) in the Delta; to Prehistoric researches in Upper Egypt, e.g. in Nazlet Khâtir and Zaweida (Naqâda), and to researches in the Western Oases. Indexes on p. 409-412.

J.J.J.

79093 LECLANT, Jean, Les sagesses de l'Égypte pharaonique. État de la bibliographie récente, *in*: *Sagesse et religion*. Colloque de Strasbourg (octobre 1976), Paris, Presses Universitaires de France [1979] (at head of title: Bibliothèque des Centres d'Études Supérieures spécialisés. Travaux du Centre d'Études Supérieures spécialisé d'Histoire des Religions de Strasbourg), 7-19.

Sequel to our number 63312. The bibliography is arranged after the following headings: I. Re-edition of general works; II. Recent publications: texts, translations and commentaries, divided into: A. Text editions of wisdom texts and fragments; B. translations in anthologies; C. individual wisdom texts: text editions, translations, studies and commentaries of text passages (notably Amenemope); III. Studies of the genre in general: analysis of themes, various approaches, the political impact, the genre in connection with O.T. proverbial and wisdom literature. See also M. Fox, *ZÄS* 107 (1980), 120-135.

79094   LESKO, Leonard H., Index of the Spells on Egyptian Middle Kingdom Coffins and Related Documents, [Berkeley, California, B.C. Scribe Publications, 1979] (13.7 x 21.4 cm; X + 110 p.).

The index presents information about the sources used by de Buck for his publication of the "Egyptian Coffin Texts", indicating the position of the spells on the coffins and on other related documents (papyri, tomb walls, etc.). Since the author proceeds from the actual documents also the P.T. spells, omitted by de Buck, are included.

After a preface and an introduction in which aims, history and scheme of the index are explained the sources are listed (p. 7-11). For each of them the combination of letters and numbers under which the source is cited is followed by mentions of its present location, the type of documents (coffin or other) and the name of its beneficiary.

The index proper indicates of each source which spells are inscribed, with their place on the document. In several instances the author has added data omitted by de Buck: inscriptions on edges that are illegible with the coffins assembled, titles and names of the owners, etc. He also indicates which parts of the texts are illegible, as well as a few errors in de Buck's publication.

At the end concordances between C.T. numbers and Lacau's Textes religieux égyptiens, vol. I (Paris, 1910 = partial reprint from *Rec. Trav.* 26-37).   J.J.J.

79095   Lexikon der Ägyptologie. Begründet von Wolfgang Helck und Eberhard Otto. Lieferung 20-23 (Band III, Lieferung 4-7). Herausgegeben von Wolfgang Helck und Wolfhart Westendorf unter Mitwirkung von Rosemarie Drenkhahn, Wiesbaden, Otto Harrassowitz, 1979 (20 x 28 cm; 640 col. [= col. 481-1120], 3 maps, 9 plans, 5 ill. and 20 fig.).

Sequel to our number 78488.

The four fascicles published this year once more contain a wide range of subjects, such as places (e.g. Kom Ombo, Koptos, Lisht, Luxor), objects (e.g. Korb, Lampe, Leier), materials (e.g. Kupfer), plants (Kornblume) and animals (Krokodil), and concepts (Krankheit, Löhne, Maat).

The first fasc. (No. 20) entirely consists of lemmata composed

with König: Königsbrief, -dogma, -grab, -gräbertal, -ideologie, -kult, -listen, -mutter, -namen (with a list of full royal names, from Dynasty I-XXXI), -plastik, -sohn, ending with the viceroy (Königssohn) of Kush, This is continued in fasc. 21 with Königstitulatur. In that fascicle one further finds lemmata on Coptic matters (literature, music, language).
From fasc. 22 we mention lemmata on cult and compounds with cult (Kultbild, -spiele, -statue, -symbole), and on land (Landessymbole, -verwaltung, Landkarte, Landwirtschaft, etc.). In fasc. 23 one i.a. finds the instructions (Lehre), in general as well as each famous one in particular; Libya and Libyans; love (Liebe) and love-songs; literature in general; lions and -heads and -statues.   J.J.J.

79096   MEIER-BRÜGGER, Michael, Ein Buchstabenindex zu den karischen Schriftdenkmälern aus Ägypten, *Kadmos*, Berlin 18 (1979), 130-177.

The author first presents the Carian texts found in Egypt in transcription, arranged after those from the Nubian Expedition of Psammetichus II in 591 B.C., those of the years 550-500 B.C. from Memphis-Saqqâra, and undated ones. He then presents an index of the individual signs in their contexts (also in transcription).

79097   PORTER, the late Bertha and Rosalind L.B. MOSS, Assisted by Ethel W. BURNEY, Topographical Bibliography of Ancient Egyptian Hieroglyphic Texts, Reliefs, and Paintings. III². Memphis. Part 2. Saqqâra to Dashûr. Fascicle 2 (III². 575-776). Second Edition Revised and Augmented by Jaromir Málek, Oxford, Griffith Institute Ashmolean Museum, [1979] (18.8 x 27.3 cm; [IV +] 202 p. [= p. 575-776], 10 plans [nos. LVIII-LXVIII]).

Sequel to our number 78640.
The present fascicle covers in seven chapters the tombs within the Step Pyramid, the areas East and West of it, that around the Unas Pyramid and the wider area between the monastery of Apa Jeremias and the Enclosure of Sekhemkhet, the area around the pyramids of Pepi I, Merenrē I and Isesi and around the pyramids of Ibi and Pepi II, the Mastabat Faraʿûn and the pyramid of Userkarēʿ Khenzer. Two more deal with the numerous tombs of which the position is unknown (p. 689-720) and with objects from the Saqqâra tombs, some from these tombs, others of not exactly known provenance (720-775). The latter chapter (of 55 pages) is entirely new, once more an indication for the enormous improvement compared with the first edition.   J.J.J.

79098   SACHS, J. and G.J. TOOMER, Otto Neugebauer, Bibliography, 1925-1979, *Centaurus*, Copenhagen 22 (1979), 258-280, with 1 pl.

The bibliography contains 28 numbers pertaining to Ancient Egyptian mathematics and astronomy, which are arranged in one section. Index is added.

79099 SCHOTT, Erika und Alfred GRIMM, Index zu Schott, S., Mythe und Mythenbildung im Alten Ägypten, UGAÄ 15, Leipzig 1945, *GM* Heft 32 (1979), 75-91.

Der 1017 Belege umfassende Index enhält die in Schott, S., Mythe und Mythenbildung im Alten Ägypten behandelten Pyramidentextstellen aus den Pyramiden der Könige Unas, Merenre, Tetj, Pepj I und Pepj II, zitiert nach K. Sethe, Die altägyptischen Pyramidentexte, aus der Pyramide der Königin Neith, zitiert nach G. Jéquier, Les pyramides des reines Neit et Apouit und aus der Pyramide des Königs Ibj, zitiert nach G. Jéquier, La pyramide d'Aba, sowie auch die zahlreichen Verweise auf den Dramatischen Ramesseum-Papyrus, zitiert nach K. Sethe, Dramatische Texte zu altägyptischen Mysterienspielen. *Inge Hofmann*

79100 SÉE, G., Index. Un urbanisme pour les morts, les vivants et les dieux. Tome I - La naissance de l'urbanisme dans la vallée du Nil. Tome II - Grandes villes de l'Égypte antique, no place, no publisher, no year (xerox-copy, 21 x 30 cm; 27 unnumbered p.).

An index to our numbers 73662 and 74663, which comprises indexes of personal and geographical names, of museums, of terms in urbanism and architecture, and of names of authors.

79101 SEYFRIED, Karl-Joachim, Verzeichnisse, *in: Festschrift Elmar Edel* 478-488.

Indexes to the Festschrift, Simpson's article (our number 79634) excepted. *J.J.J.*

79102 TRAD, May, Bibliographie de Charles Kuentz, *BIFAO* 79 (1979), V-XVI.

The list of publications, books, articles and reviews, consists of 151 items and goes from 1916 to 1979. *J.J.J.*

79103 UPHILL, E.P., The Bibliography of Thomas Eric Peet (1882-1934), *JEA* 65 (1979), 144-150.

Contains the first full list of this Egyptologist's works, consisting of 190 nos. These comprise 14 books, 21 parts of books, 1 lecture, 61 articles, 91 reviews and 2 obituaries. *E.P.Uphill*

79104 VITTMANN, G.,[Bibliographie.] Ägypten, *AfO* 26 (1978/1979), 408-409.

Sequel to our number 77773. One subject heading has been at the end: Meroitics.

79105 WERNER, Edward K., The Amarna Period of Eighteenth Dynasty Egypt. Bibliography Supplement 1978, *Newsletter ARCE* No. 110 (Fall 1979), 24-39.

Fourth supplement to our number 76831. For the other three, compare our numbers 76832, 77795 and 78850.

d. Egypt's legacy and aftermath; Hellenistic world; classical authors

See also our numbers 79315; 79318; 79458; 79668; 79812; 79860; 79927; 79943 and 791050.

79106   BEINLICH, Horst, Die Nilquellen nach Herodot, *ZÄS* 106 (1979), 11-14.

Der Bericht im zweiten Buch, *Kap. 28*, wird hier erörtert. Die überlieferte Auskunft ist, auch in Einzelheiten, richtig, sei es von Herodot zum Teil missverstanden.

M. Heerma v. Voss

79107   BITRAKOVA-GROZDANOVA, Vera. Египетски култови во Македонија, *in*: Akta I-og naučnog skupa "Antika i antičko nasledje kod nas". Ohrid - Bitolj September 25th-29th, 1977= *Živa antika. Antiquité vivante*, Skoplje 38 (1978), 331-337, with 7 ill. on 4 pl., and a French summary on p. 337.

"Egyptian Cults in Macedonia".
The penetration of Egyptian cults into Macedonia (within Yugoslavia) is indicated by two Serapis heads and, in addition to the two Isis statues of our number 76520, by six Graeco-Roman figures of her (bronzes and a gem). On the basis of stylistic analysis, these objects have been mainly dated between the 1st century B.C. and the 2nd century A.D.

S.P. Tutundžić

79108   CHADEFAUD, Catherine, Un monument témoin d'une influence grecque et hebraïque. Le tombeau de Petosiris, *Le Monde de la Bible*, Paris No. 8 (Mars-Avril 1979), 26-28.

A note on the tomb of Petosiris, particularly the Greek influence in its reliefs and the Hebrew influence in its wisdom texts. See also our number 79829.

79109   CLÉMENT, Catherine, La jeune morte ou l'Oedipe égyptien, *in*: *Le rêve égyptien*, 115-118, with 1 ill.

The author discusses Sigmund Freud's interest in the Isis-Horus-Osiris configuration.

79110   DAVIS, Whitney M., Plato on Egyptian Art, *JEA* 65 (1979), 121-127.

The writer discusses all the possible ways by which Plato could have become familiar with art and studies the passage in which he contrasts the laws governing the educative-playful function of the Muses in the known world outside Egypt with those prevailing in Egypt. The latter he showed caused a system that could produce art thousands of years before that was as good as now. The questions of religious background, illusion, 'aspective' concepts and idealizing, are all reviewed, and it is suggested that Plato admired this art. *E.P. Uphill*

79111 DOBROVITS, A., Válogatott tanulmányai. I: Egyptom és az antik világ. Red. von L. Kákosy, Budapest, Akadémiai Kiadó, 1979 (203 p., 13 fig. and ill.) = Apollo Bibliothek, 7; rev. *Acta Archaeologica Academiae Scientiarum Hungaricae* 32 (1980), 469 (L. Castiglione).

"Ausgewählte Studien. I: Ägypten und die antike Welt."

79112 DUNAND, Françoise, Religion populaire en Égypte romaine. Les terres cuites isiaques du Musée du Caire, Leiden, E.J. Brill, 1979 (15.5 x 24.5 cm; XII + 287 p., frontispiece, 128 pl., 1 map) = Études préliminaires aux religions orientales dans l'Empire romain, 76; rev. *BiOr* 37 (1980), 174-175 (V. Wessetzky).

The study consists of two parts. In the first, the introduction, the author discusses all kinds of aspects of the collection of Isis terracottas from the Roman Period in Egypt, now in the Egyptian Museum in Cairo, such as origin, typology, destination, style, technique, date, the gods represented, their functions and their cult (Isis, Harpocrates, Sarapis, Osiris), but also their priesthood and the religious beliefs in the period. The second part contains the catalogue arranged after the gods or persons represented. A concordance between the catalogue numbers and the museum inventory nos. concludes the volume.

79113 FROIDEFOND, Claude, L'hellénisme et l'Égypte ou les avatars de l'espace, *in*: *Le rêve égyptien*, 26-33, with 2 ill.

The author discusses some aspects of how authors such as Homer, Euripides, Aeschylos, Herodotus and Plutarch conceived Egypt.

79114 GAUDIBERT, Pierre, Du retour d'Hermès ..., *in*: *Le rêve égyptien*, 137-142, with 1 ill.

The author sketches the Western esoteric interest in the Corpus Hermeticum, particularly the aspect of initiation.

79115 GODWIN, Joscelyn, Athanasius Kircher. A Renaissance Man and the Quest for Lost Knowledge, [London], Thames & Hudson, [1979] (20.5 x 28 cm; 96 p., 105 fig. and ill. including a frontispiece).

After the introduction in which the author stresses Kircher's belief in Egypt as the origin of all civilizations, and his firm

roots in the Hermetic tradition, the author deals in separate chapters with his major, archaeological subjects, among which a commentary on his *Oedipus Aegyptiacus*. The text is accompanied by many engravings taken from his works.
Select bibliography at the end.

79116 HARI, Robert, Châteaux en Égypte ou la quête du merveilleux, *in*: *Le rêve égyptien*, 119-125, with 2 ill.

The author discusses the esoteric interest in ancient Egyptian monuments, particularly the Great Pyramid.

79117 HARTMANN, B., Kanttekeningen bij Herodotus de godsdiensthistoricus, *Nederlands Theologisch Tijdschrift*, Den Haag 33 (1979), 265-274.

The author makes some remarks on Herodotus' interpretatio graeca of the Egyptian religion on p. 269-270.

79118 HUMBERT, Jean, L'égyptomanie dans l'art occidental, *in*: *Le rêve égyptien*, 105-114, with 11 ill.

The author briefly sketches the history of the interest in Egypt as expressed in various aspects of Western culture including Hollywood movies.

79119 IVERSEN, Erik, La tradition hermétique, *in*: *Le rêve égyptien*, 52-58, with 1 ill.

The author briefly surveys the influence of the Hermetic writings, particularly the tractates Asklepios and Poimandres and their connections with Neo-Platonism in Medieval and Renaissance thought.

79120 JAHN, Samia al Azharia, Zwillinge und ihr Tiergestaltiges Alter Ego im Volksglauben der Sudaneraber und Nubier. Wechselwirkungen zwischen altägyptischen, orientalischen und afrikanischen Elementen, *Paideuma*, Wiesbaden 25 (1979), 159-172.

Proceeding from the widely spread belief in the Sudan that twins can assume the shape of a cat during the night the author also discusses the origin of this conception and the customs related to this. Some ancient Egyptian elements are noticed in this connection: the twin gods Shu and Tefnut with a feline reference; the principle of duality; but also the ka which is still present in the modern Qarin/Qarina, twin spirits of both sexes from the underworld, the female partner of whom can take the shape of a cat at night. Two more sections are devoted to the cult of the cat-goddess Bastet in ancient Egypt and Nubia, and to cats in the solar cult of the Late Period.

79121 JOLY, Henri, Platon égyptologue, *in*: *Le rêve égyptien*, 34-42, with 1 fig.

The author discusses some aspects of the ancient Egyptian civilization as they were conceived by Plato and characterized in his works: the grammatology of Thoth, the archaeology of the priests of Sais, and the canons of Egyptian art and the educational qualities of the laws.

79122 KACMAREK, Hieronim, Menes w tradycji antycznej i w świetle badan współczesnych, *Meander*, Warszawa 33, 1 (1978), 33-43, with 5 fig. and ill. and a summary in Latin on p. 43.

"Menes in the classical tradition."

79123 KLAKOWICZ, Beatrix E., Osirian Funeral Concept in an Etruscan Tomb, *Orientalia* 48 (1979), 332-334.

A small vase, found in an Etruscan tomb at Orvieto, in the shape of a dove's body with human head, may represent the Egyptian *ba*, in shape as well as in concept.

79124 KUSPIT, Donald B., Our Egypt, *Art in America*, New York 67, No. 2 (March-April 1979), 86-93, with 12 ill. (3 in colour; 1 on cover).

On the influence of ancient Egyptian design on Western art and architecture.

79125 LAMOURETTE, Christiane, À propos de trois romans "pharaoniques" de Naǧīb Maḥfūẓ, *in*: *Hommages Sauneron* II, 329-363.

The author discusses three novels by Naǧīb Maḥfūẓ (born 1912) of which the scene is laid in Pharaonic Egypt. They deal with Khufu, Merenre and Kamosis-Ahmosis, but reflect modern Egyptian ideas.
                                                                    J.J.J.

79126 LECLANT, Jean, À propos des antiquités égyptiennes découvertes dans les sanctuaires isiaques d'Asie Mineure, *in*: *Florilegium anatolicum*. Mélanges offerts à Emmanuel Laroche, Paris, Éditions E. de Boccard, 1979, 207-217.

Dealing with the objects discovered in Turkey that testify to the Isis cult the author discusses two shawabtis found in Kyme and an Isis statue from Ephesos. Except for coins and inscriptions, the provenance of other isiaca in Turkey is uncertain. At the end the author states that a corpus of aegyptiaca found in Turkey is a desideratum of Egyptology.
                                                                    J.J.J.

79127 LECLANT, Jean, Les sanctuaires isiaques, un aspect de l'exotisme gréco-romain, *in*: *Le rêve égyptien*, 43-51, with 1 ill.

The author offers a rapid, but annotated survey particularly about the elements of Egyptian architectural style in the Isis sanctuaries of the Roman world.

79128 LORING, John, Egyptomania: The Nile Style, *The Connoisseur*, London 200, No. 804 (February 1979), 114-121, with 21 ill. (11 in colour).

On an exhibition held in the Metropolitan Museum of Art, beginning of 1979, having as subject Egyptomania from the 18th to the 20th centuries in Western civilization.

79129 MESHCHERSKY, N.A., Египетские имена в Славяно-Русских месяцесловах, *in*: Шампольон и Дешифровка, 117-128.

"Egyptian Names in the Slavo-Russian Calendar of Saints." Study of the origin of those names in the Church Slavonic calendar of saints that are derived from Egyptian or Coptic names. Thirty-eight instances are listed, with the days to which they are attached and their etymology.

J.J.J.

79130 MUSSIES, Gerard, The interpretatio judaica of Sarapis, *in*: *Studies in Hellenistic Religions*. Edited by M.J. Vermaseren, Leiden, E.J. Brill, 1979 (= Études préliminaires aux religions orientales dans l'empire romain, 78), 189-214.

In connection with the statement in some classical and Jewish sources that Sarapis and Joseph are the same the author discusses the reasons for this identification by the Jews on p. 199-213. On account of the Osiris and the Apis components in the figure of Sarapis he demonstrates that they had features with which Joseph could be assimilated.

79131 PÉPIN, Jean, Utilisations philosophiques du Mythe d'Isis et Osiris dans la tradition platonicienne, *in*: *Sagesse et religion*. Colloque de Strasbourg (octobre 1976), Paris, Presses Universitaires de France, [1979] (at head of title: Bibliothèque des Centres d'Études Supérieures spécialisés. Travaux du Centre d'Études Supérieures spécialisé d'Histoire des Religions de Strasbourg), 51-64.

The author studies the utilisation of the myth of Osiris and Isis in some writings of the Neo-platonian authors Porphyry and Damascius.

79132 REDFORD, Donald B., Osorkho . . . called Herakles, *JSSEA* 9 (1978-1979), 33-36.

Discussing the remark by Manetho that Osorkon (III) was called by the Egyptians "Herakles", the author points out the ubiquity of the king's epitnet $s3-\overline{I}st$, his numerous monuments at Thebes, where Knonsu was revered, and the later mistake to read his name as $Wsr-\underline{H}n(s)$. So he became "Khonsu", Greek "Herakles".   J.J.J.

79133 SELEM, Petar, Nekoliko zapažanja o difuziji egipatskih kultova po rimskoj Dalmaciji, *Vjesnik za arheologiju i historiju dalmatinsku. Bulletin d'archéologie et d'histoire dalmates*, Split 72-73 (1979), 79-89, with 1 ill., 2 pl., and a French summary on p. 90-92.

"Quelques remarques concernant la diffusion des divinités égyptiennes en Dalmatie".
The author tries to penetrate deeper into the extent and character of the Egyptian cults in Roman Dalmatia. In this context are analysed unpublished statuettes: two shawabtis and a bronze Isis figure from the Franciscan Monastery at Sinj, and a mummy-form figurine with the head lost, in a private collection, on the Island Hvar.

S.P. Tutundžić

79134 SOLMSEN, Friedrich, Isis among the Greeks and Romans. Published for Oberlin College by Harvard University Press, Cambridge, Mass. and London, 1979 (13.5 x 20.5 cm; XI + 157 p.) = Martin Classical Lectures, 25.

In the light of the impression that of all oriental deities whose power expanded in Late Antiquity, Isis established by far the closest contacts with the traditions of classical civilizations the author investigates some major stages of her reception and assimilation. Chapter 1 is devoted to the adoption and interpretatio graeca of Isis by the Greeks in Egypt. Chapter 2 is concerned with her further rise by assimilation with and absorption of other goddesses, this being connected with the Greek interest in the beginning of civilization. Chapter 3 deals with the Hellenistic Period and is called: Isis in Greek thought and Roman feeling. In the last chapter the author studies some aspects of Apuleius, Metamorphoses XI.
Index at the end of the book.

79135 STÖRK, Lothar, Magdi Youssef: Brecht in Ägypten. Versuch einer literatursoziologischen Deutung unter besonderer Berücksichtigung der Rezeption des Stückes "Herr Puntila und sein Knecht Matti", Bochum, 1976; Studienverlag Dr. N. Brockmeyer, 149.S., DM 12.80, *GM* Heft 31 (1979), 85-86.

Remarks on the above mentioned sociological dissertation, which may be of interest to Egyptologists.

79136 STRICKER, B.H., De Oorsprong van het Romeinse Amphitheater, *OMRO* 59-60 (1978-1979), 297-301.

Sequel to our numbers 4262 and 70519.
Discussing the origin of the Roman amphitheatre the author proceeds from the mention of the island-in-the-middle (*p3 iw ḥry-ib*) in the Story of Horus and Seth (Pap. Ch. Beatty I, recto V, 3-6).

79137   SZENTLÉLEKY, T., Iseums of the Roman Imperial Period, Some Problems, *in*: *Acts 1st ICE*, 621-627.

The author discusses some general problems of the spread of the Isis cult and, more particularly, the Savarian Iseum at Szombathely, Hungary.

79138   TRAN TAM TINH, [V], Sarapis debout: un problème iconographique, *in*: *Acts 1st ICE*, 645-649.

The author briefly discusses the problem of the standing-Sarapis statuary, about which subject he is preparing a study which will appear in the series of the Études préliminaires aux religions orientales dans l'Empire romain.

e. Varia

See also our numbers 79612; 79623; 79635 and 791001.

79139   *The Art Gallery. The International Magazine of Art and Culture*, Ivoryton, Conn. 22, No. 2 (December/January, 1979), p. 15-16, 24-112 and 117-119, with numerous ill. [many in colour, 1 on cover].

The issue of the periodical is almost completely devoted to Ancient Egypt. The introduction, called Kaleidoscope, is by the hand of Sally Devaney. We mention the other articles:
Cissy Grossman, Out of Egypt (very brief; on the Egyptian connections with Israel);
William C. Bendig, The Ancient Art of Egypt. A Photo Essay;
Sally G. Devaney, Dendur Temple, The Metropolitan Museum of Art. A Gift from Egypt;
Bernard V. Bothmer, Across the Bridge to Egypt (on the Egyptian collection in the Brooklyn Museum);
James Manning, The Valley of the Kings (on the work in the Valley of the Kings by the Theban Expedition of the Brooklyn Museum);
Richard Fazzini, The Precinct of Mut (on the work in the Mut temple by the Theban Expedition of the Brooklyn Museum);
James F. Romano, The Newest Museum of Egyptian Art (on the Luxor Museum);
Floyd Lattin, Up the Nile to Nubia (on the exhibition "Africa in Antiquity");
Jules Taylor, Brooklyn's Own Nubians (on artifacts from Nubia in the Brooklyn Museum);
Victoria Landy, Mendes: A Contemporary Dig (on the excavations at Mendes by the American Joint Expedition);
Deborah J. Mcleod, Abu Dign, Bearing Gifts from Egypt (on Charles Edwin Wilbour);
Robert S. Bianchi, Collecting & Collectors (on the objects and

the contributors to the Egyptian Collection at the Brooklyn Museum);
Diane Guzman, The Wilbour Library of Egyptology.

79140   ASAAD, Hany and Daniel KOLOS, The Name of the Dead. Hieroglyphic Inscriptions of the Treasures of Tutankhamun Translated, Mississauga, Ontario, Benben Publications, 1979 (21.5 x 28 cm; 129 p., 5 colour pl., map); rev. *JSSEA* 9 (1978-1979), 241-245 (Ronald J. Leprohon).

This book is designed as a practical, easy-to-use guide for reading the hieroglyphs on the treasures of Tutankhamun which have been on exhibition in the U.S.A. and elsewhere. The objects are translated in the order in which they appear in the exhibit as well as the numerical order of the Metropolitan Museum of Art Catalogue (our number 76782). The inscriptions of the objects are given in hieroglyphs, transliteration, approximate pronounciation and translation. Background information on the writing system is added. At the end of the booklet a glossary of occurring signs.

79141   BENS, Jacques, La semence d'Horus (Contes de l'Égypte des Pharaons), Paris, Éditions Garnier Frères, 1979 (14 x 20.5 cm; 185 p., 1 ill. on cover); series: collection "Légendaires".

The author presents in his own words several well-known stories from ancient Egypt.

79142   DEWACHTER, Michel, Nubie - Notes diverses (II). §§ 6 à 8, *BIFAO* 79 (1979), 311-326, with 1 pl. and 1 table.

Sequel to our number 71154.
(§ 6). Several documents are listed and discussed of the chief of the archers of Kush Nakhtmin, from the reign of Ramses II. His genealogy is dealt with, and the author stresses that he has to be distinguished from the *mr mšꜥ wr* Nakhtmin, from the time of Tutankhamun and Eye, who was no viceroy of Kush, as has been suggested.
(§ 7). As regards the succession of the viceroys Huy (1) and Paser (1), the latter may probably have been a son of the former.
(§ 8). The fragmentary sandstone statue in the Musée de Grenoble, Inv. 1962 (see the catalogue, our number 79601, No. 33), is a Meroitic *ba*-statue brought by de Saint-Ferriol from Nubia, possibly from Gebel Adda.   *J.J.J.*

79143   DOBROVITS, A., Válogatott tanulmányai. II: Irodalom és vallás az ókori Egyiptomban. Red. von L. Kákosy, Budapest, Akadémiai Kiadó, 1979 (317 p., 37 fig. and ill.) = Apollo Bibliothek, 8; rev. *Acta Archaeologica Academiae Scientiarum Hungaricae* 32 (1980), 469-470 (L. Castiglione).

"Ausgewählte Studien. II: Literatur und Religion im alten Ägypten."

79144 FINEGAN, Jack, Archaeological History of the Ancient Middle East, Boulder Colorado, Westview Press/Folkestone, Dawson, 1979 (15 x 23.5 cm; XXV + 456 p., 118 ill., 3 maps, 40 tables, ill. on cover); rev. *ZAW* 92 (1980), 174 (Georg Fohrer).

In the second part of the book the author presents a history of Ancient Egypt from the Prehistoric Period to the coming of Alexander the Great, with the usual excursuses. The author devotes some attention to the archaeology as a source for historical knowledge.

79145 KATSNELSON, I.S., Тутанхамон и сокровища его гробницы, Moscow, Издательство "Наука", 1979 (11 x 20 cm; 152 p., 31 ill., 1 fig., 1 plan); at head of title: Академия Наук СССР. Институт востоковедов.   Pr. 25 коп.

'Tutankhamun and the Treasures of his Tomb'.
A reprint of our number 77401 (which appeared in 1976).

79146 MRSICH, Tycho, Ein Beitrag zum "Hieroglyphischen Denken" (2. Teil), *SAK* 7 (1979), 163-225.

Sequel to our number 78566.
In this second part the author first deals with the conception by foreigners of hieroglyphic writing, and then with the way in which modern thought conceives concept, with symbol and meaning, and other philosophical problems.
                                                              J.J.J.

79147 SMITH, H.S., Varia Ptolemaica, *in*: *Glimpses of Ancient Egypt*, 161-166.

Three brief notes dealing with: 1. words with *mim* prefix, of which a list is presented; those for which the earliest attestation is from the Ptolemaic Period may have been ancient formations, nevertheless; 2. the Greek Νεῖλος that is derived from *n3 itrw* (*ꜥ3w*); 3. the four to six Ptolemaic temples, now largely destroyed, that stood on the escarpment of the Memphite necropolis overlooking the city and have been the object of recent excavations.   J.J.J.

79148 STIERLIN, Henri, De Farao's, Alphen aan de Rijn, Uitgeverij Septuaginta/ICOB, 1979 (23 x 32.5 cm; 96 p., 2 colour ill. on endpapers, 1 colour frontispiece, numerous colour ill., 2 colour ill. on cover).

A book for the general reader exclusively illustrated with colour illustrations, which deals with Ancient Egypt in a chronological order.

79149 YOSHIMURA, Sakuji, Sand, Sweat and the 1978 A.D. Pyramid, *PHP. A Forum for a Better World*, Tokyo 10, No.4 (103) (April 1979), 19-34 and 72-74, with 13 ill. and 2 fig.

Article about a pyramid built by the Japanese at Gîza.

79150 ZAMAROVSKÝ, Vojtěch, Bohové a kralové starého Egypta, Praha, Mlada fronta, 1979 (405 p., 16 colour pl.).

"Götter und Könige Altägyptens."
Populärwissenschaftliches Buch, angelegt in Form eines Lexikons mit über 500 Stichworten zu Geschichte, Kultur und Religion Altägyptens. Das Buch vervollständigen Schwarzweiss- und Farbfotos, Zeichnungen, Tafeln, indices ägyptischer Herrscher und Gaue sowie eine Bibliographie mit der wichtigsten ägyptologischen Fachliteratur.

B. Vachala

II. SCRIPT AND LANGUAGE

a. Scripts

See also our numbers 79025; 79096; 79140; 79146; 79203; 79264; 79346; 79377; 79410; 79424; 79517; 79612; 79623; 79640; 79645; 79779; 79817; 79898 and 79968.

79151 CAZELLES, H., Les inscriptions dites proto-sinaïtiques, *Le Monde de la Bible*, Paris No. 10 (Août-Septembre 1979), 30-31, with 2 ill.

Brief note on the Sinai inscriptions.

79152 CROSS, Frank Moore, Early Alphabetic Scripts, *in : Symposia Celebrating the Seventy-Fifth Anniversary of the Founding of the American Schools of Oriental Research (1900-1975)*. Edited by Frank Moore Cross, Cambridge, Mass., American Schools of Oriental Research, 1979 (= Zion Research Foundation Occasional Publications, 1-2), 97-123, with 12 ill. and fig.

Reconsidering the problem of the early alphabetic scripts in Canaan and Phoenicia the author criticizes in section 2, sub 3 Helck's attempt to derive the Phoenician alpabet from Egyptian Hieratic (our number 72312).

79153 FISCHER, Henry George, Ancient Egyptian Calligraphy. A Beginner's Guide to Writing Hieroglyphs, New York, The Metropolitan Museum of Art, 1979 (22 x 30.5 cm; XIII + 63 p., numerous fig.).

In the introduction the author points out that it is his aim to encourage a better standard in writing hieroglyphs. His selection of signs emphasises those that require most practice, those whose form particularly requires explanation and those that require comment additional to that in the sign list of Gardiner's grammar. The last two objectives are primarily accomplished by the addition of mainly O.K. examples. The changes in form and proportions of hieroglyphs are considered, and a checklist of sources for palaeographic comparisons is given.
The author presents all alphabetic (monoconsonantal) signs and a selection of others arranged after the categories of Gardiner's grammar. Apart from the types in Gardiner are many others, accompanied by drawings of and references to the originals. In the case of signs difficult to draw he presents the successive stages for drawing a clear handwritten hieroglyph.
At the end of the book there are given addenda and a list of sources of figures and supplementary references.

79154 GRIMM, Alfred, Zu einer kryptographischen (änigmatischen) Schreibung des Substantivums *kkw* "Finsternis" im Höhlenbuch (Livre des Quererts), Livre des Quererts (3), *GM* Heft 32 (1979), 23-26.

Die im sogenannten Höhlenbuch belegte ungewöhnliche Schreibung des Substantivs *kkw* "Finsternis" mit einer Doppelsetzung der Hieroglyphe des Rinderfelles sowie nachfolgender *w*- Hieroglyphe mit dem Determinativ der Hieroglyphe des Himmels, von dem ein Gegenstand herabhängt, geht auf die im Spruch 373 (C.T. V, 35c) und Spruch 335 (C.T. IV, 320 c) aussergewöhnliche Determinierung des Substantivs *kkw* "Finsternis" mit einem Rinderfell zurück.
Inge Hofmann

79155 KRUCHTEN, J.-M., Que vient faire la couronne de Basse Egypte dans le second cartouche d'Horemheb?, *GM* Heft 35 (1979), 25-30.

Die zweite Kartusche des Haremheb wird mit dem Falken *Ḥr*, *m* und *ḥb* geschrieben, wobei in vielen Fällen zwischen das Zeichen des Falken und *m* ein zunächst überflüssig erscheinendes Zeichen der Roten Krone eingeschoben wird. Dieses hat nicht den Lautwert *n*, sondern *mḥ(w)* als Alternative zu *m-ḥb*, da das finale *b* bereits im Neuen Reich nicht mehr gesprochen wurde.
Inge Hofmann

79156 LABIB, Abdel Masih, The Formation of the Hieroglyphic Writing, *Archaeological & Historical Studies*. The Archaeological Society of Alexandria, Alexandria 6 (1979), 35-38, with 1 table.

A brief note in which the author points out that writing in Egypt existed earlier than in any other country, and that the invention was made at Naqada as early as 4000 B.C.

79157 LEAHY, Anthony, The Name of Osiris Written 𓊨𓀀, *SAK* 7 (1979), 141-153.

Studying the occurrences of the spellings of the name of Osiris with 𓀀 as the determinative, the author argues that they all belong either to the reign of Hatshepsut and the early years of Tuthmosis III (the "Deir el-Bahari era") or to the Kushite Period. He demonstrates by some examples how this spelling can be used as a dating criterion.
In an appendix monuments from the XXIInd to the XXVth Dynasties on which the name of Osiris occurs are listed. A postscript on an isolated spelling with 𓀀 from the M.K. J.J.J.

79158 LEAHY, Anthony, An unusual spelling of $krŝt$, *GM* Heft 31 (1979), 67-74, with 1 pl.

Das Wörterbuch enthält ein Wort $k3ŝ$ das als Variante des Verbes $krŝ$ "begraben" angesehen wird. Dieses findet sich in Texten der 26. Dynastie, die vorgestellt werden. Dabei wird auch die bisher unpublizierte Stele Philadelphia U.M.E. 15994 herangezogen. Das in Frage stehende Wort ist das Nomen $krŝt$, nicht das Verb $krŝ$ und entspricht dem Koptischen ⲔⲀⲒⲤⲈ, ⲔⲀⲒⲤⲒ. Problematisch ist dass r durch 3 und nicht wie üblich durch j repräsentiert wird, so dass es sich vielleicht um eine Edfu-Besonderheit handeln mag.
Inge Hofmann

79159 LIZANA SALAFRANCA, Joaquín G., Introducción Elemental a la Escritura Jeroglífica Egipcia, Huesca, [no publisher], 1979 (21.5 x 31 cm; IV + 24 p.); at head of title: Colegio Universitario de Huesca; rev. *Boletín de la Asociacion Española de Orientalistas* 15 (1979), 288-289 (Lorenzo Baqués).

Short introduction for students to the hieroglyphic script, with sections on hieratic and Demotic writing and on the decipherment of the hieroglyphs.
J.J.J.

79160 NUR-EL-DIN, M.A., Checking, Terminal, Stress Marks, Partition Indications and Margin Lines in Demotic Documents, *Enchoria* 9 (1979), 49-62.

Collection and attempt of interpretation of all kinds of markers as met with in Demotic texts.
W. Brunsch

79161 POSENER-KRIÉGER, P., Mesures des textiles à l'Ancien Empire, *in*: *Acts 1st ICE*, 523-524.

Short note on the measuring of textiles in the O.K.
The study was published in full in our number 77610.

79162 WEIDMÜLLER, Wilhelm, Die Sinai-Schrift. Nich die Urschrift, sondern eine Nachbildung des phönikischen Alphabetes, *Archiv für Geschichte des Buchwesens*, Frankfurt am Main 19 (1978), 191-223, with 7 fig. and summaries in German, English and French.

After a detailed survey of the scholarly opinions on the origin of the Latin alphabet the author discusses the problem of the Sinai script as the ancestor of the Phoenician alphabet. Proceeding from a method in which the visual presentation of scripts carries more weight than any number of words, he defends the thesis that the Sinaitic script is a formal imitation or remodeling a variant or an analogon of the ancient Phoenician alphabet.

79163 de WIT, Constant, Les valeurs du signe de l'oeil dans le système hiéroglyphique, *in*: *Festschrift Elmar Edel*, 446-455.

The author lists a large number of possibilities to use the eye in the hieroglyphic writing, with various values.
J.J.J.

79164 ZAWADOWSKI, Y.N., Les systèmes d'écriture égyptienne et méroitique: parallèles et conclusions, *in*: Шампольон и Дешифровка, 34-36.

Stating that the Meroitic script is principally syllabic, each sign representing the combination CV - although a zero value for C or V also occurs - the author argues that the Egyptian writing also had no pure vocals, and demonstrates that this statement helps us to understand the evolution from Egyptian to Semitic and Meroitic writings.
J.J.J.

b. Grammar

See also our numbers 79069; 79155; 79219; 79277; 79322; 79391; 79401 and 79517.

79165 ALLEN, J.P., Is the "Emphatic" Sentence an Adverbial-Predicate Construction ?, *GM* Heft 32 (1979), 7-15.

Nach seiner Untersuchung kommt der Verfasser zu dem Ergebnis, dass der "emphatische" Satz keine adverbial-prädikative Konstruktion ist, wenn auch die Bedeutung der adverbialen Adjunkte im "emphatischen" Satz nicht übersehen wird.
Für eine Erwiderung siehe unsere Nummer 79182.
Inge Hofmann

79166 BÖHLIG, Alexander, Zur Stellung des adjektivischen Attributs im Koptischen, *in*: *Festschrift Elmar Edel*, 42-53.

The author argues that the Coptic construction in which the attribute precedes a noun, connected by N̄, which is already found in O.Eg., serves to delimit the noun. The construction proceeded from general words and led to clearer delimitation of special characteristics.

J.J.J.

79167   BORGHOUTS, Joris F., A New Approach to the Late Egyptian Conjunctive, ZÄS 106 (1979), 14-24.

Viewing the conjunctive in context with other Late Egyptian 'narrative' verb forms, the author stresses its primary interest in thematic development. Giving 22 representative examples, he discusses its future orientation, its 'customary' function, and (observed by the author) its recording presumed facts.

M. Heerma v. Voss

79168   BORGHOUTS, J.F., A New Grammar of Late Egyptian, BiOr 36 (1979), 1-10.

Review article of M. Korostovtsev, Grammaire du néo-égyptien (our number 73411).

79169   BORGHOUTS, J.F., Some Remarks on Relativization in Late Egyptian, GM Heft 31 (1979), 9-18.

The author presents a systematic and integrated treatment of the three types of relative clauses (participle, relative form, nty). He considers them as the result of a fusion process between two originally independent sentences, one of which becomes embedded in the other. It is a condition for the fusion that in both sentences there is an identical and coreferential noun, which is surrounded by other elements. In the process the second sentence is put behind that noun in the first sentence, the noun in the second sentence is moved leftward to initial position, but is replaced by the (abstract) relative pronoun and assumes the form correlating with the initial element of the second sentence itself. The place of the noun in the second sentence being taken by a resumptive pronoun is a matter of its boundedness to an element to its left (e.g. preposition, genitive n, infinitive). The formula is given in tagmemic terminology and is exemplified by three examples with short comments.
The same topic is dealt with at more length by the same author in JNES 40 (1981), 99-117.

79170   BORGHOUTS, J.F., A Tagmemic Analysis of Late Egyptian, in: Acts 1st ICE, 111-116.

After explaining how tagmemic analysis of a language works and stating that it is open to transformational procedures, the author argues that tagmemics is particularly suitable for describing Late Egyptian. He indicates some problems on which tagmemic analysis can be applied with profit.

J.J.J.

79171 BRUNNER, Hellmut, An Outline of Middle Egyptian Grammar. For Use in Academic Instruction, Graz, Akademische Druck- u. Verlagsanstalt, 1979 (17 x 24 cm; 122 p.).

English translation of our number 67102.
In the preface to the present edition the author acknowledges the great value of the studies of H.J. Polotsky in the field of M.Eg. grammar but states not to be able to incorporate their results in this traditional grammar which takes the form of verbs as a starting point.
Some straight errors in the text were corrected, but others in the exercises were not.

79172 CHETVERUKHIN, A.S., О главных члеиак староегипетского именного предложения, in: Письменные памятники и проблемы истории культуры народов востока. XIV Годичная научная сессия ло ив АН СССР (Доклады и сообщения) Декабрь 1978 Г. Часть II, Moscow, [Издательство "Наука". Главная редакция восточной литературы], 1979, 259-265.

'The main constituents of the ancient Egyptian nominal sentence'. After a survey of the various non-verbal constructions with *pw* as a copula, the author gives a logical analysis of the absence of the pattern 'participle + *pw* + participle/adjective' and 'adjective + *pw* + participle/adjective'. None of these constituents would qualify for subjecthood, the presence of a subject (i.e., the element over which something else is predicated) being a basic requirement.

J.F. Borghouts

79173 CRUZ-URIBE, Eugene, An Archaic Use of the Impersonal Pronoun in Demotic, *Sarapis* 5, No. 1 (1979), 15-16.

Although the 3rd ps. plur. .*w* replaced *tw* as impersonal pronoun during Late Egyptian, the author points out five instances of the archaic use of *tw* (written *tw.tw*) in Demotic texts, namely Dem. Pap. Cairo 50059 (three times), Dem. Pap. Cairo 50070 and Pap. Ryl. IX.

J.J.J.

79174 DORET, Eric, La forme *sḏm.n.f* narrative, *Bulletin Société d'Egyptologie*, Genève No. 2 (Novembre 1979), 13-22.

After presenting a survey of the four *sḏm.f* forms (see author's article, *JNES* 39, 1980, 25-30) and the two *sḏm.n.f* forms, the author attempts to determine the morphological character of the "continuative" *sḏm.n.f* in a narration. He argues that it is the circumstantial form. It functions as expression of the indicative, and is preceded by an auxiliary in initial position in the first sentence of a series.

J.J.J.

79175 DORET, E., The Reading of the Negation ⌒𓄡𓄿, *JEA* 65 (1979), 161-163.

It is suggested here that the reading by James in our number 62290 be emended from *n wnn.f* to *n wn.n.f*. examples in support of this being found in the C.T.
E.P.Uphill

79176 ELANSKAYA, A.I., La construction dite "connection adverbiale" et le rôle de ⲞⲨⲚ̄/ⲘⲚ̄ en Copte, *in*: Шампольон и Дешифровка, 29-33.

After having pointed out the adverbial and not genuine verbal character of the verb forms (infinitive, qualitative) the author studies the obligatory character of ⲞⲨⲚ̄/ⲘⲚ̄ in Present I and Future I constructions having no preformant and an undefined substantival subject. She concludes that in these constructions we have a purely nominative predication which expresses the constatation of the presence/absence of a thing and that the verb form or adverb plays no predicative, but a circumstantial role. ⲞⲨⲚ̄ turns out to be a participle, which is explained by the substantive in apposition: "which is, (namely) a thing", with the verb-form/adverb as circumstantial description. At the end follows an explication of the element *t* in certain persons of the Present I and Future I as originating from the M. Eg. particle *ty*.

79177 ELANSKAYA, A.I., Упраление глаголов с отрицательным значением в Коптском языке, *in*: Письменные памятники и проблемы истории культуры народов востока. XIV Годичная научная сессия ло ив АН СССР (Доклады и сообщения), Декабрь 1978 Г., Часть II, Moscow, [Издательсиво "Наука". Главная редакция восточной литературы], 1979, 237-241.

'Rule of verbs with negative meaning in Coptic'.
1. A purpose clause dominated by a higher clause containing a verb of prevention or defence, must contain a negation, e.g. ⲀⲨⲬⲒⲢⲰϤ ⲈⲦⲘ̄ϢⲀϪⲈ 'they prevented him to speak'.
2. Conversely, if such a higher clause is negative itself, the subordinate purpose clause is nonnegative, e.g. Ⲛ̄ⲄⲚⲀⲔⲰⲀⲨ Ⲙ̄ⲘⲞⲒ ⲀⲚ ⲈⲂⲰⲔ 'you won't hinder me from going'.
3. If a nonnegative prevention clause is followed by a nonnegative subordinate one, the latter obviously does not set forth the consequences of the former, e.g. ⲦⲀϨⲚⲞ Ⲙ̄ⲘⲞⲔ ⲈⲐⲢⲒϢⲈⲚⲔ̄ 'keep yourself in check, that I may visit you'. That is, negative intention results negatively, while negated negative intention ends up positively. Biblical translations either follow the above Coptic rules or else closely follow the Greek original. Finally, Besa breaks down rule I if the consequence clause is interrogative: ⲚⲒⲘ ⲠⲈⲦⲔⲰⲀⲨⲈ Ⲙ̄ⲘⲞϤ ⲈϪⲞⲞϤ 'who prevents him from saying it?'.
J.F.Borghouts

79178 FAULKNER, R.O., The Prospective sḏm.f in the Coffin Texts, in: *Glimpses of Ancient Egypt*, 1-3.

The author lists a number of occurrences of the prospective sḏm.f in the C.T. They appear in main clauses expressing an intention or a promise; in noun clauses as objects of verbs (rdy, imy, wḥm and the vetitive m); in subordinate clauses of purpose; in future conditional clauses. Usually the form can only be recognized in the case of ultimae infirmae verbs, but three instances of an -y attached to triliteral verbs are noted.

J.J.J.

79179 GASKINS, Leanna, Notes on Middle Egyptian Syntax, [privately published], 1978 (21.6 x 27.9 cm; X + 217 loose p.).

The present notes on Middle Egyptian syntax are the product of current and on-going work at the University of California, Berkeley on the application of modern linguistics to Egyptian syntax, particularly of the transformational-generative theories of Noam Chomsky.
The prevailing notion of a non-verbal sentence type is abandoned in favour of a strict verb-subject-object structure in Middle Egyptian, with copula deletion in sentences where the copula is unmarked. The syntactic analyses are processed by phrase-structure and transformational rules, which are given as a set in the summary at the end of the book. Another feature of the present study is its treatment of higher predicates: the sentence-markers among which iw, the negations n and nn, and some particles (Gardiner's terminology). The many examples are each time presented with the tree diagrams of the deep structure and their surface structure (in handwritten hieroglyphs). They are a mixture of made-up and actual examples. For the latter group no source references are given.
The appendix contains a concordance table to topics discussed in Gardiner's Grammar.
Index at the end of the book. No bibliography and notes.

79180 GRAEFE, Erhart, Ein unbekannter Gebrauch des indirekten Genitivs in Zahlkonstruktionen, in: *Festschrift Elmar Edel*, 174-184.

Besides the constructions noun + number and number + indirect genitive + noun there occur instances of the order noun + n(y) + number, some of which the author mentions. The construction is particularly used where the number indicates the sum total of the parts of what is counted, either an object or a general concept (e.g. cattle-tax or persons).
An appendix is devoted to the place of the word "arura" when occurring with a number.

J.J.J.

79181 GREEN, Michael, A Use of the Independent Pronoun in Late Egyptian, *Oriens Antiquus* 18 (1979), 295-300.

The author argues, with the help of ten examples almost all from the late XXth Dynasty or later, that the independent pronouns also seem to convey the nuance of: 'to A belongs the legal or moral responsibility/answerability for B", apart from its well-known appearance in "A is B" and "to A belongs B" expressions.

79182 JUNGE, Friedrich, Adverbialsatz und emphatische Formen, Nominalsatz und Negation. Eine "Gegendarstellung", *GM* Heft 33 (1979), 69-88.

Der Verfasser nimmt Stellung zu unserer Nr. 79165 und überprüft die vorgebrachten Argumente hinsichtlich der Fragen, ob die Distribution der "emphatischen" Sätze nicht mit den Adverbialsätzen identisch ist, sondern mehr der der Nominalsätze gleicht, ob die emphatischen Formen eher "nominale Prädikate" als Subjekte eines adverbiellen Prädikates sind, ob die den emphatischen Formen notwendigen adverbiellen Bestimmungen deren verbale Rektionen und ihre Bestimmung als "logische" Prädikate für die grammatische Struktur grundsätzlich wenig relevant sind. Nach einer gründlichen Untersuchung kann er feststellen, dass kein Grund dafür besteht, die Richtigkeit der Theorie der emphatischen Formen in Zweifel zu ziehen.

Inge Hofmann

79183 JUNGE, Friedrich, Der Gebrauch von jw im mittelägyptischen Satz, *in*: *Festschrift Elmar Edel*, 263-271.

The author studies the function of initial iw preceding a $sḏm.n.f$, a $sḏm.f$, and an adverbial sentence. He concludes that iw characterizes the following verb-form as the predicate - hence it cannot be followed by the emphatic $sḏm.f$ which by its nature is subject of the sentences. The same rule applies for the adverbial sentence with iw: here too the following noun is predicate, while when used without iw the adverbial adjunct is predicate. This explains the difference between $mk\ iw.i\ ii.kw$, stressing the action, and $iw.i\ ii.kw$, stressing the person, and between $iw\ sḏm.f$ and $iw.f\ sḏm.f$.

J.J.J.

79184 JUNGE, F., Zur Syntax des $sḏm.f$, *in*: *Acts 1st ICE*, 337-345.

The author argues against the current conceptions that the $sḏm.f$ fulfills all syntactic tasks. In the survey of the Egyptian verb here presented the use of one of the three $sḏm.f$ forms, emphatic circumstantial or prospective (the indicative $sḏm.f$ actually does not occur) is defined by the position within a paradigma consisting of the noun, the $sḏm.n.f$ (seldom as object) and the clause. In the position of the subject the emphatic, in the position of predicate the circumstantial, in the position of object of a verb the prospective *sḏm.f* is used. These forms thus contain no information primarily usable for the syntax.

J.J.J.

79185 KASSER, Rodolphe, Relations de généalogie dialectale dans le domain lycopolitain, *Bulletin Société d'Égyptologie*, Genève No. 2 (Novembre 1979), 31-36.

Proceeding his studies of the Coptic dialect L (see our number 74385) the author discusses the development of the dialects in the Lycopolitan area.

J.J.J.

79186 KOROSTOVTSEV, M.A., Попытки обозн ачения гласных и поздней Египетской иероглифике, *in*: Шампольон и Дешифровка, 37-40.

"Attempts to Designate the Vowels in Late Egyptian Hieroglyphics." The author deals with the history of the problem of Egyptian vocalization. Since in Graeco-Roman texts, under the influence of the Greek, the consonants *i*, *w*, *ꜣ* and *ꜥ* were also used as vowels, Champollion conceived them as these. Sethe and Drioton demonstrated that this is wrong.

J.J.J.

79187 LIVERANI, Mario, Farsi Ḫabiru, *Vicino Oriente*, Roma 2 (1979), 65-77.

The author discusses possible influence of the Egyptian on the language of the Amarna Letters, particularly of the phrase *iri m/n/mi*, "behave oneself like".

J.J.J.

79188 MELTZER, Edmund S., Desiderata for the Historical and Comparative Study of Egyptian, *in*: Acts 1st ICE, 465-476.

The author surveys the problems connected with the historical and comparative study of Egyptian, devoting much attention to its place in the Afroasiatic family.
Extensive critical apparatus in the notes.

79189 MUELLER, Dieter, A Concise Introduction to Middle Egyptian Grammar, Lethbridge, 1975 (A-4 format; XI + 276 p.; p. 239 missing).

In the preface the author points out that the present grammar is meant for the instruction of undergraduate students and has incorporated particularly the more recent views of Polotsky on the M. Eg. verbal system and its syntax. For the sake of the demands to be made of a textbook for the academic class-room it consists of 20 chapters of somewhat equal length.
All chapters are subdivided in sections of varying length, 69 in total, and are provided with exercises, except for the first two.

These exercises consist primarily of genuine text units, particularly taken from the C.T. and Urk. IV, but also from literary and medical texts, with explanatory notes added. Only those to the first chapters utilize loose sentences,
Not only the inclusion of Polotsky's views, but also the author's treatment of the modes of negation make clear that this grammar is well up-to-date and meets the needs of both students and the teacher. It takes an intermediary position between a comprehensive and didactic grammar like Gardiner's and a concise and not up-to date one like Brunner's.
The grammar is concluded by an index of Egyptian sources with references of text passages to the sections in which they occur; a selective bibliography; a sign list which is an abbreviated version of the one in Gardiner's grammar but which also contains a few variants (Gardiner's sign numbers are extended with two zeros); and an index to the foregoing sign-list.
Since the grammar is as yet still unpublished, it being under final review, studies and commentary by others, and field use, enquiries should be made to The Society for the Study of Egyptian Antiquities, 6 Glencairn Ave., Toronto, Ontario M4R 1N5, Canada.

79190 OSING, Jürgen, Zur Entstehung der mittelägyptischen Negation ⌢⌣, in: *Festschrift Elmar Edel*, 302-313.

The author demonstrates that M.Eg ⌢⌣ is indeed *nn*; the alleged instances of *ny* are all inconclusive. He then raises the question of the origin of *nn*. From some C.T. Spells (186 and 187) he draws the conclusion that it originates from the particle *in* + *n*. The last part of the paper discusses the vocalization of *nn* and its development.
See also our number 79199.   *J.J.J.*

79191 ROCCATI, Alessandro, Abgeleitete Konstruktionen des Ägyptischen, *GM* Heft 36 (1979), 39-49.

Da der ägyptische Satz die Voranstellung des Subjektes wie auch des Prädikates erlaubt, ist die Unterscheidung zwischen "Nominalsatz" und "Verbalsatz" sehr schwierig. Das Verbalelement scheint mehr eine allgemeine Aussage der "Aktion" zu enthalten, als einer festen Klasse "Verbum" zuzugehören. Ein Sprachstadium, das auf der Aktionsart beruht, ist altertümlich. Die ägyptische Sprache im Alten und Mittleren Reich scheint in einem solchen Stadium zu sein, während im Neuägyptischen differenzierte Bedeutungen aus Konstruktionsverschiebungen sichtbar werden, die ein Verbalsystem voraussetzen. Es werden verschiedene Konstruktionsarten vorgestellt, aus denen hervorgeht, dass die ägyptische Sprache versucht, ein Verbalsystem zu entwickeln.
Inge Hofmann

79192 ROQUET, Gérard, Chronologie relative des changements phonétiques affectant [z] et [r] et dialectalismes provinciaux à l'ancien

Empire. *tꜣ zrf* et *mrzt* à Ḥawārta/Tahna, *in*: Hommages Sauneron I, 437-462, with 3 pl.

The author proceeds from two uncommon spellings in the so-called "Fraser Tombs" at Tihna, occuring in offering lists, namely *tꜣ zrf* (instead of *tꜣ zif*) and *mrzt* (instead of *mizt*), "liver." To the former he adds the writings *z(.)f* and *sr.f*. With a wealth of examples he discusses the palatalization of [r] as second of three consonants, arguing that it had arrived earlier elsewhere than at Tihna. The date of the development [z] to [s] is less clear.
In three excursuses Roquet deals with [rꜣ] as transitional form between [r] and [j] with archaism in compound nouns, and with ○̣, ○̣ *tꜣ*.

J.J.J.

79193 SALEH, A., Notes on the Phonetic Values of Some Egyptian Letters, *in*: *Acts 1st ICE*, 557-564.

The author discusses the *w*, *ꜣ*, the feminine *t*, and the *ḏ* of the Egyptian alphabet against a Semitic background. Many identifications with Arabic words including proper and geographical names are given.

79194 SATZINGER, Helmut, Phonologie des koptischen Verbs (Saʕidischer Dialekt), *in*: *Festschrift Elmar Edel*, 343-368.

Study of the phonological system in Sahidic on the basis of the infinitive in the stat. pron. and the qualitative. The author deals with the various vowels and consonants, presenting his results in section 22 (p. 353-354). In a long appendix (354-368) the various verbal classes are dealt with.

J.J.J.

79195 SCHENKEL, Wolfgang, Kritische Anmerkungen zur Methode der Bestimmung von Lautgesetzen für die Rekonstruktion ägyptischer Nachtonvokale, *in*: *Festschrift Elmar Edel*, 369-389, with 2 tables.

The author begins with a critical review of Osing's reconstruction of the vowels in post-stress position (see our number 76611), with special attention to its methodological shortcomings. He then presents a scheme which explains the regularities, while some irregularities can be eliminated along different ways.

J.J.J.

79196 SPALINGER, Anthony, The Negatives ⌒ and ⌒ in the Piye (Piankhy) Stela, *RdE* 31 (1979), 66-80.

L'auteur a relevé que ⌒ se trouve devant le prospectif *sḏm.f*, tandis que ⌒ n'y est jamais. On peut donc obtenir de nouvelles précisions dans la traduction.
En gros, on peut conclure que ⌒ correspond à M. Eg. ⌒ et ⌒

à M. Eg. —, dans que cela implique de rapports phonétiques ou grammaticaux entre les deux époques.

Ph. Derchain

79197 THÉODORIDÈS, Aristide, À propos du sḏm.f passif introduit par une préposition et des formes verbales à réduplication, *Annuaire de l'Institut de Philologie et d'Histoire Orientales et Slaves*, Bruxelles 23 (1979), 95-111.

The author discusses the verb form r mȝiw.f from Pap. Pushkin 127, 4,12, which Caminos (our number 77147, p. 58) explains as an instance of the rare construction of a passive sḏm.f after a preposition. He argues that the form is here an infinitive used, as often, after words such as ꜥȝ, wr, wrḏ, wdn etc., plus r. The second part is devoted to the form šdd.tw in O. Nash 2, 14, which Frandsen (our number 74207, §81) explained as a "that-form". Théodoridès argues from the context that this cannot be correct, but that the scribe wanted to stress by the second d (pronounced as t) the following t of tw. Several other instances of this scribal custom are mentioned.

J.J.J.

79198 WATSON, P.J., Consonantal Patterning in Egyptian Triliteral Verbal Roots, *in*: *Glimpses of Ancient Egypt*, 100-106, with 3 tables.

The author analyses the distribution of consonants in Egyptian triliteral roots (see also our number 73612) and compares his conclusions with the patterning in Semitic. He concludes that the same type of patterning occurs in both, e.g. identical consonants are excluded in position I-II and I-III, whilst the *IIae-gem.* type with identical consonants in II-III is found. On the other hand, Semitic languages possess roughly twice as many *med.-gem.* verbal roots as would occur on a chance basis and Egyptian the expected number. The conclusions may lead to modification of the view of some Egyptian consonants and helps to locate the Egyptian's historical position within Hamito-Semitic.

J.J.J.

79199 WESTENDORF, Wolfhart, Zur Lesung der mittelägyptischen (prädikativen) Negation (Teil 1), *GM* Heft 36 (1979), 61-67.

Der Verfasser nimmt weiterhin an, dass es eine einheitliche Negation *inj* gibt, die sich zunächst lautlich, dann aber auch orthographisch grammatikalisiert auseinanderentwickelt hat, ausgelöst durch die unterschiedlichen Betonungsverhältnisse in den verschiedenen Gebrauchsweisen. Es werden eine Reihe von Beispielen angeführt, die Diskussion soll fortgesetzt werden.
Siehe auch unsere Nummer 79199.

Inge Hofmann

79200 YOUSSEF, Ahmad Abdel-Hamid, The Stative Participle - An Arabic Approach to Egyptian Grammar, *BIFAO* 79 (1979), 441-449.

The author compares the use of the Pseudoparticiple (Old Perfective) with that of the Arabic verbal measure *faʿīl-faʿōl*, arguing that there is a close resemblance between them. This is illustrated by a large number of examples from hieroglyphic texts, to which are added an English as well as an Arabic translation.

J.J.J.

c. Lexicography, expressions, proper names, epithets

See also our numbers 79039; 79043; 79065; 79075; 79087; 79129; 79136; 79147; 79161; 79241; 79262; 79264; 79271; 79274; 79283; 79377; 79384; 79394; 79542; 79640; 79658; 79718; 79720; 79727; 79751; 79821; 79842; 79843; 79859; 79877; 79881; 79897; 79951; 79956; 79964; 79976 and 79986.

79201 ABD ER-RAZIQ, Mahmud, Die altägyptischen Weingarten *(k3nw/k3mw)* bis zum Ende des Neuen Reiches, *MDAIK* 35 (1979), 227-247.

The author successively discusses *k3nw* on cylinder seals from the O.K., *k3mw / k3nw* until the N.K. and during that period (the latter divided geographically into five groups: the Delta, Heliopolis, Memphis, Hermopolis and Thebes), the products of the *k3mw* gardens (wine and fruit), their irrigation, the gardener, and the words *k3mw-k3nw-k3ry* (see the catalogue of writings, p. 242-247). In the summary (240-241) the author i.a. concludes that the original word for vineyard was **k3lw*, superseded during the N.K. by the Semitic *k3mw*. *K3ry* indicates the professional gardener, *k3myw* the personnel of the vineyard in general.

J.J.J.

79202 ANDREU, Guillemette, An Etymological Problem, *JEA* 65 (1979), 166-167.

The writer proposes a different word *tk* as the ancestor of the Demotic *tk* to that of *dg3* "razor" of Davies (our number 77184).

E.P. Uphill

79203 BARTA, Winfried, Das Jahr in Datumsangaben und seine Bezeichnungen, *in: Festschrift Elmar Edel*, 35-41.

The author once more studies the reading of 𓆳, arguing against von Beckerath (see our number 69060) that it was read in the O.K. as *rnpt zp*, which became *rnpt ḥsbt* in the M.K. and later on *ḥsbt*. He also argues that, except those XIIth Dynasty rulers who began their reign as coregent, no pharaoh after the VIth Dynasty antedated his years to the New Year's day of his first year, until the Late Period when *rnpt* (calendar year) and *rnpt ḥsbt* (reigning year) are again distinguished.

J.J.J.

79204 BERLEV, O.D., "Золотое имя" Египетского царя, in: Шампольон и Дешифровка, 41-59.

"The 'Golden Name' of the Egyptian King."
The author presents an important discussion of the "Golden Horus" name of the Pharaohs and its interpretations through the ages, down to the Roman Period. His most interesting point is that originally "golden" here indicates the flesh of the god, the main proof being derived from Amenemhat's titulary on the Leiden stela V4, which Berlev reads as Ḥr m3ˁ-ḫrw m (sic!) nbw (see p. 50); m3ˁ-ḫrw is the variable part, normally written after Ḥr (m) nbw, "Horus in the Flesh".
It is only in the XIIIth Dynasty that nbw acquires in some instances the meaning "Golden", while in the Late Period the interpretation "Horus on the golden" (= his enemy) occurs.
J.J.J.

79205 de CENIVAL, Françoise, En marge du P. dém. Lille 99. Quelques nouveaux exemples d'une variante du nom théophore Ns-nḥmt.t ˁw3j, Enchoria 9 (1979), 139-140.

The theophorous proper name Ns-nḥm-ˁn that occurs in P. dem. Lille 99 is a variant of the well-known name Ns-nḥm.t-ˁw3j.
W. Brunsch

79206 CLÈRE, Jacques J., Recherches sur le mot ⲟ̓ⲥ des textes gréco-romains et sur d'autres mots apparentés, BIFAO 79 (1979), 285-310, with 2 tables and 1 ill.

Listing a large number of occurrences in texts from the Graeco-Roman Period of the word written ⲟ̓ⲥ and varr., the author argues from its use in the Pap. Bremner Rhind and the Litany of the Sun that it is probably to be read as ḥsbw, certainly not as š3w. It probably indicates a mineral substance of green colour in the earlier texts; its various meanings in expressions from the Graeco-Roman Period are still uncertain.
J.J.J.

79207 COUROYER, B., A propos de Luc. II, 52, Revue Biblique, Paris 86 (1979), 92-101.

On account of a New Testament passage in Luke II 52 the author discusses the N.K. epistolary expression "the favour in the presence of (ḥst m-b3ḥ) gods and men" and the expression spd-ḥr "alert(ness)", occurring in funerary offering formulae. The connection between "favour" and "love" is briefly touched upon. Some concluding remarks are devoted to the influence of Egyptian wisdom literature on the Hebrew proverbial wisdom texts.

79208 DĄBROWSKA-SMEKTAŁA, E., ḥtp di n<y>swt Formula, New Variant from Meir, in: Acts 1st ICE, 131-132.

A hitherto unknown variant of the ḥtp-dỉ-nswt formula, occurring on a coffin from Meir in the museum at Warsaw (Inv. No. 139 937), is here presented in hieroglyphs with transliteration, translation and notes.

J.J.J.

79209 DAUMAS, François, Remarques sur l'absinthe et le gattilier dans l'Égypte antique, in: Festschrift Elmar Edel, 66-89.

The author discusses the plant names sꜥm and sꜥꜣm, both occurring in medical and other texts, sꜣꜥm i.a. Pap. Harris 500, 7,7. On account of vocalization, medical applications and symbolic use in religious and literary texts he identifies sꜣꜥm as σούρε (ἄγνος Vitex Agnus Castus L., and sꜥm as σόμι (= αψίνθιον), mainly Artemisia Absinthum L., but also indicating other species of Artemisia.

J.J.J.

79210 DEVAUCHELLE, Didier, A propos du nom Pn-ḥj, Enchoria 9 (1979), 141-142.

According to the author the proper names Pa-ḥj and Ta-ḥj (Παχοις Ταχοις) are not to be translated as 'He/she-of-the-height', but are abbreviations of Pa-/Ta-(ḏd-)ḥnsw-(iw=f-ꜥnḥ).

W. Brunsch

79211 DION, Paul-E., Les types épistolaires hébréo-araméens jusqu'au temps de Bar Kokhbah, Revue Biblique, Paris 86 (1979), 544-579.

Some remarks to Demotic epistolary formulae on p. 570-571.

79212 GERMER, Renate, Untersuchung über Arzneimittelpflanzen im Alten Ägypten. Dissertation zur Erlangung der Würde des Doktors der Philosophie der Universität Hamburg, Hamburg, [no publisher], 1979 (14.5 x 20.5 cm; [IV +] 400 p.).

The author, who is a biologist as well as an egyptologist, discusses in this thesis the words for plants that occur in the medical papyri, the veterinary papyrus Kahun, and a few papyrus fragments and ostraca.
The study consists of two parts. In the four introductory chapters (p. 1-12) Mrs Germer deals with the present state of our knowledge, the means of identifying the plants, the difficulties of the Egyptian physician to judge the effectivity of the drugs (e.g. the placebo effect), and the reasons why particular plants have been used in the pharmacopoeia.
The body of the book consists of a discussion of each separate plant, first those of which the identification is fairly certain, tain, and then those that cannot at present be identified. Of the separate plants the botanical name is given (if known), its Egyptian name in hieroglyphs (with variants), references to the medical texts and to its pharmaceutical applications, and a thorough

discussion in which its possible or certain identification is argued. The author attempts from the point of view of natural science to evaluate the identifications brought forward by egyptologists and to determine the pharmacological effectivity of the drugs.
A summary of the results (no more than 31 plants are definitively identified) on p. 372-381. Indexes p. 388-400.

J.J.J.

79213   GOEDICKE, Hans, An Old Kingdom Word, *in*: *Festschrift Elmar Edel*, 142-151, with 2 plans.

Against Brovarski (see our number 76114) the author argues that the word ḥr in the Abusir Papyri and elsewhere in O.K. texts does not denote the pyramid as architecture, but is rather a general designation of the high-lying section of the funerary complex, thus denoting primarily the compound of the mortuary temple with its cult-installations.
See also Mme Posener's commentary on the Abusir Papyri, our number 76639, 22-24, not quoted by Goedicke.

J.J.J.

79214   GÖRG, Manfred, *Piggul* und *pilaegaeš* - Experimente zur Etymologie, *Biblische Notizen*, Bamberg Heft 10 (1979), 7-11.

The author investigates the possibility whether Hebrew פגול, "impure (meat)" can be derived from Egyptian *pꜣ grg*, and פלגש, "sexual partner" from the rather neutral Egyptian word *pꜣ iry-gs*.

79215   GÖRG, Manfred, *Ṯ(w)tpt* - eine fast vergessene Deutung, *Biblische Notizen*, Bamberg Heft 8 (1979), 11-13.

Short note on the possible connection between Hebrew *ṯ(w)tpt* and Egyptian *ḏdft*, "Uraeus".

79216   GÖRG, Manfred, Ein vermeintliches Fremdwort, *ZÄS* 106 (1979), 175-176.

Das Kausativ *sḥrꜥ* in *WB* IV, 261, 7 (Gruppenschreibung) ist identisch mit *sḥri-ꜥ* in *WB* IV, 271, 1-3. Es handelt sich also nicht um ein Fremdwort (so in unserer Nummer 71263, Nr. 203).

M. Heerma v. Voss

79217   GÖRG, Manfred, Zwei bautechnische Begriffe in 1 Kön 6,9, *Biblische Notizen*, Bamberg Heft 10 (1979), 12-15.

In a discussion of the architectural expression גבים ושדרת (1 Kings 6,9) the author draws attention to the possibility that the first element containing the consonants *g + b* may be connected with Egyptain *gbꜣ*, "arm", and to the fact that the second element *šdrt* appears in Egyptian as a loan-word 𓊃𓂧𓂋𓏏𓉐, "columned hall".

79218 GRAEFE, Erhart, *wnḫ*, "lösen" (pHarris 500,5.12-6.2 und pD'Orb. 5.1-2). Mit einem Nachtrag von Phillippe Derchain, *SAK* 7 (1979), 53-63.

Proceeding from an article of Derchain (our number 75179) in which the passages mentioned in the title are studied, the author argues that *wnḫ* does not mean "to clothe", but "to unfasten". He adduces several instances where this is clearly meant.
In the appendix Derchain agrees with his suggestion, which with a slight emendation strengthens his former solutions.

J.J.J.

79219 GREEN, M.A., *B3w* Expressions in Late Egyptian, *in: Glimpses of Ancient Egypt*, 107-115.

The author studies the distribution of some L.Eg. expressions involving the word *b3w*. His basic material consists of eleven occurrences in Deir el-Medîna ostraca in eight texts, divided into three instances of the phrase *b3w nṯr ḫpr* and eight of the oath formula *p3 nty bin b3w.f r mwt*. To them are added two other expressions with *b3w* from ostraca and six more from inscriptional sources not from the workmen's village.
The author studies meaning and context of the expressions, concluding that even such a restricted inquiry can help in understanding the development of L.Eg. A particular section is added concerning *ꜥḥꜥ.n* in colloquial L.Eg.

J.J.J.

79220 HASSAN, Ali, Die Wörter *šbd* und *m3wḏ*, *MDAIK* 35 (1979), 119-124.

The author conceives both words mentioned in the title as Semitic loanwords. He gives a number of different writings of each and presents in hand-copy and translation sentences in which they occur. The former he translates as "stick" or "staff", the latter as "carrying-pole" or "yoke", with a derivative meaning used for a piece of land.

J.J.J.

79221 HELCK, Wolfgang, Doch noch einmal der angebliche Kult des Kugelfisches im 1. o. äg. Gau, *GM* Heft 36 (1979), 31-36.

Vgl. die Diskussion in unseren Nummern 78355 und 78237. Eine neuerliche Untersuchung ergibt, dass die *zḥw špt* als topographischer Punkt zu werten sind, wobei die Grundbedeutung von *zḥ* "Laube" ist. Der Verfasser vertritt die Meinung, dass es sich um Lauben handelt, in denen die Fischer die gefangenen Kugelfische verarbeiteten, da entgegen der üblichen Annahme die Kugelfische essbar sind, sofern sie von den Eierstöcken, der Galle und der Leber befreit werden. So wurden sie auch bei der Versorgung der Toten verwendet. Die *zḥw špt* sind die für das Gebiet des 1. Kataraktes typischen Fischerlauben und nicht Wallfahrtskapellen, in denen der Kugelfisch kultisch verehrt wurde.

Inge Hofmann

79222 KASSER, Rodolphe, Un lexème copte oublié. TKHN akhmimique (Nahum 3, 19), *Bulletin Société d'Egyptologie*, Genève No. 1 (Mai 1979), 23-25.

The author, discussing the word TKHN in the Akhmimic version of *Nahum* 3, 19, suggests that it occurs in F. and M. as TKλN and is connected with S. TWϨN "to push, repel". The sentence in *Nahum* is to be translated: "Your wound is swollen".

J.J.J.

79223 KITCHEN, K.A., Egypt, Ugarit, Qatna and Covenant, *Ugarit-Forschungen* 11 (1979), 453-464.

The author discusses the term *bĕrit* attested in various Semitic cultures, and in Egypt as a loanword. The earliest Egyptian textual evidence for *br(y)t* is the Nauri Decree (*KRI* I, 51,6; 52,16; 53,5; 57,9), where the term could be used for contract, compact, agreement, in the economic sphere for hired labour. From Pap. Anastasi II, 8,2 it appears that it can denote a group of *brt* women, so probably women hired on contract. In the inscriptions of year II of Ramses III (the Victory over the Libyans) at Medinet Habu (*KRI* V, 64,4; 65, 14) *brt* is attested in the political realm, as compact, agreement, covenant among tribal groups, and as vassal-treaty, covenant between the conquerors and the defeated. The author is sceptical about Görg's proposal to take *bryt* as the equivalent of *mryt*, and as a plural collective of *mrt*, "serfs". At the end of the article remarks on its general meaning obligation, treaty, covenant.

79224 LALOUETTE, Claire, Le "firmament de cuivre". Contribution à l'étude du mot *biꜣ*, *BIFAO* 79 (1979), 333-353.

The author studies the problem how the word *biꜣ*, certainly meaning "copper", came to be connected with the concept "heaven". She points out that according to the P.T. the king, having become a star, can return to the earth along a string of copper, a poetic transposition of the streaks made by meteors in the sky. Hence the celestial throne is said to consist of copper, and even heaven itself. This also explains why in the O.K. royal statues were made of that metal, which bears a certain ideological value.

J.J.J.

79225 LUBETSKY, Meir, The Early Bronze Age Origin of Greek and Hebrew *limen*, "Harbour", *Jewish Quarterly Review*, Leiden 69 (1978/79), 158-180.

Contrary to the prevalent view, the author proposes to derive Hebrew *lmn*, Greek *limên* from ancient Egyptian *m(i)ni*, under

change of Egyptian $\dot{\imath}$ to corresponding Semitic l and under metathesis from *mnl into lmn, this transposition being common owing to the liquidity of l, m, n and r.
Assuming that limên is an Egypto-Semitic word, the author attempts to solve the question how it did reach the Greeks: either through the Northwestern Semites, or through Greek and Semitic populations in Lower Egypt. Supporting evidence comes from the Arabic word for port, almînâ(h), which is derived from Coptic words ultimately deriving from Eg. mnỉ.
The author further corroborates his argument by examining the closely related connotations of Eg. mnỉ, Hebrew lmn and Greek limên.

79226 MACDONALD, John, An Assembly at Ugarit ?, *Ugarit-Forschungen* 11 (1979), 515-526.

Discussing the possibility of a citizen's assembly at Ugarit, the author refers to the Egyptian loanword mw-ꜥdwt, Hebrew môꜥēd, "assembly", in the Story of Wenamun.

79227 OCKINGA, Boyo G., rōš wĕzānāb kippāh wĕʼagmôn in Jes 9, 13 und 19, 15, *Biblische Notizen*, Bamberg Heft 10 (1979), 31.

The author investigates the possibility to compare an expression in Isa. 9, 13 and 19, 15 with Egyptian ḥ3t and pḥwy, and swt/šmꜥw "Upper Egypt" and w3ḏ/mḥw, "Lower Egypt" as expressions of dualistic totality.

79228 OGDON, Jorge Roberto, The Desert of the Beautiful Goddess of the West (Apropos of Two Old Kingdom Tombstones), *JSSEA* 9 (1978-1979), 107-110, with 2 fig.

Proceeding from two O.K. monuments, a stela formerly in the Collection Meux and the false-door Cairo Cat. gén. 56994, the author suggests to render S(my)t nt ʼImntt as "The Desert of the (Goddess of the) West", conceiving ʼImntt as an abbreviation of ʼImntt-nfrt, the name of a female deity. The pattern, a locality plus the name of a deity, is known from other instances too.
See now Goedicke, *JSSEA* 10 (1979-1980), 61.

J.J.J.

79229 OGDON, Jorge Roberto, Un nuevo ejemplo de la formula šdỉt s3ḫw en proskinemas del primer periodo intermedio (Dins. VII-X), *Boletin de la Asociación Española de Orientalistas*, Madrid 15 (1979), 230-232.

The author publishes another instance of the expression šdỉt s3ḫw, "recitation of glorifications" occurring in an offering formula on the coffin of a Gemniemhat, from the IXth Dynasty and originating from Saqqara, but now in the Ny Carlsberg Glyptotek, Copenhagen (Inv. No. AEIN 1615).

79230 el-SAYED, Ramadan, Un nom populaire à l'époque ptolemaïque, GM Heft 35 (1979), 51-58.

80 Belege für den Namen Padehorpare und seiner Varianten Horpare, Neshorpare und Tadithorpare werden zusammengestellt. Sie stammen alle aus der ptolemäischen oder römischen Periode und sind auf die thebanische Region beschränkt. Ihre Träger scheinen zu den Notabeln der Gegend gehört zu haben. Der Name Padehorpare und Horpare lebt weiter als der von Heiligen und Märtyrern.

Inge Hofmann

79231 SCHULMAN, Alan R., (ṯȝrt): Cabin, Forecastle, Enclosed Structure, BES 1 (1979), 29-40, with 1 fig.

The author disputes Glanville's generally accepted opinion on the word ṯȝrt designating the cabin of a ship. Although reconsidering the complete evidence on the word., the discussion focuses on a legend to a scene in the tomb of Neferhotep (Theban Tomb No. 49). the Carnarvon Tablet I, 11 and depictions of warships from the scenes of the naval battle against the Sea Peoples at Medinet Habu. The author proposes to identify the ṯȝrt with the fore- and sterncastle of a ship, it having the more general meaning "enclosed structure". The Dockyard Papyrus vso 3, 3-4 makes clear that the structure could have windows.

79232 THÉODORIDÈS, Aristide, "Parler avec (une femme)", *Annuaire de l'Institut de Philologie et d'Histoire Orientales et Slaves*, Bruxelles 22 (1978), 77-96.

Proceeding from a passage in the Tale of the Two Brothers (Pap. d'Orbiney 4, 10), where the husband asks his wife m.nym mdt m-dỉ.t, lit. "who has spoken with you?", the author argues that this phrase means, when used in connection with a woman, "to seduce". In connection with men, particularly authorities, it means "to press (people)". The author adduces a number of passages supporting his argument.

J.J.J.

79233 THIRION, Michelle, Notes d'onomastique. Contribution à une révision de Ranke PN, RdE 31 (1979), 81-96.

L'auteur propose des séries de noms répertoriés par Ranke, Personennamen qui seraient à regrouper (ce qui amènerait la suppression de certaines notices, de noms fantômes dus à des erreurs de lecture et de lectures à rectifier).

Ph. Derchain

III. TEXTS AND PHILOLOGY

a. Epigraphy

See also our numbers 79275; 79446; 79451; 79508; 79509; 79519; 79524; 79526; 79549; 79570; 79601; 79604; 79618; 79619; 79620; 79621; 79626; 79638; 79690; 79705; 79790; 79900; 79904; 79906; 79981 and 791015.

79234 CORTEGGIANI, Jean-Pierre, Une stèle héliopolitaine d'époque saïte, in: Hommages Sauneron I, 115-153, with 1 fig. and 7 pl. (1 folding).

Publication of a limestone funerary stela of a priest Djedatumiufankh, found in el-Matarîya (Heliopolis) and dating from the Saite Period. It is in a bad state of conservation, the uncommon inscription being only partly legible. The text, arranged in vertical and horizontal columns, consists of traditional parts and an actual biographical part.
The author presents the text in hieroglyphs and translation, with a commentary.

J.J.J.

79235 FISCHER, Henry G., The Old Kingdom Inscriptions Restored, *JEA 65* (1979), 42-46, with 4 fig.

Restores the inscriptions and corrects previous readings of the great false door from Mariette's Saqqâra mastaba D 13 now in Cairo Museum (CG 1379). This belongs to a Judge and King's Acquaintance called $Špsỉ$, and also refers to two wives of his son called $Df3t.sn$ and $Ḥtp-ḥr.s$. These two ladies also appear on the false door of the adjacent mastaba D 70 belonging to the Vizier $Pḥ.n-w(ỉ)-k3.(ỉ)$, and the conclusion is reached that the latter made the false door in D 13 for his parents. It is therefore suggested that the p at the end of the line of text in D 13 belongs to the vizier's name although it remains uncertain whether the term father was used before $Špsỉ$. The date of the tomb of the earlier Mry at Hagarsa is also discussed and the inscription restored as : "(My Lord) made (this) for me (as befits my state of reverence) with the Majesty of . . . $Nfr-k3-Rˁ$, thus suggesting that the tomb was built in this reign.
See now also Fischer *GM* Heft 42 (1981), 19-21.

E.P. Uphill

79236 GABALLA, G.A., False-Door Stelae of Some Memphite Personnel, *SAK* 7 (1979), 41-52, with 3 fig. and 3 pl.

Publication of three N.K. false-door stelae in the Cairo Museum, namely of the $ḥry-nfw$ n $M3ˁt$ Suty (JE 8781), from Saqqâra; the $ḥry-ỉrw$ $ḫsbḏ$ Hatiay (JE 25641), also from Saqqâra; and the $ḥry$ $ḥmwy$ m $Ptḥ$ Hatiay (TR 2/11/24/1), from Abydos. On all three Os-

iris is adored, each time with another companion. In the lower registers members of the family are represented.
The three men belong to Memphite families who were employed in mundane aspects of known Memphite cults. Apart from a description of the stelae and a translation of the texts the author discusses the owners, their functions and families.

J.J.J.

79237 GABALLA, G.A., Monuments of Prominent Men of Memphis, Abydos and Thebes, in: *Glimpses of Ancient Egypt*, 42-49, with 3 fig. and 3 ill.

Publication of three monuments now in Cairo Museum. 1. The limestone stela found S. of the pyramid of Unas and belonging to the chief of the fattened (?$i\overset{?}{r}w$) fowl Huya (JdE 27958). Apart from the unusual title the stela is of importance since it mentions two wives of Huya.
2. The upper half of a sandstone stela of the famous first prophet of Osiris Wennofer, from the reign of Ramses and found in Abydos (JdE 32025). The author presents a summary genealogy of Wennofer and discusses the title of Osiris $wr \ d\overset{?}{i}w$, "Great of the Five".
3. A limestone stela-fragment mentioning the vizier Amenmose, from Deir el-Medîna (TR 9/6/26/3). The vizier belongs to the time of Amenmesse and hence the chief workman whose name is lost on the fragment may have been Neferhotep.   J.J.J.

79238 GABALLA, G.A., Three Funerary Stelae from the New Kingdom, *MDAIK* 35 (1979), 75-85, with 4 fig. and 1 pl.

The three stelae from the Cairo Museum here published are: TN 11. 11.24.5, from Abydos, of the sculptor Se and the scribe Smentawi; JdE 18925, from Saqqâra, of a woman called Aati and her husbands Praemhab and Amenemhab (or is this one person?); TN 29.4.24.2, from Abydos, depicting three (related?) families. The stelae, of which the latter two are of fairly rare round-topped type, are described and presented in photograph, while the texts are given in hand-copies and translation. The author pays particular attention to the relations between the persons who are mentioned.

J.J.J.

79239 GOHARY, S.G., The Doorway of the Priest Hori-em-hab of Athribis, in: *Glimpses of Ancient Egypt*, 75-79, with 2 fig. and 2 ill.

Publication of two limestone blocks from Athribis, a lintel (Cairo TR 14/6/24/6) and part of the left hand jamb of a doorway (Cairo TR 2/2/21/12), both from the time of Ramses III. The first piece has also been published by Vernus (our number 78817, p. 52-53 and pl. 7 [No. 57].

J.J.J.

79240 GOURLAY, Yvon J.-L., Trois stèles memphites au Musée de Grenoble, *BIFAO* 79 (1979), 87-101, with 3 pl.

Discussion of three Memphite stelae in the Museum of Grenoble (see also our number 79601). 1. The XVIIIth Dynasty stela of the overseer of the goldsmiths, Amenemhat (Inv. 1963; cat. no. 20). Added are remarks on the necropolis of goldsmiths from the N.K. 2. The Ramesside stela of the w^cb of "Amon of the Porch", Ptahmai (Inv. 1953; cat. no. 24). 3. The Saito-Persian stela of Pedese (Inv. 1950; cat. no. 25). J.J.J.

79241 GRAEFE, Erhart und Mohga WASSEF, Eine fromme Stiftung für den Gott Osiris-der-seinen-Anhänger-in-der-Unterwelt-rettet aus dem Jahre 21 des Taharqa (670 v. Chr.), *MDAIK* 35 (1979), 103-118, with 1 fig. and 1 pl.

The stela here published was seen in 1976 with an antiquities dealer in Luxor. It shows in the arch at the left side Taharqa before Amon, right Taharqa followed by the Divine Consort Shepenupet before Osiris-who-saves-his-servant-in-the-Netherworld ($W\!s\!\underset{\smile}{i}r$ $\acute{s}d\ \d{h}m.f\ n\ dw3t$). The text, in 25 lines, contains the essentials of a deed of donation to this Osiris by the servant of the Divine Adoratrice $P3\text{-}n\text{-}P$. Among the donations are a chapel, a field, food, amulets, bronze temple furniture, but also five persons. The text is given in photograph and facsimile, with a translation and a commentary. In their general comments the authors i.a. point out that the text is of a unique character, only resembling Taharqa's Kawa stelae. Where in Thebes the chapel (in which the stela has been standing) was situated is unknown.
An excursus deals with a possible derivation of $m\underline{h}$, "room (?)", while a list of hitherto unknown names and addenda and corrigenda to the Wb. are added at the end.
J.J.J.

79242 GUIDOTTI, Cristina M., Un frammento di stele della XVIII dinastia nel Museo Archaeologico di Firenze, *Egitto e Vicino Oriente* 2 (1979), 39-48, with 1 pl. and 16 fig.

Le fragment de stèle calcaire 12271 du Musée de Florence, provenant de la collection Wladimir de Grüneisen, restait inédit. C'est la partie droite du registre inférieur; elle montre deux porteuses d'offrandes à perruque enveloppante et "tunique" descendant jusqu'aux pieds. La figure de gauche, précédée d'un grand vase, tient un oiseau dans la main conservée. L'autre porteuse ($s3t\ Mryt\ w\underline{h}m$ $^cn\underline{h}$) présente un brasier allumé. Les divers indices font songer à une origine thébaine et proposer comme date la XVIIIe dynastie. Entre les deux dames est posée "sur" une corbeille une offrande portant des traces de couleur rouge: des ovales empilés en pyramide. Ce tracé apparaît dans 3 tombes de Gourna parmi les offrandes à Renenoutet. Il doit s'agir de pains entassés, sculptés comme de simples couches décroissantes en vue latérale, que la peinture venait préciser, plus le pain du sommet, vu d'en haut. La tombe de Rekhmirê offre la même disposition et la même stylisation pour les anneaux d'or, détaillés après coup.

J. Custers

79243 HABACHI, Labib, Rock-Inscriptions from the Reign of Ramesses II on and around Elephantine Island, in: *Festschrift Elmar Edel*, 227-237, with 5 fig. and 1 pl.

The author publishes four hitherto unknown rock-inscriptions from the time of Ramses II discovered by him in the neighbourhood of Elephantine: one from prince Khaemwast mentioning the fifth jubilee, two from the chief of the bowmen and overseer of the works Nebinakhtu, and one from the stable-master and royal messenger Nekhmontu. Discussing the events, e.g. the building of a temple on Elephantine by Nebinakhtu, and the persons here mentioned he also points at other rock-inscriptions elsewhere which have been published previously.

J.J.J.

79244 JACQUET-GORDON, Helen, Deux graffiti de l'époque libyenne sur le toit du temple de Khonsou à Karnak, in: *Hommages Sauneron* I, 167-183, with 4 fig.

The author publishes two of the numerous graffiti from the roof of the Khonsu temple at Karnak (Nos 10 and 11). The texts are presented in facsimile and transcription, with translations and comments. They are dated in year 4 of Pharaoh Sheshonq (No. 10) and year 5 of Pharaoh Iny (No. 11), while both mention a priest $Ddi-ich$, one being the grandfather of the other (see genealogy on p. 178). Mrs Jacquet argues that the Sheshonq may be Sheshonq III, the name of Pharaoh Iny being unknown from other sources. In this discussion she suggests on account of the expression $Pr-c3$ that the larger Dâkhla stela dates from the reign of Sheshonq III.

J.J.J.

79245 KOŁODKO, Monika, Stele Nowego Państwa w zbiorach Museum Narodowego w Warszawie, *Rocznik Museum Narodowego w Warszawie*, Warszawa 23 (1979), 7-39, with 20 ill. and summaries in Russian and French.

The author publishes six N.K. stelae from the National Museum at Warsaw. We mention: Inv.No. 141280 MN, Memphite, of excellent quality; Inv. No. 143341 MN, from Deir el-Medîna, XIXth Dynasty; Inv. No. 141279 MN, rectangular, end XVIIIth Dynasty; Inv. No. 142294 MN, XIXth Dynasty, belonging to the guard of the tomb of the chief treasurer Maia; Inv. No. 139328 MN, fragmentary, from Edfu, XVIIIth Dynasty?; Inv. No. 199203 MN, fragmentary, N.K., stela dedicated to Sakhmet of Abusir.

79246 KURZ, M., Graffiti de la montagne thébaine. II, 5. Plans de position, Le Caire, Centre de documentation et d'études sur l'ancienne Égypte, 1974 (21 x 27 cm; portfolio containing p. 26-32 and plans 166-197); at head of title: Collection scientifique.   Pr. LE 3

Sequel to our number 73423.
The text pages contain concordance lists of the graffiti. The plans pertain to the sectors A 10, C 2-5, E, the Valley of the Kings (A) and the Valley of the Queens (B), sections 183-215.

79247 KURZ, M., Graffiti de la montagne thébaine. II, 6. Plans de position, Le Caire, Centre d'étude et de documentation sur l'ancienne Égypte, 1977 (21 x 27 cm; portfolio containing p. 33-40 and plans 198-215); at head of title: Collection scientifique. Pr. LE 2,25

Sequel to our preceding number.
The text pages contain concordance lists of the graffiti. The plans pertain to the sectors E 2-4, sections 216-233.

79248 LOWLE, D.A., A Nineteenth Dynasty Stela in the Louvre, *in*: *Glimpses of Ancient Egypt*, 50-54, with 1 fig. and 1 ill.

Publication of Louvre stela C. 148, perhaps from Memphis, which dates from the reign of Ramses II and belonged to the scribe of the offering table of the Lord of the Two Lands Neferhotep, son of the charioteer Raiay. A statue of Neferhotep may perhaps be preserved in the Museo del Sannio in Benevento (see Porter-Moss VII, 418 and Müller, our number 69430, 92-93 and pl. 29,1). The author studies the family of Neferhotep, who was attached to the royal wine cellar.

J.J.J.

79249 MÁLEK, Jaromír, The statue of Sebkhotpe in the Fondation Martin Bodmer in Cologny: An additional note, *GM* Heft 31 (1979), 75-76.

Unter Heranziehung der Arbeiten von John Williams, die zwischen 1830 und 1840 gemacht wurden und sich im Griffith Institute in Oxford befinden, konnte der Text auf dem Rückenpfeiler der Statue des Sebkhotpe, die kürzlich von R. Hari veröffentlicht wurde (vgl. unsere Nr. 78344) korrigiert werden.

Inge Hofmann

79250 MEEKS, Dimitri, Une fondation Memphite de Taharqa (Stèle du Caire JE 36861), *in*: *Hommages Sauneron* I, 221-259, with 1 fig. and 1 pl.

Publication of the large stela Cairo J.E. 36861 that from internal evidence is suggested to have been erected near the S. dromos of the Ptah temple at Memphis. It was dedicated by Taharqa, dealing with the rebuilding of the small Amon temple, the renewal of its furniture, and the donation of funds among which some fields. The author presents the text in photograph and drawing, and in printed hieroglyphs, with a translation and an extensive commentary. On p. 257-259 an analysis of its contents.

J.J.J.

79251 MOUSSA, Ahmed M. and Mahassen NASSAR, Two Old Kingdom Falsedoors from the Causeway of King Unas at Saqqara, *SAK* 7 (1979), 155-161, with 2 fig. and 1 pl.

Publication of two falsedoor stelae found in the Unas causeway and now in the magazine of Saqqâra. The first one (Reg. No. 17083) belonged to a certain *Nṯr-(pw-)nswt* and represents i.a. the owner and his family; the other (Reg. No. 17084) belonged to his wife *Ḥnws*. They date from the time of Niuserre.
The pieces are described and presented in line drawings, the texts transliterated and translated. *J.J.J.*

79252 ROCCATI, Alessandro, Per un "capace spirito di Ra", *in*: *Hommages Sauneron* I, 281-283, with 1 pl.

The stela Turin 50015 (cfr Tosi-Roccati, our number 72710, p. 50-51 and 267), of the *ȝḥ-iḳr-n-Rʿ* Pahatia, bears on both small sides a badly legible text, here published. They mention the *sš-ḳd* Amennakhte and his father Ipuy. Since Amennakhte is here not yet a scribe the stela dates from the early XXth Dynasty.
J.J.J.

79253 ROSENVASSER, A., Aksha: la estela de la "Bendición de Ptah", *Revista del Instituto de Historia Antigua Oriental*, Buenos Aires 4 (1978), 9-61, with 8 pl. (2 folding).

The author publishes in full the duplicate text of the 'Blessing of Ptah for Ramesses II', known in the version of the great hall of the Abu Simbel temple, discovered by the Franco-Argentine Archaeological Expedition in the Sudan during the 1961 campaign at the Aksha temple of Ramesses II.
By reassembling the different fragments, the author is able to give an extensive philogical discussion of the text and to reconstruct its former appearance. After these comments, it clearly arises that the Aksha stela presents better readings for several words, which should be preferred to those of the Abu Simbel version; e.g., *bnȝw* (AS, 1.12 for *bngȝw/bng* (AK., 1.11), or *ḥwtí* (AS, 1. 32) for *ḥws.tí* (AK., 1. 31). The author presents a new translation of the text of the 'Blessings' in the light of these emendations.

J.R. Ogdon

79254 el-SAYED, Ramadan, Quelques précisions sur l'histoire de la province d'Edfou à la 2e période intermédiaire (Étude des stèles JE 38917 et 46988 du Musée du Caire), *BIFAO* 79 (1979), 167-207, with 2 pl.

The author publishes two limestone stelae from the S.I.P. and from Edfu (Cairo JdE 38917 and JdE 46988), presenting the texts in printed hieroglyphs with epigraphical remarks, a translation and an extensive commentary. In both texts a king Dedumose is mentioned.

In the second section el-Sayed presents remarks as to the finds in the area of Edfu in general; the style and epigraphy of the stelae here published; the titles and names occurring in the texts; their religious particularities and historical importance. He deals with the two rulers called Dedumose ($Dd-nfr-R\zc$ and $Dd-ḥtp-R\zc$), suggesting that, though being local rulers and remaining vassals of the Theban kings, the rulers of the provinces of Edfu and Gebelein were powerful as a result of the prosperity of the region.
J.J.J.

79255 el-SAYED, Ramadan, Stèles de particuliers relatives au culte rendu aux statues royales de la XVIIIe dynastie à la XXe dynastie, *BIFAO* 79 (1979), 155-166, with 1 pl.

Publication of the limestone stela Cairo JdE 20395, from Abydos representing in the upper register Ramses III adoring the triad of Abydos and in the lower register the $w\zc b$-priest of king Sethnakht, $Mr-sw-it.f$, in adoration before the sitting statues of Sethnakht and his wife.
In a second section the author draws up a list of N.K. stelae on which a private person adores a cult statue of a king, arranged in the order of the kings.
J.J.J.

79256 SCHULMAN, Alan R., The King's Son in the Wâdi Naṭrûn, *The Bulletin of the American Society of Papyrologists*, New York 15 (1978), 103-113, with 1 pl.

Publication of a later N.K. stela in the University Museum, Philadelphia (Inv. No. E 13608), although now actually missing, and originating from the Museum's excavations at Memphis (Find Nr. M-2834). After a description of the scene in the top of the stela of which only a small portion is preserved, the author presents the text, which primarily consists of the offering formula and the owner's name and titles, in transliteration and translation followed by a commentary. The problem of the identity of the owner of the stela and his titles among which those of "King's Son in the Wâdi Naṭrûn" ($s\ʒ-nswt\ m\ sḫt-ḥmʒt$) and $s\ʒ-nswt\ tpy\ n\ Nḫn$ is discussed.

79257 SHIMY, M., avec la collaboration de Pierre du BOURGUET, Graffiti de la montagne thébaine. III, 7. Fac-similés, Le Caire, Centre d'études et de documentation sur l'ancienne Égypte, 1977 (21 x 27 cm; portfolio containing p. 21-23 and pl. 293-308); at head of title: Collection scientifique.   Pr. LE 1,875

Sequel to our number 74629.
The fascicle contains the facsimiles of the graffiti nos. 3839-3973.

79258 SIMPSON, William Kelly, Two Stelae of the Overseer of Goldworkers of Amun, Amunemhab, at Yale and the Oriental Institute, *BES* 1 (1979), 47-53, with 1 fig. and 2 pl.

The author publishes the two almost similar stelae Oriental Institute Chicago Inv. No. 10789 and Yale University Art Gallery Acc. No. 1937.144, both belonging to the overseer of goldworkers of Amun, Amunemhab and possibly from Thebes. He describes the representations on the stelae, gives their texts in transliteration and translation without notes, and compares the use of the available space on the stelae, which are likely to have been carved by the same artist, or at least in the same workshop, although the inscriptions are by different hands.

79259 SIST, Loredana, Stele magica con figurazione di dea serpente da Antinoe, *Vicino Oriente*, Roma 2 (1979), 93-97, with 1 pl.

Publication of a limestone block from the Ptolemaic Period, found at Antinoe. It bears a relief representing a snake-shaped divinity with a human head and the emblem of Nefertem protected by a scorpion, as well as a fragmentary inscription mentioning Isis. The piece has obviously the same function as the magical stelae of Horus on the crocodile.

J.J.J.

79260 ŚLIWA, Joachim, Representations of the Triumphant Ruler in the Temple of Queen Hatshepsut at Deir el-Bahari, *Folia Orientalia*, Kraków 20 (1979), 165-169, with 1 plan and 1 fig.

In the "Portico of Birth" in the Deir el-Bahri temple some graffiti occur, one of which represents the queen smiting an enemy, executed in red ochre. It may date from the Saite Period. *J.J.J.*

79261 TRAUNECKER, C., Manifestations de piété personnelle à Karnak, *BSFE* No. 85 (Juin 1979), 22-31, with 2 fig.

La dévotion des humbles a laissé à Karnak des témoignages discrets. Parmi 1428 "graffiti" figurent seulement 244 textes, souvent pures mentions nominales. Les 186 auteurs, en majorité d'époque ramesside, sont soit illettrés soit fonctionnaires secondaires des temples. L'Égyptien s'exprimait peu dans les sanctuaires principaux; des exemples éclairants sont répandus dans le secteur de l'allée processionnelle. Une façade de pylône porte sans signature des épithètes d'Amon-Rê. Un départ d'escalier, lieu effacé, recèle tel petit tableau soigneusement sculpté: un bossu, wˁb ou artisan, faisant offrande devant la stèle d'Horus-Shed "de la bourgade de Rahotep". A l'escalier d'un autre pylône, la triade thébaine, une Thouéris, Aménophis Ier et Ahmès Néfertari comme divinité "des greniers" reçoivent l'adoration du chef-pâtissier Nebbouneb. Un brasseur prend la même reine secourable pour médiatrice auprès d'Amon. Dans un couloir, le grand-prêtre Amenhotep officie; une inscription nomme un pâtissier, pour qui le supérieur hiérarchique sert d'intercesseur. Sur un pylône, un haut personnage non accompagné de légende reçoit le culte d'un subalterne. Traunecker reconnaît dans ces improvisations de touchants témoins de la piété des humbles et un ingénieux remède aux inconvénients de leur condition.

J. Custers

79262 WILD, Henri, Une stèle memphite du règne d'Amenophis III à Lausanne, *in*: *Hommages Sauneron* I, 305-318, with 1 fig. and 1 pl.

Publication of a stela from Memphis preserved in the Musée Cantonnal d'Archéologie et d'Histoire at Lausanne (No.3376). It represents the *ꜥꜣ-n-bꜣḥ* called *Twk-ꜥꜣ* with his family and dates from the time of Amenophis III. The author presents the stela in photograph and drawing, with description, translation and comments, particularly on the word *bꜣḥ*.

J.J.J.

79263 YOUSSEF, Ahmed Abdel-Hamid, A Hymm of Ramses II at Abu Simbel, *ASAE* 63 (1979), 183-202, with 10 p. of hieroglyphic text (= p. 184-194) and 2 pl.

The author studies the twin stelae (C 20 and 22) in the recesses flanking the Great Temple of Abu Simbel, presenting the text (see now also Kitchen, Ramesside Inscriptions II, 315-321) with translation and some notes.

J.J.J.

79264 ŽÁBA †, Zbyněk, The Rock Inscriptions of Lower Nubia (Czechoslovak Concession). With Contributions by Fritz Hintze (Meroitic and Carian Inscriptions), Latin Inscriptions and those in Greek contributed by the Author. Followed by a Palaeography of Ancient Egyptian Rock Texts here published by † Zbyněk Žába and Miroslav Verner, Prague, [Universita Karlova], 1974 [1979] (24.3 x 33.6 cm; 351 p., frontispiece, 12 maps, 239 pl. with 418 ill. and fig.) = Charles University of Prague. Czechoslovak Institute of Egyptology in Prague and in Cairo Publications, Volume 1.

This is the first volume publishing the results of the Czechoslovak epigraphical expedition to Nubia (1963-1964); that on the rock drawings will follow. The inscriptions here published have been discovered in the two areas of which the Czechoslovak concession consisted, one from Nagˆ el-Bîr (c. 11 km downstream of the temple of Amada) to the temple of Wâdî el-Sebua, and the other from the temple of Gerf Hussein to that of Kalâbsha.
In the preface the history of the Czechoslovak institute in Cairo and of the expedition to Nubia is sketched and aims and techniques of the publication explained. Most of the 243 inscriptions are in Egyptian (No. 199 in Coptic), some in Greek (No. 196 in Carian), and a few in Latin, Meroitic and Aramaic (see the list on p. 12). They are divided into eleven groups, five areas in the Southern and six in the Northern part of the concession.
The Egyptian texts are given in printed hieroglyphs and translation, preceded by indications about their exact location and a description and followed by notes and comments as well as indications of their date. The non-Egyptian texts are treated in a similar way. Moreover, the plates bear illustrations of the inscriptions and, in several instances, their direct surroundings.
An appendix (p. 223-242) is devoted to 30 hieroglyphic rock inscriptions (numbered A 1 - A 30) discovered by members of the expedit-

ion along the road from Marsa Alam on the Red Sea to Edfu.
Three excursuses deal with the dates of the inscriptions from the
area of el-Girgâwi (near Korosko), personal names and filiations,
and the formal aspect of the rock texts.
There follows a palaeography of the texts (259-325) by Žába and
Verner, preceded by general remarks and a note to signs G 39 and
H 8. The catalogue itself follows the order of Gardiner's Sign-
list, with the numbers of Moller's list added.
Indexes to various subjects on p. 329-345.

J.J.J.

79265 ZIEGLER, Christiane, La fausse-porte du prince Kanefer, "Fils de Snéfrou", *RdE* 31 (1979), 120-134, with 3 pl. and 2 fig.

Reconstitution d'une fausse-porte découverte par de Morgan à Dah-chour et dont les fragments ont été dispersés depuis lors dans divers musées.
L'auteur cherche alors à identifier les personnages mentionnés et se préoccupe de la date du personnage, qui pourrait avoir vécu sous le règne de Chéphren, mais une date plus tardive, allant jusqu'à la VIIIe dyn. paraît ne pas être impossible.

Ph. Derchain

79266 ZIVIE, Alain-Pierre, La tombe d'un officier de la XVIIIe dynastie à Saqqara, *RdE* 31 (1979), 134-151, with 2 pl.

Il s'agit d'une inscription inédite lue par l'auteur à l'entrée d'une tombe du "Bubasteion à Saqqara". Photographie et transcription ac-compagnent un commentaire qui s'attache pratiquement à chaque mot.
Il s'agissait en apparence d'un officier de marine.

Ph. Derchain

b. Literary, historical and autobiographical

See also our numbers 79032; 79065; 79093; 79209; 79218; 79223; 79226; 79231; 79232; 79243; 79362; 79366; 79372; 79389; 79451; 79466; 79538; 79540; 79619; 79636; 79642; 79748; 79781; 79825; 79826; 79927 and 79972.

79267 BRUNNER, Hellmut, Zitate aus Lebenslehren, *in: Studien zu altägyp-tischen Lebenslehren*, 105-171.

In the introduction the author points out the various questions con-cerning citations from wisdom literature: the original instruction from which there is cited, the social class to which the documents containing citations belong and the influence of the instruction, the renderings of the passages and their meaning, and problems of text criticism. The author offers here only a representative selec-tion from the vast material, giving for each instruction the vari-ous passages and their citations in hieroglyphs with mention of the sources, and adding to each entry a commentary, except for the first one, the Instruction of Imhotep, and the last, the Wisdom of Amenemope which he discusses in general. The texts dealt with are

the Instructions of Djedefhor, Ptahhotep, Amenemhat and the Loyalist Instruction.
After having pointed out that the term "citation" was used in a broad sense, the author discusses in his conclusion his criteria of the presence of at least two original key words and a relation in train of thought between original and citation. He concludes that older passages were incorporated in younger instructions, that the instructions are closely related to the autobiographies, that some passages were used in a juridical sense and that particularly the royal inscriptions amply use the instructions.

79268 BRUNNER-TRAUT, Emma, Wechselbeziehungen zwischen schriftlicher und mündlicher Überlieferung im Alten Ägypten, *Fabula. Zeitschrift für Erzählforschung*, Berlin - New York 20 (1979), 34-46.

Discussing the mutual relation between the oral and literary fixed tradition, which latter is strictly regulated by the rules of Maʿat, the author stresses the power of the word and of eloquence, as they are present on the one hand in the wisdom and related literature such as the Eloquent Peasant, the Prophecy of Neferty, the Instruction of Ptahhotep, the Mythus vom Sonnenauge and other Demotic fables, and on the other hand in the stories such as the Pap. Westcar, the myth of the divine royal birth, Wenamun and Demotic literature.

79269 BRYAN, Betsy M., The Hero of the "Shipwrecked Sailor", *Sarapis* 5, No. 1 (1979), 3-13.

Proceeding from Otto's description of the Story of the Shipwrecked Sailor as a "didactic piece" (our number 66461) the author argues that its true hero is the snake, not the sailor, who appears in many respects not to meet the requirements of the Wisdom literature. In that light the concluding words of the story are clear: the sailor is an inept storyteller.

J.J.J.

79270 CHAPPAZ, Jean-Luc, Un manifeste littéraire du Moyen Empire. Les lamentations de Kha-khêper-rê-séneb, *Bulletin Société d'Égyptologie*, Genève No. 2 (Novembre 1979), 3-12.

French translation of the Complaints of Kha-khêper-re-seneb, with philological notes and commentary. The author particularly points out the uniqueness of the introduction (rt. 2-9).
For an English translation, see our number 73372.

J.J.J.

79271 CODY, Aelred, The Phoenician Ecstatic in Wenamūn. A Professional Oracular Medium, *JEA* 65 (1979), 99-106.

The writer discusses the passage in 1, 38-40, where it is related that an oracular message was communicated to the ruler of Byblos. It is suggested that the translations 'page' or 'noble

youth' are an inadequate rendering of the term used of the one
who had the divine-seizure, and that the word is really a North-
west Semitic one denoting a person who functions as an oracular
medium. The difficulty of the orthography is explained as due
to confusion with the word for a youth in Egyptian, i.e. ꜥdd for
ꜥdd. The extract would thus refer to royal sacrifices followed
by a consultation with a professional oracular body, an extra
nuance being that it is Amun, not a local god who works through
them.

E.P. Uphill

79272 COSTA, Alvimar, A literatura Egípcia do primeiro período inter-
mediário (2.154-2.052 a.C.), *Studia*, Passos 2 (1979), 163-218.

Survey of the Egyptian literature of the F.I.P., with translations
in Portugese of parts of some works, e.g. the Instruction for
Merikare and the Dialogue between a Man and his Soul.

J.J.J.

79273 van DIJK, Jac., The Luxor Building Inscription of Ramesses III,
GM Heft 33 (1979), 19-29, with 3 ill. on 2 pl.

Es wird ein neuer Text der bereits zweimal publizierten Bauin-
schrift von 10 Zeilen vorgelegt, übersetzt und mit Anmerkungen
versehen. Die Lage der von Ramses III. erbauten Kapelle wird
diskutiert und das im Text genannte Erscheinen des Amun am ersten
jeder Dekade besprochen.

Inge Hofmann

79274 EDEL, Elmar, Bemerkungen zu den Schiesssporttexten der Könige der
18. Dynastie, *SAK* 7 (1979), 23-39, with 1 fig.

In the first section the author argues that a word $m\underline{d}d$, "target",
does not exist (against Helck and Decker; see our number 71144,
103-105); $stỉ\ r\ m\underline{d}d$ means "shooting to hit", the reverse of $stỉ\ r\ tht$, "shooting wide". The second section presents a restoration and translation of *Urk.* IV, 1322, 16-18. In the third the
author discusses the form $stt.f$ in *Urk.* IV, 1245, 3-4; 1321, 17-18;
and 1318, 10. Each time it is an emphatic form which leads to a
new translation. The fourth is devoted to *Urk.* IV, 2047, 6-9.
In the final section Edel presents a survey of the shooting achievements ascribed to the kings, which he strongly doubts to be indeed according to truth.

J.J.J.

79275 EDEL, Elmar, Zum Verständnis der Inschrift des *Jzj* aus Saqqara.
Zu Helcks Bearbeitung dieser Inschrift in *ZÄS* 104, 89-93, *ZÄS*
106 (1979), 105-116, with 1 fig. and 1 pl.

Neubearbeitung des Textes unserer Nummer 77336. Im Nachtrag (115-
116) findet man Fechts Metrisierung der Inschrift.

M. Heerma v. Voss

79276 ENGEL, Helmut, Die Siegesstele des Merenptah. Kritischer Überblick über die verschiedenen Versuche historischer Auswertung des Schlussabschnitts, *Biblica*, Roma 60 (1979), 373-399.

The author offers a historical survey of the most important studies on the end of the Israel Stela of Merenptah and discusses their explanations as far as the Israel question is involved. As for the military activity of Merenptah he puts the question of one or two invasions of the Libyans and his presence in Syria-Palestine in his first years. Then he discusses the philological problems of line 27 of the stela, whether should be read "Israel *fkt*" or "Israel *rmṯ.f kt*", and the geographical questions. Much room is devoted to the attempts to use the stela in connection with the Exodus and its date. Lastly, he deals with the relation between "the ancestors of Israel in Egypt" and "Israel" on the stela.

79272 FECHT, Gerhard, Die Berichte des *Ḥrw=ḫwj.f* über seine drei Reisen nach *I3m*, *in: Festschrift Elmar Edel*, 105-134.

The author presents the transliteration of Harkhuf's accounts of his expeditions (the letter of the king is excluded) in its metric scheme, with a translation and extensive comments on grammatical points, geography and the literary qualities of the text.

J.J.J.

79278 GOEDICKE, Hans, "Irsu, the Kharu" in Papyrus Harris, *WZKM* 71 (1979), 1-17.

The author translates and discusses the first section of Pap. Harris I,75 (lines 1-6), presenting an entirely new rendering (see p. 9). He e.g. does not read "*Trsw*, a Kharu", but *Sw*, whom he calls the prototype of king Saul, since, after his interpretation, the events described took place outside the geographical limits of Egypt itself. This is mainly based on his interpretation of *p3 t3 n kmt*, *p3 t3* (as against *t3*) referring to a political entity (see the Excursus, p. 14-17).

J.J.J.

79279 GREEN, Michael, Wenamun's Demand for Compensation, *ZÄS* 106 (1979), 116-120.

Transliteration, translation and discussion of *Wenamun*, 1, 14-21. Wenamun's claim accords with the *Hammurabi Codex*, the prince's rejection of it with the Ugaritic tablets.

M. Heerma v. Voss

79280 GUNDLACH, Rolf, Der Obelisk Tuthmosis I. Textthematik und Funktion, *in: Festschrift Elmar Edel*, 192-226, with 6 tables.

The author presents a profound analysis of the texts of Tuthmosis I's obelisk at Karnak, demonstrating that they contain two connec-

ted elements: a program for his government and information about a historical event, the erection of both obelisks.
After an introduction and discussion of the methods applied in the article the author deals with the sequentional and positional structure of the texts and their contents. Various themes pass the review: the relations between the king and the gods, the world and the Egyptians; obelisk and *ished*-tree, etc. A summary of the scheme of the texts in section 5, followed by a discussion of the qualities and actions of the king and his program for his government as here formulated, and a comparison with other occurrences of the titulary of Tuthmosis I. Conclusions on p. 220.

J.J.J.

79281 GUNDLACH, R., Strukturfragen bei der Analyse und Interpretation ägyptischer historischer Texte, *in*: *Acts 1st ICE*, 265-270, with 1 diagram.

The author describes the methods of analysing historical texts, and presents then two examples: the Konosso stela of Tuthmosis IV and the "Königsnovelle" of Sethi I in the Kanais temple. At the end a comparison of the structures of these texts.

J.J.J.

79282 HORNUNG, Erik, Lehren über das Jenseits?, *in*: *Studien zu altägyptischen Lebenslehren*, 217-224.

The author briefly discusses the complementary character of the Books of the Netherworld and wisdom literature, with respect to their function, namely to provide information, knowledge about the hereafter respectively the present world. But the objectives of both genres are different: for the Instructions to give a man his proper place in the world order, and for the Books of the Netherworld to incorporate the deceased king in the cycle of the sun god.

79283 IVERSEN, E., The Chester Beatty Papyrus, No. 1, Recto XVI, 9 - XVII, 13, *JEA* 65 (1979), 78-88, with 9 fig.

The writer takes these poems published half a century ago by Gardiner and offers some new renderings in the translations. Detailed notes are given and comparisons made with words used in other texts including both Hebrew and Coptic. Certain words such as $hg3i$ 'doorlatch' are translated for the first time.

E.P. Uphill

79284 KEEL, Othmar, Eine Diskussion um die Bedeutung polarer Begriffspaare in den Lebenslehren, *in*: *Studien zu altägyptischen Lebenslehren*, 225-234.

The author contests the opinion expressed in our number 66534 that there is a shift from an early cosmos-oriented principle of i.a. Egyptian wisdom literature to an anthropological, as is particularly clear from the polarity of just versus guilty in the O.T. He

argues that this phenomenon is typical of Late Period wisdom literature in general.
The discussion afterwards is briefly summarized.

79285 KITCHEN, K.A., Ramesside Inscriptions. Historical and Biographical. II: 4, Oxford, B.H. Blackwell Ltd, [1979] (20.5 x 28.8 cm; 32 p. [= II, 193-224]); rev. *BiOr* 38 (1981), 28-30 (W. Helck).

Sequel to our number 70313 and continued by our number 71323. Although the fascicles 5-12 of volume II have been published already in the years 1971, 1976, 1977 and 1979, this fascicle 4 has appeared at a much later date. It contains the conclusion of the records in Upper Egypt of the Wars of Ramses II at Abydos and minor fragments from Lower Egypt. Then follow the Undated War Scenes and Lists in the Nubian Temples: Beit el-Wali, Gerf Husein, Wadi es-Sebua, Derr, Abu Simbel, Aksha, Amarah West. The fascicle ends with three stelae from Syria-Palestine.

79286 KITCHEN, K.A., Ramesside Inscriptions. Historical and Biographical. II: 10, Oxford, B.H. Blackwell Ltd, [1979] (20 x 29 cm; 32 p. [= p. II, 481-512]); rev. *BiOr* 37 (1980), 142-143 (Wolfgang Helck).

This tenth fascicle of the royal inscriptions of Ramses II is a sequel to our number 77421. It continues the Other Royal Monuments - Geographical Series. After having first finished the series on monuments from Heliopolis, the author proceeds with those from Memphis, most of which come from the Ptah temple, and includes minor remains from Gîza and Saqqâra. Next follow those from Middle to upper Egypt namely from Heracleopolis, Hermopolis, Sheikh Zibeida, Matmar and el-Birbâ. The fascicle ends with inscriptions from the temples of Sethi I and Ramses II (first Pylon) at Abydos.

79287 KITCHEN, K.A., Ramesside Inscriptions. Historical and Biographical. II: 11, Oxford, B.H. Blackwell Ltd, [1979] (20 x 29 cm; 32 p. [= p. II, 513-544]); rev. *BiOr* 37 (1980), 142-143 (Wolfgang Helck).

Sequel to our preceding number.
The fascicle is completely devoted to the temple of Ramses II at Abydos. It continues first the inscriptions from the forecourt and pylons, and then presents those of the Festival Calendar on the exterior of the South Wall, of the Festival Court, the Table of Kings in Portico-room II, and those of the Portico-rooms. On the last page the beginning of the texts of the 1st Octostyle Hall.

79288 KITCHEN, K.A., Ramesside Inscriptions. Historical and Biographical. II: 12 Oxford, B.H. Blackwell Ltd, [1979] (20 x 29 cm; 32 p. [= p. II, 545-576]); rev. *BiOr* 37 (1980), 142-143 (Wolfgang Helck).

Sequel to our preceding number.
After the inscriptions of the 1st Octostyle Hall have been continued those of the dependencies of the 1st and 2nd Octostyle Hall are presented, together with some other fragments and those of the

'Metropolitan' Temple and other sites at Abydos. Next follow minor inscriptions from Dendera, the Wâdî Hammâmât, and a triad from Koptos (CGC 555). The rest of the fascicle is devoted to Thebes, first to fragments and statuary from the Montu and Maʕat Precincts at Karnak, and then to the inscriptions from the Great Temple of Amon at Karnak. They start with statuary at the 2nd Pylon and proceed with dedications, mainly on the architraves, in the Great Hypostyle Hall. The fascicle is terminated by the scenes of the Opet and the Valley Festivals in the same hall.

79289 KITCHEN, K.A., Ramesside Inscriptions. Historical and Biographical. II: 13, Oxford, B.H. Blackwell Ltd, [1979] (20.5 x 28.8 cm; 32 p. [= p. II, 577-608]); rev. *BiOr* 38 (1981), 28-30 (W. Helck).

Sequel to our preceding number.
In this fascicle the Geographical Series of Other Royal Monuments is continued with the conclusion of the inscriptions in the Great Temple of Amon at Karnak, in which are included those from the temple of Mut at Karnak. Next follows the other main temple at Thebes East, the temple of Amon at Luxor.

79290 KITCHEN, K.A., Ramesside Inscriptions. Historical and Biographical. II: 14, Oxford, B.H. Blackwell Ltd, [1979] (20.5 x 28.8 cm; 32 p. [= II, 609-640]); rev. *BiOr* 38 (1981), 28-30 (W. Helck).

Sequel to our preceding number.
The Geographical Series of Other Royal Monuments at Thebes East is concluded by various inscriptions in the Temple of Amon at Luxor, mainly the forecourt. Then follow those of the West side of Thebes with the Temple of Sethi I at Qurna.

79291 KITCHEN, K.A., Ramesside Inscriptions. Historical and Biographical. II: 15, Oxford, B.H. Blackwell Ltd, [1979] (20.5 x 28.8 cm; 32 p. [= II, 641-672]); rev. *BiOr* 38 (1981), 28-30 (W. Helck).

Sequel to our preceding number.
The inscriptions of the temple of Sethi I at Qurna, with which the Geographical Series of Other Royal Monuments at Thebes West started, are concluded and followed by minor works from both temples at Deir el-Bahri. The fascicle ends with various inscriptions from the Ramesseum, among which fragments at Medinet Habu.

79292 KITCHEN, K.A., Ramesside Inscriptions. Historical and Biographical. II: 16, Oxford B.H. Blackwell Ltd, [1979] (20.5 x 28.8 cm; 32 p. [= p. II, 673-704]); rev. *BiOr* 38 (1981), 28-30 (W. Helck).

Sequel to our preceding number.
The Geographical Series of Other Royal Monuments on the West Side of Thebes in the Ramesseum is continued with the rather large section of the jar-sealings and ostraca (mainly wine dockets). The wine dockets on ostraca are subdivided after formula, date or vintners. The fascicle is concluded by the Official Works at Deir el-Medîna, among which the Hathor temple.

79293 KITCHEN, K.A., Ramesside Inscriptions. Historical and Biographical. II: 17, Oxford, B.H. Blackwell Ltd, *[1979]* (20.5 x 28.8 cm; 32 p. *[=* p. II, 705-736*]*); rev. *BiOr* 38 (1981), 28-30 (W. Helck).

Sequel to our preceding number.
This fascicle first continues the Geographical Series of Other Royal Monuments at the West Side of Thebes with the rest of the official works at Deir el-Medîna and minor records therefrom. After Thebes follow inscriptions from i.a. Armant, el-Kab and Elephantine. The same geographical series starts for Nubia with inscriptions from the rock-temples of Beit el-Wali, Gerf Husein and Wadi es-Sebua.

79294 KITCHEN, K.A., Ramesside Inscriptions. Historical and Biographical. II: 18, Oxford, B.H. Blackwell Ltd, *[1979]* (20.5 x 28.8 cm; 32 p. *[=* p. II, 737-768*]*); rev. *BiOr* 38 (1981), 28-30 (W. Helck).

Sequel to our preceding number.
In the Geographical Series of Other Royal Monuments in Nubia are first the inscriptions from Wadi es-Sebua continued. Next follow the rock temple of Derr, and Aniba, temple as well as town. The major part of the fascicle is taken by the Great Temple of Abu Simbel, but also the small temple of Abu Simbel is partly dealt with.

79295 KITCHEN, K.A., Ramesside Inscriptions. Historical and Biographical. II: 19, Oxford, B.H. Blackwell Ltd, *[1979]* (20.5 x 28.8 cm; 32 p. *[=* p. II, 769-800*]*; rev. *BiOr* 38 (1981), 28-30 (W. Helck).

Sequel to our preceding number.
In the Geographical Series of Other Royal Monuments in Nubia follow after the finishing of the inscriptions from the small temple and the smaller rock-stelae at Abu Simbel, those from Faras, Aksha, Buhen, Amarah West, and even Kawa and Napata. The fascicle continues with a short section called Miscellaneous and Minor Royal Monuments, and ends with the Documents of the Reign, which section begins with the Louvre Leather Roll from year 5.

79296 KITCHEN, K.A., Ramesside Inscriptions. Historical and Biographical. II: 20, Oxford, B.H. Blackwell Ltd, *[1979]* (20.5 x 28.8 cm; 32 p. *[=* p. II, 801-832*]*); rev. *BiOr* 38 (1981), 28-30 (W. Helck).

Sequel to our preceding number.
The Documents of the Reign of Ramses II continue with the lawsuit over a slave-girl already started in the previous fascicle (Pap. Cairo J. 65739; see Gardiner, *JEA* 21, 1935, 140-146), that over landholding (Pap. Berlin P. 3047; see our number 63218), a ship's log (Pap. Leiden I 350 vso; see our number 61368), and The Royal Canon of Turin (Pap. Turin N. 1874), the recto of which contains an administrative text. The verso, bearing the famous kings' list will be continued in the next fascicle.

79297 KITCHEN, K.A., Ramesside Inscriptions. Historical and Biographical. II: 21, Oxford, B.H. Blackwell Ltd, *[1979]* (20.2 x 29 cm; 32 p. *[=* II, 833-864*]*).

Sequel to our preceding number.
The Royal Canon of Turin is continued. Next follow monuments of the royal family, first those of queen mother Tuya and then those of the queens consort: Nefertari, Isetnofret, Henutmire, and Maathorneferure and her sister. Monuments of the princess-queens will be recorded somewhere else, while those of princesses and the king's sister will appear in volume III, on the contemporaries of Ramses II.
The section on the princes starts with several synopses of lists of princes: one on the sources (with bibliography and sigla), one numbering the about 50 princes, and lastly a synopsis of the standard lists in the Ramesseum, the Luxor temple, Abu Simbel, Derr, and Wadi es-Sebua.

79298 KITCHEN, K.A., Ramesside Inscriptions. Historical and Biographical. II: 22, Oxford, B.H. Blackwell Ltd, *[1979]* (20.2 x 29 cm; 32 p. *[=* II, 865-896*]*).

Sequel to our preceding number.
The synopsis on the standard lists of princes is concluded. Then follow four others: the lists from Abydos, Tanis (Pi-Ramesse), Medinet Habu copied from the Ramesseum and O. Cairo J. 72503.
Next come the monuments of individual princes, notably Kha emwaset, with at the end an insertion on monuments of his subordinates.

79299 KITCHEN, K.A., Ramesside Inscriptions. Historical and Biographical. II: 23, Oxford, B.H. Blackwell Ltd, *[1979]* (20.2 x 29 cm; 32 p. *[=* II, 897-928*]*).

Sequel to our preceding number.
The monuments of individual princes are continued, among which eight of Merenptah as a prince.
For the princesses the procedure as in our two preceding numbers is followed: first a synopsis of lists of princesses in which the formal numbering of the princesses, the sources and their concordances are given and then those of lists recorded at individual places. The synopses of the lists of princesses are concluded by the supplementary documents: the "List of Osirians" (Pap. Turin Pleyte-Rossi, pl. 12) and O. Louvre 666.
The volume is completed with the monuments of individual princesses and minor addenda. In the conclusion the author refers for further addenda and corrigenda to volume VII and for the private monuments from the reign of Ramses III to volume III.

79300 KITCHEN, K.A., Ramesside Inscriptions. Historical and Biographical. II:24, Oxford, B.H. Blackwell Ltd, *[1979]* (20.2 x 29 cm; XXXII p.).

Sequel to our preceding number.
This last fascicle of the second volume contains 30 preliminary pages. P. V-XXI present the contents: over 400 numbers on more than 900 pages. Then follow the literary and textual abbreviations. The last three pages are devoted to the preface in which the author sets forth his ideas on the work.

79301 KITCHEN, K.A., Ramesside Inscriptions. Historical and Biographical. III: 5, Oxford, B.H. Blackwell Ltd, [1979](20 x 29 cm; 32 p. [= p. 129-160]); rev. *BiOr* 37 (1980), 142-143 (Wolfgang Helck).

Sequel to our number 78442.
The Private Monuments of Contemporaries of Ramses II in the Civil and Royal Administration (labeled section A) are continued with those of the Subordinates of Nubian Viceroys (labeled Category III). On the first page those of the local artists and craftsmen (sub F) are finished. Category III closes with heading G: Temples and Cults in Nubia.
Then follow in the new categories IV the chiefs of the Treasury (sub A) and their subordinates (sub B) and in V the Superintendents of the Granaries of the South and the North (sub A) and other staff (sub B). Category VI (mayors of Thebes) starts at the end of the fascicle with Paser, mayor of East Thebes.

79302 KNAUF, Ernst A., Zum "Einzelkämpfer" Sinuhe B 110 und 1. Sam. 17, 4. 23, *GM* Heft 33 (1979), 33.

Der ägyptische Begriff *pry* betont das Herausgehen des Einzelkämpfers aus der Schlachtreihe, der hebräische *īš hab-bēnayim* das Ergebnis dieses Vorgangs. Dieser sachlichen Parallele wird eine terminologische aus dem arabischen Bereich hinzugefügt: "zweikämpfen" heisst *bāraza*, dem 3. Stamm von *baraza* "hinausgehen", während der Zweikampf selbst stattfindet "zwischen den Schlachtreihen", also eine terminologische Verbindung zum Hebräischen herstellt.

Inge Hofmann

79303 KRUCHTEN, Jean-Marie, Une révolte du vizir sous Ramsès III à Athribis?, *Annuaire de l'Institut de Philologie et d'Histoire Orientales et Slaves*, Bruxelles 23 (1979), 39-51.

The author studies the passage of Pap. Harris I, 59-10 - 60, 1, from which Breasted and others have concluded to a revolt of a vizier. He rejects this explanation and argues that the sentences refer to a juridical reorganization of the temple of Athribis constituting its autonomy. The article contains a careful analysis of some key words and phrases.

J.J.J.

79304 LAFFONT, Élisabeth, Les livres de sagesses des pharaons, [Paris], Gallimard [1979](10.8 x 17.7 cm; 156 p., 1 colour ill. on cover); series: Collection Idées.

After a general introduction on the Egyptian conceptions and
those aspects of the civilization important for understanding
the wisdom literature, which also contains remarks on the broader context of the Old Testament, the author presents after short
introductions translations without notes of the Wisdoms of Ptahhotep,
Kagemni, Amenemope, Any and Petosiris, the Admonitions of
Ipuwer (consistently called Iuper), the Instruction for Merikare
and that of Amenemhat and the Prophecy of Neferty.
No bibliography or indexes are given.

79305 MIOSI, F.T., Horus as a Trickster, *JSSEA* 9 (1978-1979), 75-78.

Proceeding from Goedicke's article "Seth as a Fool" (our number
61290) the author presents a different interpretation of the pertinent passage in the Story of Horus and Seth (13,2-13). Horus
deceived Seth by building a wooden boat plastered with gypsum,
so that it looked like a transport vessel of stone. See now also
Goedicke, *JSSEA* 10 (1979-1980), 59-61.

J.J.J.

79306 ODEN, Robert A., Jr., "The Contendings of Horus and Seth" (Chester Beatty Papyrus No. 1): A Structural Interpretation, *History of Religions*, Chicago 18 (1979), 352-369.

The author attempts to apply in a consistent way the structural
approach to myth to a particular myth, namely the "Story of the
Contendings of Horus and Seth" in Pap. Chester Beatty I. First
the author presents a summary of the story itself and its interpretation (notably those of Spiegel from 1937 and of Griffiths,
our number 60300) and points out the central concern of the myth:
Horus and Seth and their relationship.
He then presents his own structural analysis. After a list of binary contrasts between the two protagonists he makes an attempt
to explain why each element in the myth has significance. He construes a semantic rectangle of the relationships of Osiris, Isis,
Horus and Seth based on kinship terminology: the relationship
between Seth and Horus (maternal uncle and nephew) and between
Seth and Isis (brother and sister) are wholly negative,
while those between Horus and Osiris (son and father) and Osiris
and Isis (husband and wife) are wholly positive. The various contests in the central part of the narrative fit into this scheme
of the protagonists and their characteristics. After remarks on
the ultimate conflict between culture and nature, here symbolized
by right of inheritance and strength and maturity, which in its
turn conflicts with the Egyptian preference of elder above younger the author points out that in the story this opposition is
encountered by fitting it into a series of similarly irresolvable
conflicts. The author ends with the conclusion that the meaning of
the tale is its structure.
For a reaction, see our number 79320.

79307 O'MARA, Patrick F., The Palermo Stone and the Archaic Kings of Egypt, La Canada, Calif., Paulette Publishing Co., *[1979]* (20.4 x 26.1 cm; XVII + 208 p., 49 fig., 9 tables, 1 diagram) = Studies in the Structural Archaeology of Ancient Egypt, *[1]*.   Pr. $ 22

In the preface the author points out that this volume is the first of a series treating of the mathematical archaeological approach to ancient Egyptian monuments. In all volumes the author will proceed from the conception of an inherently architectonic structure of the Egyptian mind. In this volume the author exhaustively analyses the physical structure of the Palermo Stone in order to reconstruct its original appearance and to identify the kings recorded, and investigates the associated Cairo Stone.
The book consists of four parts: the stone itself and the creators of its records; the reconstruction; the Cairo Stone; and the kings of the Archaic Period. In the first chapter the author relates the discovery of the Palermo Stone and the earlier attempts at reconstruction, particularly that of Borchardt, criticizing the traditional methodology, while in chapter 2 he devotes his attention to the various draftsmen engaged in its carving, making comparisons with other ancient Egyptian material.
In six following chapters (3-8), constituting part 2, he makes his attempt to reconstruct the original appearance of the stone. In chapter 9 (= part 3) he argues that the Cairo Stone was not drawn according to the Egyptian canon and tentatively concludes that it is a modern fake.
In the subsequent part 4 (= chapters 10-13) the author sets forth in chapter 11, on the 1st Dynasty, his ideas on the order of the kings listed on the Palermo Stone, concentrating his argument on the identification of king Kenkenes = king Samti-Den with the unifier of the two lands. Chapters 12 and 13 are respectively devoted to the kings of the IInd and IIIrd Dynasties. At the end of chapter 13 the author presents a summary of his results, correlating the archaeological data with those of the Palermo Stone, the Turin Royal Canon and Manetho.
The book is concluded by an appendix in which the Cairo Stone is tested for palm distances.
Compare our numbers 79312 and 79313.
The second volume in the series by the same author, The Chronology of the Palermo and Turin Canons, has appeared in 1980.

79308 POSENER, Georges, L'Enseignement d'un homme à son fils, *in*: *Studien zu altägyptischen Lebenslehren*, 307-316.

The author sketches the reconstruction problems of the Instruction of a Man to his Son. He is able to add to the text a new piece which deals first with Pharaoh's domination over foreign countries and respect for his name, and then abruptly followed by a new topic treating wisdom themes. In this respect the present instruction resembles the Loyalist Instruction. Several ostraca containing lines of unknown texts could be placed now. One of the themes in the wisdom part seemed to be that of the advantage of indifference of character, and this reminded the author of the contents of what he once called "The Final Section of an Unknown Wisdom Text". This led him to new identifications and connections.

79309 POSENER, Georges, Les malheurs d'un prêtre égyptien. Un récit sous forme de lettre, *Journal des Savants*, Paris, 1979, 199-205.

Review of our number 77147.

79310 REDFORD, Donald B., A Gate Inscription from Karnak and Egyptian Involvement in Western Asia During the Early 18th Dynasty, *JAOS* 99 (1979), 270-287, with 2 fig.

The author publishes some blocks from the Sheikh Labib storeroom at Karnak which have been part of a gateway. The inscription, which could be partly restored, mentions inw, while male figures are represented beside the text, with on their heads crenelated rectangles inscribed with Syrian toponyms: Kedem, Tunip and $D3i-wny$. The gate is dated to the reign of Amenophis I. In this connection the author discusses the foreign policy of the early XVIIIth Dynasty, arguing that the inscription reflects the first instance of Egyptian penetration into Northern Syria, probably between years 12 and 21 of Amenophis I. The evidence about campaigns in Syria of Tuthmosis I is also studied.

J.J.J.

79311 REDFORD, Donald B., The Historical Retrospective at the Beginning of Thutmose III's Annals, *in*: *Festschrift Elmar Edel*, 338-342, with 1 fig.

The author demonstrates that Sethe's restorations of lines 9-10 of the Annals of Tuthmosis III (*Urk*. IV, 648, 2-3) are not correct. Collation of the text leads to a different restoration. It appears to follow the same pattern as the historical pericope of Pap. Harris I, 75, 2-5, describing anarchous conditions in Asia which looks to be the historical truth.

J.J.J.

79312 REEVES, [C.N.], A Fragment of Fifth Dynasty Annals at University College London, *GM* Heft 32 (1979), 47-52, with 1 fig. and 1 pl.

Es handelt sich um das von Petrie falsch interpretierte Fragment (U.C. 15508) auf der Rückseite des sogenannten Palermo-Steines im University College in London. Der Text wird vorgestellt und eine Interpretation vorgeschlagen.
Siehe auch unsere Nummer 79307.

Inge Hofmann

79313 RIDLEY, R.T., The World's Earliest Annals: A Modern Journey in Comprehension, *Acta Antiqua Academiae Scientiarum Hungaricae*, Budapest 27 (1979), 39-48.

The author presents a survey of Egyptological interpretation and understanding of the Palermo Stone.
Compare our numbers 79307 and 79312.

79314 SHIRUN-GRUMACH, Irene, Bemerkungen zu Rhythmus, Form und Inhalt in der Weisheit, *in*: *Studien zu altägyptischen Lebenslehren*, 317-352.

In the first section the author explains her attempt to reconcile Fecht's metrical rules and the parallellismus membororum or thought couplet rule. Modifying Fecht's metrics slightly, and taking the thought couplet as the basic unit, but without a completely free verse, she prefers to utilize the term "(bound) rhythm" (compare also our number 77701).
Next she exemplifies her system on account of various form types of bound language in the Wisdom of Amenemope: the admonition, the admonition with promise, the pure promise, the motivation by a general statement or by the illustration of certain human types through typical actions or attitudes (called "predication"), and a particular form of predication, namely that introduced by *ir* (called "gloss"). From this some relation between rhythm and form types is demonstrated.
The last section is devoted to the study of rhythm in a particular chapter of the Wisdom of Amenemope, chapter 25.

79315 SPIES, Otto, Eine altägyptische Quelle zum Märchen "Die Beiden Wanderer" der Brüder Grimm, *in*: *Festschrift Elmar Edel*, 397-408.

The author presents an analysis of the motifs in the "Tale of Two Travellers" that occurs with many peoples, relating in full a modern Egyptian version. He points out that the oldest known version is the "Tale of the Blinding of Truth" from Pap. Chester Beatty II so that an Egyptian origin is more probable than the Indian that is usually suggested.
J.J.J.

79316 VACHALA, Břetislav, Staroegyptská pastýřská píseň, *Nový Orient*, Praha 34, No. 4 (1979), 109.

"Ein altägyptisches Hirtenlied".
Tschechische Übersetzung des Hirtenliedes aus der Mastabas des Ti und Mereruka.
B. Vachala

79317 VERNUS, Pascal, Un décret de Thoutmosis III relatif à la santé publique (P.Berlin 3049,vo XVIII-XIX), *Orientalia* 48 (1979), 176-184, with 1 folding pl.

Ce document fragmentaire publié dès 1905 mérite de retenir l'attention. Le texte est en hiératique "sacerdotal", d'une autre main que les hymnes qui précèdent. Il s'ouvre par une titulature de Thoutmosis III sans date. Notre "décret royal" serait une version

incomplète destinée à la propagande. Son but seul est indiqué:
"guérir celui qui (souffre) physiquement de son mal, après que Sa
Majesté eut vu un livre de protection du temps des ancêtres ...
à cause de la souffrance des pauvres"..."Ceux de la salle *dryt*
l'initièrent [aux carac]téristiques de ce pays (?). Ce pays sera-
t-il donc exempt de maladie...?" On voit le roi intervenir en mati-
ère médicale, et le titre *wḥm mswt* désigne ici un aspect de la
fonction monarchique : son expression se limite ailleurs à des cas
individuels, sauf une fois sous Ramsès III, pour protéger les cara-
vanes allant vers l'isthme de Suez. Notre papyrus semble témoig-
ner d'un souci d'hygiène publique, s'étendant à l'Égypte entière.
La graphie "*km-m-n-nw*-petit oiseau" noterait le mot *kámenou* ; *sḏb*
est traduit "élément pathogène". Plusieurs indices convergents
laissent sous-entendre chez Thoutmosis III une politique systéma-
tique de réorganisation des archives de temple.

J. Custers

79318 VYCICHL, Werner, La femme au cheveux d'or, *Bulletin Société
d'Égyptologie*, Genève No. 1 (Mai 1979), 13-15.

The author points out that the motif of the woman with the frag-
rant locks of hair occurring in the Tale of the Two Brothers is
also found in a story of the Ubykhs (formerly living in the Cauca-
sus). He lists no less than ten correspondences.

J.J.J.

79319 WATTERSON, Barbara, The Use of Alliteration in Ptolemaic, *in*:
Glimpses of Ancient Egypt, 167-169.

The author discusses alliteration in texts inscribed on the E.
and W. walls of the naos exterior of Edfu. She presents examples
(in hieroglyphs, with translation) of alliteration based on each
of the consonants except t which does not occur there, while q
is found alliterating with k.

J.J.J.

79320 WENTE, Edward F., Response to Robert A. Oden's "The Contendings of
Horus and Seth" (Chester Beatty Papyrus No. 1): A Structural Interpretation, *History of Religions*, Chicago 18 (1979), 370-372.

The author criticizes the validity of the structural analysis of
myth as applied to the Contendings of Horus and Seth (Pap. Ch.
Beatty I) in our number 79306. He stresses the tale-like character
of the story.

c. **Religious, magical**

See also our numbers 79046; 79088; 79094; 79099; 79154; 79209; 79253; 79263; 79282; 79319; 79362; 79364; 79382; 79517; 79544; 79606; 79619; 79636; 79638; 79640; 79647; 79659; 79674; 79714; 79718; 79720; 79748; 79762; 79770; 79782; 79963 and 79976.

79321 ALTENMÜLLER, Hartwig, Ein Zauberspruch zum "Schutz des Leibes", *GM* Heft 33 (1979), 7-12.

Spruch VI von der Rückseite der sog. "magischen" Statue Ramses III. (Kairo JE 69771) ist auf 3 weiteren Denkmälern enthalten. Es handelt sich um einen "Spruch für den Schutz des Leibes gegen jede männliche Schlange und gegen jede weibliche Schlange", der hier in seinen vier Varianten in Synopse untereinander zusammengestellt übersetzt und interpretiert wird.
Inge Hofmann

79322 ASSMANN, Jan, Harfnerlied und Horussöhne. Zwei Blöcke aus dem verschollenen Grab des Bürgermeisters Amenemḥēt (Theben Nr. 163) im Britischen Museum, *JEA* 65 (1979), 54-77, with 2 pl. and 4 fig.

A discussion of two blocks from the lost tomb of the mayor Amenemḥēt (Theban tomb no. 163) now in the British Museum. The blocks BM 55336-7, show the Harper playing before the dead man and his wife who are seated in a funerary pavilion. Using Spiegelberg's squeezes of the scenes in the Griffith Institute the writer analyzes the layout and gives copies of the inscriptions with translations and copious notes. Details such as the sizes of the blocks and colours used on the figures are also included.
E.P. Uphill

79323 BARTA, Winfried, Bemerkungen zur Bedeutung der im Pyramidenspruch 273/274 geschilderten Anthropophagie, *ZÄS* 106 (1979), 89-94.

Verfasser vergleicht die charakteristischen Aussagen des Spruches mit den Erkenntnissen der Ethnologie. Es handelt sich um einen rituell-magischen Kannibalismus. Dieser veranlasste die Identifikation des toten Königs mit seinen vergöttlichten Ahnen und deswegen seine Auferstehung.
M. Heerma v. Voss

79324 FAULKNER, R.O., Coffin Texts III, 317r: A Correction, *JEA* 65 (1979), 161.

In C.T. Spell 238 it is suggested that the previous reading of $\dot{i}w$ $sf3$ $ḫt.\dot{i}$ "hatred (?) is behind me" is emended to nn $\dot{i}zft$ $ḫt.\dot{i}$ "no wrongdoing pursues me.
E.P. Uphill

79325 FOSTER, John L., Some Observations on Pyramid Texts 273-274, the So-Called "Cannibal-Hymn", *JSSEA* 9 (1978-1979), 51-63.

The author presents a translation in the form of a poem of the "Cannibal Hymn" (P.T. Utt. 273-274), with an introduction. He discusses the divergences between the versions of Unas and Teti, the poetic structure of the hymn: 114 verse lines, constituting couplets and stanzas; the language he himself used in his rendering, and some difficult points. At the end a discussion of the theme of the hymn.
J.J.J.

79326 GEORGE, Beate, Ein Text der Ptolemäerzeit über das Dasein in Unterwelt und Grab, *Medelhavsmuseet Bulletin*, Stockholm 14 (1979), 16-23, with 2 ill. and 6 fig.

Discussion of the inscription on the lid of a wooden anthropoid coffin (NME 7) that belonged to a certain $Ns-w\underline{s}iw$. The text, known from three other coffins from the Late Period and here presented in hieroglyphs and translation with a commentary, describes the entry of Re into the netherworld and his activities there on behalf of all the dead as well as those on behalf of $Ns-w\underline{s}iw$ in particular.
J.J.J.

79327 GERMOND, Philippe, En marge des litanies de Sekhmet à Edfou: flèches et messagers, *Bulletin Société d'Égyptologie*, Genève No. 2 (Novembre 1979), 23-29.

It is the function of the litanies of Sakhmet in Edfu in which her arrows and messengers are mentioned to prevent her to send them against the Living Falcon, that is, to demonstrate her dangerous side at the end of the year. See now the same author, Sekhmet et la protection du monde = Aegyptiaca Helvetica 9/1981.
J.J.J.

79328 GRIMM, Alfred, Ein Zitat aus den Pyramidentexten in einem ptolemäischen Ritualtext des Horus-Tempels von Edfu. Edfou III, 130. 14-15 = Pyr. 376 b (Spr. 269). Zur Tradition altägyptischer Texte. Voruntersuchungen zu einer Theorie der Gattungen, *GM* Heft 31 (1979), 35-46.

Der Edfu-Text wird dargelegt, transkribiert, übersetzt und kommentiert, desgleichen der Anfang von Spruch 269 (Pyr. 376 b-c). Er ist Bestandteil eines Ritualtextes, der eine Opferzeremonie, das Darbringen von Weihrauch, begleitete. Das zeigt, dass die Redaktoren der ptolemäischen Tempelinschriften mit den Inschriften aus den Pyramiden des Alten Reiches bzw. den diesen zugrundeliegenden auf Papyrus geschriebenen Textvorlagen, vertraut gewesen sind, dass also die Texttradition über einen Zeitraum von mehr als zweitausend Jahren ungebrochen war.
Inge Hofmann

79329 HAEKAL, Fayza Mohammed Hussein, Another Version of the Book of the Dead (Chap. 128-134) from Papyrus Cairo Museum S.R. 640, *ASAE* 63 (1979), 51-78, with 12 p. of hieroglyphic text (= p. 67-78).

After a description of the papyrus here studied, which belonged to a prophet of Montu Ankhefenkhonsu from the T.I.P. (probably the son of Besenmut) and very likely came from the Deir el-Bahri cachette, the author presents a translation of the text (B.D. Ch. 128-134) with some comments. There follows a clear hand-written transliteration of the 25 columns.

J.J.J.

79330 HORNUNG, Erik, Das Totenbuch der Ägypter, Eingeleitet, übersetzt und erläutert, Zürich und München, Artemis Verlag, 1979 (10.2 x 17 cm; 544 p., 92 fig.); series: Die Bibliothek der alten Welt. Reihe der Alten Orient ; rev. *BiOr* 38 (1981), 30-31 (M. Heerma van Voss); *CdE* LIV, No. 108 (1979), 245-248 (J. Gwyn Griffiths).

Pr. S.F. 78/DM 85

In the introduction the author discusses earlier editions and translations of the B.D., the principles on which the present translation is based, and the history and meaning of the text. He i.a. points out the importance of the regnal periods of Sesostris II and III for the development of the funerary literature since it is that time that a change from heavenly spheres to those of the underworld took place, as reflected in the C.T. He also stresses the free order in which the texts occur in various copies; that they did not contain mysterious wisdom but were available to everyone who could afford to buy a copy; that they show a cooperation and not a contrast of magic and religion.
There follows a translation in verses of those chapters that occur in the N.K. copies, accompanied by vignettes. The last part contains notes to the introduction and short discussions of the separate spells, preceded by mentions of the copies on which the translation was based, bibliographical references, and parallels in the C.T., if any. In the discussion the author also defends where necessary his translation of difficult sentences, and he describes the meaning of the vignettes.
A list of the copies of the B.D. here used on p. 525-528; a bibliography on p. 530-532; an index on p. 535-543.

J.J.J.

79331 HORNUNG, Erik, unter Mitarbeit von Andreas BRODBECK und Elisabeth STAEHELIN, Das Buch von den Pforten des Jenseits. Nach den Versionen des Neuen Reiches. Teil I: Text autographiert von Andreas Brodbeck, [Genève, Éditions de Belles-Lettres], 1979 (21 x 30 cm; XII + 410 p.) = Aegyptiaca Helvetica. Herausgegeben von/publié par Ägyptologisches Seminar der Universität Basel et Faculté des Lettres de l'Université de Genève, 7.

Like the first part of the edition of the Sun litany in this series (see our number 75347) the present volume consists of a brief introduction and the text in its various versions, given in handwritten hieroglyphs.
The edition is a substantial enlargement and improvement on Piankoff's edition of the Book of Gates (see our numbers 61546, 62465

and 62466), presenting in parallel columns all the known copies from the N.K.: those in the royal tombs, from Horemheb to Ramses VII; that in the tomb of Tjanefer (Theban Tomb No. 158); those on the coffins of Sethi I and Merenptah; and that in the Osireion at Abydos.
Translation and commentary as well as discussion of the illustrations will follow.
J.J.J.

79332 IBRAHIM, Mohiy el-Din, The God of the Great Temple of Edfu, in: Glimpses of Ancient Egypt, 170-173.

The author deals with an inscription on the exterior W. wall of the Edfu temple in which the god is presented as one of the Mythical Ancestors. The next text is given in hieroglyphs, transliteration and translation.
J.J.J.

79333 IBRAHIM, Mohiy E.A.E., Two Jubilee Texts from the temple of Edfu, ASAE 63 (1979), 89-101, with 1 folding pl.

The texts here discussed occur on the exterior of the east enclosure wall of the Edfu temple in two adjoining scenes, one being concerned with the proclamation of the decree to the gods, the other with the proclamation to the people. The texts are presented in hieroglyphs with a translation, and the conclusions at the end.
J.J.J.

79334 IVERSEN, Erik, Remarks on Some Passages from the Shabaka Stone, in: Festschrift Elmar Edel, 253-262, with 1 fig.

The author contests Sethe's theory that the text of the Shabaka Stone is a mystery play containing stage directions; he considers it an example of mythical historiography.
Iversen argues that the words of 10b, 11b and 12b are to be read after line 9; that the lines 10c - 12c continue the narrative after Geb's speech in 10a-12a; that 13-18 contain two different speeches, that of Geb in the upper-part and that of Horus in the lower part. The division of Seth's speech (lines 13a-18a) over six lines by a redactor indicates that, though the Ennead was addressed as a body, six gods were present.
J.J.J.

79335 JANKUHN, D., Der Spruch: "Die Häuser im Wasser zu bauen" (CT VI, Sp. 571) (Zur Frage der Lokalisierung der Nekropole von Buto-Sais), in: Acts 1st ICE, 327-321.

Proceeding from the O.K. title ẖrp ḥwt (nt) mw the author deals with C.T. Sp. 571 about the ḥwt imywt mw. He presents a translation of this text and argues that it relates to the regional necropolis of Sais and Buto situated on a "turtle-back".
J.J.J.

79336 KADISH, Gerald E., The Scatophagous Egyptian, *JSSEA* 9 (1978-1979), 203-217.

The author discusses texts in which the deceased denies eating excrement or drinking urine, or even harbouring any intentions to do so. He particularly deals with C.T. Spell 173, of which he presents a translation. He explains the refusal of the deceased not only from his intention to be ritually pure, but referring to Mary Douglas' study "Purity and Danger" (New York, Praeger, 1966) he sets forth that dirt means danger, disorder and chaos. Non-scatophagous utterances are a means to commit oneself to the idea of the integrated universe.

J.J.J.

79337 KOENIG, Yvan, Un revenant inconvenant? (Papyrus Deir el-Medineh 37), *BIFAO* 79 (1979), 103-119, with 2 fig. (1 folding) and 2 pl.

The amuletic papyrus here published, consisting of three lines, is a partly double of Pap. Louvre 3233a (see our number 77296). It mentions a lady T-dit-p-bik and probably dates from the early XXVIth Dynasty. The parallel passages are presented in hieroglyphs, with a translation and comments. The author interprets the invocation as being directed against malicious dead. Notes to the publication of Pap. Louvre 3233a are added.

J.J.J.

79338 LECLANT, Jean, Les textes de la pyramide de Pepi Ier, IV: le passage A:S, *in*: *Festschrift Elmar Edel*, 285-301, with 1 table and 7 fig.

Sequel to our numbers 75437, 77469 and 79517.
The author here deals with the reconstruction of the N. and S. walls of the passage between the antechamber and the serdab in the Pepi Pyramid. The texts which deal with the shroud of Pharaoh and its cosmetics are partly known from other pyramids and partly new, e.g. cols. 10-13 of the S. wall. The author discusses their contents so far as they have now been reconstructed; of the N. wall only a small bit has been recovered.

J.J.J.

79339 Papyrus Ani. BM 10.470. Vollständige Faksimile-Ausgabe im Originalformat des Totenbuches aus dem Besitz des British Museum, Graz-Austria, Akademische Druck- und Verlagsanstalt, 1979 (81 x 42.5 cm; portfolio containing title page + 37 sheets of colour photographs) = Codices Selecti. Phototypice Impressi. Volumen 62.

Reedition in colour photographs of the entire B.D. of Ani in the British Museum, without introduction or text.

J.J.J.

79340 ROCCATI, A., Procédés employés dans l'assemblage des papyrus de Turin, *in*: *Acts 1st ICE*, 553-556.

The author makes some remarks on the magical papyri in the collection of the Egyptian Museum in Turin.

79341 RÖSSLER-KÖHLER, Ursula, Kapitel 17 des ägyptischen Totenbuches. Untersuchungen zur Textgeschichte und Funktion eines Textes der altägyptischen Totenliteratur, Wiesbaden, Otto Harrassowitz, 1979 (17 x 24 cm; XIII + 388 p.) = Göttinger Orientforschungen. Veröffentlichungen des Sonderforschungsbereiches Orientalistik an der Georg-August-Universität Göttingen. IV. Reihe: Ägypten, 10. Pr. DM 66

In the introduction the author points out that this textcritical study of B.D. Ch. 17 had to be limited to the probably decisive early stage of the textual sources (XVIIth-XIXth Dynasties) and that the application of the textcritical method on the text material enabled the reconstruction of the original text.
Chapter 1 is devoted to the textcritical investigation of B.D. Ch. 17. After having listed the text sources the author extensively studies the text according to the three constituent parts of the textcritical method. First the *recensio*, i.e. the reconstruction of the mutual relations of the various text sources in a text stemma, which is based on the process of eliminating the various types of text corruption by a set of rules. Then follow the *examinatio* and *emendatio*, in which the author checks whether the text resulting from the *recensio* can be considered original and reconstructs the text of the archetype in transliteration (with *apparatus criticus*) and in translation (accompanied by the parallels). Summary at the end of the chapter.
In chapter 2 the author studies, with the help of C.T. Spell 335 and the reconstructed text of B.D. Ch. 17, the stage of the text redaction proper in order to elucidate its principles and aim. The redaction procedure is most conspicuous in the explanatory glosses. The author concludes that the text of B.D. Chapter 17 can be considered a reworking of C.T. Spell 335 and that this redaction originates from Upper Egypt, most probably from the XIIIth Dynasty. Goal was the production of some kind of encyclopaedia of the text utterances of C.T. Spell 335, which gained quickly a canonical character.
The last and brief chapter 3 is concerned with the function of B.D. Ch. 17: it served as a compendium of contemporary funerary literature which guaranteed the deceased the possession of the in this respect most important utterances and conceptions. At the end of the chapter a brief evaluation of the present result for the study of syncretistic processes.
Index to gods, sources, and some Egyptian words.

79342 ROSSITER, Evelyn, Le Livre des Morts. Papyrus d'Ani, Hunefer, Anhai. Commentaires, [Paris], Seghers, [1979](21 x 27.7 cm; 122 p., 122 ill, [116 in colour], colour ill. on cover).

After an introduction on the B.D. called "Reu Nu Pert Em Rhu ou les chapitres de l'A-Venir quotidien" dealing with background in-

formation on the subject, and an illustrated repertory of symbols, gods and objects, all vignettes of the B.D. of Ani, Hunefer and Anhai are reproduced in their original order with captions. Various spells are translated completely in separate sections.
There is also an English edition: The Book of the Dead. Papyri of Ani, Hunefer, Anhaï, New York, Miller Graphics, 1979.

79343 RUBINSTEIN, R.I., Книга Мертвых и отношение древних Египтян к смерти, *in*: Шампольон и Дешифровка, 72-87.

"The Book of the Dead and the Relation of the Ancient Egyptians with the Dead."
Survey of the Egyptological literature concerning the Egyptian conceptions of death and their expression in the B.D.

J.J.J.

79344 SADEK, Ashraf I., Glimpses of Popular Religion in New Kingdom Egypt 1. Mourning for Amenophis 1 at Deir el Medina, *GM* Heft 36 (1979), 51-56.

Es wird das Ostrakon Gardiner 31 vorgestellt, das, mit anderen Daten kombiniert, Hinweise gibt für das Fest des Trauerns für Amenophis 1., wie es von den Arbeitern in Deir el-Medina durchgeführt wurde. Acht Festtage für Amenophis sind bekannt, für OG 31 scheint der 9. Tag, d.h. der 3. Peret 21 in Frage zu kommen. Zu den Klageriten gehörten das Weinen und das Schlagen ins Gesicht wie es auch aus Herodot (II, 85) überliefert ist. Die gleichen Klageriten wie für gewöhnliche Leute gelten also auch für einen königlichen Verstorbenen.

Inge Hofmann

79345 VALLOGGIA, Michel, Le papyrus Lausanne No 3391, *in*: *Hommages Sauneron* I, 285-304, with 3 pl.

Publication in photograph and transcription, with notes to the palaeography and particularities of its writing and discussion of its original owner, of Pap. Lausanne No. 3391, a complete copy of the First Book of Respirations. The copy may date from the 2nd century B.C.

J.J.J.

79346 VERNUS, Pascal, Un hymne à Amon, protecteur de Tanis, sur une tablette hiératique (Caire J.E. 87889), *RdE* 31 (1979), 101-119, with 1 pl. and 2 tables.

La tablette de calcaire (6 x 9 cm), présentée en photographie agrandie, pratiquement illisible au recto a fourni pourtant un texte cohérent au verso. Elle est comparable à de nombreux objets similaires appartenant à la liturgie, dont Vernus dresse l'inventaire.
Une minutieuse analyse paléographique, occupant la moitié de l'article, expose la méthode de datation. La tablette serait de

la fin du 1er siècle a.C., mais sa date pourrait être abaissée jusqu'à la fin du 2e p.C.

Ph. Derchain

d. Socio-economic, juridical, administrative

See also our numbers 79231; 79518; 79841; 79875; 79905 and 79976.

79347 EYRE, C.J., A 'Strike' Text from the Theban Necropolis, in: Glimpses of Ancient Egypt, 80-91, with 2 ill.

Publication of O. Nicholson Museum, Sydney, R. 97, from the mid-XXth Dynasty and probably written by the scribe of the necropolis Amennakhte. The text records a visit of high officials to the necropolis on account of a "walkout" of the workmen complaining of hunger and the non-payment of part of their wages. The author particularly studies the palaeography of the text.

J.J.J.

79348 GITTON, Michel, Nouvelles remarques sur la stèle de donation d'Ahmes Néfertary, BIFAO 79 (1979), 327-331.

Proceeding his discussion with Mme Menu about the donation of queen Ahmose-Nofertari (see our numbers 71403, 76284 and 77526), the author once more weighs the major arguments. Does the text mean that the function of second prophet of Amon was yielded by the Queen in exchange for an indemnification, or was the function acquired by her? The author again defends the former explanation.

J.J.J.

79349 JANSSEN, J.J., Background Information on the Strikes of Year 29 of Ramses III, Oriens Antiquus 18 (1979), 301-308, with 1 table.

The author discusses O. Turin 57072, formerly No. 6365, recently published in our number 78498. After having given the translation and the philogical notes the author points out its relevance as an illustration of the events among the necropolis workmen of Deir el-Medîna in year 29 of Ramesses III about which the Turin Strike Papyrus gives such a vivid account. In an excursus the author criticizes Žaba's conclusions in our number 2651.

79350 JANSSEN, Jac. J., The Water Supply of a Desert Village, Medelhavsmuseet Bulletin, Stockholm 14 (1979), 9-15, with 3 ill. and 1 fig.

The author publishes O. MM 14126 vso (for the rto see our number 73554, no. 17). The text contains a list of house owners in the first column and a quantity expressed in khar in the second. The author first dates the ostracon to the end of the XIXth Dynasty on account of the names and then points out that the text is probably concerned with the water supply of the village of Deir el Medîna.

79351 KOENIG, Yvan, Catalogue des étiquettes de jarres hiératiques de Deir el-Médineh. Fascicule 1. Nos 6000-6241, *[Le Caire]*, Publications de l'Institut français d'Archéologie orientale, 1979 (15 x 22 cm; [VI +] 44 p., 27 pl.) = Documents de fouilles, XXI/1.

The first fascicle of the publication of the hieratic jar labels found during the excavations of Deir el-Medîna follows the usual system of the series: in the first part, the description and technical data of the texts, in the second, the plates, hieroglyphic transliterations of all texts, accompanied in many, but not in all instances by facsimiles on the opposite page.
The texts are arranged according to the subjects indicated by their wording. They deal with various kinds of food: olive oil (nos. 6000-6085), *nḥḥ* oil (6086-6103), *mrḥt* oil (6104-6124), fat (6125-6142), *sgnn* (6143), *srmt* (6144-6153), *smỉ* (6154-6160), meat (6161-6165), fowl (6166-6181), honey (6182-6196), incense (6197-6205), *bš?* (6233-6235), *irwyt* (6236-6238), other products (6239-6241, to be continued in fascicle 2). Group 13 (6206-6232) constitutes an exception since it consists of products stated to be transported by *ḥryw mnšw*.
The publication of the texts is continued in fascicle 2 (it has appeared in 1980), while fascicle 3 will contain the discussion of the material.

J.J.J.

79352 KOENIG, Yvan, Livraisons d'or et de galène du trésor du temple d'Amon sous la XXe dynastie, *in*: *Hommages Sauneron* I, 185-220, with 8 double pl.

Publication of two fragmentary papyri written by the same scribe, of unknown provenance and at present preserved in the IFAO. The author presents a careful description of their outer appearance, writing and language, as well as a translation with commentary. The documents came from the archive of the Treasurer of the Amon Temple at Karnak and record the results of expeditions sent in order to procure gold and galena (*msdmt*) in the Eastern Desert. The dates, the years 1 and 2, may belong to the reign of Ramses VII.

J.J.J.

79353 MARCINIAK, Marek, Ostraca hiératiques de Deir el-Bahari, *in*: *Acts 1st ICE*, 453-455.

Discussion of five ostraca concerned with the building activities of Tuthmosis III at Deir el-Bahri, which complement the ones published in our number 60325.

79354 MEEKS, Dimitri, Les donations aux temples dans l'Égypte du Ier millénaire avant J.-C., *in*: *State and Temple Economy in the Ancient Near East* .II, 605-687, with 1 map.

Documentation about the temples and their economy during the T.I.P. is scanty, donation stelae constituting almost the only source. The author here presents a comprehensive study of this class of texts, based on about 130 instances (some of which unpublished) he has been able to collect. They range in time from the XVIIth Dynasty to the end of the XXVIth Dynasty (the Ptolemaic material is here excluded) and can be divided into two groups: 26 from the N.K., over 100 from the later periods. The latter group is particularly the subject of this study.
Only four came from Thebes, all others from the Delta and the adjoining area of Upper Egypt. The former bear different formulae, testifying to a different juridical development. The author discusses the northern larger group, their geographical distribution and their economic background. Comparing them with the 8 N.K. stelae from Nubia he suggests that they reflect the exploitation of newly conquered areas.
Studying minutely the representations and texts of the stelae the author draws a large number of conclusions, e.g.: that the transport of the fields took always place through an administrative intermediary; that the original ownership of the fields is unknown; that the beneficiary is either the divine offering or a member of the temple personnel; that private donations were essentially destined for the funerary cult, royal donations for the maintenance of the temple economy; that the reason why the type of stelae disappears at the end of the XXVIth Dynasty is not clear. Many historical suggestions are made throughout, also in the notes. On p. 657-687 the author presents a catalogue of donation stelae, preceded by an introduction. He i.a. lists: donation stelae proper (arranged after their dates); doubtful instances; those wrongly included in former lists and discussions; post-Saitic stelae; stelae with donations to lions; boundary stelae.

J.J.J.

79355 MENU, Bernadette, La fondation cultuelle accordée à Sheshonq, *CRIPEL* 5 *[1979]*, 183-189.

The author studies stela Cairo JE 66285 (published by Blackman in *JEA* 27 [1941], 83-95) which records the foundations by Psusennes II of a funerary cult for Nimrod, on request of his son Sheshonq. She analyses the contents of the text, particularly the specification of properties and personnel, and concludes that not the transfer of properties, but the rights on usufruct and services is recorded.

J.J.J.

79356 POSENER- KRIÉGER, P., Les papyrus d'Abousir et l'économie des temples funéraires de l'Ancien Empire, *in*: *State and Temple Economy in the Ancient Near East*. I, 133-151.

The author presents a survey of her study on the Abusir papyri (our number 76639), particularly their importance for our knowledge about the economy of the O.K. She sets forth the system of provisioning the temples, discussing i.a. the provenance of the provisions. They came partly from the sun-temple of Neferirkare and partly from the residence, where the entire system, also the supply of products for the sun-temple, was concentrated. The funerary domains of Neferirkare, however, seem to be almost absent from this system, unless they were represented by an institution called R_3-$\check{s}$-K_3k_3i as their central organization. The quantities daily consumed by the temples were enormous, and the number of persons living from them, clerical and lay personnel of the temple as well as funerary priests of the tombs in this area, was equally large. Hence the necessity for the residence to keep control of the whole system. The archive proves that, despite the derelict state of the temple, the funerary cult of the king long time after his death still played an active role in the economic structure of the O.K.

J.J.J.

79357 POSENER-KRIÉGER, Paule, Le prix des étoffes, in: *Festschrift Elmar Edel*, 318-331, with 7 fig.

After quoting some examples of high "prices" of cloth in the O.K. the author publishes two short texts from the archive of Gebelein, very similar to each other and resembling the famous "Hauskauf" -stela from Gîza (*Urk*. I, 157-158). The Gebelein texts, one of which is fragmentary, are presented in facsimile, transliteration and translation, with a commentary. The author i.a. suggests that the *pr* exchanged for a number of cubits of cloth is actually a funerary chapel.

J.J.J.

79358 THÉODORIDÈS, Aristide, L'acte de vente d'Ancien Empire (26e s. av. J.C.), *Revue internationale des droits de l'antiquité*, Bruxelles, 3e série, 26 (1979), 31-85, with 2 pl.

The author discusses the O.K. block of stone Cairo J.E. 42787 which was presumed to be inscribed with a deed of sale of a house. After an introduction on the position of the common person in the O.K. and a survey of Egyptological opinion on sale, money, value and related problems the author quotes some texts on selling and buying. He then extensively comments upon Pirenne's translation of the text, its edition by Sethe and the points of view of Goedicke (our number 70213) and K. Gödecken (our number 76291) on the text. In a new translation he presents his own interpretation and arrangement of the text.
The author concludes that two parties speak in the text, one reminding past events, the other announcing future engagements, and that, consequently, the text does not constitute a deed of sale. He also draws a second conclusion as regards the sale and the general situation of O.K. institutions from the juridical, social and

economic points of view and points out that the magico-religious stage of law and that of the primitive conception of formalism were already passed.

79359 VERNER, Miroslav, Neue Papyrusfunde in Abusir, *RdE* 31 (1979), 97-100, with 1 fig.

Présentation d'un fragment provenant d'un groupe d'environ 200 qui pourraient completer les textes publiés par Posener-Kriéger-de Cenival (notre No. 68486).

Ph. Derchain

79360 VINOGRADOV, I.V., Данные Папируса Вилвбур о ха-та фараона, *in*: Шампольон и Дешифровка, 60-71.

"Evidence from the Papyrus Wilbour concerning the Khato-lands of Pharaoh."
The author argues that the *khato*-lands of Pharaoh, to which are devoted 15 paragraphs of Text A of the Papyrus Wilbour and the entire Text B, are lots cultivated by persons, mostly temple-personnel, who received part of their yield. The Text B is composed from the material in Text A, as e.g. comparison of A §44 with B §7 demonstrates. That the amounts of *arourai* mentioned in Text B are mostly larger than those of Text A is explained by the incomplete state of Text A. Probably Text B was a copy of an older list made some years before; hence the numerous corrections.

J.J.J.

79361 ZONHOVEN, L.M.J., The Inspection of a Tomb at Deir El-Medîna (O. Wien Aeg. 1), *JEA* 65 (1979), 89-98, with 1 pl. and 1 fig.

This ostracon was acquired by H. Junker in 1911 and measures 30 x 25cm. It seems to be written by Amennakhte, son of Ipuy, the famous scribe of the time of Ramesses III, and he appears as a witness on it. It is dated to year 25 and concerns a tomb survey, workmen and guardians being mentioned as well as a detailed list of the contents. A very detailed commentary is given and places where Černý's transcription differs from that of the author are indicated.

E.P. Uphill

e. Demotic and related material

See also our numbers 79081; 79205; 79211; 79241; 79250; 79268; 79458; 79524; 79528; 79574; 79726; 79745; 79748; 79896 and 791035.

79362 BONNEAU, Danielle, Didier DEVAUCHELLE, Michel PEZIN, Les Papyrus Leconte, *in*: *Actes du XVe Congrès International de Papyrologie*. Troisième partie. Problèmes généraux - Papyrologie littéraire, [Bruxelles - Louvain 29 août - 3 septembre 1977. Edités par Jean Bingen et Georges Nachtergael], Bruxelles, Fondation Egyptologique Reine Elisabeth, 1979 (= Papyrologica Bruxellensia, 18), 25-26.

The authors introduce a collection of Demotic and Greek papyri belonging to Leconte: juridical texts, three contracts of sale, a Demotic literary text, and a Demotic hymn to Sobek.

79363 BRESCIANI, E., Progretto di pubblicazione degli ostraka demotici e greco-demotici di Medinet Madi (Scavi A. Vogliano, Università di Milano, 1939), *in*: *Acts 1st ICE*, 125-126.

Short report on the progress of the publication of Demotic ostraca from Medinet Madi. *J.J.J.*

79364 BRESCIANI, Edda, Elsa BEDINI, Lucia PAOLINI and Flora SILVANO, Una domanda oracolare demotica con responso scritto, il Pap. Dem. Cairo CG 31212 riconsiderato, *Egitto e Vicino Oriente* 2 (1979), 57-68, with 2 ill. and 2 fig. on 2 pl.

En Égypte, les consultations oraculaires (savoir) ressemblent beaucoup aux lettres aux dieux (obtenir); la différence apparaît dans les formules oraculaires, communes au démotique, au grec et au copte. Le dieu est censé choisir entre deux feuillets, l'un affirmatif, l'autre négatif. Mais déjà un papyrus de Dîmé portait, outre la formule du choix, une réponse écrite. Le papyrus de Tebtynis ici réédité date comme l'autre du IIe siècle av. J.-C. Mesurant 32 cm, il pouvait constituer la seule forme de questions posées. Ces réponses écrites présupposent chez l'interprète la connaissance du contenu; le dieu pouvait lui manifester son avis par un mouvement de la statue ou par un songe. Ici Sobekemheb fils de Pabo, "le magasinier" (de Sobek ?) pose une vingtaine de questions réparties en trois groupes. Le premier concerne la cause de ses malheurs: le dieu ou diverses personnes, un autre l'état de sa future sépulture ; le dernier concerne sa famille et ses serviteurs, habitant peut-être au temple Nord de Sobek. Une épidémie pourrait avoir affolé l'interrogateur insatiable ; Sobek se contenterait d'assumer la responsabilité des malheurs, envoyant le consultant vérifier les faits sur place. La mention d'Osir-Apis précède une courte lacune.

J.Custers

79365 BRESCIANI Edda, Maria Carmela BETRÓ and Sergio PERNIGOTTI, Ostraka demotici da Ossirinco, *Egitto e Vicino Oriente* 2 (1979), 69-84, with 4 pl.

Sequel to our number 78123.
The authors present 15 texts, mainly letters and accounts, in photograph, facsimile, transliteration and translation with comments.

79366 BRUNSCH, Wolfgang, Die bilingue Stele des Moschion (Berlin Inv. Nr. 2135 - Cairo J. d'E. Nr. 63160). Mit einem Exkurs von G. Amendt, *Enchoria* 9 (1979), 5-32, with 8 pl. (3 folding; 1 unnumbered).

Republication of the different, highly artificial, Greek-Demotic texts of this bilingual stela, a dedication to Osiris in Xois of late Roman date by an Egyptian named Moschion, on behalf of the healing of his foot. The Demotic texts are probably also metrically formed like the Greek ones, but according to the rules of the Egyptian qualitative accent. Two of the texts (SD and SG) are arranged in a sort of 'crossword puzzle', the system of which is mathematically studied by G.Amendt.

W. Brunsch

79367 CRUZ-URIBE, Eugene, A Transfer of Property during the Reign of Darius I (P.Bibl.Nat. 216 and 217), *Enchoria* 9 (1979), 33-44, with 3 pl. (2 folding), 2 tables and 1 facsimile on an unnumbered pl.

Republication of two papyri which come from Thebes and are dated to the fifth year of Darius I (=516 B.C.). The texts belong to an archive, and deal with the transfer of the property of the woman $T3-sn.t\ -hr$ to her son $P3-dj-imn-htp$ and her daughter $Rwrw$ in equal shares.

W. Brunsch

79368 CRUZ-URIBE, Eugene and George R. HUGHES, A Strike Papyrus from the Reign of Amasis, *Sarapis* 5, No 1 (1979), 21-26.

The authors present a new transliteration and translation with a commentary of Dem.Pap. Berlin 13616, originally studied by Erichsen (our number 3854). It dates from year 13 of Amasis and deals with a strike of the quarrymen of Elephantine.

J.J.J.

79369 DEVAUCHELLE, Didier, Le papyrus démotique Louvre E 9415. Un partage de biens, *RdE* 31 (1979), 29-35, with 1 pl.

Photographie, translittération, traduction et commentaire très bref du papyrus mentionné dans le titre, daté par l'auteur des alentours de 200 a.C. La parenté du formulaire avec celui du pap. Turin No 28 de Botti (daté de 110-109) paraît certaine.

Ph. Derchain

79370 GRUNERT, Stefan, Ägyptische Erscheinungsformen des Privateigentums zur Zeit der Ptolemäer: Liturgietage, *ZÄS* 106 (1979), 60-79.

Verfasser untersucht eine spezifische Form individualisierten Privateigentums. Er stellt 25 Urkunden aus dem Totoes-Archiv vor. Bei diesen Rechtsvereinbarungen sind Objekt Liturgietage am Hathor-Tempel in der Nekropole, am Isis-Heiligtum, am Hathor-Temple auf dem Berg, am Kultraum des Arensnuphis, bzw. an der Pyramide des Amenophis, Sohn des Hapu. Zum Schluss bespricht Grunert den Wert der Liturgietage.

M. Heerma v. Voss

79371 JARITZ, Horst, Herwig MAEHLER, und Karl-Theodor ZAUZICH, Inschriften und Graffiti von der Brüstung der Chnumtempel-Terrasse in Elephantine, *MDAIK* 35 (1979), 125-154, with 11 pl.

On the balustrade along the terrace of the Khnum temple in Elephantine a number of graffiti have been discovered. The present study first discusses the balustrade itself on which three naoi, two altars and two pairs of obelisks had been standing (see fig. 1). Then the graffiti are published, 51 written in Greek, 7 in Demotic, some accompanied by a figure (e.g. a hand or an animal head). Most texts are given in facsimile and all are discussed. At the end a list of private names occurring in these texts.

J.J.J.

79372 LICHTHEIM, Miriam, Observations on Papyrus Insinger, *in*: *Studien zu altägyptischen Lebenslehren*, 283-305.

On account of the wisdom text of the Demotic Pap. Insinger the author discusses four points: 1. the sentences of Demotic Instructions (Ankhsheshonqi; Pap. Insinger and Pap. dém. Louvre 2414) consist of single lines, which are grammatically and logically complete and self-contained. The conspicuous difference in this respect with the older Egyptian wisdom literature which is structured in couplets is explained by her as resulting from the reluctance of Demotic writers to adapt the vernacular to the requirements of the elevated poetic style; 2. some key terms of the vocabulary of Pap. Insinger which are more abstract than those of the earlier instructions and denote the contrast between the wise and the fool; 3. Pap. Insinger's views on fate and fortune and their expression by means of paradoxes; 4. Hebrew (Qohelet and the Wisdom of Ben-Sira) and Greek (Sentences of Menander) parallels.

79373 MENU, Bernadette, La colonne 2 du "Code d'Hermopolis", *in*: *Actes du XVe Congrès International de Papyrologie. Quatrième partie. Papyrologie documentaire, [Bruxelles - Louvain 29 août - 3 septembre 1977. Édités par Jean Bingen et Georges Nachtergael]*, Bruxelles, Fondation Egyptologique Reine Elisabeth (= Papyrologica Bruxellensia, 19), 214-221.

The author reinterprets the Legal Code of Hermopolis sections Col. 2, 12-22 and Col. 2, 22 - Col. 3, 2 (see already our numbers 73664 and 75490). She points out that the first section is not an excursus outside the subject dealt with, concerned with a public protest (Demotic šʿr), but the description of the first stage of a procedure which takes an end in the following section in Col. 2. It is concerned with the setting free of an immovable (house or plot of land), given by a debtor to his creditor as a guarantee for his debt (money or cereals). A transliteration and translation of the sections conclude the article.

79374 MENU, Bernadette, Reçus démotiques gréco-romains provenant d'Edfou, in: Hommages Sauneron I, 261-280, with 5 double pl.

Publication of 30 Demotic ostraca from Edfu, 24 dealing with capitation (ḥmt ʿp.t), 3 with taxes for the maintenance of dykes (pꜣ wš nbj) and 2 with taxes on ships (ḥḏ n tks), while no. 30 is of uncertain nature. All texts are given in photograph, facsimile, transliteration and translation, with some comments. In three appendices: a table of various writings of ḥmt ʿp.t, a discussion of the amount of the taxes, and an index of proper names.
J.J.J.

79375 MENU, Bernadette, Reçus démotiques romains provenant d'Edfou (O.D. IFAO: 2ᵉ série), BIFAO 79 (1979), 121-141, with 5 double pl.

Sequel to our preceding number.
Thirty more Demotic ostraca from Edfu bearing tax receipts are here published. The author also makes general remarks on the capitation (p. 129-130), the dyke tax (133-135), and the fruit tax (136). At the end a note by P.W. Pestman on the double date of O.D. 622 (No. 28 in our preceding number).
J.J.J.

79376 NUR-EL-DIN, M.A., The Collection of the Demotic Ostraca in Cairo Museum, in: Acts 1st ICE, 499-501.

The author gives some details about the collection of Demotic ostraca in the Cairo Museum, such as provenance and the contents of the more interesting ones.

79377 NUR-EL-DIN, M.A., The Proper Names in Mattha's Demotic Ostraka: a Reconsideration, Enchoria 9 (1979), 45-48.

The author proposes new readings for proper names of some fifty ostraka of Mattha's publication (Cairo 1945).
W. Brunsch

79378 PERNIGOTTI, Sergio, Ancora sulla stele Firenze 1639 (2507), Egitto e Vicino Oriente 2 (1979), 21-37.

En 1975, Malinine avait attribué à ce texte une datation nouvelle. Deux règnes y étaient évoqués en effet, cette stèle hiéroglyphique transcrivant un contrat démotique originel et le datant d'un Wahib-Rê sans autre cartouche. Malinine avait compris Apriès, se fondant sur l'emploi du cartouche isolé et sur la paléographie. La datation proposée antérieurement (règne de Psamétik Iᵉʳ), à laquelle Malinine était revenu, devrait être abandonnée, pense Pernigotti, sous réserve d'une révélation de parallèles contemporains. L'auteur passe en revue les rares documents analogues, puis présente une traduction, une reconstitution du texte démotique et son interprétation. Parmi les données onomastiques figurerait la mention d'un

Grand chef des Ma(shaouash): Khari = (P3) H3ry. L'examen détaillé aboutit à trois conclusions. I. Le texte reste relativement correct malgré la difficulté de transposer le démotique en hiéroglyphes, l'inexpérience du lapicide et la mauvaise préparation de la pierre employée. II. L'élimination de quelques mots par souci de concision s'expliquerait assez logiquement, mais le moins bien aux première et avant-dernière lignes. III. L'original ne paraît pas antérieur au début du VIe siècle.

J. Custers

79379 PEZIN, Michel, Un ostracon démotique inédit r rḫ.w r, *Enchoria* 9 (1979), 143, with 1 pl.

Publication of a very fragmentary ostracon of the type of $r.rḫ=w\ r$ (land allotment).

W. Brunsch

79380 QUAEGEBEUR, J., De nouvelles archives de familles thébaines à l'aube de l'époque ptolémaïque, *in*: Actes du XVe Congrès International de Papyrologie. Quatrième partie. Papyrologie documentaire, [Bruxelles - Louvain 29 août - 3 septembre 1977. Édités par Jean Bingen et Georges Nachtergael], Bruxelles, Fondation Égyptologique Reine Élisabeth, 1979 (= Papyrologica Bruxellensia, 19), 40-48.

The author presents a group of Demotic texts belonging to one archive from Thebes and dating from the time of Alexander the Great and his son, which were recently acquired by the Musées Royaux d'Art et d'Histoire at Brussels. Two of the more important papyri (Inv. Nos. E 8552 and 8253) are documents concerning a payment in silver, while the other (Inv. No. 8253) is concerned with a transfer of property. The Inv. Nos. E. 8255 and E. 8256 form two sets of papyrus strips consisting respectively of 4 and 5 texts.
The author traces the family relations between the contracting parties and points out the importance of the archive, its information about the position of the Egyptians in the local administration and its ties with other Theban archives.

79381 SEIDL, Erwin, Eine demotische Juristenarbeit, *Zeitschrift der Savigny-Stiftung für Rechtsgeschichte*. Romanistische Abteilung, Weimar 96 (1979), 17-30.

Review article of Mattha-Hughes, The Demotic Legal Code of Hermopolis West (our number 75490).

J.J.J.

79382 SMITH, M., A Demotic Version of a Hymn to Amon, *in*: *Acts 1st ICE*, 587-592.

The author makes remarks on a Demotic version of a hymn to Amon which is preserved on an ostracon from the collection Hess, which is now in the collection of the University of Zürich. The text of which 31 lines are preserved on the ostracon is also known from other versions in the Isis temple of Philae and the Hibis temple in the oasis of Khârga. The text dates from the late-Ptolemaic - early Roman Period.

79383 TAIT, W.J., The Offices of the House of Pharaoh, in: *Actes du XVe Congrès International de Papyrologie* - Quatrième partie. Papyrologie documentaire, [Bruxelles - Louvain 29 août - 3 septembre 1977. Édités par Jean Bingen et Georges Nachtergael], Bruxelles, Fondation Égyptologique Reine Élisabeth, 1979 (= Papyrologica Bruxellensia, 19), 49-50.

The author briefly reports on a fragment of a Demotic onomasticon from Tebtynis, which provides new evidence for the pharaonic Egyptian administration at the end of the Late Period, now in the collection of the Egyptological Institute of Copenhagen University.

79384 THISSEN, Heinz-Josef, Demotische Graffiti des Paneions im Wadi Hammamat, *Enchoria* 9 (1979), 63-92, with 15 pl. and 7 facsimiles on 2 unnumbered pl.

Publication of 40 proskynemata respectively visitors' inscriptions of the Paneion in the Wadi Hammamat. The texts date to Ptolemaic times and have mostly been incised by workers of the quarries there. Two excursuses on the group *prs tmstm* and on the formulars of these inscriptions in general close the paper.

W. Brunsch

79385 THISSEN, Heinz-Josef, Die "nördliche" Hathor, *GM* Heft 35 (1979), 77-79.

Durch eine Zusammenstellung einer Reihe von Epitheta der Hathor in demotischen Texten wird wahrscheinlich gemacht, dass statt der "nördlichen" Hathor eine "Herrin" Hathor zu lesen ist.

Inge Hofmann

79386 WÅNGSTEDT, Sten V., Demotische Quittungen über Salzsteuer, *Orientalia Suecana*, Stockholm 27-28 (1978-1979), 5-27, with 5 ill. and 17 facsimiles.

The author publishes 20 Demotic ostraca on the taxation of salt, 15 of which come from the British Museum, London and the 5 others from major collections in Europe. They all date from the 3rd century B.C. and originate from Thebes. The texts are presented either in facsimile or in photograph (in two instances even both), with transliteration, translation and short comments.

79387 WOLFF, Hans Julius, Neue Juristische Urkunden, *Zeitschrift der Savigny Stiftung für Rechtsgeschichte*. Romanistische Abteilung, Weimar 96 (1979), 258-271.

Nr. 6 (p. 268-271: P. Oxyrhynchus (ed. J.R. Rea) Nr. 3285 contains part of a Greek version of our number 75490.

79388 ZAUZICH, Karl-Theodor, Einige Bemerkungen zu den demotischen Papyri Louvre E. 3333 und E. 3334, *Enchoria* 9 (1979), 121-124, with 1 ill. and 1 fig.

Several corrections to our number 77635, 97 ff.

W. Brunsch

79389 ZAUZICH, K.-Th., Neue literarische Texte in demotischer Schrift, *in*: *Acts 1st ICE*, 691.

Abstract of a paper. For the complete text see our number 78889.

79390 ZAUZICH, K.-Th., Zwei vermeintliche Ortsnamen, *Enchoria* 9 (1979), 145.

Two corrections of Spiegelberg's readings:
1) P. Loeb 1, vso. 2: instead of "*Swn*" read "*wꜥ iwn*" (a cargo).
2) P. Loeb 6, 20; 26, 9; 26, 10: instead of a toponym "*Snmḥ*" read "*snf*" (the year before).

W. Brunsch

f. Coptic

See also our numbers 79573; 79745 and 79828.

79391 BELLET, P., Bibliographical Glosses and Grammar in Ogdoad (VI: 62, 33 - 63,9.31-32), *Enchoria* 9 (1979), 1-4.

Some grammatical and interpretative notes on several places in Codex VI of Nag Hammadi ("The Ogdoad"), a "preprint of the translations from the eleven-volume English edition" of which has already appeared (J.M. Robinson ed., The Nag Hammadi Library, San Francisco 1977).

W. Brunsch

79392 BROWNE, Gerald M., Michigan Coptic Texts, Barcelona, Papyrologica Castroctaviana, 1979 (16 x 22 cm; XVI + 79 p., 4 pl. [1 folding]) = Papyrologica Castroctaviana. Studia et textus, 7.

This edition of Coptic texts from the Michigan collection is distributed by the Biblical Institute Press, Piazza della Pilotta, 35, I-00187 Roma, Italia (Lire 10,000 = $ 12.50).
The publication contains texts with textual annotations on papyrus, parchment and paper of a theological nature, dating from A.D. 300-1000. Nos 1-8 contain Coptic translations of the Bible: P. Mich. Inv. No. 3589 (Psalm 115 (116), 3-7); Inv. No. 5421 (Job 30.21-30), which was hitherto unidentified, with translation, compared with the Sahidic and Bohairic versions; Inv. No. 4951 (I Corinthians 4.9-5.3); Inv. No. 4563 (I Corinthians 11.10-28); Inv. No. 552 (II Corinthians 12.21-13.12); Inv. No. 3535a (Galatians 5.11-6.1), also provided with reconstructed Akhmimic and

Sahidic versions; Inv. No. 4962.2 (Hebrews 2.11-15); Inv. No. 4538c (Revelation 18.7-10).
The rest of the volume includes the beginning of Gregory's Encomium on Basil of Caesarea (P. Mich. Inv. No. 5567a + Louvain Ms. 44, ed. Lefort), with translation; a hymn to the Archangel Michael (Inv. No. 4567a), with translation; fragment of an early Bohairic text dealing with the Archangel Raphael (Inv. 4162); a Christian amulet (Inv. No. 1559), with translation; an almanac (Kalandologion; Inv. No. 590), compared with a version at present in Vienna, with translation. The appendix contains a revision of Till, Eine koptische Bauernpraktik, *MDAIK* 6 (1936). At the end indexes of proper names, Coptic and Greek words.

79393 BROWNE, Gerald M., Notes on the Fayumic John, *Enchoria* 9 (1979), 135-137.

Some critical remarks upon our number 62234.
W. Brunsch

79394 BRUNSCH, Wolfgang, Drei koptische Ostrakonbriefe aus der Sammlung des ägyptologischen Instituts in Heidelberg, *ZÄS* 106 (1979), 25-36, with 5 ill.

Verfasser gibt Beschreibung, Aufnahme(n), Text mit App. crit., Übersetzung und Kommentar jedes Briefes. Es betrifft Inv. Nr. 297 (Bitte), 774 (Quittung) und 773 (Eingabe).
Am Schluss allgemeine Bemerkungen über Aufbau und Formular der koptischen Briefe. *M. Heerma v. Voss*

79395 COQUIN, René-Georges, Un complément aux *Vies sahidiques de Pachôme*: Le manuscrit IFAO, copte 3, *BIFAO* 79 (1979), 209-247, with 2 pl.

Publication of the Ms. IFAO, copte 3, twelve pages from a Sahidic codex designated by Lefort as S^5 in his edition of the Life of St. Pakhom. The ms. comes from the White Monastery, and the text is here presented with a translation and a commentary, followed by the Arabic version from Ms. Vat. ar. ff° 33^v-39^v.
J.J.J.

79396 DEMBSKA, A., Coptic Liturgical Manuscripts from Polish Collection, *in*: *Acts 1st ICE*, 155-161.

The author enumerates and briefly describes the Coptic liturgical mss. preserved in Polish collections.
J.J.J.

79397 The Facsimile Edition of the Nag Hammadi Codices. Cartonnage. Published under the Auspices of the Department of Antiquities of the Arab Republic of Egypt in Conjunction with the United Nations Educational, Scientific and Cultural Organization, Leiden, E.J. Brill, 1979 (24 x 33 cm; XXIV p., 72 pl.); rev. *CdE* LV, No. 109-110 (1980), 343 (Jean Bingen). Pr. fl. 180

Sequel to our numbers 77222 and 77223.
In the preface, in English with a shorter Arabic version on opposite pages, James M. Robinson describes the recent history of the papyri of which the photographs are here published and which were used to produce the cartonnage in the leathern covers of the twelve extant Nag Hammadi Codices. The Greek and Coptic Texts will be published at a later date.
The papyri provide information that may be relevant to the location of the production of the codices in time and space. The already suggested association with Chenoboskion, or rather Chenoboskia, appears to be confirmed and there is more evidence for their monastic provenance. The author summarizes recent literature about the bindings, date and place of origin of the codices.
J.J.J.

79398 GASCOU, Jean, Ostraca de Djêmê, *BIFAO* 79 (1979), 77-86, with 2 pl.

Publication of six Coptic ostraca from Djeme, five tax receipts and a list of names.
In an appendix some improvements on the readings of ostraca already published.
J.J.J.

79399 LAFONTAINE, G., Un éloge copte de Saint Michel, attribué à Macaire de Tkow, *Le Muséon*, Louvain 92 (1979), 301-320.

The author publishes a Coptic eulogy of the archangel Michael attributed to Macarius bishop of Tkow (Antaeopolis), at present preserved in the Pierpont Morgan Library, New York (Inv. No. M 592, 27v-37r). The text is presented with a Latin translation having the Greek words in the Coptic text in between brackets, and a few textcritical notes.

79400 LAFONTAINE, Guy, Une homélie copte sur le diable et sur Michel, attribuée à Grégoire le théologien, *Le Muséon*, Louvain 92 (1979), 37-60.

The author publishes a Coptic homily on the archangel Michael and the devil, at present preserved in the Pierpont Morgan Library, New York (Inv. No. M 592, 8r-16v). The text is presented with textcritical notes and a translation in Latin, with the Greek words in the Coptic text in brackets.

79401 LAYTON, Bentley, The Gnostic Treatise on Resurrection from Nag Hammadi, Edited with Translation and Commentary, Missoula, Scholars Press, 1979 (13.5 x 22 cm; X + 220 p.) = Harvard Theological Review. Harvard Dissertations in Religion, 12; rev. *BiOr* 28 (1981), 6-11 (Jacques E. Menard); *Rivista* 54 (1980), 390-391 (Tito Orlandi).
Pr. $ 7.50

In the preface the author explains that he has largely rewritten the translation and commentary of his original dissertation (Harvard 1971) and in the introduction that his new translation of

and commentary on the Treatise on Resurrection (also known as the Epistle to Rheginus; Nag Hammadi Codex I = Codex Jung, p. 43,25 - 50,18) differs very substantially from previous ones, apart from a brief general discussion and the date.
He then presents in chapter 1 the text and both his modern and precise literal translation interspersed with the Greek words on opposite pages. This is followed in chapter 2 by a commentary containing the specific comments, in which each section is headed by a synopsis of the essential line of thought of the treatise and (sometimes) the author's pertinent remarks. The third chapter is devoted to the general commentary on the content and the arrangement of the treatise, while the fourth deals with the grammatical notes.
After nine grammatical appendices (the use of the forms spelled ΠΙ, ΤΙ, ΝΙ; the use of connective particles in the text; clauses of purpose, cause and command; the word ΠШΗΡΕ Ν̄- followed by either an attributive or genitive construction; the asyndetic first perfect construction ΑϤСШΤΜ̄ ΑϤШΤΟΡΤΡ̄; the interrogative phrase ΕΤΒΕ ΕΥ ; the periodic structure of the very difficult lines 167-175 = 49,16 ff; line 183 = 49, 36; and the inflection of conjugations and suffixed pronouns) follow the complete indexes to the Coptic text (proper names; Greek and Coptic words) and a concordance between the author's line numbering and that of the manuscript.

79402 LUCCHESI, Enzo, Localisation d'une pièce manuscrite isolée dans la littérature chenoutienne, ZÄS 106 (1979), 80-81.

L'auteur a réimprimé le folio K 9243 de la Bibliothèque Nationale de Vienne, publié par Wessely en 1909. Ce manuscript constitue les pages 365-366 du codex A de notre n° 3437, pp. 59-71. Le texte est accompagné d'un apparat critique et d'une traduction latine du passage correspondant offert par le codex B.
M. Heerma v. Voss

79403 MacCOULL, Leslie S.B., Coptic Marriage Contract, *in*: Acts du XVe Congrès International de Papyrologie. Deuxième partie: Papyrus inédits (P. XV. Congr.) [Bruxelles-Louvain 29 août - 3 septembre 1977. Edités par Jean Bingen et Georges Nachtergael], Bruxelles, Fondation Égyptologique Reine Élisabeth, 1979 (= Papyrologica Bruxellensia, 17), 116-123.

Publication of the text and translation with notes of a Coptic marriage contract (Pap. Pierpont Morgan Inv. 660.B.12), of which the provenance is unknown, and which dates from the late 6-7th centuries A.D.

79404 MacCOULL, Leslie S.B., The Martyrdom of St Sergius of Benha, *in*: *Coptic Studies Presented to Mirrit Boutros Ghali* for the Forty-Fifth Anniversary of the Founding of the Society for Coptic Archaeology. Edited by Leslie S.B. MacCoull, Cairo, 1979, 11-25, with 1 ill.

The author presents a hand-written text of the Martyrdom of St. Sergius of Benha, and a translation with notes.

79405 Nag Hammadi Codices V, *2-5* and VI with Papyrus Berolinensis 8502, *1* and *4*. Contributors James Brashler - Peter A. Dirkse - Charles W. Hedrick - George W. MacRae - William R. Murdock - Douglas M. Parrott - James M. Robinson - William R. Schoedel - R. McL. Wilson - Francis E. Williams - Frederik Wisse. Volume editor Douglas M. Parrott, Leiden, E.J. Brill, 1979 (15.5 x 24.5 cm; XXII + 553 p.) = Nag Hammadi Studies, 11; at head of title: The Coptic Gnostic Library. Edited with English Translation, Introduction and Notes Published under the Auspices of the Institute for Antiquity and Christianity; rev. *Biblical Archaeologist* 42 (1979), 251-252 (Birger A. Pearson); *BiOr* 37 (1980), 181-183 (Philippe Luisier); *ZDMG* 131 (1981), 202-203 (M[artin] K[rause]).
Pr. fl. 180

In the foreword J.M. Robinson points out that it is the aim of the Coptic Gnostic Library to present the Nag Hammadi texts in a uniform edition that will promptly follow the appearance of the Facsimile Edition of the Nag Hammadi Texts.
After a table of tractates in the Nag Hammadi codices and Pap. Berolinensis 8502, and a list of abbreviations and short titles follows the Introduction dealing with Codices V and VI in general. Codex V includes five tractates: Eugnostos; Apocalypse of Paul; First and Second Apocalypse of James; and the Apocalypse of Adam, while Codex VI contains eight tractates of which three Hermetic: Acts of Peter and Twelve Apostles; the Thunder; Perfect Mind; Authoritative Teaching; Concept of One Great Power; Plato, Republic 588b-589b; Discourse of the Eighth and Ninth; Prayer of Thanksgiving, and Asclepius 21-29. Then J.A. Robinson presents the codicological data of both codices.
Most room is devoted to the various tractates, with texts and translations on opposite pages, and provided with short bibliographies, discussions and notes at the bottom of the page.
On the tractates mentioned above follow two more: the Gospel according to Mary and the Act of Peter, both from Pap. Berolinensis 8502.
The volume ends with elaborate indexes and references.

79406 PERNIGOTTI, S., Il codice copto (= Edda Bresciani, Nuovi papiri magici in copto, greco e aramaico, I), *Studi classici e orientali*, Pisa 29 (1979), 15-53, with 3 pl.

After an introduction by Edda Bresciani about a group of papyri (Coptic, Greek and Aramaic) in a private collection the author publishes a Coptic codex from the 5th century A.D. Of twelve small pages of papyrus only six are inscribed, with three texts of a magical nature. The author presents them in photograph, facsimile and translation, with notes and commentary.
The second text is a very small Coptic fragment.
Index on p. 50-53.
J.J.J.

79407 QUECKE, Hans, Ein faijumisches Fragment aus Ps 90(91) P. Heid. Kopt. 184), in: *Festschrift Elmar Edel*, 332-337.

Publication of a papyrus sheet bearing a fragment of Ps. 90 (91) in the Faijumic dialect. Since only the recto is written on, it did not come from a codex but served as an amulet. The author presents the text and discusses its writing and language and the relation to the S. and B. versions.
J.J.J.

79408 ROBINSON, James M., The Discovery of the Nag Hammadi Codices, *Biblical Archaeologist*, Cambridge, MA 42 (1979), 206-224, with 16 ill. (1 in colour), 1 map and 1 fig.

The author presents the story of the discovery of the Nag Hammadi Codices.
See our numbers 79542, and 79556.

79409 SHORE, A.F., Extracts of Besa's *Life of Shenoute* in Sahidic, *JEA* 65 (1979), 134-143, with 2 pl.

Extracts are edited here of the Sahidic version containing passages hitherto unrecorded and contributing to what Leipoldt termed 'die Urform der Biographie'. They are found on a single vellum bifolio in the British Museum (BM 10820) and of unknown provenance. The leaf measures 13 in. high by 10 in. wide and has two columns of thirty four lines to the page. The text concerns among other things a letter that Apa Shenoute received from the emperor Theodosius. A copy of the text, translation and commentary are given.
E.P. Uphill

79410 WISSE, Frederik, Language Mysticism in the Nag Hammadi Texts and in early Coptic Monasticism I: Cryptography, *Enchoria* 9 (1979), 101-120.

The author studies twenty cryptographic Coptic inscriptions and gives an outline of Coptic cryptography in general.
W. Brunsch

g. Relations between Egyptian and Biblical literature

See also our numbers 79093; 79108; 79207; 79211; 79227; 79278; 79284; 79304; 79449; 79586; 79755; 79827; 79854 and 79918.

79411 BRYCE, Glendon E., A Legacy of Wisdom. The Egyptian Contribution to the Wisdom of Israel, Lewisburg, Bucknell University Press/ London, Associated University Presses, *[1979]*(13.6 x 21.5 cm; 336 p.); rev. *Liber Annuus. Studium Biblicum Franciscanum* 30 (1980), 424-428 (A. Niccacci); *Revue Biblique* 87 (1980), 139-145 (B. Couroyer); *ZDMG* 130 (1980), 634-635 (Leo Prijs). Pr. £10/$19.50

As for the Egyptian sources, this book on the legacy of wisdom of
Egypt to Israel concentrates on the wisdom of Amenemope. In the
first two chapters the author offers an extensive survey of the
theories on the Semitic or Egyptian direct dependence of Amenemope
and the refutations thereof, although there are no longer reasons
for the assumption of a Semitic original on account of the recent
Egyptian evidence. Instead of the former approach, the author
studies the case for the mutual dependence of both cultures and
posites as his central thesis that three stages marking the transmission and development of Egyptian materials can be isolated:
adaptation, assimilation and integration. These stages are successively discussed in the next three chapters. In chapter 3 he
demonstrates that the Israelite wisdom schools adopted Egyptian
ideas, proverbs and literary forms along the pattern of their own
culture.
He observes in chapter 4 that assimilation involves a creative
utilization of the source materials and combines Egyptian motifs
with other materials for the production of genuine, uniquely Israelite literary works. Since in the integrative stage mostly no direct relationship between source and product can be postulated,
the link can only be recognised through the phases of adaptation
and assimilation, thus the history of the tradition. Three types
of material can be distinguished, one of which can be related to
Egyptian traditions only by a thematic study, while the other two
betray the relationship by their relatedness to materials that
derived from the same source, directly or indirectly. Discussing
the setting of this borrowing in chapter 6 and 7, the author identifies it with the royal Israelite court, which on account of
similarity of setting and ideology, used themes and conceptions
from other cultures. Chapter 8 is devoted to the relationship between wisdom and the religion of Israel.
Notes on p. 211-249, bibliography on p. 255-285, a general
index on p. 287-323, and indexes to O.T. and other sources.

79412 CAZELLES, Henri, Les nouvelles études sur Sumer (Alster) et Mari
(Marzal) nous aident-elles à situer les origines de la sagesse israé
lite, in: La Sagesse de l'Ancien Testament par M. Gilbert, Gembloux, Éditions J. Duculot S.A./Leuven, University Press, [1979]
(= Bibliotheca Ephemeridum Theologicarum Lovaniensium, 51), 17-27.

Discussing some new studies on Sumer and Mari in the light of the
origin of the Israelite wisdom literature the author devotes some
remarks to the age of the Instruction of Hardjedef.

79413 GÖRG, Manfred, Ptolemäische Theologie in der Septuaginta, *Kairos*,
Salzburg 20 (1978), 208-217.

The author studies the Egyptian-Ptolemaic influence on the redaction of the LXX. In this connection he discusses i.a. the Greek
rendering of the name of Moses and the theological system of the
Hermopolitan Ogdoad.

79414 KITCHEN, Kenneth A., The Basic Literary Forms and Formulations of Ancient Instructional Writings in Egypt and Western Asia, *in*: *Studien zu altägyptischen Lebenslehren*, 235-282.

In this broad overall picture of instructions in the Ancient Near East the author starts by pointing out two spheres of the instructions, the practical aspect and the reflective. In the first section, on wisdom and "social" literature he sketches the shift from the older practical, prescriptive instructions to the M.K. reflective literature and argues that it is essential for the outline of the history of the entire genre, that the whole compositions, as well as their constituent parts and their literary techniques, should be studied, while in the second section he divides them in two types, both having a formal title, but one with and the other without prologue (see tables I-III). In the third section he discusses the constituent features: the content and structure of titles, their lengths in the various periods (IV); sub-titles, titular interjections and recurrent cross-headings (V); length and nature of prologues (VI); the various possibilities in the segmentation of the texts (VII); epilogues and conclusions (VIII). The fourth section is devoted to structural detail, dealing with the length of units (the two-line unit is by far the commonest and operates with parallellism and antithesis; table IX), and the atomistic units and those built into larger organic entities.
In the concluding survey the results are summarised. Table No. X offers a key to the literature on the sources and abbreviations, after a geographical division.

79415 von NORDHEIM, Eckhard, Der grosse Hymnus des Echnaton und Psalm 104. Gott und Mensch im Ägypten der Amarnazeit und in Israel, *SAK* 7 (1979), 227-241.

Discussing the suggested relations between the Akhenaton Hymn and Psalm 104 (see, e.g., Assmann, our number 72037), the author first presents a translation of both texts. He then deals with the evident non-Egyptian traditions in the psalm and its scheme, and points at the resemblances and distinctions of the texts. He concludes that the psalm has more Mesopotamian-Canaanite than Egyptian characteristics.

J.J.J.

79416 RUFFLE, John, The Teaching of Amenemope and its Connection with the Book of Proverbs (The Tyndale Biblical Archaeology Lecture, 1975), *Tyndale Bulletin* 28 (1977), [1979], 29-68.

After a survey of the scholarly opinion on the connections between the Teaching of Amenemope and the O.T. Proverbs 21.17 - 24.22 the author discusses the date and authorship of the two works and the general points of connection between Biblical and Ancient Egyptian wisdom texts on account of a large number of passages. He then carefully compares the pertinent passages in Proverbs and Amenemope. In the conclusion he expresses his doubts on a direct connection between Proverbs and Amenemope since the resemblance is only superficial. It seems more reasonable to him that king Solomon had questioned about wisdom a cultured Egyptian at his court, who had knowledge of the Egyptian wisdom through his scribal training.

79417 RUPRECHT, Eberhard, Der traditionsgeschichtliche Hintergrund der einzelnen Elemente von Genesis XII:213, *Vetus Testamentum*, Leiden 29 (1979), 444-464.

The promises of a great nation and a great name made in Genesis 12, 2-3 are compared with phrases from Egyptian texts.

79418 WALTKE, Bruce K., The Book of Proverbs and Ancient Wisdom Literature, *Bibliotheca Sacra*, Dallas 136, No. 543 (July-September 1979) 221-228.

In this discussion of the relations between the O.T. Book of Proverbs and Ancient Near Eastern Wisdom literature several aspects are reviewed: literary forms, structure of literature and arrangement, transmission of the text, the history of the Wisdom tradition, the setting, the meaning and the theology of the Book of Proverbs. Special attention is devoted to the relations between Proverbs and the Wisdom of Amenemope.

79419 WHITLEY, Charles F., Koheleth, His Language and Thought, Berlin-New York, Walter de Gruyter, 1979 (15 x 23.5 cm; VIII + 199 p.)= Beihefte zur Zeitschrift für die alttestamentliche Wissenschaft, 148; rev. *ZAW* 91 (1979), 474-475 (*[Georg Fohrer]*).

Chapter D, section 2 (p. 152-157) is devoted to the supposed Egyptian influence in the O.T. Book of Koheleth (Ecclesiastes). The author concludes that the author borrowed from other cultures as well.

79420 WRIGHT, G.R. H, The Passage of the Sea, *GM* Heft 33 (1979), 55-68.

Der Zug der Juden durch das Meer wird eingehend erörtert hinsichtlich der Frage, wo dieses "Schilfmeer", in den englischen Übersetzungen oft als "Rotes Meer" geschrieben, eigentlich lag. Der Name "Rotes Meer" kommt allerdings bereits in der Vulgata vor, während die hebräische Bibel eindeutig von einem "Schilfmeer" spricht. Verfasser identifiziert dieses mit dem ägyptischen "Schilffeld" (*sekhet iaru*), das der Tote auf seinem Weg ins Jenseits durchqueren musste. Eben diesen Übergang von einer Existenz in eine andere wird auch für den Durchzug der Juden angenommen, die so für ein neues Leben gereinigt wurden. Die Lokation des Schilfmeeres kann daher überall gesucht werden, da es in den Herzen der Menschen ist.

Inge Hofmann

79421 YAMAUCHI, Edwin M., Documents from Old Testament Times: A Survey of Recent Discoveries, *The Westminster Theological Journal*, Philadelphia 41 (1978/79), 1-32.

The author lists documentary evidence in Ancient Egyptian, from Egypt itself and elsewhere, which is of importance for the biblical historian.

h. General and varia

See also our numbers 79096; 79151; 79264; 79372; 79470; 79479; 79481; 79528; 79597; 79606; 79775 and 79912.

79422 BRACK, A. und A., Hieratische Ostraka vom Grab des Tjanuni, Theben Nr. 74, Funde von der Schweizerischen Grabung 1975, *in*: *Acts 1st ICE*, 121-124.

For the four ostraca here described, with translation and commentary, see now our number 77106, 73-78 and pl. 54-56.

J.J.J.

79423 CHACE, Arnold Buffum, The Rhind Mathematical Papyrus. Free Translation and Commentary with Selected Photographs, Transcriptions, Transliterations and Literal Translations, Reston, The National Council of Teachers of Mathematics, *[1979]* (28.9 x 22.5 cm; XII + 140 p., 8 pl., 1 fig.)= Classics in Mathematics Education *[A Series]*, 8.

On p. 65-66 there is added a list of selected bibliographical references to literature after 1929, the year of publication of the original edition.

79424 MASSON, Olivier, Remarques sur les graffites cariens d'Abou-Simbel, *in*: *Hommages Sauneron* II, 35-49, with 8 fig. and 3 pl.

Study of eight Carian graffiti on the feet of the colossi at Abu Simbel, with publication of their photographs made in 1956. In an index remarks on the pretended Carian signs in a Greek text from the same place. An index of Carian words on p. 49.

J.J.J.

IV. HISTORY

a. Up to the New Kingdom

See also our numbers 79067; 79122; 79254; 79470; 79681; 79697; 79751; 79867; 79869 and 79920.

79425 BARTA, Winfried, Bemerkungen zu den Summenangaben der Turiner Königspapyrus für die Frühzeit und das Alte Reich, *MDAIK* 35 (1979), 11-14.

Proceeding from his conclusion that the totals for the XIIth Dynasty given by the Turin Canon are correct, the author argues that also the total of 955 years for the O.K. is reliable, provided that it reckons from the beginning of a dynasty 0 (3092 B.C.).

J.J.J.

79426 BARTA, Winfried, Chronologie der 12. Dynastie nach den Angaben des Turiner Königspapyrus, *SAK* 7 (1979), 1-9.

Since the total of years the Turin Royal Canon ascribes to the XIIth Dynasty does not appear to agree with what we know from the sources about the various reigns (cfr our number 76064) the author first suggests the possibility of a coregency between Amenemhat III and IV of over 5 years. Then the total is only 1 year too high, which may be a scribal error.
It is also possible that Parker's second hypothesis that the seventh year of Sesostris III was Jul. 1872, not 1875, is correct. Barta calculates the dates anew and shows that then the Canon was correct.

J.J.J.

79427 BERLANDINI, Jocelyne, La pyramide "ruinée" de Sakkara-Nord et le roi Ikaouhor-Menkaouhor, *RdE* 31 (1979), 3-28, with 2 ill. and 4 pl.

Un article de vingt-cinq pages, dans lesquelles après avoir fait l'historique d'un mo.ument qui n'existe plus, l'auteur tente de l'attribuer à un roi dont on ne sait sauf qu'on lui attribue quelques monuments anépigraphes, pour la plupart de provenance rarement assurée. Voir aussi notre no. 78078.

Ph. Derchain

79428 DELIA, Robert D., A New Look at Some Old Dates: A Reexamination of Twelfth Dynasty Double Dated Inscriptions, *BES* 1 (1979), 15-28, with 2 fig.

The author reconsiders three XIIth Dynasty double dated private inscriptions which name two kings: the stelae Cairo 20516 and

Leiden V4 and the rock inscription of Hepu at Aswân (Porter-Moss, V, 247). On account of a comparison with mainly XIIth Dynasty undated private monuments which name two kings and arguing that the above inscriptions bear each a different character he interprets them as referring to two separate dates in a period of time spent under kings. This brings the M.K. monuments so far considered to refer to coregencies into tune with those of the O. and N.K., which do not provide "double dated" texts naming two kings either.

79429 HELCK, Wolfgang, Die Datierung der Gefässaufschriften aus der Djoserpyramide, *ZÄS* 106 (1979), 120-132, with 1 table.

Betrachtung der Inschriften unserer Nummern 59360, 61421 und 65299. Helcks Tabelle 1 ist eine Zusammenstellung über Zahl, Art und Herkunft der Einritzungen, die Königsnamem enthalten. Daraus zieht er Schlüsse, unter andern zur Anordnung der Könige.
Es folgt die Besprechung der Aufschriften mit nichtköniglichen Namen und Ämtern. In einer Übersicht (S. 125) stellt Verfasser die Personen auf, die sowohl in Abydos wie in Saqqara belegt sind. Es zeigt sich, dass es bereits unter *Nj-nṯr* ein Vezirat und den Beginn der Gauverwaltung gab.
Anhangweise bespricht Helck die Abfolge der Könige am Ende der 2. Dynastie.

M. Heerma v. Voss

79430 KANAWATI, N., The Provincial Movement in the Sixth Dynasty of Egypt, *in*: *Acts 1st ICE*, 353-358, with 2 fig.

The author compares the sizes of eight tombs of Expedition Leaders from Aswân (VIth Dynasty), after arranging them in a chronological order, and concludes that they demonstrate the same trend as the tombs of the viziers in the capital.
For a more extensive argument, see now Kanawati's publication, our number 77393.

J.J.J.

79431 KAPLAN, Haya Ritter, The Problem of the Dynastic Position of Meryet-Nit, *JNES* 38 (1979), 23-27, with 3 fig. and 1 table.

Contrary to the general view expressed by scholars the writer suggests that this First Dynasty queen should be placed *before* king Zer rather than after. The lack of "Abydos ware" pottery in her tomb and other archaeological evidence is cited and the relevant EB levels in Palestine discussed in this context.

E.P. Uphill

79432 KUCHAM, Lisa, Titles of Queenship. Part II: The Eleventh Dynasty and the Beginning of the Middle Kingdom: The Wives of Nebhepetre Mentuhotep, *JSSEA* 9 (1978-1979), 21-25.

Sequel to our number 77447.
Listing and studying the titles of the eight wives of Nebhepetre

Montuhotep the author concludes that *Tm* stressed her position of mother of the king's successor, while *Nfrw* carries O.K. titles and the other six woman seem to have filled a strictly cultic position.

J.J.J.

79433 LILYQUIST, Christine, A Note on the Date of Senebtisi and other Middle Kingdom Groups, *Sarapis* 5, No. 1 (1979), 27-28.

Commenting upon Williams' article on the chronology of major groups and deposits from the M.K. (our number 76842), the author mentions three points in which she thinks that he was too categorical.

J.J.J.

79434 TROY, Lana, Ahhotep - A Source Evaluation, *GM* Heft 35 (1979), 81-91, with 2 fig.

Zwei Königinnen mit dem Namen Ahhotep lebten während der 17. und frühen 18. Dynastie, deren Existenz durch zwei Särge sowie durch andere Objekte gesichert ist, wobei Ahhotep I. als Gemahlin von Tao II. und Ahhotep II. als Gemahlin Amenophis I. galt. Eine erneute Untersuchung des Quellenmaterials - es ist in einem Appendix aufgelistet - ergab, dass die beiden Frauen die Gemahlinnen der Könige der 17. Dynastie Kamose und Tao II. waren; letztere erlangte als Mutter des ersten Königs der 18. Dynastie Ahmose Berühmtheit.

Inge Hofmann

b. From the New Kingdom

See also our numbers 79067; 79105; 79142; 79244; 79354; 79434; 79459; 79538; 79626; 79633; 79636; 79645; 79686; 79791; 79805; 79867; 79904; 79905; 79917 and 791007.

79435 ALDRED, Cyril, More Light on the Ramesside Tomb Robberies, *in*: *Glimpses of Ancient Egypt*, 92-99, with 2 ill.

The author attempts to reconstruct the events in Thebes at the end of the XXth Dynasty. It is likely that between years 16 of Ramses IX and 1 of the *Wḥm-mswt* era no important tomb robbery has been recorded, although those of the tombs of Sethi 1 and Ramses II probably took place during these years, full of upheavals (e.g. the expulsion of the high priest Amenhotep). The *Wḥm-mswt* era, however, was a period during which order was restituted. The expulsion of Paiankh after officiating at Thebes for some years was done by Ramses XI himself, and this happened with some bitter fighting. It is during these events that the royal tombs were robbed in daytime by large bodies of ruffians who i.a. shifted and broke the coffins of Ramses VI.

J.J.J.

79436 BARTA, Winfried, Die ägyptischen Monddaten und der 25-Jahr-Zyklus der Papyrus Carlsberg 9, *ZÄS* 106 (1979), 1-10.

Verfasser verwendet das Schema des demotischen *Pap. Carlsberg 9* zur Berechnung und zyklischen Festlegung aller überlieferten Monddaten. Er leitet die Zyklusanfänge während der Ramessidenzeit ab und ermittelt die julianischen Jahre für zwei Neumonde, im 3. Jahr Ramses' X., bzw. im 25. Ramses' XI.

M. Heerma v. Voss

79437 von BECKERATH, J., Zur dritten Zwischenzeit Ägyptens, *OLZ* 74 (1979), 5-10.

Review article of our number 73405.

79438 BONHÊME, Marie-Ange, Hérihor fut-il effectivement roi?, *BIFAO* (1979), 267-283.

The author expresses her doubts whether indeed Herihor has been a king, arguing that no genealogical inscriptions mention his parents as usually also for usurpers; that he is absent in the tradition of Manetho; that not a single inscription is dated after his reign; that his prenomen *ḥm-nṯr tpy n 'Imn*, although written in a cartouche is not a real one. Although he had adopted a royal titulary composed after the normal model its contents are not according to the tradition. Certainly Herihor appropriated part of the royal functions, but like the later God's Wives he combined them with a priestly function.
For Herihor, see also Wente's introduction to our number 79636.

J.J.J.

79439 GRAEFE, Erhart, Zu *Pjj*, der angeblichen Nebenfrau des Achanjati, *GM* Heft 33 (1979), 17-18.

Die neuerdings in der Literatur erwähnte *Pjj* als Nebenfrau des Achanjati ist eine Legende. Titel und Name lauten: "Geliebte Gelobte des Wa-en-Re, Hofdame, *Pjj*". Es handelt sich somit um eine konventionelle "Hoftitulatur", für die ein weiterer Beleg gegeben wird.

Inge Hofmann

79440 HARI, Robert, Mout-Nefertari, épouse de Ramses II: une descendante de l'hérétique Ai ?, *Aegyptus* 59 (1979), 3-7, with 1 pl.

On account of a button of a case found by Schiaparelli in the tomb of Nefertari (Relazione 1, fig. 89, 6) and at present in the Egyptian Museum in Turin, which bears the prenomen of Ay the author poses the question whether Nefertari is the granddaughter of Nefertiti and was married to Ramses II in the first period of his reign for reasons of legitimation.

79441 HORNUNG, Erik, Chronologie in Bewegung, *in: Festschrift Elmar Edel*, 247-252.

Proceeding from Edel's suggestion (see our number 76218) that Khattushilish III reigned until year 42 + x of Ramses II, the author evaluates recent theories about a shorter chronology of the N.K. He accepts a beginning of Ramses' II reign in 1279 and of the reign of Tuthmosis III in 1479 (against Wente-van Siclen, our number 76830). Possibly this will appear to have consequences for the chronology of the N.K. that has to be reconsidered.

J.J.J.

79442 KITCHEN, K.A., Aspects of Ramesside Egypt, in: Acts 1st ICE, 383-389.

The author argues that close observation of known sources and fuller availability of texts may lead to extension of our knowledge. Illustrating the first point, he demonstrates that the titles of the first three rulers of the XIXth Dynasty were modelled on those of the kings of the early XVIIIth Dynasty, and, also, that from the Thebaid into Nubia the name of Ramses II was spelt until year 20 with -ss, after that with -s-sw, which may be a dating criterion. The second point is illustrated by new evidence from the tomb-chapel of Paser (Theban Tomb No. 106) which proves that the pontificate of his father Nebneteru dates from the time of Sethi I. The well-known limestone flake mentioning his name and dating from year 17 of Ramses II actually is a fragmentary "tourist graffito" recording a visit of Paser in that year.

J.J.J.

79443 KRAUSS, R., Meritaten as Ruling Queen of Egypt and Successor of Her Father Nipkhururia-Akhenaten, in: Acts 1st ICE, 403-406.

The thesis here defended is subject of a monograph, our number 78453.

79444 LEAHY, Anthony, Nespamedu, "King of Thinis", GM Heft 35 (1979), 31-39.

Der Rassam-Zylinder Ashurbanipals nennt unter anderen "Königen" den Iš-pi-ma-a-tu von Ta-a-a-ni. Der "König" kann identifiziert werden als Ns-p3-mdw; in der Ortschaft muss man Thinis sehen. Der "König" ist der bekannte Vezir Nespamedu, dessen Vorfahren thinitischen Ursprungs sind und von dort nach Theben zogen. Nespamedu, der möglicherweise schon 671 v. Chr. Vezir war, ist in Abydos Grab D. 57 bestattet. Bereits sein Vater hatte das Amt von Montemhet übernommen, Nespamedu kann es an seinen Sohn weitergeben, aber das "Königreich" von Thinis dürfte mit Nespamedu begonnen und geendet haben.

Inge Hofmann

79445 MURNANE, William J., The Bark of Amun on the Third Pylon at Karnak, JARCE 16 (1979), 11-27, with 5 pl. (containing 8 photographs and 2 drawings) and 1 table.

The large relief of the bark of Amun on the east face of the third pylon in Karnak (PM II^2, 61 = (183)) shows two, largely expunged, small, king-like figures behind the two of the protagonist and builder of the pylon, Amenophis III. Stylistically datable to the Amarna period, these two additions have been quoted as evidence for a coregency between Amenophis III and IV. Closer scrutiny of the cutting reveals, that (1) they were shaved back by Horemheb, (2) they were superimpositions themselves by a predecessor, most likely Tutankamun, to judge by scanty hieroglyphic evidence, who (3) cut his barge-frontal figure over an existing offering table, while for the other free space was available so that (4) Horemheb's recutting the table went to greater depth than in the other case, where Tutankhamun's figure was replaced by a large ankh-sign. Furthermore, the style of certain attendant figures foreshadows Amarna conventions, but it can be found elsewhere in the reign of Amenophis III, such as in the Theban tomb of Nefersekheru (no. 107); it does not necessarily imply an early Atenist tendency. An appendix (pp. 18-21) lists instances of the iconography of the Userhet barge from the XIth dynasty until the early Ptolemaic period and in an addendum (21-22) comments are offered on our no. 76251.

J.F. Borghouts

79446 NIWIŃSKI, Andrzej, Problems in the Chronology and Genealogy of the XXIst Dynasty: New Proposals for their Interpretation, *JARCE* 16 (1979), 49-68, with 4 tables.

Typological similarities between coffins from the two Deir el Bahari *caches* of the XXIst Dynasty may lead to genealogical, hence also chronological, regroupings of their owners. A. Pinudjem I, Henuttaui (daughter of Tantamun) and Nodjmet: Tantamun may have been Ramses XI's consort (not of his Tanite plenipotentiary, Smendes) and Henuttaui their daughter. The latter links the XXth and XXIth dynasties, as she was married to the high priest and 'king' Pinudjem I. Pinudjem had a later wife Isitemkheb, and daughters from these two marriages occur in a Luxor graffito (PM II², 307 = (27) III.2), here (p. 51-52) reanalyzed. Nodjmet, sister of Pinudjem and wife to Hrihor, died in a year 1 of Pinudjem, which is best attributed to Psusennes I. Being a $mw.t-nsw.t$ herself, her son may have been Nefercheres (Neferkarē). B. Remarks on coffins of high women in Thebes (Tayuheret, Nauny, Faiaenmut, Djedmutesᶜankh) and several descendants of the h.p. Menkheperrēᶜ (Meritamun, Gautseshni and Hori, children; Harweben and Menkheperrēᶜ, grandchildren; a great granddaughter Gautseshni). Coffins CG 61030 and 61031 must belong to different Isitemkhebs. To account for Menkheperrēᶜ's many children, a second wife (unknown, so far) is proposed for him. C. Relationships of the owners of gilded coffins (2nd *cache*) to the family of the high priests: Nesamun (coffin no. 148), the chantresses Taudjatrēᶜ (144), Menakhonsupakhered (JdE 29622) and Maatkarēᶜ (132). D. The vexed 49 year reign, mentioned on a Theban mummy bandage: Psusennes or Amenemope? The final interpretation given is '(year 2 of) king Amenemope, year 49 (of the h.p. Menkheperrēᶜ)'. Historical conclusions are, that the two sons of the h.p. Pinudjem I were almost simultaneously raised to their high offices, viz. Menkheperrēᶜ

as h.p. in Thebes and Psusennes I as king in Tanis, with Nefercheres remaining as co-king in Thebes for a few years.
Later, a son Smendes of Menkheperrēʿ first served as h.p. in
Tanis and afterwards succeeded his father in Thebes. Some modifications in an addendum, following remarks by K.Kitchen and J.
von Beckerath.

J.F. Borghouts

79447 OSING, Jürgen, Zur Geschichte der späten 19. Dynastie, *SAK* 7
(1979), 253-271.

Critical review of the article of Krauss about the reign of king
Amenmesse in *SAK* 4 and 5 (our numbers 76467 and 77438). The major
conclusion of Osing is that the problem whether Amenmesse preceded
Sethi II or whether his reign falls within that of the latter is
still undecided, the evidence being insufficient. Osing i.a. argues that Krauss' dating of some of the relevant ostraca cannot
be correct; neither his reconstruction of the building history
of Sethi's tomb. The mentions of an "enemy" do not necessarily
point at Amenmesse, and the evidence that this king was identical
with the viceroy of Kush Messui is not conclusive.

J.J.J.

79448 PEREPELKIN, Yu. Y., Кэйе и Семнех-ке-рэ. К исходу солнче-
поклоннического переворота в Египте, Moscow, Издательство
"Наука", 1979 (22.2 x 15 cm; 310 p.).   Pr. 2 P. 20 коп.

'Kiya and Smenchkarēʿ On the end of the solar cult revolution
in Egypt'
A study based on egyptological literature (listed on p. 296- 309)
in eleven chapters, of the following contents: 1. the role of
queen Nefertiti (p. 6-30); 2. the ownership of the $mȝrw\ itn$ and the
northern palace at Amarna (31-50); 3. the provenance of the Hermopolis reliefs (51-70); 4. the ownership of the gold coffin from
the so-called tomb of Teye (Th. T. 55), with a full translation
of its texts; 5. the enigma of Smenchkarēʿ (94-110); 6. on the
rival queen Kiya (111-134); 7. on the identity of a daughter of
Kiya and Amenophis IV (135-154); 8. co-regency and titles of
Smenchkarēʿ (155-183); 9. further documentary information on Smenchkarēʿ (184-213); 10. the solar cult of Smenchkarēʿ (214-236); 11.
the body of the so-called Akhenaten coffin (237-257); and, finally,
an appendix with the names of the Aten (258-295).

J.F. Borghouts

79449 RATIÉ, Suzanne, La Reine Hatchepsout. Sources et problèmes, Lugdu-
num Batavorum, E.J. Brill, 1979 (20 x 27 cm; 372 p., 16 pl.) =
Orientalia Monspeliensa 1. Institut d'Égyptologie - Université
Paul Valéry.   Pr. fl. 178

The present study constitutes the scholarly complement to a mono-

graph intended for the general public which the author has published in 1972 (see our number 72582).
In the foreword the author discusses the damnatio memoriae of the queen in the later Egyptian history and her rediscovery in modern times. She also deals with the queens in Egypt in general and the reigning queens in particular, stating that among the latter the reigns of queens Tausert and Cleopatra VII show some analogy to that of Hatshepsut.
The twenty-five chapters of the book are devoted in detail to all possible aspects of Hatshepsut's reign: family relations in the early XVIIIth Dynasty; chronology and date of the queen's reign (including a section on Hatshepsut and the Bible); the historical facts of the period (four chapters, devoted i.a. to Hatshepsut's youth, the alleged coregency with Tuthmosis I, the marriage with Tuthmosis II, the years preceding her reign; the relationship with Tuthmosis III; the building activities of the first years); mythical elements of the reign (e.g. the texts and representations of the Divine Birth); the queen in representations and in priestly functions); the Punt expedition; the temple of Deir el-Bahri; building activities in the country (i.a. the Speos Artemidos) and in Thebes; the expedition to Sinai of year 13; years 15 (*sed*-festival and obelisks) and year 16 (i.a., the second tomb of Senenmut and Nefrure, Tuthmosis' wife); foreign policy; public life and festivals; private life (hardly anything known); courtiers (Senenmut and his brothers, Ineni, Hapuseneb, and several others); the last years and the queen's death; the persecution of her memory. The last two chapters present an attempt to interpret the facts (i.a. indicating resemblance between the religion in this period and the Aton cult) and an evaluation of the reign.
Additions and corrections on p. 341-352 (i.a. references to the recent publication of the "Chapelle Rouge"; see our number 77453 and, for the plate volume, our number 79628). Index of names on p. 353-363.

J.J.J.

79450 REDFORD, Donald B., Once Again the Filiation of Tutankhamun, *JSSEA* 9 (1978-1979), 107-115.

The author denies that there is any proof of Tutankhamun being the physical son of Amenophis III, whereas the name $Twt-ʿnḫw-itn$ clearly reflects the beliefs of the Amarna Period. Although he is once called (in Hermopolis) "the king's bodily son" he may be a relative of Akhenaton once or twice removed, but other explanations are also possible.

J.J.J.

79451 ROSENVASSER, A., La Estela del Año 400, *Revista del Instituto de Historia Antigua Oriental*, Buenos Aires 4 (1978), 63-85, with 1 fig.

The author translates anew 'Stela of Year 400' and deals with current views concerning the contents and their implications. He concludes that the theories recently advanced by Schott, Stadelmann and Goedicke lack any sound basis and just only complicate the understanding of an already complex matter. He follows the original theory of Sethe. He discusses the location of Avaris, the antiquity of the cult of Seth in the Eastern Delta, and the chronological problems posed by the enigmatic reference to a 'year 400'.

J.R. Ogdon

79452 SAMSON, Julia, Akhenaten's Successor, *GM* Heft 32 (1979), 53-58.

Ausgehend von der Namensgebung wird darauf verwiesen, dass es weder sicher sei dass ein junger Mann namens Smenkhkare existierte noch dass er Meritaten heiratete und Nachfolger Echnatons wurde. Meritaten ist mit dem König *Ankhkheprure-mry-Neferkheprure-Nefernefruaten-mry-w3-en-re* verbunden.

Inge Hofmann

79453 SEIPEL, W., Zur Chronologie der Verfehmung Hatschepsuts durch Thutmosis III., *in*: *Acts 1st ICE*, 581-582.

The author contests the dating of the inscription of Tuthmosis III on the South Wall of the Hatshepsut building in the Karnak Temple in his 42nd year, and consequently the beginning of her dishonouring. The complete article will appear in a forthcoming issue of *MDAIK*.

79454 SPALINGER, A.J., The Civil War Between Amasis and Apries and the Babylonian Attack Against Egypt, *in*: *Acts 1st ICE*, 593-604.

Proceeding from the year 570 B.C. as the one in which Amasis became king after his victory in the civil war against Apries, the author restudies the invasion of Egypt by Nabuchadnezzar, which the late traditions placed under the reign of Apries. He presumes that the Babylonian attack took place in the first months of Amasis' reign, when Apries had not yet died.
Chart 1 presents the list of the dated inscriptions of Apries and Amasis, chart 2 the data concerning *Putu*=Libya and chart 3 his chronological arrangement.
Extensive notes.

79455 SPALINGER, Anthony, The Military Background of the Campaign of Piye (Piankhy), *SAK* 7 (1979), 273-301, with 5 maps.

Thorough analysis of Piye's famous campaign and the counter-moves of his enemies, in which the author discusses the events in their chronological order, paying ample attention to their geographical, political, and religious aspects. In the summation (p. 292-296) remarks about the "medieval" aspects of the Egyptian civilization in this period, e.g. the regard for horses and the lack of nationalism

J.J.J.

79456 SPALINGER, Anthony, Traces of the Early Career of Ramesses II, *JNES* 38 (1979), 271-286, with 2 fig.

Deals with the period when the young Ramesses was associated in the kingship of his father Seti I, often wrongly called a coregency, and mainly uses the evidence from the temple of Beit el Wali. It is noted that the carving of the scenes in this temple must be subsequent to the events shown, and that those of the entrance hall were begun in raised relief but completed later in incised. Even the latter have the earlier simpler form of the cartouche. Three wars are depicted, Asiatic, Nubian and Libyan, that showing the Shosu being probably the same as Seti's campaign shown in the Karnak scenes. It is further suggested that all the Beit el Wali Asiatic war scenes refer to the campaign of Year I of Seti, although conclusive data is not yet available. Ramesses also appears to have participated with his father in a Libyan campaign and subsequently had his figure carved over that of Mehy in the Karnak scenes. The article concludes with the fact that Ramesses was born before the accession of Seti and by the latter's year eight was old enough to father four children, the regency beginning after this in the ninth regnal year.

E.P. Uphill

79457 SPALINGER, Anthony J., Traces of the Early Career of Seti I, *JSSEA* 9 (1978-1979), 227-240.

The author deals with the early career as (co-) regent of Sethi I, proceeding from the words of the Abydos Dedicatory Stela of this Pharaoh. The most important event of his preroyal days was his campaign to the *Fnḫw* lands, which was also referred to on his father's and his own Buhen stelae.
In this connection the author extensively discusses the uncertain date of accession of Seti I, quoting several of his stelae. He suggests that it may be close to IV *šmw* 23.

J.J.J.

79458 TRAUNECKER, Claude, Essai sur l'histoire de la XXIXe dynastie, *BIFAO* 79 (1979), 395-436.

On account of the available evidence the author, who is preparing the publication of the bark-shrine of Psammuthis and Achoris in front of the Karnak temple, presents a minute study of the XXIXth Dynasty (399-380 B.C.).
In the first section he deals with the preceding Persian occupation and the wars of liberation against this people. Then, in two sections, he discusses the evidence for the period related by Greek authors, and that in the Demotic Chronicle and with Manetho. The latter incorrectly places Psammuthis after Achoris. In the fourth section the dated monuments and documents from the dynasty are listed. They date from three rulers only, Nepheritis I, Psammuthis and Achoris, the other two, Muthis and Nepheritis II, being ephemeral.

Based on the assembled material, the author then discusses the history and chronology of the dynasty.
For the publication of the bark shrine, see now C. Traunecker, F. Le Saout and O. Masson, La chapelle d'Achôris à Karnak, 2 vols, Paris, 1981.

J.J.J.

c. International affairs

See also our numbers 79009; 79421; 79444; 79449; 79454; 79455; 79456; 79457; 79458; 79574; 79616; 79648; 79722; 79755; 79756; 79776; 79912; 79923; 79958 and 791017.

79459 The Cambridge History of Africa, Volume 2. From c. 500 B.C. to A.D. 1050. Edited by J.D. Fage, Cambridge-London-New York-Melbourne, Cambridge University Press, 1978 (14.5 x 23.5 cm; XVII + 840 p., 67 fig and maps, 38 pl.).

We mention the chapters and sections which are of interest for Egyptology and Meroitics.
Chapter 2 (p. 87-147), North Africa in the period of Phoenician and Greek colonization, c. 800 to 323 B.C., by R.C.C. Law: The Saite Dynasty in Egypt; Persian rule in Egypt; the last native dynasties and the establishment of Greek rule in Egypt.
Chapter 3 (p. 148-209), North Africa in the Hellenistic and Roman Periods, 323 B.C. to A.D. 305, by R.C.C.Law: Egypt under the Ptolemaic Dynasty; Cyrenaica under Ptolemaic rule; Egypt and Cyrenaica under Roman rule.
Chapter 4 (p. 210-271), The Nilotic Sudan and Ethiopia, c. 660 B.C. to c. A.D. 600, by P.L. Shinnie: the origins of Meroitic civilization Meroe from c. 300 B.C. to the Roman invasion; Meroe and the Roman empire; the later culture at Meroe; the rise of Aksum; the end of Meroe.
Chapter 9 (p. 556-588), Christian Nubia, by P.L. Shinnie.

79460 CAZELLES, Henri, L'Égypte et la Bible, *in*: *Le rêve égyptien*, 13-18, with 1 ill.

The author offers a concise survey of the history of the relations between Egypt and the Biblical world. At the end some attention for cultural influences.

79461 COHEN, Rudolph, The Iron Age Fortresses in the Central Negev, *BASOR* No. 236 (Fall 1979), 61-79, with 1 map, 1 fig., 8 ill. and 4 plans.

The author assumes that the fortress network along the principal routes in the Negev, dating from the 10th century B.C., was deliberately destroyed during pharaoh Shishak's campaign into Palestine.

79462 DOTHAN, Moshe, Ashdod at the End of the Late Bronze Age and the Beginning of the Iron Age, *in*: *Symposia Celebrating the Seventy-Fifth Anniversary of the Founding of the American Schools of Oriental Re-*

search (1900-1975). Edited by Frank Moore Cross, Cambridge, Mass., American Schools of Oriental Research, 1979 (= Zion Research Foundation Occasional Publications, 1-2), 125-134, with 1 plan and 3 ill.

Rich Egyptian finds attest to continued Egyptian supremacy in Ashdod as late as the second half of the 13th century B.C.

79463 FAGE, J.D., A History of Africa, London, Hutchinson, 1979 (15 x 24 cm; X + 534 p., 8 pl., 12 maps); series: The History of Human Society.

In chapter 2, Africa and the Ancient Civilizations of the Near East and the Mediterranean (p. 34-56) the author deals with: cultural contacts between Egypt and the African hinterland in general, the Kushite rule and Egypt, the Meroitic civilization, the Roman rule in Africa, and the Axumite kingdom.

79464 FRANDSEN, Paul, Egyptian Imperialism, *in*: *Power and Propaganda*. A Symposium on Ancient Empires. Edited by Mogens Trolle Larsen (= Mesopotamia 7), Copenhagen ?, Akademisk Forlag, [1979], 167-190.

The author presents in this paper a revaluation of the Egyptian policy towards Nubia and Syro-Palestine, mainly during the N.K., arguing that the methods adopted in these two areas are quite different. Nubia was no more exploited than any region in Egypt itself, though the control assumed a more overt and ideologically more intensive form. The area was clearly the objective of a conscious Egyptianization policy. In Asia, however, maintenance of ordered relations between the separate societies was the primary objective, the outcome being a relationship based on a system of international law. The Egyptians retained the existing political organization, adding only what was necessary for the preservation of their suzerainty. Retenu seems not to have been structurally integrated into the Egyptian economy, as Nubia was, and there are no traces of cultural imperialism.
How the two types of imperial rule came about is uncertain. Several reasons why Egypt responded to the phenomena from outside as it did can be given, but the internal reasons to choose this twofold system are unknown.

J.J.J.

79465 GEORGIOU, Hara, Relations between Cyprus and the Near East in the Middle and Late Bronze Age, *Levant*, London 11 (1979), 84-100, with 1 table.

The author devotes a section to Alašiya in the Egyptian texts, mainly dealing with the evidence from the Amarna Letters apart from brief mentions in the reigns of Tuthmosis III, Sethos I and the Ramessides. In the conclusion the author remarks that Cyprus seems to have retained some measure of independence from the great powers of Egypt and the Hittites during its period of active trade.

79466 GÖRG, Manfred, Ausweisung oder Befreiung? Neue Perspektiven zum sogenannten Exodus, *Kairos*, Salzburg 20 (1978), 272-280.

The author reconsiders the O.T. Exodus story. The ambiguous attitude of Pharaoh in the story may be an echo of Pharaoh Siamun's behaviour towards Israel in the time of Solomon. He also considers the possibility of a banishment of this Hebrew ethnic group of which many members occupied high positions in the Egyptian army in the time of Sethnakht, on account of possible evidence from his Elephantine stela.
For the last subject, see now R. Drenkhahn, Die Elephantine-Stele de Sethnakht und ihr historischer Hintergrund, Wiesbaden, Otto Harrassowitz, 1980 (Pr. DM 42).

79467 GÖRG, M., Bevölkerungspolitische Strukturen in Südpalästina (mit Nor östl. Sinai) zum ausgehenden 13. Jh. (im Lichte ausserbiblischer Quellen) ("Kadesch in Geschichte und Überlieferung." Materialien zur Tagung der Arbeitsgemeinschaft der deutschsprachigen Kath. Alttestamentler vom 23.-27. Sept. 1979 in Bamberg), *Biblische Notizen*, Bamberg Heft 9 (1979), 51-53.

The author presents some texts relating to the possible presence of š3sw-Bedouins in Southern Palestine/Sinai and Northern Palestine/ Syria before the XIXth Dynasty and their attested presence in the first mentioned area in the Ramesside Period.

79468 GÖRG, Manfred, Tuthmosis III ind die š3sw-Region, *JNES* 38 (1979), 190-202.

The presence of the š3sw Bedouin in Southern Palestine under Tuthmosis III is demonstrated in the contemporary texts according to previous authorities.
Evidence is quoted here, however, suggesting a location in northern Palestine, or even connections with the Orontes at this period.
E.P. Uphill

79469 GREEN, Alberto R., Israelite Influence at Shishak's Court ?, *BASOR* No. 233 (Winter 1979), 59-62.

Proceeding from Redford's thesis (see our number 72589) that the taxation system of Solomon corresponded closely to that employed by Sheshonq I on behalf of the temple of Arsaphes the author explains the correspondence by derivation by Sheshonq from Israel, for which he adduces several arguments.
J.J.J.

79470 HELLBING, Lennard, Alasia Problems, Göteborg, Paul Åströms Forlag, 1979 (22.5 x 30.3 cm; XII + 112 p., 2 maps, 21 ill. [8 in colour]) = Studies in Mediterranean Archaeology, 57.

This thesis (Göteborg, 1979) is devoted to problems concerning Alasia, a kingdom mentioned from the 18th to the 11th century B.C.

In chapter 1 the background is sketched, mainly the Amarna Tablets
and their dates, but also containing a section on Egypt under Akhenaton. Chapter 2 deals with the letters from Alasia to Egypt,
discussing their sequence and the problem to whose reign they belong. The author argues that the correspondence covers most of Akhenaton's reign and that the number of wives and children of the
Pharaoh mentioned, is an indication of the letters' order.
Chapter 3, on EA 35, deals with the god Nergal (Reshef), and the
ox and "good oil" referred to, suggesting that the ox was actually
a statue sent because of a plague in Alasia for which also the oil
was intended. The same letter also mentions an "eagle-conjurer"
from Egypt (chapter 4). Since bird sorcery was not familiar there
it may be that "eagle" was a symbol for "evil" and that the sor-
cerer was an oracle-priest required by Alasia in connection with the
plague.
In chapter 5 the evidence about Alasia from the Amarna Tablets is
put together, with a section on its trade with Egypt. The author
concludes that Alasia was not a single city but a country.
The same subject is discussed in chapter 6, but here on account
of other sources, among which those from Egypt (i.a. the Story
of Wenamon, Annals and other inscriptions of Tuthmosis III, etc.).
For a summary of all sources, see p. 57-59 with the table on p.60.
Chapter 7 and 8 present the conclusions to the location of Alasia
on account of the written sources and the archaeological evidence.
The author suggests that the name indicated the whole of Cyprus,
but a definite solution of the problem is as yet impossible.
Bibliography and indexes at the end.

J.J.J.

79471 JAROŠ, Karl, Geschichte und Vermächtnis des Königreiches Israel
von 926 bis 722 v. Chr., Bern - Frankfurt am Main - Las Vegas,
Peter Lang, [1979] (15 x 21 cm; 146 p., 25 maps, plans, ill. and fig.)
= Europäische Hochschulschriften, Reihe XXIII, 136.

Section 2.2 (p. 16-17) is concerned with the campaign of Sheshonq
I to Palestine.

79472 KATZENSTEIN, H. Jacob, Tyre in the Early Persian Period (539-486
B.C.E.), *Biblical Archaeologist*, Cambridge, MA 42 (1979), 23-34,
with 8 ill., 2 fig. and 3 maps.

The author states that the Tyrians had settled in Memphis some
time before Herodotus' visit.

79473 KUSCHKE, Arnulf, Das Terrain der Schlacht bei Qadeš und die Anmarsch-
wege Ramses' II. Summarium einer ebenso kritischen wie selbstkriti-
schen Bestandsaufnahme, vorwiegend im Hinblick auf die geographi-
schen Gegebenheiten, *Zeitschrift des Deutschen Palästina-Vereins*,
Wiesbaden 95 (1979), 7-35, with 3 maps.

The author attempts to shed more light on the level approaches,
the camp, the battle positions, the area and the course of the

Kadesh battle of Ramses II by confronting the data extracted by autopsis from the geography of the area with the report in the Egyptian texts. He extensively surveys and criticises the scholarly literature on the subject (i.a. by Alt), paying particular attention to the interpretation of the so-called "Letter of the General", which is instructive in this respect (see our numbers 71115 and 71588).

79474 LEHMANN, G.A., Die Šikalājū - ein neues Zeugnis zu den "Seevölker" - Heerfahrten im späten 13. Jh. v. Chr. (RS 34.129), *Ugarit-Forschungen* 11 (1979), 481-494.

Discussing the historical background of a royal Hittite letter (RS 34.129), which dates from the time of the destruction of the Hittite and Ugaritic power by the Sea-Peoples, the author occupies himself with Helck's theory of the Sea Peoples as troops of prisoners of war recruited from captured sea pirates (our number 76357) and the textual and representational Egyptian evidence for the various peoples together constituting the Sea Peoples.

79475 LIVERANI, Mario, Three Amarna Essays, Malibu, Undena Publications, 1979 (21.7 x 28.2 cm; 34 p.) = Monographs on the Ancient Near East vol. I, fasc. 5, p. 75-106; series: Series and Monographs on the Ancient Near East.

Two of the three articles are within the scope of the AEB. They were published before in Italian in our numbers 71372 and 72443 and are now translated in English by Matthew L. Jaffe, who also wrote the introduction. Selected bibliography of the author at the end.

79476 MALAMAT, Abraham, The First Peace Treaty Between Israel and Egypt, *Biblical Archaeological Review*, 5, No. 4 (September-October 1979), 58-61, with 1 ill. and 1 fig.

The author discusses the peace treaty between Solomon and, probably, Pharaoh Siamun, stressing i.a. that it was an exception that the Egyptian king gave his daughter in marriage to a foreign ruler.

J.J.J.

79477 MELLAART, James, Egyptian and Near Eastern Chronology: A Dilemma ?, *Antiquity* 53 (1979), 6-20, with 2 tables.

The usual historical chronologies of Ancient Egypt and Mesopotamia either the low or the middle chronology, appear to be incompatible with the evidence acquired by the dendrochronology-corrected C14 method.
In the first section the author points out the uncertainties in the Egyptian chronology of the M.K. and the S.I.P., suggesting that the latter may have lasted substantially longer than usually stated and that the "fixed" date of year 1872 B.C. for the 7th year of

Sesostris III may be wrong. For the F.I.P. and the O.K. he also
suggests a longer duration, reaching a date c. 3400 B.C. for the
beginning of the 1st Dynasty.
After having dealt with Mesopotamian chronology he returns to Egypt,
comparing what is known of calibrated radiocarbon dates with historical dates. Although full of inconsistencies the former appear
best to suit a high chronology, and this is confirmed by correla-
tions between Egyptian evidence and Palestinian radiocarbon dates.
J.J.J.

79478 NA'AMAN, Nadav, The Brook of Egypt and Assyrian Policy on the Bor-
ders of Egypt, *Tel Aviv*, Tel Aviv 6 (1979), 68-90.

The article is devoted mainly to the events that occurred in Southern Palestine during the late 8th-7th centuries B.C., particularly
to the problem of the location of the Brook of Egypt. On account
of the Assyrian inscriptions, the evidence from the O.T. and a discussion of the objectives and policy of the Assyrians on the Egyptian border the author proposes to identify the Brook of Egypt with
the Nahal Besor (i.a. assuming an equation of the places Yurza and
Arza), and not with Wadi el-ʿArish, generally accepted as such, which
identification is primarily based on late sources.

79479 NA'AMAN, N., The Origin and Historical Background of Several Amarna
Letters, *Ugarit-Forschungen* 11 (1979), 673-684.

The author re-groups some Amarna Letters to other regions of origin than assumed by Knudtzon in his edition of Amarna tablets.

79480 NA'AMAN, N., Sennacherib's Campaign to Judah and the Date of the
$lmlk$ Stamps, *Vetus Testamentum*, Leiden 29 (1979), 61-86.

The author cites on p. 65 from the section concerning his campaign
in Philistia in the Annals of Sennacherib's expedition to the West,
which relates the battle of Eltekeh between the Assyrian and Egyptian armed forces. The passage implies that the rulers of the Delta headed this expedition, joined by an Ethiopian army despatched
by one of the kings of the XXVth Dynasty, and that this expedition
is not the same as that mentioned in 2 Kings 19,9, but an earlier
one.

79481 OTTEN, Heinrich, Ein weiterer Ramses-Brief aus Boğazköy, *in*: *Festschrift Elmar Edel*, 314-316.

Publication of the text of a fragmentary letter from Ramses II recently found in Boğazköy. It is addressed to an unknown person
called "my son", for which two parallels are quoted from other unpublished letters of Ramses.
J.J.J.

79482 SCHACHERMEYR, Fritz, Die ägäische Frühzeit: Die Ausgrabungen und
ihre Ergebnisse für unser Geschichtsbild. 3. Band: Kreta zur Zeit

der Wanderungen vom Ausgang der minoischen Ära bis zur Dorisierung der Insel, Wien, Verlag der Österreichischen Akademie der Wissenschaften,1979 (15 x 23.5 cm; 374 p., 106 fig., 30 pl., 1 folding map) = Mykenische Studien. Veröffentlichungen der Kommission für mykenische Forschung, 7 = Österreichische Akademie der Wissenschaften. Philosophisch-historische Klasse. Sitzungsberichte, 355.

The chapters 2-4 are concerned with the transition of Late Minoan I to Late Minoan II which is visible in the new Mycenean costume of the Cretans on Egyptian N.K. reliefs, and with Late Minoan III A and III B, during which last phase the second Mycenean invasion took place and which is conspicuous for its ceramic import products found at contemporary Tell el-Amarna. Chapter 11 is devoted to the Sea Peoples and Crete (p. 109-121).

79483 SCHULMAN, Alan R., Beyond the Fringe: Sources for Old Kingdom Foreign Affairs, *JSSEA* 9 (1978-1979), 79-104.

The author discusses the nature and interpretation of the sources for foreign relations of the O.K. Leaving aside the Libyans with whom neither trade nor diplomacy seems to have existed, as well as Upper Nubia, he deals with the relations with Lower Nubia, Byblos and the Sinai, and Crete and Anatolia. He stresses that scenes as that of Sahure smiting down his foes have propagandistic rather than historical value, and that objects not found in a sealed or stratified context are no reliable indications. In the last part of his study Goedicke enumerates what we know about the subject, suggesting that the period from the reign of Snofru until the beginning of the VIth Dynasty was relatively devoid of major warfare.
J.J.J.

79484 SCHULMAN, Alan R., Diplomatic Marriage in the Egyptian New Kingdom, *JNES* 38 (1979), 177-193.

The article deals with a number of well known foreign marriages especially those of Ankhesenamūn, Amūnhotpe III and Ramesses II. While the diplomatic advantages of such alliances are pointed out it is also stressed that Amūnhotpe III took an equivocal attitude to them, apparently acquiring foreign princesses as wives but citing the lack of precedent for giving his own daughters in return. The Hyksos marriage of the early XVIIIth Dynasty kings is also discussed, it being suggested that this took place while the XVIIIth Dynasty Theban kings were still vassals. Thutmose III is also shown to have had at least three foreign wives, possibly the daughters of minor Syrian rulers. Ramesses II is credited with at least four diplomatic marriages, two with Hittite princesses, one with a Babylonian bride and one with a North Syrian ruler's daughter. The conclusion is that in the XVIIIth Dynasty Egypt initiated these marriages as the great power in the Near East, apparently calling them "tribute" from the foreign powers.
E.P. Uphill

79485 SHEA, William H., The Conquests of Sharuhen and Megiddo Reconsidered, *Israel Exploration Journal*, Jerusalem 29 (1979), 1-5.

The author argues that since there is no destruction layer at Sharuhen between the Hyksos Period and the XVIIIth Dynasty strata, either the identification of Tell el-Farʿah with Sharuhen is not correct, or that it was not burned after the conquest of Ahmose. He also points out that it is unlikely that Tuthmosis III destroyed it instead of captured Megiddo in his first Asiatic campaign.

79486 SPALINGER, Anthony J., Egyptian-Hittite Relations at the Close of the Amarna Period and Some Notes on Hittite Military Strategy in North Syria, *BES* 1 (1979), 55-89.

The lengthy article on the historical situation in North Syria at the end of the Amarna Period and slightly later is divided into four sections. After some introductory words in section 1 the author analyses in detail in section 2 the account of the warfare in Mursili II's annals for his years 7 and 9 as regards Northern Syria.
The author argues that although Mursili II was faced by in his years 7 and 9 with revolts in Nuḫasse, the key of the Syrian confederacy on which consequently his attention was focused, he did not personally intervene in North Syria, his strategy being to avoid a confrontation with the Egyptian army active there at that time, and to deal only with the rebels in Nuḫasse. The author notes that Assyria as well as Egypt could have caused the threat to Nuḫasse as the key of the Hittite state system.
In section 3 the author studies the Hittite policy under Mursili II's successor Muwatalli. Partly on account of the evidence from Seti I's Karnak reliefs concerning his campaigns in Phoenicia and Syria, he is able to reconstruct that in spite of Seti I's regaining control over the area and his victory over a Hittite army, Muwatalli did continue the policy of Mursili by not intervening personally. The great confrontation only took place in year 5 of Ramses II on the occurrence of the Kadesh battle. Going back to the time of Suppiluliuma in section 4, the author concentrates primarily on the Hittite king's reaction to the ill-fated outcome of the agreement between Egypt and Hatti, i.e. the killing of his son, Zannanza, by the Egyptians. In the last section 5 the author discusses the Egyptian evidence concerning their activities in Syria from the time of Horemheb to the reign of Seti I.

79487 SPALINGER, Anthony J., The Northern Wars of Seti I: An Integrative Study, *JARCE* 16 (1979), 29-47, with 1 fig.

I. An analysis of the sequence of Seti's war representations on the outer wall of the Karnak hypostyle (PM II^2, 53 foll. = (166)-(170); *KRI* I, 6 foll.), differing in points from our number 76267, 100-06 (pp. 29-37). II. Topographical lists relating to the various campaigns (37-39). III. The Hittite reactions, analyzed from

cuneiform sources, including the reigns of Suppiluliuma and Muwa-
tallis (39-41). IV. The chronological framework of the campaigns,
including those to Libya and Nubia (41-43).

                      J.F. Borghouts

79488 SPALINGER, A., Some Additional Remarks on the Battle of Megiddo, *GM* Heft 33 (1979), 47-54.

Es wird erörtert, ob das Datum der Schlacht von Megiddo vom 21. Tag in Tag 20 verbessert werden müsse. Der Verfasser setzt sich eingehend mit einer Untersuchung von Lello (vgl. unsere Nr. 78482) auseinander; er nimmt an, dass sich die Zeitangabe auf die erste Nachmittagsstunde des 19. Tages bezieht, als die Soldaten das Kina-Tal erreichten. Thutmosis hielt einen Nachmittagsschlaf und erhielt nach diesem die Nachricht über die Nähe des Feindes. Der Bericht über die Schlacht bezieht sich auf das "Erscheinen des Königs" am Morgen des nächsten, d.h. des 20. Tages.

                      Inge Hofmann

79489 TADMOR, Hayim, The Decline of Empires in Western Asia ca. 1200 B.C.E., *in*: *Symposia Celebrating the Seventy-Fifth Anniversary of the Founding of the American Schools of Oriental Research (1900-1975)*. Edited by Frank Moore Cross, Cambridge Mass., American Schools of Oriental Research, 1979 (=Zion Research Foundation Occasional Publications, 1-2), 1-14, with 1 folding map.

The author evaluates the political situation and events in the ancient Near East in the second half of the second millennium, the period of "the club of the great powers" among which Egypt, up to around 1200 B.C., the chronological milestone marking the dissolution of the political and social order of that time which occurred with the advent of the "Sea Peoples", the Israelites and the Arameans.

79490 WARD, William A., Remarks on Some Middle Kingdom Statuary Found at Ugarit, *Ugarit-Forschungen* 11 (1979), 799-806.

The author reconsiders Helck's analysis of the M.K. statuary from Ugarit (our number 76353) on account of the fragments of a statuette of an anonymous XIIth Dynasty princess, a triad of the vizier Senusert-ankh, both associated with level II at Ugarit (the whole range of the M.B. phase), which is roughly contemporary to the M.K., and a sphinx of Amenemhat III, possibly also associated with the MB phase, although found in the LB phase of the Baal temple. The problem is that so far conclusive evidence is missing which allows us to determine absolute dates for the various MB phases, since its relative chronology cannot be related to some absolute dates in Egyptian chronology.

79491 WEIPPERT, Manfred, The Israelite "Conquest" and the Evidence from Transjordan, *in*: *Symposia Celebrating the Seventy-Fifth Anniversary of the Founding of the American Schools of Oriental Research*

(1900-1975). Edited by Frank Moore Cross, Cambridge, Mass., American Schools of Oriental Research, 1979 (= Zion Research Foundation Occasional Publications, 1-2), 15-34.

The author studies the settlement of the Israelites and Transjordanian neighbours, which marked the end of the Late Bronze Age and the beginning of the Iron Age. Section 2 is concerned with Transjordan, where the $\check{S}^{y}sw$ of the Egyptian sources played an important role.

79492 WITAKOWSKI, Witold, The Origins of the Jewish Colony at Elephantine, *Orientalia Suecana*, Stockholm 27-28 (1978-1979), 34-41.

After a survey of the scholarly opinions on the origin of the Jewish colony at Elephantine the author reconstructs the events as follows: the first Jewish immigrants came to Elephantine in the 8th century B.C. after the defeat of Israel by Assyria; the second wave after the fall of the Judaic state in 587 B.C.; service of the Jews in the Egyptian army from the Persian times onwards.

79493 ZADOK, Ran, On Some Foreign Population Groups in First Millennium Babylonia, *Tel Aviv*, Tel Aviv 6 (1979), 164-181.

The article supplies information on the minor foreign elements in Babylonia during the Chaldaean and Achaemenid Periods, among which Egyptians (p.172-173). Although only a small ethnic group there in that time, they seem to have been the most influential.

V. ART AND ARCHAEOLOGY

a. Methodology of archaeology and museology; technological research

See also our numbers 79028; 79029; 79062; 79063; 79067; 79523 and 79612.

79494 BIETAK, Manfred, Urban Archaeology and the "Town Problem" in Ancient Egypt, *in*: *Egyptology and the Social Sciences*, 97-144, with 2 maps, 8 plans, 2 fig. and 1 table.

Stating that, from the view of cultural history, ancient Egypt had an urban civilization, the author presents in this article his arguments for that opinion which is relatively new in Egyptology. After discussing the literary and the archaeological evidence (thesis and antithesis) he draws up a list of qualities which are required for a site to be a town. He distinguishes various types of Egyptian towns (gezira-, levee- and tell-towns, and settlements at the rim of the desert). Then those towns that have been excavated to some extent pass the review: Hierakonpolis, Elephantine, Edfu, Abydos, Kahun, Deir el-Medîna, Tell el-Dabaʿ-Qantir and el-ʿAmarna; while the scantiness of our knowledge about Thebes and Memphis is stressed and that concerning the fortress-towns in Nubia is briefly summarized. In the last sections Bietak presents his synthesis and makes remarks about some peculiarities of ancient Egyptian urbanism, stating that our picture is still largely theoretical and that we need far more data. In this connection he briefly mentions the aims of urban archaeology. Two excursuses deal with the archaeological problems of stratigraphy in a townsite and the excavation techniques there required.

J.J.J.

79495 ČEJKA, Jiří, Eva KAPRÁLOVÁ, Zdenek URBANEČ and Eugen STROUHAL, Contribution to the Physico-chemical Research on Ancient Egyptian Materials, in: *ICOM Committee for Conservation*. 5th Triennial Meeting, Zagreb, 1-18 October 1978. Preprints, No. 78/116, 10 p., with abstract.

Results of a study of materials from ancient Egypt such as inorganic coatings (metallic and mineral), mineral filling and synthetic eyes of mummies deposited in Czechoslovak collections, ceramics from Nubian cemeteries from the 4th and 6th centuries A.D. at Wadi Qitna and Kalabsha-South, and a calcified myoma uteri found in a cemetery at Sayala.
The examination through various techniques yielded data which became a basis for objective archaeological examination and conservation treatment.

79496 CURTO, S., Museum Problems, in: *Acts 1st ICE*, 127-129.

Important remarks as regards the problem of an archaeological museum in our time and their solutions, demonstrated on the example of the Turin Museum.

J.J.J.

79497 FLEMING, S.J. and J. CROWFOOT PAYNE, PIXE. Analyses of some Egyptian Bronzes of the Late Period, *MASCA Journal*, Philadelphia 1, No. 2 (June 1979), 46-47, with 1 ill. and 1 table.

Short report on lead isotope analysis of ancient Egyptian bronzes.

79498 GÖDECKEN, K.B., Trade in the Near and Middle East and the Chronological Problems of the Late 2nd Millennium: An Approach by Neutron Activation Analysis, in: *Acts 1st ICE*, 229-235, with 3 tables.

In order to get reliable data the author analysed some 350 pot sherds from Ugarit of Ugaritic and other origin, among them so-called Mycenean and Kamares ware. The methods she used are here described, the results presented in the tables.

J.J.J.

79499 HAENY, Gerhard, New Kingdom Architecture, in: *Egyptology and the Social Sciences*, 85-94 and 83.

Convinced that Egyptology needs to reassess it scholarly attitude towards architectural monuments and to reform the methods currently employed in fieldwork, the author presents a survey of this present attitude and the methods at present employed. He points out the necessity to pay attention to scattered monuments of provincial sites and to study seriously the major monuments from an architectural viewpoint. He stresses that much evidence has been lost by lack of architectural experience among egyptologists; that the present appearance of buildings is often misleading by the disappearance of walls or roofs; that some usual translations of Egyptian architectonic terms are wrong; that architecture is not a technique but an art, the expression of a society for the immaterial concepts housed in buildings such as temples and tombs, visible manifestation of the principles governing the society. The rules, however, have to be decoded; reliefs and inscriptions are "labels" referring to the "contents" of a building, while the architectural forms refer to its contents and the specific functions of its rooms.
J.J.J.

79500 HASSAN, Ali, Neue Formen der Kooperation zwischen Ägyptologie und Naturwissenschaft (Neue Forschungen an den Giza-Pyramiden), *ASAE* 63 (1979), 79-87, with 3 pl.

The author i.a. mentions possibilities of drawing historical conclusions from the measurements of the pyramids, and particularly deals with the search for hidden chambers in the Chephren pyramid (the Cosmic Ray Project and the Electromagnetic Sounder Experiment).
J.J.J.

79501 KISCHKEWITZ, H., Neue Technik bei der Darstellung traditioneller Objekte, in: *Acts 1st ICE*, 371-375, with 2 pl.

Remarks on some major museological problems, illustrated from the new arrangement of the objects in the Berlin Museum.
J.J.J.

79502 MOMMSEN, H., K.G. BAUER, Q. FAZLY, T. MAYER-KUCKUK und P. SCHÜRKES, mit einem Anhang von Elmar EDEL, Analyse altägyptischer Metallfundstücke durch alphainduzierte Röntgenemission, Anhang: Beschreibung der untersuchten Objekte, *ZÄS* 106 (1979), 137-148, with 5 fig. and 2 tables.

Der Leiter und die Mitarbeiter des Instituts für Strahlen- und Kernphysik der Universität Bonn haben 14 Metallgegenstände untersucht, von denen 12 aus den Gräbern der Qubbet el-Hawa stammen. Der Beitrag erklärt ihre Methode und zeigt die Ergebnisse. In einem Anhang, *Beschreibung der untersuchten Objekte*, ordnet Elmar Edel die Assuanstücke nach ihren Objektnummern. Sie gehören jetzt der Sammlung des Bonner Ägyptologischen Seminars, S. 147-148.
M. Heerma v. Voss

79503 STÓS-FERTNER, Z., and N.H. GALE†, Chemical and Lead Isotope Analysis of Ancient Egyptian Gold, Silver and Lead, *in*: *Proceedings of the 18th International Symposium on Archaeometry and Archaeological Prospection*. Bonn, 14-17 March 1978, Köln, Rheinland-Verlag GmbH, in Kommission bei Rudolf Habelt Verlag GmbH, Bonn, 1979 (= Archaeo-Physika. Herausgegeben vom Landschaftsverband Rheinland Rheinisches Landesmuseum Bonn, 10), 299-315, with 2 maps, 7 fig. and 1 table.

After remarks on the mineralogical and geographical source of the gold, electrum, silver and lead of the ancient Egyptians, the authors present their chemical analyses and their interesting conclusions.

79504 TEFNIN, Roland, Image et histoire. Réflexions sur l'usage documentaire de l'image égyptienne, *CdE* LIV, No. 108 (1979), 218-244, with 1 fig.

Plaidoyer en faveur d'une analyse des documents figurés égyptiens selon des méthodes inspirées de la linguistique (necessité de créer une sémiologie égyptienne), pour dépasser enfin la conception actuellement encore trop répandue de l'objectivité historique des scènes représentées, et arriver à la reconnaissance de l'implication poétique de toute représentation.
Ph. Derchain

79505 WILDUNG, D., Herkunftsbestimmung altägyptischen Steinmaterials, *in*: *Acts 1st ICE*, 683-686.

The author reports on a research project, in which the University of München and Staatliche Sammlung cooperate, on the determination and analysis of the various Egyptian kinds of stone and their provenance from Egypt and its neighbouring regions.

b. Excavation reports

1. Lower Egypt and Memphis and surroundings

See also our numbers 79027; 79035; 79036; 79037; 79058; 79064; 79092; 79139; 79147; 79587 and 79620.

79506 ABOU-GHAZI, Dia', Discoveries of Selim Hassan at Saqqarah, *ASAE* 63 (1979), 1-4, with 2 pl.

The first part of the article contains a few addenda to our number 64001, referring to our numbers 75314-75316.
The second part deals with the painted wooden statue of $Ḥwf-Rˁ$ (Cairo JE 93164), from the Vth Dynasty. It has been found by Selim Hassan at Saqqâra and has now been restored.
J.J.J.

79507 BADAWY, Alexander, Preliminary Report about Fieldwork at the Tombs of Nyhetep-Ptah (Giza) and ʿAnkhmʿahor (Saqqara), *ASAE* 63 (1979), 5-26, with 7 pl. including 1 plan.

Preliminary report on the fieldwork of the University of California in 1974. The first part is devoted to the poorly preserved tomb chapel of Ni-hetep-Ptah (Lepsius 25 = G 2430; see Porter-Moss III.1, 2nd edition, 94-95). The chapel is briefly described.
The second, larger part (p. 7-26) deals with the famous tomb of ʿAnkhmaʿhor-Sesi in Saqqara (see Porter-Moss III.2, 2nd edition, 512-515). The wall-scenes are described and a few general remarks added, e.g. about the family of the tomb owner and his relations with his sculptors.
For Badawy's discussion of ʿAnkhmaʿhor's jewellery, see our number 75032.

J.J.J.

79508 BALBOUSH, Motawi, Preliminary Report on the New Discovery of the Temple of Ramesses II at Heliopolis (Seasons 1964-1967), *ASAE* 63 (1979), 27-33, with 5 fig. and 14 pl.

The author publishes some of the finds from his excavations at Tell el-Hisn (see also our number 75528), namely: the texts of the two limestone door-jambs with the names of Ramses II, Ramses IX and his son Nb-$m3$ ʿt-$Rʿ$ (see already our number 72503, p. 75), a scarab, a mummification bed, and pottery pipes. More objects are represented in photograph on the plates.

J.J.J.

79509 BASTA, Mounir, Excavations West of Kôm Firin (1966-1967), *CdE* LIV, No. 108 (1979), 183-196, with 3 ill. and 5 fig.

A l'occasion de la mise en valeur d'un territoire situé à l'ouest de Kôm Firin, dans le Delta occidental, a été découverte une nécropole qui fut fouillée en 1966-67. Les tombes les plus importantes sont mentionnées ici, tandis que quelques inscriptions de parois et d'objets mis au jour sont publiées en fac-simile.

Ph. Derchain

79510 BASTA, Mounir, Preliminary Report on the Excavations at Saqqara (1964) & the Discovery of a Tomb of the 5th Dynasty, *ASAE* 63 (1979), 35-50, with 36 pl.

In the first part the author deals with some finds made during the excavations in 1964 in the middle of the Unas causeway, e.g. three Late Period coffins and some shafts and burial chambers from the O.K.
The second part is devoted to his main discovery, the tomb of Niʿankh-Khnum and Khnemhotep, now published by Moussa and Altenmüller (see our number 77542).

J.J.J.

79511 COULSON, William D.E. and Albert LEONARD, Jr., A Preliminary Survey of the Naukratis Region in the Western Nile Delta, *Journal of Field Archaeology*, Boston 6 (1979), 151-168, with 26 maps, fig. and ill.

The Naukratis Project concerns work in the western Nile Delta, specifically along the Canopic branch of the Nile from el-Barnugi in the North to Kom el-Hisn in the South. In the initial phase of this project 10 sites were examined and sherded: Kom Ge'if (Naukratis); el-Neqrash; Nebire; Kom Firin; Kom Dahab; Kalabt Shafiq; el-Barnugi; Kom el-Hisn; Teh el-Barud; Silvagou and Kom Dillangat. The authors summarize i.a. the Pharaonic evidence from Kom el-Hisn.

79512 EIWANGER, Josef, Zweiter Vorbericht über die Wiederaufnahme der Grabungen in der neolithischen Siedlung Merimde-Benisalâme, *MDAIK* 35 (1979), 23-57, with 16 fig. including 1 map, and 4 pl.

Sequel to our number 78240.
Apart from a survey of the second campaign which led to the distinction of four, probably five phases, with a clear break between phases I and II, the author systematically deals with the aspects of the excavation: traces of buildings and burials; ceramic and its typology; flint implements (a group from S V-1978 is separately discussed), and some small objects among which an anthropomorphic idol. Investigations in the surroundings are recorded. At the end a summary of the results.   J.J.J.

79513 el-HALIM, N.M.A., Archaeological Site of Alexandria Before Alexander, *in: Acts 1st ICE*, 285-287.

The author briefly discusses the Alexandrian area during the Pharaonic Period and argues that Rakwtis village and Pharos island are archaeological sites dating back to that period.
                                                                                       J.J.J.

79514 HARRISON, Margaret, Excavation at Mendes, *Newletter ARCE* No. 17 (Winter 1978/79), 15-17, with 1 ill.

Short report on the excavations at Mendes carried out by the Institute of Fine Arts of the University of New York and Brooklyn Museum under the directorship of Donald P. Hansen and Edward L. Ochsenschlager.

79515 HAWWASS, Zaki A., Preliminary Report on the Excavations at Kom Abou Bellou, *SAK* 7 (1979), 75-87, with 1 map and 4 fig.

From 1970 to 1975 Kôm Abû Billo (Terenuthis) has been the object of excavation campaigns. In this preliminary report the author briefly deals with the history of the site (in the Pharaonic Period known as Mafket), which flourished in the Graeco-Roman and early Coptic Periods, and presents the major results of work in a cemetery from that later time.   J.J.J.

79516 LAUER, Jean-Philippe, Travaux et recherches à Saqqarah (15 Décembre 1974 - 28 Mars 1975), *ASAE* 63 (1979), 137-142, with 3 pl.

Continuing his preliminary reports on the work at Saqqâra (for the season 1972-1973, see our number 73430) the author deals with the reconstruction works in the Djeser complex, the excavations in the complex of Sekhemkhet, researches in the Pyramid Temple of Unas (see our number 77452) and in the pyramids of Pepi I and Merenre.
J.J.J.

79517 LECLANT, Jean, Recherches dans la pyramide et au temple haut du pharaon Pépi Ier, à Saqqara, Leiden, Nederlands Instituut voor het Nabije Oosten, 1979 (19.5 x 26.5 cm; [IV +] 23 p., 3 plans, 1 folding table, 1 loose folding sheet with hieroglyphic texts, 17 pl.) = Scholae Adriani de Buck Memoriae Dicatae, 6; rev. *BiOr* 38 (1981), 36-38 (Vilmos Wessetzky); *Oriens Antiquus* 19 (1980), 317-319 (Claudio Barocas).

The first section of this enlarged lecture presents a survey of the site of the Pepi pyramid and the history of the study of its texts, followed by a description of the author's excavation together with M. Lauer. The second section deals with an example of the results, namely the P.T. on the East wall of the sarcophagus chamber (indicated as P/F/E/). The text is presented on a loose sheet, a table of concordances as a folding plate. The author describes the reconstruction of the wall and makes various remarks to the text, e.g. to its palaeography and grammar. Section 3 is devoted to the excavation of the Pyramid Temple, describing its various rooms.
J.J.J.

79518 MARTIN, Geoffrey T., Excavations at the Memphite Tomb of Ḥoremḥeb, 1978: Preliminary Report, *JEA* 65 (1979), 13-16, with 2 pl. and 1 plan.

The clearance of the subterranean galleries was completed and the full extent of those served by shaft IV is shown. The burial complexes were originally for Ḥoremḥeb and his queen. Room H had walls with shallow recessed panels like a palace facade design, and two false doorways, the decoration being carried out in red and black. Room K had a false window over the east door. Among the many sherds from the burial chamber P was a hieratic docket dated to the 13th year of Ḥoremḥeb. Another miniature stela of king Ay was found. A summary is given of the archaeological development of the tomb structure.
E.P. Uphill

79519 MARTIN, Geoffrey Thorndike, The Tomb of Ḥetepka and Other Reliefs and Inscriptions from the Sacred Animal Necropolis North Saqqâra. 1964-1973. With Chapters by Alan B. Lloyd and J.J. Wilkes and a Contribution by R.V. Nicholls, London, Egypt Exploration Society, 1979 (25 x 31 cm; XVI + 142 p., 1 plan, 4 fig., 86 pl. [3 folding], colour frontispiece) = Texts from Excavations. Fourth Memoir = Excavations at North Saqqâra. Documentary Series, 2.

Publication of the inscribed and written material found during the excavations of 1964-1973 in North Saqqâra, with exclusion of the hieroglyphic texts on Carian stelae (see Masson, our number 78537) and the texts from the galleries and the objects there found.
After a general introduction eight groups of texts are dealt with. In section A the Vth Dynasty tomb of Ḥetepka (no. 3509): its architecture, its date, the name, title and family of its owner and the other names mentioned, and, particularly, the reliefs and the inscriptions. At the end the unplaced fragments are listed and described.
Section B deals with three archaic inscriptions (on a bowl, on a vase, and a seal impression). In section C 113 objects from the O.K.: seal impressions, stelae, relief blocks, offering bases and -tables, and so on.
Section D is devoted to the material dating from the N.K. to the Ptolemaic Period; inscriptions and reliefs, stelae, statuettes, etc. (nos. 118-339). Particular attention draws a painted wooden panel from the XXVIIth Dynasty showing a procession of foreigners with cattle in an un-Egyptian style (no. 284), discussed by Nicholls (p. 74-78). Section E contains a catalogue with data of inscriptions on blocks and relief fragments from the Main Temple Complex of Nectanebo II.
In the short section F Lloyd publishes two figured ostraca, one with a representation of a Carian soldier, the other with that of a war-galley. Section G, also by Lloyd, presents the Greek inscriptions and sealings, section H, by Wilkes, a Latin inscription on a stela.
On p. 125-127 some remarks concerning chronological and other point e.g. that the O.K. material dates from the Vth and the VIth Dynasties, and that Horus appears to play a prominent role in texts and reliefs of the destroyed temple of Nectanebo II.
Three concordances to various series of numbers and extensive indexes on p. 128-142. On the plates a plan of North Saqqâra, plans of the O.K. tombs, drawings of the inscriptions and reliefs, and a few photographs.   J.J.J.

79520   MÜLLER, H.W., Zur Archäologie der Vor- und Frühgeschichte des Deltas, *in*: *Acts 1st ICE*, 483-487.

After some remarks on the problem of the cultural influence of the Delta in the early history of Egypt the author briefly describes the excavation of and some objects from el-Sabʕa Banât near Minshât Abu Omar. The objects turned out to be from the Naqâda culture and were brought there by colonists. The genuine Delta culture must be in a deeper stratum.

79521   MÜLLER-MEHLIS, R., Zeugnisse einer der ältesten Hochkulturen der Erde, *Antike Welt*, Feldmeilen 10, Heft 1 (1979), 61.

Short report on the German expedition to Tell es-Sabᶜa Banat near the village Minshat Abu Omar, on the Eastern edge of the Delta, where, under the direction of H.W. Müller, a First Dynasty necropolis was discovered. One of the vessels there found bears the name of Narmer.

79522 OCHSENSCHLAGER, E.L., Taposiris Magna: 1975 Season, in: Acts 1st ICE, 503-506.

Short report on the 1975 excavation season at Taposiris Magna (Abu Sir), west of Alexandria on the Mediterranean shore.

79523 Preliminary Report on Czechoslovak Excavations in the Mastaba of Ptahshepses at Abusir, Prague, Charles University, 1976 [1979] (20.5 x 21 cm; 126 p., 58 pl. bearing plans, ill. and fig.).
Pr. Kčs 33

The preliminary publication of the result of the Czechoslovak expedition to Abusir contains short studies by various authors, all dedicated to various aspects of the mastaba of Ptahshepses. This tomb has been discovered and partly excavated by de Morgan in 1893, but he appears not to have surmised the extent and complexity of the building.
After a foreword by Zdeněk Uherek and an introduction by Miroslav Verner there follow seven short reports on the seasons between 1960 and 1974, the first six by the late Zbyněk Žába and a longer one on the last season by Verner. Then Vladimír Martinák presents a technical report on the geodetic documentation survey.
The mastaba is described in two chapters. Vladimír Fiala discusses its architecture (p. 47-60), dealing i.a. with the stages of its building, and Verner writes on the reliefs (61-73): first some general remarks, then a brief description of each wall and column, ending with remarks on Ptahshepses' sons on account of the carved-off reliefs. Verner also devotes a chapter to the mason-marks and similar inscriptions, containing i.a. titles and names of Ptahshepses.
In the last chapter Eugen Strouhal deals with the secondary burials found in the tomb area (remains of about 275 persons, mostly from the Saite and later Periods); Ladislav Bareš with some coffins of these burials; Petr Charvát with the pottery from all periods found on the site; and Miroslav Korecký with the pillar system in the pillar court and the columns of the East portico.
The plates contain plans and photographs of details of the tomb and of its reliefs as well as some illustrations to the later chapters, i.a. human remains, a coffin, and drawings of the pottery types.
J.J.J.

79524 RAY, J.D., The World of North Saqqâra, World Archaeology, Henley-on-Thames 10 (1978-1979), 149-157.

After introductory remarks on the special position of Egyptian archaeology, the importance of philology, and a short history of the excavations in the animal necropolis, the author sketches the settlement of North-Saqqâra as a whole. He deals with the configuration (Osiris)-Apis-Isis-Thoth-Horus and explains how the role of Osiris-Apis as a medium led to the birth of a true religious centre for the pilgrims of the Late Period. The last part of the article is devoted to the various kinds of documents there found such as the Serapeum stelae and the archive of Hor.

79525   el-SAWI, Ahmad, Excavations at Tell Basta. Report of Seasons 1967-1971 and Catalogue of Finds, Prague, Charles University, 1979 (16.5 x 24.5 cm; 107 p., 243 plans, ill. and fig. on 86 pl., 1 map, 1 loose folding plan, ill. on wrappers).   Pr. Kčs 54

In the introduction the author presents a survey of previous excavations at Tell Basta (Zagazig) and summarizes the most important discoveries. The following chapters are each devoted to the publication of the finds of one of the four excavation seasons. After a note on the excavation area follow brief descriptions of the burials and the objects found with them which for a large part consisted of amulets, beads and vessels (Registration nos. noted) and, at the end of each chapter, the finds from the general debris. The three sites of the 1968 season yielded the burials nos. 1-48; the 1969 season nos. 49-136; the 1970 season nos. 137-164; and the 1970-1971 season nos. 165-210. Apart from the burials excavated during the 1970 season, among which several from the O.K., almost all were from the N.K. During the 1970 season there were also dis covered a great building from the O.K., possibly connected with the collection of taxes, where several vessels were found, a temp of king Teti to the North of that of king Pepi I, a cemetery of cats, and a M.K. palace.
Index at the end of the book.

79526   el-SAWI, Ahmed, Some Objects Found at Tell Basta (Season 1966-67) *ASAE* 63 (1979), 155-159, with 10 pl. (1 folding).

After a survey of areas excavated at Tell Basta since 1961 (for the first season, see our number 64142) the author publishes some finds from the campaign 1966-67: two limestone offering tables, a jar with the representation of Bastet in Osiride form, and severa beads and amulets.

J.J.J.

79527   SIMPSON, William Kelly, The Pennsylvania-Yale Giza Project [The University Museum in Egypt. The Present], *Expedition*, Philadelphia, Penn. 21, No. 2 (Winter 1979), 60-63, with 5 ill. and 1 fig

Short on the University Museum - Yale University Expedition for the recording of Gîza Mastabas. For the history and other activities of the University Museum, see our numbers 79001, 79021, 7902 79535, 79547, 79548 and 79550.

79528   SMITH, H.S. and D.G. JEFFREYS, The Anubieion, North Saqqâra, Pre liminary Report, 1977-1978, *JEA* 65 (1979), 17-29, with 1 plan and 6 fig.

Seven major construction and occupation phases of post-Old Kingdom date were identified in Area 5, ranging in time from N.K. to the first centuries A.D. Remains of a brick mastaba probably of O.K. date were found in Area 13, as well as one constructed of stone blocks. In Area 12 traces of a processional way can be equated with the Serapeum dromos recorded by Mariette. Fragments of Greek papyri (N. Saq. 77/8-317/321) found in the uppermost level (phase V) have been dated to the first century A.D., while Demotic ostraka are probably Ptolemaic. An ostrakon with three Aramaic letters (N. Saq. 77/8-235) belongs to the late sixth or early fifth century B.C. and the hieroglyphic fragments relate to tomb-scenes of the Old and Middle Kingdom necropoleis. A rich and homogeneous pottery sherd collection was obtained and seven coins of Roman and Byzantine emperors in addition to Ptolemaic.

E.P. Uphill

79529 SPENCER, Jeffrey, Expedition to Saqqara, *The British Museum Society Bulletin*, London No. 28 (July 1978), 13-15, with 5 ill.

On the 1977 season of the British Museum's expedition to Saqqâra.

79530 VACHALA, Břetislav, Pod abúsírskými pyramidami, *Lide a země*, Praha 28, No. 12 (1979), 529-533.

"Unter den Pyramiden von Abusir."
Verfasser gibt einen Überblick über die Ergebnisse der tschechoslowakischen Grabungsarbeiten in Abusir seit dem Jahre 1960. Bei der letzten, 12., Expedition des Tschechoslowakischen Ägyptologischen Instituts der Karlsuniversität Prag auf dem Südfeld von Abusir sind südlich der Neferirkare-Pyramide, Totentempel und Pyramide der Königin Khentkaus (ḥt Ḥr, m33t Ḥr Stḥ, Ḥnt-k3w.s) und in der Nachbarschaft der Mastaba der Prinzessin Khekeretnebti weitere Mastabas aus der 5. und 6. Dynastie freigelegt worden, deren Inhaber der Prinz Neserkauhor, der Verwalter der Königskinder Idu und seine Gattin Khenti sowie der Einzige Freund des Königs, der Palastverwalter Merneferu waren. Einzigartig ist der Fund eines Baukomplexes des zentralisierten Totenkultes vom Ende der 6. Dynastie, der aus einem Hof mit Kreisförmigen Opfertischen, Libationsbassins und drei gewölbten Räumen besteht.

B. Vachala

79531 VACHALA, Břetislav, Zpráva o činnosti Čs. egyptologického ístavu UK, odd. Katedry věd o zemích Asie a Afriky FF UK v roce 1978, *Zprávy Československé společnosti orientalistické při ČSAV*, Praha 16, No.2 (1979), 26-29.

"Bericht über die Tätigkeit des Tschechoslowakischen Ägyptologischen Instituts der Karlsuniversität, Bereich Asien- und Afrikawissenschaften, für den Zeitraum 1978."
Verfasser berichtet über die Ergebnisse der 12. Expedition des tschechoslowakischen Ägyptologischen Instituts in Abusir.

B. Vachala

79532 VERNER, M., Czechoslovak Excavations at Abusir, *in*: *Acts 1st ICE*, 671-675.

Short report on the Czechoslovak excavations at Abusir. For a full report see our number 78813 and *ZÄS* 107 (1980), 158-169.

b. **Excavation reports**

2. **Upper Egypt**

See also our numbers 79027; 79035; 79036; 79037; 79058; 79092; 79139; 79587; 79624 and 79959.

79533 ALMAGRO, M. and F.J. PRESEDO, Les fouilles à Hérakléopolis Magna (1976), *in*: *Acts 1st ICE*, 67-71, with 1 plan.

Preliminary report on the campaign of 1976, during which investigations in the necropolis discovered in 1968 were continued. Some tombs were described and dated either to the Late Period or to the early M.K. and the F.I.P.

J.J.J.

79534 Anonymous, Fieldnotes, *Newsletter ARCE* No. 108 (Spring 1979), 18-20.

Short notes on the Hierakonpolis and Mut Temple, Karnak expeditions, under the auspices of the American Research Center in Egypt.

79535 Anonymous, The University Museum Expedition to Dra Abu el Naga [The University Museum in Egypt. The Present], *Expedition*, Philadelphia, Penn. 21, No. 2 (Winter 1979), 50-51, with 2 ill. and 1 map.

Short note to the University Museum Expedition to Dra Abu el Naga.
For the history and other activities of the University Museum, see our numbers 79001, 79021, 79026, 79527, 79547, 79548 and 79550.

79536 ARNOLD, Dieter, The Temple of Mentuhotep at Deir el-Bahari. From the Notes of Herbert Winlock, New York, 1979 (26.5 x 35.5 cm; XV + 73 p., frontispiece, 53 pl. [7 folding], 13 plans and fig.) = Publications of the Metropolitan Museum of Art Egyptian Expedition, 21; at head of title: The Metropolitan Museum of Art Egyptian Expedition; rev. *BiOr* 38 (1981), 43-46 (Erhart Graefe).

In the introduction the author points out that the present publication is both an excavation report of the temple of Mentuhotep Neb-hepet-re at Deir el-Bahari from the notebook containing the records concerning the main temple and from that devoted to the intramural tombs by Herbert Winlock, the director of the Metropolitan Museum of Art Expedition to Deir el-Bahari, and at the same time an updated review in which criticism and even rejection of Winlock's theories and conclusions is included when necessary. In the following chapters there is in each section referred to the pertinent pages in these manuscripts. Chapter 1 gives a topographical description of buildings and excavation, which comprises the causeway, the rough fieldstone wall and those of the various courts, the fill of the middle terrace of Hatshepsut's temple and that east of the court, the gardens, the gigantic tomb structure in the forecourt of the temple complex called Bab el-Hosan, and some varia. Chapter 2 is concerned with the reconstruction of the main temple after Winlock. All differences with the reconstruction of the present author (see our number 74040) are presented and discussed once more, while Winlock's remarks on items where both he and the present author came to the same conclusions are omitted. Chapter 3, devoted to the four building phases of the temple, contains no references to the Winlock manuscripts, since no such essay has appeared so far, but relies on the documentation of the expedition. In chapter 4 the author discusses the finds: the seated and standing statues of the king, the four foundation deposits, the bread deposits and bread moulds, the workmen's equipment, and the buried animals (one cow and several bulls). Four brief chapters (5-8) follow, respectively dealing with the sequence of work of the expedition in the temple, lists of expedition members and of brick types, and a table of contents for Winlock's notebook on the XIth Dynasty temples. After a description in chapter 9 of plates nos 38-51 follows the general index.

79537 ASFOUR, M.A.M., From One of My Old Diaries: Deir-en-Nawahid, *in*: *Glimpses of Ancient Egypt*, 4-11, with 10 ill. and 1 fig.

The author presents some information about his until today unpublished excavations from 1947 at Deir-el-Nawahid, S. of Abydos, where he discovered a plundered cemetery. Data are listed for some ten tombs and the objects they still contained, among which statuettes from the late O.K. or the early F.I.P. The major finds are illustrated by photographs.

J.J.J.

79538 BAKRY, Hassan S.K., The Sphinx Avenue of the Luxor Temple: Its Literary and Historical Importance, *in*: *Acts 1st ICE*, 79-86, with 2 pl.

The author relates the long history of the excavations of the sphinx avenue in front of the Luxor temple, which was known from 1902 onwards and excavated first in 1949 by Ghoneim and then from 1959 on by Abu el-Kader. He discusses also the sphinxes, and particularly the inscriptions on their socles, the poetic beauty of their style and their importance for the history of the XXXth Dynasty.

J.J.J.

79539 DONADONI, Sergio, Remise en état de la Tombe no 27 à l'Asasif, *in*: *Acts 1st ICE*, 175-179.

Survey of the reconstruction works in Theban Tomb No. 27 (Sheshonq).
                                                                J.J.J.

79540 EDEL, E., Die Grabungen auf der Qubbet el Hawa 1975, *in*: *Acts 1st ICE*, 193-197, with 1 pl.

Brief report on the continuation of the clearing of the double tomb of M$\hat{q}$w and S3bn$\hat{i}$ in Qubbet el-Hâwa. There were i.a. found an undisturbed burial room of a child and a fine wooden coffin that originally belonged to S3bn$\hat{i}$'s wife St-K3 but was used for a male corpse.
The author reports also on his study of the texts from the tomb which shows parallels to the already known text of S3bn$\hat{i}$, and he draws some historical conclusions from them. He mentions further that the wood from the excavations is analysed; two hitherto in Egypt unknown African trees are identified.   J.J.J.

79541 GINTER, Bolesław, Janusz K. KOZŁOWSKI, Joachim ŚLIWA, Excavation Report on the Prehistoric and Predynastic Settlement in el-Tarif During 1978, *MDAIK* 35 (1979), 87-102, with 7 fig. including 1 plan, and 2 pl.

In the area of el-Tarif extensive remains from the Prehistoric and Predynastic Periods have been found, mostly in a disturbed position because of later tomb constructions. Strips between the so-called East and West Mastabas and south of the former, not touched by the German excavators, were the object of the researches here reported on. The article discusses the stratigraphy, the flint and ceramic finds, occurring in primary position, and the settlement structures connected with them.
                                                                J.J.J.

79542 HABACHI, Labib, Six-Dynasty Discoveries in the Jabal al-Ṭarif, *Biblical Archaeologist*, Cambridge, MA 42 (1979), 237-238, with 1 ill.

The author briefly reports about the O.K. tomb of Thauti at the Jabal al-Ṭârif near Nag Hammadi, discusses the possible connection of the name of the goddess Bat with the word Faw in the nearb Faw Qibli, and devotes some attention to the name Idi, found on an object in one of the caves.
Compare our numbers 79408 and 79556.

79543 KAISER, Werner und Peter GROSSMANN, Umm el-Qaab. Nachuntersuchungen im frühzeitlichen Königsfriedhof. 1. Vorbericht, *MDAIK* 35 (1979), 155-163, with 1 map, 1 plan and 2 pl.

Since Petrie's publication of the tombs of Umm el-Qaʕab did not answer all questions the authors began new researches in the

area in 1977. Here they mainly discuss cemetery B, where the
plan of tomb 17/18 could be improved (see fig. 2). Whether B 10,
15 and 19 belong together is not quite certain; for B 7 and 9
this is clear, however. All these tombs are investigated so far
as possible, as was the tomb of Peribsen and cemetery U
that may actually be part of cemetery B.

J.J.J.

79544 KARKOWSKI, Janusz, Deir el-Bahari 1974-1975 (Travaux égyptologiques), *Études et Travaux* 11 (1979), 217-220, with 3 fig. (1 folding).

Sequel to our number 78416.
The egyptological works in the Hatshepsut temple at Deir el-Bahri in the 1974-1975 season concentrated on the classification of the blocks in the open magazines, the continuation of researches into various elements of the temple and the analysis of the finds from preceding seasons. One was able to identify the disposition of fragments on various walls, especially the West part of the South Wall of the Upper Court (purification of the king), as well as the East Wall of the vestible of the Solar Sanctuary (cosmological text).
Compare our number 79558.

79545 KEMP, Barry J., Preliminary Report on the el-rAmarna Survey, 1978, *JEA* 65 (1979), 5-12, with 1 pl. and 2 fig.

The archaeological survey was begun in the North City at the northernmost occupation limits and linked up with last year's surveying points, using the scale 1:2500. Further work was carried on at the gateways of the North Riverside Palace.
Buildings to the north of the Great Temple in the Central City were also mapped in outline. Broken pottery bread moulds were noted in the Temple Magazines to the South. Roman remains were located in the storm-water channel just north of El-Till. A stone weight in the bakery of the temple magazines refers to an overseer of the kitchens and of the chapel (?) of the Aten in the House of Rejoicing of the Aten.

E.P. Uphill

79546 LAUFFRAY, J., Karnak d'Égypte. Domaine du divin. Dix ans de recherches archéologiques et de travaux de maintenance en coopération avec l'Égypte. Préface de Ch. Desroches-Noblecourt, Paris, Éditions du Centre National de la Recherche Scientifique, 1979 (24 x 30 cm; 246 p., 1 table, 12 plans, 30 fig., 106 ill., 43 colour ill. [2 folding], colour ill. on cover). Pr. FF 190

This study presents a survey of ten years of activities of the Franco-Egyptian Centre in Karnak. Although intended for the general public - most subjects have been dealt with in scientific articles, particularly in Kêmi and in *Karnak V* (see our volume

1975), while others will be studied in *Karnak VI* (published in 1980)- there are made original scientific remarks on various pages. Moreover, the book is of importance because of its very rich and splendid illustration.

After the introduction by Mme Desroches-Noblecourt and the author's preface in which the members of the Centre are mentioned the material is presented in four parts, together fourteen chapters.

In part 1 the topography, architecture and history of the Karnak complex is described, a survey given of the way in which the temple functioned in antiquity, and of the work of the Centre.

The other parts are devoted each to activities in a special part of the building. Those in front of the temple (the dromos, the basin of the sacred barks, the chapel of Akhoris), those in the Forecourt (the Colonnade of Taharqa) and those in the main temple and the Akh-menu are discussed in part 2. Works in the transverse axis, particularly those on the XIth Pylon, in part 3.

This part also contains a chapter on the Aton heresy, and another on the reconstruction of the walls of the Aton temple from talatat. In part 4 are presented activities outside the main temple in the area of the Sacred Lake (e.g. the houses discovered East of it) and in the vicinity of the Khonsu and Opet temples. In the last chapter some remarks on various subjects, particularly on metrology. The postface presents a program for future researches. Index on p. 231-232. Bibliography (general and to each part in particular) on p. 241-246.

J.J.J.

79547 O'CONNOR, David, Abydos: The University Museum-Yale University Expedition [The University Museum in Egypt. The Present], *Expedition*, Philadelphia, Penn. 21, No. 2 (Winter 1979), 46-49, with 3 fig., 1 map, 1 plan and 1 ill.

Short report on the University Museum - Yale University Expedition activities at Abydos. For the history and other activities of the University Museum, see our numbers 79001, 79021, 79026, 79527, 79535, 79548 and 79550.

79548 O'CONNOR, David, The University Museum Excavations at the Palace-City of Malkata [The University Museum in Egypt. The Present], *Expedition*, Philadelphia, Penn. 21, No. 2 (Winter 1979), 52-53, with 1 fig., 2 ill., 1 map and 1 plan.

Short note to the University Museum Excavations at Malkata, Thebes. For the history and other activities of the University Museum, see our numbers 79001, 79021, 79026, 79527, 79535, 79547 and 79550.

79549 PRESEDO VELO, F.J., Les dernières découvertes à Hérakléopolis Magna, *in*: *Acts 1st ICE*, 525-532, with 4 fig.

The author presents the most important finds made during the 1976 excavations at Herakleopolis Magna: several false-door stelae, and a list of offerings brought by offering bearers.

79550 REDFORD, Donald, The Akhenaten Temple Project and Karnak Excavations [The University Museum in Egypt. The Present], *Expedition*, Philadelphia, Penn. 21, No. 2 (Winter 1979), 54-59, with 5 ill. and 1 plan.

Report on the Akhenaten Temple Project at Karnak.
For the history of other activities of the University Museum, see our numbers 79001, 79021, 79026, 79527, 79535, 79547 and 79548.

79551 ROMER, John, The Theban Royal Tomb Project, *Newsletter ARCE* No. 109 (Summer 1979), 6-7.

Abstract of a preliminary report.

79552 el-SAYED, Abdullah, A Prehistoric Cemetery in the Abydos Area, *MDAIK* 35 (1979), 249-301, with 33 fig. including 1 map and 1 plan.

Publication of the results of excavations near Abydos in 1965-1968, mainly in the South near Salmâni (site S). After an introduction one section is devoted to earlier prehistoric researches in the area, listing the more important discoveries. The author draws the conclusion that the town grew in size and importance to an important place at the end of the Prehistoric Period.
The other section deals with the author's own excavations, particularly the 136 graves found on site S, studying their chronological distribution. The author concludes that the cemetery began in Naqâda Ib, grew considerably during the Naqâda II period, while the number of burials sharply diminished during Naqâda III. On p. 260-273 the tomb register indicating the data (i.a. the Sequence Dates) of each grave; on p. 274-301 drawings constituting the pottery corpus.   J.J.J.

79553 SCHADEN, Otto J., Preliminary Report on the Re-clearance of Tomb 25 in the Western Valley of the Kings (WV 25). University of Minnesota Egyptian Expedition January 1976, *ASAE* 63 (1979), 161-168, with 9 pl.

Report on the re-clearance of the unfinished tomb no. 25 in the Western Valley of the Kings near the tomb of Eye, discovered by Belzoni and since then examined many times. No inscriptional material or deposits have been discovered. The tomb seems to have been constructed in the late XVIIIth Dynasty and is of royal design. It was reused for the burial of eight bodies in the late N.K.
                                                                                J.J.J.

79554   SHAʿRAWI, Galal, Clearance of a New Kingdom Cemetery at el-Shutb (near Kom Ombo Temple), *ASAE* 63 (1979), 169-176, with 7 pl. and 27 fig.

The N.K. cemetery of el-Shutb, about half a kilometer East of the Kom Ombo temple, has partly been excavated in 1965-1967. The author presents a survey of the seven types of tombs, a list of objects found inside them, and brief descriptions of six major tombs.

J.J.J.

79555   VALBELLE, D., Le village de Deir el-Médineh: Essai de chronologie schématique, *in*: *Acts 1st ICE*, 661-663.

The author briefly sketches the subsequent stages in the history of the village of Deir el-Medîna.

79556   VAN ELDEREN, Bastiaan, The Nag Hammadi Excavation, *Biblical Archaeologist*, Cambridge, MA 42 (1979), 225-231, with 8 ill.

A short survey of the Nag Hammadi excavation which started in 1975.
Compare our numbers 79408 and 79542.

79557   VERMEERSCH, P.M., E. PAULISSEN, M. OTTE, G. GIJSELINGS and D. DRAPPIER, Prehistoric and Geomorphologic Research in Middle Egypt, *in*: *Palaeoecology of Africa and the Surrounding Islands*. Volume 11 Covering the 1975-1977, edited by E.M. van Zinderen Bakker [and] J.A. Coetzee, Rotterdam, A.A. Balkema, 1979, 111-115, with 1 map.

This paper is a progress report of the activities of the Belgian Middle Egypt Prehistoric Project. The studied sites belong to the Acheulean, the Middle and the Upper Palaeolithic Periods. Important characteristics of the sites and their industries are mentioned. A threefold subdivision of the Nile Valley is presented.

Authors' summary

79558   WYSOCKI, Zygmunt, Deir el-Bahari 1974-1975, *Études et Travaux* 11 (1979), 207-216, with 3 ill.

Sequel to our number 78874.
This is the technical report of the director of the Polish Mission at Deir el-Baḥri in the season 1974-1975. Blocks from the West wall of the Upper Portico were arranged, identified or recognized. Reconstruction of this wall beginning from the South end has been started. According to the same technique the South Wall of the Upper Court was completed.

79559   WYSOCKI, Zygmunt, Deir el-Bahari 1975-1976, *Études et Travaux* 11 (1979), 221-228, with 3 ill.

Sequel to our preceding number.
In this season the works of conservation have been continued: conservation of the wall behind the North Colonnade of the Middle Terrace; construction of the masonry of the West Wall of the Upper Portico; re-integration of the protodoric columns into the interior line of the Upper Portico; reconstruction of the central part of the rock platform above the Upper Terrace of the temple.

b. Excavation reports

3. Surrounding areas and countries

See also our numbers 79035; 79065; 79073; 79074; 79092, 79587 and 791015.

79560 DOTHAN, Trude, Excavations at the Cemetery of Deir el-Balaḥ, [Jerusalem, The Institute of Archaeology, The Hebrew University, 1979] (19 x 28 cm; [IX +] 114 p., frontispiece, 224 ill., fig., maps and plan, 6 tables) = Qedem. Monographs of the Institute of Archaeology. The Hebrew University of Jerusalem, 10; rev. AJA 84 (1980), 379-380 (Saul S. Weinberg).

After an introduction on Deir el-Balah and the excavations there in general, the author discusses in three separate chapters the anthropoid clay coffins and the related finds in the Late Bronze Age burials Nos. 114, 116 and 118. Of each tomb she describes the burial, the anthropoid clay coffin, the pottery and vessels, metal objects, jewellery and other artifacts, and scarabs and seals. For tomb No. 114 this is done in collaboration with I. Beit-Arieh; the section on scarab and seals in tomb No. 116 is by the hand of B. Brandl, as well as that on the scarabs, beads, amulets and finger rings in tomb 118.
Then follows a chapter by B. Arensburg and Patricia Smith, on the human remains which were more like the N.K. Lower Egyptian population and different from the typical Mediterranean population of Israel. In the conclusions the author presents an evaluation of the chronology and the strongly Egyptian affinities of the burial gifts; technique and the typology of the anthropoid coffins; anthropoid coffins in Egypt; and those from Canaan.
Catalogue of finds at the end of the book.

79561 EMERY†, Walter B., H.S. SMITH and A. MILLARD, The Fortress of Buhen. The Archaeological Report. With Contributions by D.M. Dixon, J. Clutton-Brock, R. Burleigh, and R.M.F. Preston, London, Egypt Exploration Society, 1979 (35 x 44.5 cm; XVI + 225 p., 48 fig. including plans, 107 pl., frontispiece) = Forty-Ninth Excavation Memoir = Excavations at Buhen, vol. I.

For the second volume, on the inscriptions, see our number 76733. The first volume, still partly from the hand of the late Walter Emery, has been completed by Smith and Miss Millard.

Apart from Emery's preface and Smith's introductory note the book consists of three parts. Part I, by Emery, contains the architectural description, divided into three chapters: a short general description and a survey of the history of the fortress, and more extensive descriptions of the M.K. and N.K. fortresses.
In part II Smith presents his archaeological commentary, adding numerous details to Emery's survey. First a chapter on the outer and inner fortifications, followed by notes on metrology, construction and the manning of the fortress (at least 1500 men). Then a discussion of the buildings of the inner and outer towns, followed by some historical considerations: summaries of the stratigraphy and building history of the fortifications and of the inner town, a discussion of the latter's character of occupation and its historical development, and of the location and role of Buhen.
Part III, by Miss Millard, is devoted to the finds: tools and weapons; faience and stone vessels; objects of personal adornment; games, toys and figurines; statuary and funerary objects; miscellaneous finds. A special chapter deals with pottery. All objects are described, mostly very briefly, while their significant data are mentioned.
Part IV (p. 191-195) deals with the famous Buhen horse. After Dixon's brief introduction Mrs Clutton-Brock presents a minute description of the animal (see already our number 75141), while Richard Burleigh reports on its attempted radiocarbon dating.
In two appendices other such datings and analyses of metal ores are presented by Burleigh and Preston. There follow an index, a distribution list of the finds, and a reverse index of grid numbers and catalogue numbers.
On the plates plans of the fortress in its various stages, of details of the fortifications and of the buildings; drawings of the more important objects from the site, among which the pottery types; 138 photographs (pl. 79-101) made during the excavations, and seven plates with photographs of the objects.

J.J.J.

79562 GASCOU, Jean et Guy WAGNER, avec la collaboration de P.J. GROSSMANN, Deux voyages archéologiques dans l'oasis de Khargeh, *BIFAO* 79 (1979), 1-20, with 1 plan and 6 pl.

Report on two archaeological journeys in 1978 to the el-Khârga Oasis. The sites are briefly described in a geographical order: those south of Khârga, those near it and those north of it.

J.J.J.

79563 GIDDY, Lisa L., Balat: Rapport préliminaire des fouilles à ʿAin Aseel, 1978-1979, *BIFAO* 79 (1979), 31-39, with 3 plans (2 folding), 3 fig. (2 folding) and 7 pl.

Proceeding the researches at ʿAin Aseel (see our following number) the author excavated parts of the large building called by Fakhry a temple. Its nature is still uncertain. This time several occupation phases could be established.

In an appendix N.-C. Grimal discusses the impressions of seals
and plaquettes that have been found. The writing resembles that
of O.K. papyri.

J.J.J.

79564 GIDDY, Lisa L. et Nicholas-C. GRIMAL, Balat: Sondage sur le site
de ʿAin Aseel, Rapport préliminaire, *BIFAO* 79 (1979), 21-30,
with 1 plan, 3 fig. and 6 pl.

Preliminary report on sondages near Balât in the Oasis el-Dâkhla
in 1978. Constructions were brought to light which show two occupation phases. The relatively homogeneous pottery points to an
Egyptian occupation from the VIth Dynasty onwards until a still
uncertain period.

J.J.J.

79565 GIDDY, Lisa L. et Nicholas-C. GRIMAL, Rapport préliminaire sur
la seconde campagne de fouilles à Balat (Oasis de Dakhleh): le
secteur nord du mastaba V, *BIFAO* 79 (1979), 41-49, with 1 folding plan, 2 fig. and 4 pl.

During the campaign of 1977-1978 some thirty tombs were excavated north of mastaba V. The authors discuss their construction
techniques, burials, re-use and date (VIth Dynasty-end F.I.P.).

J.J.J.

79566 KLEMM, Dietrich und Rosemarie, Herkunftbestimmung altägyptischen
Steinmaterials, *SAK* 7 (1979), 103-140, with 3 maps (1 folding)
and 8 pl.

The article consists of two parts, the first one containing a report on the first campaign of the quarry-expedition (Sept-Oct.
1977), the other on the second campaign (Sept.-Oct. 1978). During these campaigns the stone in a number of quarries and the
conditions of the quarries themselves have been studied, while
attention is paid to the periods during which a particular quarry
was used.

J.J.J.

79567 MILLS, Anthony J., The Basis of an Oasis = *Archaeological Newsletter. Royal Ontario Museum*, Toronto, New Series, No. 168 (May
1979), 4 p.

Short report on the Dâkhleh Oasis Project by the director A.J.
Mills, containing some information on the flourishing period
of the oasis during the Roman Period.

79568 MILLS, A.J., Dakhleh Oasis Project. Report on the First Season of
Survey October - December 1978, *JSSEA* 9 (1978-1979), 163-185, with
9 pl.

The aims of the Dakhleh Oasis Project is to describe and understand the settling and development of man in the oasis, for which

the area will have to be studied in great local detail.
After briefly mentioning the very few earlier studies of the oasis
there follows a general description. During the first season the
most western part of the oasis has been surveyed. The results,
discovery of a number of settlement sites and cemeteries from
the Neolithic, Pharaonic, Roman, Christian and Islamic Periods,
are described. As regards Pharaonic times the western part of the
oasis shows extensive remains from the late VIth Dynasty and the
F.I.P., but no evidence was brought to light for the following ages
until the Roman times.

J.J.J.

79569 MILLS, Anthony J., Fieldnotes: The Dakhleh Oasis Project, *Newsletter ARCE* No. 107 (Winter 1978/79), 9-10.

Short note to the Dakhleh Oasis Project of the Royal Ontario Museum, Toronto and the Society for the Study of Egyptian Antiquities.

79570 SAYED, Abdel-Monem A.H., Discovery of the Site of the 12th Dynasty Port at Wâdi Gawâsîs on the Red Sea Shore, *in: Acts 1st ICE*, 569-577, with 1 map.

The author first draws attention to the important findings, viz. three stelae and then discusses the historical significance of the port: the name and date of the port, the problem of the situation of the land Punt, the finding of Egyptian stone anchors.
See also our number 77676.

79571 VALLOGGIA, Michel, La fouille du mastaba V de Balat (Oasis de Dakhleh), *BSFE* N° 84 (mars 1979), 6-20,with 6 ill.

A Balat, Fakhry avait pu dégager quatre mastabas; l'Institut français a fouillé plus au nord. Le splendide mobilier de *Mdw-nfr*, gouverneur de l'oasis jusqu'ici inconnu, permet de préciser la date de ses activités: un gobelet d'albâtre mentionne en effet le Premier jubilé de Pépi II. L'édifice comprenait une cour extérieure non dallée; la cour intérieure, comme l'autre percée d'un puits, gardait deux socles pour stèles et un bassin à libations. Un couloir ouvrait sur trois chapelles à voute étoilée. De bonnes peintures très détériorées représentaient l'agriculture et la vie quotidienne. La voute de décharge n'avait pas empêché un effondrement. Il a fallu démonter la superstructure pour atteindre l'appartement funéraire,inviolé. Dans le cercueil écrasé reposait Medounefer, muni de deux "palettes" de scribe, en albâtre, où étaient énumérés ses titres. Il était paré de colliers et amulettes, entre autres de cinq pendentifs en or. Le cellier conservait 99 jarres sphériques. Des coffres contenaient des outils ou des objets de toilette, dont certains en cuivre. En plus de la céramique abondante et des vases à parfum, mentionnons la guenon d'albâtre tenant son petit, enfin le babouin de diorite, portant la titulature royale.

J. Custers

79572 VALLOGGIA, Michel, Rapport préliminaire sur la deuxième campagne de fouilles du mastaba V à Balat (Oasis de Dakhleh), *BIFAO* 79 (1979), 51-61, with 6 pl.

Sequel to our number 78803.
Proceeding his studies of mastaba V the author discusses the constructions east of it, the interior court, the chapels and the substructure.
J.J.J.

79573 VERNUS, P., Douch arraché aux sables, *BSFE* N° 85 (juin 1979), 7-21, with 6 ill. and 1 fig.

Les deux campagnes menées en 1979 à Douch, à l'extrémité Sud de l'oasis de Kharga, ont déjà livré de beaux résultats. Pourtant seul le temple de grès, appuyé à la forteresse, a été dégagé. Il était dédié à Osiris *Iywy* ("bienvenue!") avec trois parèdres, plus Amon-Rê de Hibis, Thot, Shou et les trois épouses. Construit par Domitien et Trajan, décoré sous Hadrien, il abrita Sérapis et en outre une chapelle adossée. Au IVe siècle, les deux cours dallées furent intégrées à la zone urbaine ; le sanctuaire fut probablement transformé en église. La céramique découverte permettra de dresser un corpus bien daté. Plus de 400 ostraca, dont plusieurs en copte, fourniront une documentation importante sur les institutions proto-byzantines. Au Nord furent explorées six tombes ; l'une contenait encore une dizaine de momies accompagnées d'un matériel hétéroclite. Notons les perspectives ouvertes par ces découvertes pour l'étude de l'armée romaine et l'histoire des religions. Le nom même de la Kusis romaine (en égyptien Kush) inclinait les fouilleurs à dater sa fondation plus anciennement ; au cours de la troisième campagne furent découvertes des monnaies ptolémaïques et des textes démotiques.
J. Custers

79574 WHITCOMB, Donald S. and Janet H. JOHNSON, Quseir al-Qadim 1978. Preliminary Report, Cairo, American Research Center in Egypt, Inc., [1979](19.5 x 26.5 cm; [XII +] 352 p., 56 ill., 1 fig., 89 pl. containing fig., plans and maps).

In this preliminary report of the first season of the excavations at the site of Quseir el-Qadim and of the survey of the Quseir region in 1978 a large number of authors made small or more extensive contributions in the various chapters. Since Quseir al-Qadim does not predate the first century A.D. the book is almost completely outside the scope of the AEB, it being concerned with material from the Roman and Islamic Periods. In the first chapter, on the background, by J.H. Johnson and D.S. Whitcomb, there are some brief remarks on the pharaonic expeditions to the spice lands which seem to have gone via the Wadi Hammamat and a Red Sea port and on the role of the area in the Predynastic Period. In chapter 10, on the epigraphy, J.H. Johnson briefly reports on the Demotic ostracon found (p. 244). In chapter 12, on the Quseir regional survey, Martha Prickett discusses the Predynastic and Greco-Roman evidence, no pharaonic material having been identified as yet within the survey region. The closest material (M.K.) comes from the mouth of the Wadi Gasus, 52 km to the North, and the Wadi Gawâsis, while the next closest pharaonic evidence is the inscriptions from the Wadi Hammamat, 95 km to the west on the central route from Quseir to the Nile Valley.

The book is distributed by Undena Publications, Malibu, California

c. Museum collections and exhibitions

See also our numbers 79011; 79013; 79042; 79048; 79059; 79128; 79139; 79376; 79502; 79688; 79690; 79697; 79716; 79773; 79774; 79783 and 79785.

79575   ALDRED, Cyril, Scenes from Ancient Egypt in the Royal Scottish Museum Edinburgh, Edinburgh, The Royal Scottish Museum, [1979] (24.7 x 19.8 cm; 24 unnumbered p. 5 colour ill. [1 on cover], 12 fig. [1 on cover], 11 ill.).

On account of four imaginative colour scenes the author deals with the following subjects: King Scorpion Performs an Agricultural Ceremony; A Sculptor's Workshop c. 2350 B.C.; A Frontier Fortress in the Sudan c. 1860 B.C. (= Semna); A Private Mansion c. 1370 B.C. (Tell el-Amarna house).

79576   ALDRED, Cyril, The Temple of Dendur, *BMMA* 36 (1978-1979), 1-64, with 49 ill. (many in colour), 1 map and 1 cross-section.

In this article, written on the occasion of the erection of the Dendur Temple in the Metropolitan Museum, New York and profusely provided with illustrations and captions, the author first relates the more recent history of Dendur and the other Nubian monuments and discusses next the politico-religious scene at the time of founding the temple, in which were venerated Pedesi and Pihor, two sons of a chief of the Blemmyes, who were deified after their drowning in the Nile. Then he describes the gateway and the temple with its pronaos, vestibule and sanctuary in the context of a more general description of temple and rites. The article ends with some remarks on the graffiti, and the significance of Dendur as a monument in which drowned persons were venerated and which probably also contained their tomb chamber. Compare our numbers 78082 and 79615.

79577   Anonymous, Grenoble, Musée de peinture et de sculpture. Collections égyptiennes, *La Revue du Louvre et des Musées de France*, Paris 29 (1979), 333, with 1 ill.

Short note on the Egyptian collection in the Musée de Grenoble. For the catalogue see our number 79601.

79578   Anonymous, Marseille. La tombe de Nefertari, *Archeologia*, Paris No. 136 (Novembre 1979), 80, with 1 ill.

Note on an exhibition presenting the large scale photographic reconstruction of the tomb of Nefertari, held in the Musée Borély, Marseille, 1979-1980.

79579   Anonymous, The Search for Ancient Egypt, *The Pennsylvania Gazette*, Philadelphia 77, No. 5 (March 1979), 31-33, with 14 ill.

Short report on an exhibition at the University Museum, Philadelphia in 1979, the pieces of which were mainly gathered from the Museum's excavations. Many of them have never been displayed in public.

79580   BOURRIAU, Janine, Museum Acquisitions 1977. Egyptian Antiquities Acquired in 1977 by Museums in the United Kingdom, *JEA* 65 (1979), 151-155, with 2 pl.

Lists 166 objects dating from predynastic times to the Coptic period acquired by museums in Great Britain. Dimensions and donors are given.   *E.P. Uphill*

79581   The Ernest Brummer Collection. Vol. II: Ancient Art. Auction Sale from 16th to 19th October 1979 at the Grand Hotel Dolder, Zürich by Galerie Koller in Collaboration with Spink & Son, [Zürich, 1979] (20.5 x 30 cm; 435 p., 291 ill. [many in colour]).

Within the section of Egyptian and Near Eastern Antiquities and Works of Art Egypt occupies the nrs 500-528, which are presented in a colour ill. and a description with data and bibliography on opposite pages (p. 17-61).

79582   CANBY, Jean Vorys, Diana BUITRON and Andrew OLIVER, Ancient Jewelry in Baltimore, *Archaeology* 32, No. 5 (September/October 1979), 53-56, with 11 ill. (6 in colour).

On the occasion of an exhibition of the jewelry in the Walters Art Gallery, Baltimore the authors describe a carnelian pendant in the shape of a *bulti*-fish and merely mention the rest of that part of the collection.

79583   CASTIONI, Christiane, Dominique DÉROBERT, Robert HARI, Jocelyne MULLER-AUBERT, Bérengère STAHL-GUINAND, Égypte, [Genève, Musée d'Art et d'Histoire, 1977] (17 x 24 cm; 32 p., colour ill. on cover, 18 ill. on 16 pl., 2 fig.) = Images du Musée d'Art et d'Histoire de Genève, 10.

Version of our number 77153 which does not contain the homage to Charles Maystre.

79584 CORTEGGIANI, Jean-Pierre, L'Égypte des Pharaons au Musée du Caire, [Paris], Éditions Aimery Somogy, [1979] (14.5 x 21.5 cm; 256 p., 44 colour ill., 1 map, 1 plan) = Trésors des grands musées, 16.

After having sketched the history of the Egyptian Museum in Cairo and its collections, the author presents a selection of 120 objects from all periods. Data such as material, measurements, date inv. no., location no. are given, followed by a description with background information. Glossary, indexes and tables of concordances between the nos. in the present guide and various Cairo nos. at the end.
Most of the objects are well-known, but are not among the most illustrated objects in the Egyptian Museum, Cairo.

79585 DESROCHES-NOBLECOURT, Chr., Commémoration du 150e anniversaire de la fondation du "Musée égyptien" au Louvre, *La Revue du Louvre et des Musée de France*, Paris 29 (1979), 330-331, with 2 ill.

Short article on the re-opening of the crypt in the Louvre, which contains now, apart from other objects, the zodiac from Dendera in the ceiling.

79586 DONADONI ROVERI, Anna Maria, Fouilles dans le Musée de Turin. Une statuette de Tiyi-Touéris. Des cartons de tissage copte, *in*: Acts 1st ICE, 181-185, with 4 pl.

The author publishes two results of her "excavations" in the Turin Museum: an anepigraph wooden statuette (Cat. 566), which she argues to represent queen Tiyi, in the shape of a hippopotamus, probably Ipet as personification of Luxor; and some Coptic papyrus fragments (N. Suppl. 2200), possibly from Hermopolis Magna, with models for a weaving workshop.
                                                                J.J.J.

79587 Funde aus Ägypten. Österreichische Ausgrabungen seit 1961. Katalog einer Sonderausstellung der Ägyptisch-Orientalischen Sammlung, Wien, Kunsthistorisches Museum, 1979 (19 x 21 cm; 120 p., 1 map, 2 plans, 1 fig., 96 ill., colour ill. on cover).

Catalogue of an exhibition of objects that came to the museum in Vienna from excavations in Sayâla, Tell ed-Dabʿa and Asasîf (1961-1978). After a preface by Helmut Satzinger a general introduction to the three sites is given by Manfred Bietak.
To each of the three sites a chapter is dedicated, consisting of special introductions to periods or to types of objects, and descriptions of the objects in the order after which they were exhibited. This order is more or less chronological for Sayâla, roughly systematical for Tell ed-Dabʿa. Apart from photographs representing more important objects there are also several pictures of the excavations themselves.
At the end a bibliography and a list of concordances between inventory and catalogue numbers.
                                                                J.J.J.

79588 FUSCALDO, Perla, [Las piezas egipcias del Museo Etnografico de Buenos Aires (Ultima parte)]. VIII. Estatuillas y animales momificados, *Revista del Instituto de Historia Antigua Oriental*, Buenos Aires 4 (1978), 87-95, with 6 pl.

Sequel to our number 75237.
Publication of 3 bronze statuettes and 2 faience amulets representing animal deities, and of 2 mummified animals preserved at the Museo Etnográfico de Buenos Aires, with commentaries on the cult of animals in Egypt. No dates are given for the pieces.
J. R. Ogdon

79589 FUSCALDO, Perla, [Las piezas egipcias del Museo Etnografico de Buenos Aires (Ultima parte)]. IX. La tabla funeraria del ataud de Amenirdis, *Revista del Instituto de Historia Antigua Oriental*, Buenos Aires 4 (1978), 96-97, with 1 pl.

Publication of the funerary wooden tablet belonging to the coffin of Amenirdis, preserved at the Museo Etnográfico de Buenos Aires and dated to the XXIst Dynasty. Bad state of preservation. Exterior decoration lost. Interior decoration commented: few signs preserved; usual depictions of the lifting of the sky, this time by Geb instead of Nut.
J.R. Ogdon

79590 GIAMMARUSTI, Antonio e Alessandro ROCCATI, I templi di File, Torino, Museo Egizio, 1979 (21.7 x 21.7 cm; 48 unnumbered p., 2 maps, 2 plans, 2 fig., 16 ill., ill. on cover); at head of title: Ministero per i beni culturali e ambientali. Soprintendenza per le antichità egizie. Città di Torino. Assessorato per la cultura. Con la collaborazione della società Condotte Mazzi Estero s.p.a.

Booklet edited on account of an exhibition in the Egyptian Museum in Turin. First the "death of Philae", the UNESCO campaign and the removal of the monuments by the Italian firm Condotte Mazzi Estero are described. The booklet further deals with the importance of Philae, the archaeological researches preceding the removal of the monuments, the constructive elements of the temples and the resurrection on Agilkia.
J.J.J.

79591 Götter und Pharaonen. Roemer- und Pelizaeus-Museum Hildesheim, 29. Mai- 16. September 1979, [Hildesheim, Roemer- und Pelizaeus-Museum, 1979] (21 x 23.5 cm; 390 p., colour frontispiece, ill. on endpapers, 56 colour ill. [2 on covers], 197 ill., 1 map, 1 plan, 1 fig.).

Compared with the catalogue of the same exhibition at Villa Hügel, Essen and Munich (our number 78305), the main difference, apart from a different cover, endpaper illustrations and a Geleitwort, consists in the addition of 23 pieces from Hildesheim itself, numbered nos. 176-198. They range from O.K.- F.I.P. (6 pieces) through the M.K. (2), the N.K. (4), the Saite Period (1), to 16 pieces from the Greco-Roman Period, and they comprise mainly statuary and reliefs.

79592 GOLDSTEIN, Sidney M., Pre-Roman and Early Roman Glass in The Corning Museum of Glass, Corning New York, The Corning Museum of Glass 1979 (20 x 28 cm; 312 p., coloured frontispiece, 12 fig., numerous ill., 36 colour pl., 6 folding pl.).

After a glossary, a bibliography and a preface briefly surveying the history of the collection the author describes in the introduction the various techniques in glass-making and sketches briefly the history of early glass (on account of vessels in the Corning collection), especially its renaissance after 1000 B.C.
Then follows the catalogue of the objects, the more important of which are shown in (colour) ill. and are provided with data and description. We mention the most important sections: Egyptian cast and core-formed objects from the N.K. (Nos. 9-39; fragments 40-122 mainly consisting of vessels; Egyptian cast and core-formed jewelry, amulets and inlays, from the N.K. to the 7th century B.C. (Nos. 123-166); in the section on Hellenistic cast and cut glass from the 4th to 1st centuries B.C. particularly Egyptian amulets (Nos. 335-438), but also more dispersed objects bearing Egyptian motifs or in Egyptian styling, as is also the case in the section on Ptolemaic-Roman mosaic-glass inlay from the 3rd-1st centuries B.C.
The last section which has many ancient Egyptian or Egyptianizing objects is that on faience, Egyptian blue, obsidian and stone.
Extensive concordances at the end of the book. For a major acquisition (illustrated in the book but not included), a head of a XVIII Dynasty king cast in (blue?) glass, see our number 79743.

79593 GORENC, Marcel, Egipat, Zagreb, Arheološki muzej. 1979 (13 x 20 cm; 39 p., 23 ill. [3 in colour], colour ill. on cover); series: Serija vodiči.

"Egypt".
A guide to the Egyptian Collection of the Archaeological Museum in Zagreb.

79594 HESSE, Brian and Robert K. EVANS, A New Permanent Exhibition at the Smithsonian Institution, *Archaeology* 32, No. 3 (May/June 1979) 53-55, with 4 colour ill.

Egypt is well-represented in the new permanent exhibition called Western Civilization: Origins and Traditions, at the National Museum of Natural History and National Museum of Man, departments of the Smithsonian Institution at Washington.

79595 JAMES, T.G.H., An Exodus Overdue, *The British Museum Society Bulletin*, London No. 31 (July 1979), 14-19, with 4 ill. and 1 fig.

Report on the rearrangement of the Egyptian Sculpture Gallery in the British Museum.

79596   [JAMES, T.G.H.], An Introduction to Ancient Egypt, [London], Published for the Trustees of the British Museum by British Museum Publications Limited, [1979] (15.6 x 23.4 cm; 286 p., 3 maps, 3 plans, 1 fig., 94 ill., 16 colour pl.).   Pr. £8.50

This is a revised edition of our number 64130 published under a slightly different title, in a larger format and with more and different illustrations. The revision which i.a. concerns the dates has been carried out by the staff of the Egyptian Department of the British Museum.
J.J.J.

79597   JAMES, T.G.H., A Little Known Library in a Famous Museum, *PLA Report. Post Library Association*, Greenvale, N.Y. 6, No. 1 (Spring 1978), 16-20, with 6 ill.

Article for the general reader on the papyrus and ostraca collection in the British Museum.

79598   Journey to the West. Death and Afterlife in Ancient Egypt. A Catalog of the Exhibition at the Robert H. Lowie Museum of Anthropology. June 22, 1979 - March 3, 1980, The Regents of the University of California, 1979 (21.5 x 25.5 cm; 22 p., 14 ill., 1 map).

Most of the exhibited objects are derived from the excavations by George Reisner for the University of California between 1899 and 1905 (Deir el-Ballas, el-Ahaiwah and Nag' el-Deir) but some are from other excavations of Reisner (Gîza).
In fact this booklet contains an introduction to funerary and more general aspects of ancient Egypt and to the relations between Reisner, Mrs Phoebe Hearst and the University of California.

79599   KOZLOFF, Arielle P., Guessing the Unseen from the Seen, *The Bulletin of The Cleveland Museum of Art*, Cleveland, Ohio 66, No. 9 (December 1979), 334-346, with 23 ill. and 1 fig.

Publication of three pieces in the Cleveland Museum. 1. A tiny ivory giraffe head (CMA 77.146), dated on artistic grounds to the time of Amenophis III and originally part of a cosmetic spoon. 2. A painted limestone wall fragment (CMA 76.51), joining to another fragment (CMA 61.205) published by Cooney (our number 68130) and showing a fourth nome-god and the lower part of a register above it; perhaps it came from the *maru* of Amenophis III on the East bank. 3. A fragment of a feather-garmented human torso with a hand and the wrist with a bracelet (CMA 14.667), suggested to belong to the standing figure of a goddess (Sakhmet?) from the time between the XXth Dynasty and the early Ptolemaic Period.
J.J.J.

79600   KUENY, G., Le culte privé des morts en Égypte antique d'après la collection du Musée de Grenoble, Grenoble, Centre regional de documentation pedagogique, 1979 (17 x 17 cm; 28 p., 12 ill. and 15 slides).

Introduction on funerary beliefs, objects and cult, followed by commentaries to 15 slides which all show funerary objects (including a funerary stela).

79601 KUENY, Gabrielle and Jean YOYOTTE, Grenoble, Musée des Beaux-Arts. Collection égyptienne, Paris, Éditions de la réunion des musées nationaux, 1979 (18 x 24 cm; 219 p., 4 fig., 313 ill., colour ill. on cover) = Inventaire des collections publiques françaises, 23; rev. *BiOr* 37 (1980), 331-333 (M.J. Raven).
Pr. FF 100

This is an up-to-date catalogue of the Egyptian antiquities preserved in the Musée des Beaux-Arts in Grenoble, written by a group of French scholars. It contains apart from the catalogue proper a preface, an introduction by the first mentioned author, and a survey of the history of the collection which includes i.a. the collection of the Comte de Saint-Ferriol.
The objects are in ten groups: reliefs, stelae, statues and statuettes, shawabtis, coffins and mummy masks, amulets and ornaments, vases, various objects, forgeries and imitations (!; Nos. 269-274), and human and animal mummies and fruits; all together 313 numbers among which some famous ones such as the Kuban stela of Ramses II, some coffins of the F.I.P., and parts of the walls of Tuthmosid temples (Nos 1-11).
Each object is carefully described, all technical details added, and each is accompanied by one or more photographs. In a few appendices the objects mentioned by Tresson in his first catalogue of the collection (Grenoble, 1933) that have disappeared or not been included here since not being Egyptian are listed, and some information is presented from the Comte de Saint-Ferriol's travel notebooks that may throw light on the provenance of the objects. Tables of concordances between Tresson's and the present catalogue and indexes on p. 208-217.
J.J.J.

79602 LATTIN, Floyd, The Most Distant of Men. Africa in Antiquity: The Arts of Ancient Nubia and the Sudan, *The Connoisseur*, London 200, No. 804 (February 1979), 98-103, with 12 ill. (5 in colour).

On the exhibition "Africa in Antiquity", for the catalogue of which see our number 78008.

79603 [LILYQUIST, Christine and Edna R. RUSSMANN], Egyptian Art, *in*: *Notable Acquisitions*. 1975-1979. Selected by Philippe de Montebello, Director, New York, The Metropolitan Museum of Art, [1979] (21.9 x 28.2 cm; 96 p., 177 ill. [1 on cover; 34 in colour]).

The authors briefly discuss three notable acquisitions of the last five years: a M.K. royal head (Acc. No. 1978.204), a N.K. cosmetic implement (Acc. No. 1977.169), and the schist bust of a man, of the XXVIth Dynasty (Acc. No. 1976.325). All objects are depicted.

79604 LIMME, Luc, Egyptische stèles, Brussel, Koninklijke Musea voor Kunst en Geschiedenis, 1979 (16 x 23.5 cm; 56 p., 21 ill., colour ill. and plan on cover) = Wegwijzers voor de Egyptische Afdeling, 4.
Pr. BF 100

Publication of twenty stelae (actually no. 2 is a false door) preserved in the Royal Museum of Art and History in Brussels, preceded by an introduction. The booklet is intended for the general visitor of the collection. All types of stelae are represented, ranging in time from King Den to the first century B.C. Each of them is briefly described, the technical data and bibliography added in small print, while of each a clear photograph is given (with no. 9 a second one of a detail).
There is also a French version: "Stèles égyptiennes" = Guides du Département Égyptien, 4.

J.J.J.

79605 LIPIŃSKA, Jadwiga, The Egyptian Collection in the National Museum in Havana, *in*: *Acts 1st ICE*, 425-426.

Short description of the Egyptian collection in the National Museum in Havana and a note on a small collection in Santiago de Cuba. Their publication in the Corpus Antiquitatum Aegyptiacarum series is announced.

79606 LISE, Giorgio, Museo archeologico. Raccolta egizia, [Milano], Electa Editrice, [1979] (23.5 x 25 cm; 245 p., 518 ill. [many in colour] and 33 fig. on 164 pl.); series: Musei e gallerie di Milano.

After an introduction on the Egyptian collection in the Castello Sforzesco in Milan follows the catalogue proper. The objects are presented in the catalogue number order and are provided with data such as inventory numbers (old and new), provenance, bibliography (if present) and a description. The collection comprises: (fragments of) sarcophagi, mummies (nos. 1-60); stelae, mainly from the N.K. (61-67); papyri, such as B.D. or mythological, from the N.K. to the Ptolemaic Period (68-74); funerary cones and seal impressions (75-79); sculpture, among which a statue of Amenemhat III and various Graeco-Roman material (80-102); canopic jars (mostly only the lids) (103-118); two headrests (119-120); various inscribed fragments and objects (121-125); vessels of various types and from various periods (126-156); bronze statuettes (157-324); scarabs among which some heart scarabs (325-392); amulets (393-762); jewellery (763-795); shabtis (796-949); varia (950-971). An appendix to the plates shows some reproductions of a previous publication of a coffin from the Saite Period (Cat. No. 6) and of a mythological papyrus (Cat. No. 71) and drawings of funerary cones, amulets, and pottery types.

At the end a hieroglyphic index to the proper names, a concordance table, an introduction to the Egyptian chronology, a selected bibliography, and a glossary with references to various catalogue nos. See already our number 77486.

79607 The Luxor Museum of Ancient Egyptian Art. Catalogue, Cairo, American Research Center in Egypt, 1979 (21.5 x 27.8 cm; XVI + 219 p., 2 maps, 2 plans, 167 ill., 22 colour ill., frontispiece, 2 colour ill. on cover); rev. *BiOr* 38 (1981), 53-55 (Cl. Vandersleyen); *Serapis* 5, No. 2 (1980), 55-59 (Peter A. Piccione).

The catalogue of the Luxor Museum (opened December 1975), prefaced by Bernard V. Bothmer, has for the most part been written by James E. Romano, with contributions by Klaus Parlasca (Hellenistic, Roman and Early Christian objects) and J. Michael Rogers (Islamic pottery). It describes about 150 objects, although the numbers of the catalogue go up to 337, the gaps in the numbering being reserved for later additions to the collection.
All objects are minutely described, material, provenance and date are mentioned, as well as bibliographical references, so far as extant. Moreover, each object is represented by at least one, in some instances by two or more photographs, the more important ones in colour.
The objects range from the Prehistoric to the Mamluk Period and represent a large number of types: sculpture (reliefs and statues), paintings, objects of minor arts, for funerary and daily use, etc. Several of them are well known, e.g. some pieces from the treasure of Tôd, the relief of Amenophis II as an archer, the relief with the acrobats from the "Chapelle Rouge", the painting of Amenophis III formerly on display in the tomb of Ramose, some objects from Tutankhamon's tomb and a talatat wall. Others are less famous, such as a hitherto unpublished standard-bearing statue of a High Priest of Khonsu called Ramose. Several of them came from the Sobek temple at Dahamsa.
On p. 211-214 concordances.
In 1981 there has appeared a German edition: Das Museum für altägyptische Kunst in Luxor, Katalog, Mainz, Verlag Philipp von Zabern, (Pr. DM 58), in the foreword of which Bernard V. Bothmer states that the translation follows almost literally the text of the original, but that some corrections and bibliographical additions have been made.
A small-size booklet with essentially the same contents has already appeared in English, as well as in Arabic, German and French in 1978: Guidebook. The Luxor Museum of Ancient Egyptian Art, Cairo, Egyptian Antiquities Organization. Arab Republic of Egypt.
J.J.J.

79608 MESSIHA, Hishmat and Mohamed A. ELHITTA, Mallawi Antiquities Museum. A Brief Description, Cairo, General Organization for Government Printing Offices, 1979 (20 x 27.5 cm; [IV +] 36 p., folding plan, 32 pl., frontispiece); at head of title: Arab Republic of Egypt, Ministry of Culture. Antiquities Service.

After an introduction dealing with the neighbourhood of Mallawi (Ashmûnein, Tûna el-Gebel, Antinoe, etc.) from where the objects in the Mallawi Museum came the halls of the museum are briefly described. There follows a list of the major objects, arranged after categories, each with a number, a very brief description, its date and provenance. Some of them are represented on the (not too clear) plates.
Most objects date from the Graeco-Roman Period and came from Tûna el-Gebel. From earlier periods we mention; the coffins of 'Iy-m-ḥtp (Nos. 559-560; from Meir, Late Period); the double statue of Pepi-ʿankh-ib and his wife (No. 565; from Meir, VIth Dynasty); a N.K. royal head (No. 570; from Ashmûnein); the wooden coffin of 'Itf-ib (No. 566; M.K.) and other coffins from that period (Nos. 567-569), all from Asyût.
Indexes p. 27-34.

J.J.J.

79609 MUNRO, Eleanor, Ancient Nubia's Old Art with a New Past, *Art in America*, New York 67, No. 3 (May-June 1979), 116-119, with 9 ill.

On the exhibition "Africa in Antiquity" held at the Brooklyn Museum, New York. For the catalogue, see our number 78008.

79610 Nubië aan de Nijl. Voorportaal van Afrika. Haags Gemeentemuseum. 22 september - 25 november 1979, [Den Haag, Haags Gemeentemuseum, 1979] (21 x 29.5 cm; 64 p., 1 chart, 1 map, 37 colour ill. [1 on cover]).

Abbreviated version in Dutch of our number 78008, which presents only the catalogue proper.
An introduction on the various cultures and periods of Nubia is included. The catalogue briefly describes all 295 pieces. The only illustrations are a number of colour ill. from the original catalogue.

79611 Ontmoeting met het Oude Egypte. Werk van de 19e eeuwse kunstenaar David Roberts, [Leiden], Rijksmuseum van Oudheden, [1979] (20.6 x 29 cm; 71 p., colour ill. on cover).

Catalogue of an exhibition of coloured lithographs by the famous painter of architecture David Roberts (1796-1864), who visited Egypt and Nubia in 1838-'39 and made there more than 300 sketches which he afterwards has worked out. Lithographs made after them by Louis Haghe were published in six volumes between 1842 and 1849. There were two editions, one in which the lithographs were coloured by hand. The exhibition shows 55 examples of these, mostly representing buildings from Egypt and Nubia.
The catalogue deals with the life of the painter, his travels and the edition of his lithographs, and describes each of the representations. On cover Roberts' coloured view on Philae.

J.J.J.

79612 Pelizaeus-Museum Hildesheim, [Braunschweig], Westermann, [1979]
(12.8 x 18.7 cm; 128 p., 1 map, 2 plans, 6 fig., 55 ill., 16 colour
ill., colour ill. on cover); series: Museum.   Pr. DM 8

This booklet, written by Arne Eggebrecht and the members of his
staff, presents an introduction to the Egyptian collection in
Hildesheim for the general public. It does not give a catalogue of
the objects but discusses special topics,illustrating them with
objects from the collection. The various chapters are signed by
the initials of the authors. After an introduction about the foun-
der and the history of the museum the first chapter gives an abstract from the diary of an excavator, with comments. There follow
chapters on: the pyramids and their building techniques; pharaohs
and officials; tombs (particularly the mastaba of Uhemka); the
Thoth chapel of Ptolemaeus I; Greek sculpture in Egypt; textiles;
gold and jewellery; daily life and festivals; writing and language;
figures of divinities; radiological investigation of mummies; restoration problems; the educative function of the museum.
                                                              J.J.J.

79613 PÉREZ DIE, Marie Carmen, La Collection égyptienne du Musée Archéologique National de Madrid (Espagne), *in*: *Acts 1st ICE*, 515-518.

The author briefly presents the Egyptian collection of the Nationa.
Archaeological Museum in Madrid.

79614 ROOT, Margaret Cool, Faces of Immortality. Egyptian Mummy Masks,
Painted Portraits, and Canopic Jars in the Kelsey Museum of Archae-
logy. Kelsey Museum of Archaeology, The University of Michigan, An.
Arbor, September 20, 1979 - February 17, 1980, [Ann Arbor, Kelsey
Museum of Archaeology, The University of Michigan, 1979](17.5 x 27
cm; XI + 63 p., 1 map, 64 ill.[1 on cover]).

Although the majority of the pieces is formed by mummy or portrait
from the Graeco-Roman Period some pieces date from Pharaonic times
canopic jars or lids from the M.K. the N.K. and the T.I.P., and
two mummy masks of which one from the Late Period - Ptolemaic Period and the other a minature plaster mask from the M.K. The object
are presented in photograph with data and description.
In the introduction the author surveys the development of the mumm
mask from the O.K. onwards and the function of the mask, the ba an
canopic jars as means for exact likeness.
Bibliography at the end.

79615 ROSENBLATT, Arthur, Dendur in New York, *BMMA* 36 (1978-1979), 65-80
with 20 ill. (2 in colour) and 2 cross-sections.

The author relates the story of the removal of the Dendur Temple
from Nubia and its re-erection at the Metropolitan Museum, New
York.
See also our number 79576.

79616 Sahara. 10.000 Jahre zwischen Weide und Wüste, [Köln], Museen der Stadt Köln, [1978?] (21 x 27.5 cm; 472 p., numerous ill., fig., maps and pl. [many in colour]); rev. *L'Anthropologie* 83 (1979), 147-148 (M.-C. C[hamla]).

This is the catalogue to an exhibition on the Sahara held in Köln, 1978 to which many authors contributed. Among the articles there are some of interest to Egyptology: Henri Lhote: Die Felsbilder der Sahara, p. 70-97; Paul Huard, Die Felsbilder des Tibesti-Gebirges, 272-278; Pavel Červíček, Felsbilder Oberägyptens und Nubiens, 279-289; and Manfred Weber, Die alten Ägypter und die Wüste, 334-340 (the dangerous desert; hunting in the desert; economical and political significance).

79617 SCHNEIDER, Hans D., Taffeh. Rond de wederopbouw van een Nubische tempel. Uitgave ter gelegenheid van de inauguratie van de Tempel van Taffeh in het Rijksmuseum van Oudheden te Leiden op 4 april 1979. Ingeleid door H.K.H. Prinses Beatrix, 's Gravenhage, Staatsuitgeverij, 1979 (20 x 27 cm; 130 p., 1 map, 2 maps, 2 plans, 4 fig., 152 ill. [95 in colour], colour frontispiece, ill. on cover).

This lavishly illustrated book has been published on the occasion of the resurrection of the Tâfa temple in the Museum of Antiquities in Leiden. This Nubian temple has been donated to the Netherlands by the Egyptian government.
The first chapter, followed by an English translation, contains a summary of the study. Chapters 2 and 3 deal with the Nubian history till the end of the Meroitic Empire and the Nile dams; chapter 4 with the post-Meroitic history and the settlement of Shokan excavated by the Dutch; chapter 5 with the paintings in the church of Abdallah Nirqi. Chapters 5-8 are devoted to the background and surroundings of the Tâfa temple: Isis and the Dodekaschoinos, Kertassi and Taphis. In chapter 9 the travellers who passed Tâfa and described it in their journals are dealt with. The last three chapters discuss the temple itself in detail, its use from A.D. 427 as a Christian church, and its salvage and reconstruction in the Leiden Museum.
At the end a chronological table, a bibliography, and a brief survey of the history, collection and exhibitions of the museum.
J.J.J.

79618 STEINMANN, Frank, Drei verlorene Stücke des Leipziger Ägyptischen Museums, *ZÄS* 106 (1979), 168-175, with 1 fig. and 2 pl.

Veröffentlichung von Fotos und Zeichnungen, mit Übersetzungen und Besprechung, der folgenden Stücke. 1. Inv.-Nr. 5143. Pyramidion des Neuen Reiches, angefertigt von einem Thotnufer und wohl als "Grabstele" verwendet. Kalkstein, Höhe 54 cm.
2. Inv.-Nr. 399. Denkstein der 19. Dyn., gestiftet von einem Chonsemwâset. Darstellung der Prozessionsbarke des Amun; vor ihr Ramses III. Kalkstein, H. 37, Breite 50 cm.
3. Inv.-Nr. 5060. Grabstele der Spätzeit (wohl spätsaitisch-ptole-

mäisch) für einen Arzt. Dargestellt ist die Verehrung des Osiris und des Apis. Kalkstein, H. 57 cm. *M. Heerma v. Voss*

79619 STEWART, H.M., Egyptian Stelae, Reliefs and Paintings from the Petrie Collection. Part Two: Archaic Period to Second Intermediate Period, Warminster, Aris & Phillips Ltd., *[1979]* (27.5 x 29.7 cm; VIII + 44 p., 41 pl. *[a few double, 2 folding.])*; rev. *Acta Archaeologica Academiae Scientiarum Hungaricae* 32 (1980), 475 (L. Castiglione); *CdE* LV, No. 109-110 (1980), 161-162 (Herman de Meulenaere).
Pr. £15

Sequel to our number 76747.
Proceeding the publication of the stelae etc. in the Petrie collection, the author this time deals with 165 numbers, from the Archaic Period to the S.I.P. They are, i.a., 13 small stelae from the 1st Dynasty and 2 from the 2nd (from Helwân); relief fragments from the Sun-temple of Neuserre; a fragment of royal annals, probably from the Palermo Stone; relief fragments from O.K. tombs; 3 portions of P.T.; fragments of early M.K. reliefs from Koptos and from the pyramid temple of Sesostris II at el-Lâhûn; private stelae of all periods, e.g. that of Mentuhotep, a nomarch of Hermonthis (see our number 62227) and a late XIIth Dynasty stela with a hieratic inscription consisting of names and titles (see our number 71311); fragments of a stela of king Rahotep, from the S.I.P.; a few offering tables from the O. and M.K.
Each object is carefully described, while all data are listed and the text translated. Most of them are given in line drawings, one also in photograph and two in photograph only.
J.J.J.

79620 STUART, P., Rijksmuseum van Oudheden, *Nederlandse Rijksmusea*, 's Gravenhage 99 (1977), 1979, 285-298, with 8 ill.

Apart from the acquisition of four shawabtis, the Egyptian collection was enriched by an Amarna relief with a representation of a couple of horses and charioteers, a limestone false-door from the Roman Period and a limestone relief bearing the cartouches of emperor Nero.
There is also a short report on the third excavation season in the tomb of Horemheb at Saqqâra.

79621 WILDUNG, Dietrich, Staatliche Sammlung ägyptischer Kunst, *Münchner Jahrbuch der bildenden Kunst*, München 30 (1979), 199-206, with 9 ill.

Description of the accessions to the collection in the years 1977 and 1978. Among the more important are: a tripartite tomb niche from the O.K. (ÄS 6288); a cult statuette of a crocodile god from the M.K. (ÄS 6080); and a fragment from the face of one of the colossi of Akhnaton from East Karnak (ÄS 6290).

79622 WILKINSON, Charles K., Egyptian Wall Paintings: The Metropolitan Museum's Collection of Facsimiles = *BMMA* 36, No. 4 (Spring 1979), 56 p., 40 colour ill. (1 on cover), 31 ill., 1 plan and 2 maps.

After a foreword by Philippe de Montebello, director of the Metropolitan Museum of Art, the author, himself one of the members of the graphic section of the Museum's Egyptian Expedition, presents in a running story the background to the fine collection of facsimiles now on display in the Museum.

79623 [ZIEGLER, C.], Les visites éducatives dans les collections égyptiennes du Musée du Louvre, [Paris, 1979](15 x 21 cm; portfolio containing six loose leaf booklets with text pages and plans; colour ill. on cover); series: Dossiers de la direction des Musées de France.

Six loose leaf booklets, one with the introduction entitled "Champollion et la Pierre de Rosette" (with drawings illustrating the plan and lay-out of a mastaba, a chronological table, and informations about books, slides and postcards), and five, each dealing with a special subject: Le Nil, la vie rurale et fluviale; Le pharaon et ses fonctionnaires. Les grands figures d'histoire d'Égypte; Les coutumes funéraires; Les dieux d'Égypte et leur demeure; La vie quotidienne. The booklets contain (on a few loose pages) a very brief introduction on the subject and a catalogue of some objects in the exhibition relating to it, while on two folding plans (one for each floor) their present place is indicated.
                                                                    J.J.J.

d. Monuments

See also our numbers 79011; 79065; 79084; 79371; 79519; 79523; 79558; 79559; 79590; 79611; 79612; 79615; 79617; 79697; 79788 and 79959.

79624 ARNOLD, Dieter und Dorothea, Der Tempel Qasr el-Sagha. Aufnahmen unter Mitarbeit von Andreas Brodbeck, Mainz am Rhein, Verlag Philipp von Zabern, [1979](27 x 35.5 cm; 41 p., 23 fig. including 1 map, 29 pl. [2 folding]) = Archäologische Veröffentlichungen. Deutsches Archäologisches Institut Abteilung Kairo, 27; rev. *BiOr* 32 (1981), 46-48 (Alexander Badawy).   Pr. DM 84

In the first chapter Dieter Arnold describes the various architectonic elements of the temple of Qasr el-Sagha, and its vicinity, a few km north of the Birket Qarûn. In the following chapters 2-6 he respectively dates the temple to the classical period of the M.K. (reigns of Sesostris II-III), discusses its building type, explains the significance of the temple on account of its site and its scenes as a magical barrier against the Libyan desert, and briefly describes the nearby settlement, as well as the finds in the temple, the ceramics excepted. These last are described and

discussed by Dorothea Arnold, as well as the ceramics from the settlement near the temple and from the L-shaped quai.
Brief general index.

79625 BONHÊME, Marie-Ange, Un document sur la religion du Nouvel Empire égyptien: la Chapelle Rouge d'Hatshepsout à Karnak, *Revue de l'histoire des religions*, Paris 195 (1979), 117-119.

Synthèse d'une communication partant de notre No. 77453.

79626 KUHLMANN, K.P., Der Felstempel des Eje bei Akhmim, *MDAIK* 35 (1979) 165-188, with 1 plan, 1 fig. and 9 pl.

The rock-chapel of Min at el-Salâmûni near Akhmîm, from the time of Eye, has never been adequately published (see Porter-Moss, V, 17-18). The author has devoted to it one short campaign. He discusses here its position and name ($\underline{T}zt$), earlier publications, its architecture in which two phases can be distinguished, its date (Phase I: Eye and his architect Nakhtmin; phase II: the priest H. Maakheru, possibly from the XXVIth Dynasty).The decoration is described and five graffiti are discussed (the names of Tuthmosis I and Ramses II occur).
Then the author devotes sections to the origin and function of the sanctuary (probably a cult-place for the quarrymen) and to some details, the quarries of el-Salâmûni, the supposed name of a goddess *Tin-ins-Mḥyt* (see our number 79813), the goddess ꜥprt-st, the possible origin of Eye from Akhmîm. A summary on p. 187-188.

J.J.J

79627 KUHLMANN, K.P., Der Tempel Ramses II. in Abydos. Vorbericht über eine Neuaufnahme, *MDAIK* 35 (1979), 189-193, with 1 fig. and 2 pl.

Report on the preparations for a new publication of the temple of Ramses II in Abydos. The three sections deal with the cleaning of the temple, a few corrections and additions to the informations Porter-Moss VI, 33-41 about the decoration, and remarks concerning the architecture.

J.J.J

79628 LACAU, Pierre et Henri CHEVRIER, avec la collaboration de M.-A. BONHÊME et M. GITTON, Une chapelle d'Hatchepsout à Karnak. II. [Le Caire], Le Service des Antiquités de l'Égypte avec la collaboration de l'Institut français d'Archéologie orientale du Caire, 1979 (portfolio, 34 x 50 cm, containing 24 loose plates).

Sequel to our number 77453.
Plate 1 presents a scheme of the four exterior walls of the "Red Chapel" with the numbers of the blocks; pl. 2-13 rather small photographs of these blocks so far as preserved, arranged in registers provided with indications about their place on the walls; 13-18 of the vestibule, 19-24 of the sanctuary.

J.J.J

79629 LETELLIER, Bernadette, La cour à péristyle de Thoutmosis IV à Karnak, *BSFE* No 84 (mars 1979), 33-49, with 5 ill., and 2 fig. on a folding plate.

Des blocs et fragments de grès extraits du IIIe pylône depuis assez longtemps ont permis à l'auteur de reconstituer un péristyle. La moitié des blocs, sculptés sur une de leurs faces, composent six parois, correspondant à la couverture intérieure des murs. Un autre quart appartenait à 38 piliers: l'angle N-E devant le IVe pylône en garde deux en place; estimés à un total de 80, ils étaient disposés sur deux rangs. La surface empiétait sur la future grande salle hypostyle. Du monument ne subsisterait que la moitié Ouest, démontée en priorité pour construire le IIIe pylône. Le dépliant donne le réassemblage des deux parois principales. Thoutmosis IV, de taille héroïque, y présente à Amon des troupeaux et des offrandes; des tableaux plus banals couvrent deux registres superposés. Un panneau est resté inachevé, enfin Tiâa, mère du Roi, accompagne son fils dans une scène de fondation. Ces parois, plus épaisses au sommet, durent s'appuyer à des murs en calcaire, datant de Thoutmosis II, qui d'après leur ligne de dédicace conservée délimitaient une cour. Thoutmosis IV aurait tapissé de grès la cour de calcaire, matériau qui avait la préférence au début de la dynastie, et aurait ajouté des colonnades.
J. Custers

79630 LETELLIER, Bernadette, La cour à péristyle de Thoutmosis IV à Karnak (et la "cour des Fêtes" de Thoutmisis II), *in*: *Hommages Sauneron* I, 51-71, with 7 fig. (2 folding) and 3 pl.

Study of a sandstone monument of Tuthmosis IV, blocks of which came from the 3rd pylon and are preserved in the "Musée en plein air". Remains of its pillars are still in situ at the N.W. corner of the 4th pylon. Of the building, a court with an inner peristyle, about 944 blocks and 3 monolithic pillars have been identified. The author describes her reconstruction of the wall scenes, the pillars and other architectural elements, and the plan of the building which poses several problems. She suggests that it was constructed within an earlier court of Tuthmosis II, the sandstone blocks covering its inner walls; no remains of an outer wall of the later king have been discovered.
J.J.J.

79631 LORTON, David, Report on Research on Theban Tombs of the New Kingdom 1976-1977, *JSSEA* 9 (1978-1978), 27-31.

The author reports on the progress of his preparations for publishing Theban tombs on the basis of Davies' notebooks and the material assembled by Säve-Söderbergh. He has chosen for the first publication the tombs nos. 12, 13 and 247.
J.J.J.

79632 PARKER, Richard A., Jean LECLANT, Jean-Claude GOYON, The Edifice of Taharqa by the Sacred Lake of Karnak. With translations from the French by Claude Crozier-Brelot, Providence, Brown University Press /London, Lund Humphries, [1979](20.5 x 37 cm; X + 95 p., 1 plan, 20 fig., 44 pl.)= Brown Egyptological Studies, 8; rev. *ZDMG* 131 (1981), 202 (J[ürgen] v[on] B[eckerath]).

Pr. £ 30

The publication is the outcome of cooperation between the three authors, the share of each being explained by Parker in his preface.
In the first two chapters Leclant describes the history of the discovery and study of the edifice and its architecture. He presents hypotheses about the disposition of the superstructure now largely destroyed and discusses the reused blocks from which the edifice had been built.
Then follows the main chapter (p. 11-79) on the decoration, by Goyon. He studies the scenes and the inscriptions, which are given in hieroglyphs with translation and footnotes. From this chapter one is able to follow the progress of the ritual through the subterranean rooms. The last chapter (80-86), also by Goyon, presents an interpretation of the edifice. He i.a. remarks that nowhere the name of the Divine Votaress is mentioned; Taharqa alone performs the rites, the aim of which was the oneness of the divinity through the fusion of Amon and Re as creator and protector of the universe.
For the plates 1-30 with photographs and drawings of the scenes and texts Parker is responsible, while Goyon is for pl. 31-44, on which texts with parallels from other buildings are presented. Indexes on p. 93-95.

J.J.J.

79633 SETON-WILLIAMS, M.V., Ptolemaic Temples, [Cambridge, privately published, 1978](16 x 24 cm; [II] + 53 p., 1 colour ill. on cover, frontispiece = map, 4 ill., 1 fig., 9 plans).

In this booklet the author presents the most prominent Greco-Roman sanctuaries in Egypt. First she sketches the history of the Ptolemies and briefly introduces the art and architecture of the period. Then she gives descriptions of and information on the various temples: the Hathor temple at Dendera with special sections on the kiosk of the Union with the Disc and the Osiris chapels on the roof, and on the festival of Dendera; the Montu temple at Medamud; the temples of Ptah and of Mut in Asheru at Karnak; the small Ptolemaic temple in the Medinet Habu complex; that of Deir el-Medîna; Esna; Edfu; Kom Ombo; and the temple complex at Philae including the kiosk and the temple of Hathor.
Brief glossary of architectural terms at the end.

79634 SIMPSON, William Kelly, Topographical Notes on Giza Mastabas, *in Festschrift Elmar Edel*, 489-499, with 3 fig.

The author presents notes and comments to a large number of tombs all excavated by Reisner in the Western and Eastern cemeteries at Gîza. The remarks refer to the following numbers: 2337X, 2360N,

2341A, 5080 (Seshemnofer II), 7101 (Qar), 7102 (Idu), 7310-7320, 7411 (Kayemthenent), 7530 (queen Mersyankh III), 7837-7843 (Ankhmare), 7911 (*Ny-ḫȝswt-nswt*).They are partly additions to Porter-Moss, 2nd edition, III.1, and partly additions and corrections to the author's recent publications (the tombs of Qar, Idu and Mersyankh III).

J.J.J.

79635 TADEMA, Auke A. and Bob TADEMA SPORRY, Vallei der koningen. De graven van de farao's, Haarlem, Fibula-van Dishoeck, [1979](22.5 x 29.5 cm; 176 p., 11 fig., 3 plans, 2 maps, 165 fig., 28 p. with colour ill., map on endpapers, colour frontispiece, colour ill. on cover).

This is a book on the Valley of the Kings whose text, intended for the general public, does not aim at any original scientific value. Apart from the present state of the Valley of the Kings short chapters deal with the Valley of the Queens, Deir el-Medîna and the royal mortuary temples, while others are devoted to legal and illegal finds in the valley, the tomb robberies, mummification, the royal funeral, the royal mummies, and the recent decay of the tombs.
The space occupied by the text is, however, small compared by that of the numerous illustrations, the authors' own photographs, many of which show views and details not found in any other book. Of some importance for the egyptologist are also the drawings of the tombs on the last pages accompanying the data for each royal tomb.

J.J.J.

79636 The Temple of Khonsu - Volume I. Plates 1-110. Scenes of King Herihor in the Court. With Translations of Texts. By the Epigraphic Survey, Chicago, Illinois, The Oriental Institute of the University of Chicago, [1979](portfolio containing 2 unnumbered pl. with plans and elevations + 110 pl. [36 folding], and a booklet: 23.3 x 30 cm; XXVIII + 55 p.)=The University of Chicago Oriental Institute Publications. Volume 100; rev. *AJA* 85 (1981), 94-95 (William Kelly Simpson).   Pr. $ 90

In the preface of the booklet that accompanies the plates Edward F. Wente first states that the present publication is, more than any other of the Epigraphic Survey, the result of collective contribution by many (see list of names on p. VII). Work on the temple has begun in 1935 and was carried on, with interruptions, until 1973. Then Wente deals with some points of the technique used in drawing the plates. The major part of the preface is taken by what Wente calls "just a few provisory remarks concerning the possible historical significance of the scenes reproduced in this volume." He i.a. discusses whether Paiankh was Herihor's son (probably not), the position of Herihor's wife Nuteme, his origin (Libyan?), the date of the construction of Amon's sacred barge with Phoenician timber, the nature of Herihor's kingship (he probably remained high priest)(see also our number 79438). At the end remarks on

reused blocks in the court, some of which came from the mortuary temple of Amenophis III (see pl. 110).
The second half of the booklet (p. 1-55) contains translations of and commentary on the texts of the scenes.
The plates bear, apart from plans and three photographs (nos 1 and 2), drawings of all scenes, executed in the best tradition of the Epigraphic Survey.

J.J.J.

79637 VALBELLE, Dominique, La porte de Tibère dans le complexe religieux de Médamoud, *in*: Hommages Sauneron 1, 73-85, with 4 fig. and 1 pl.

Study on the remaining blocks of the Gate of Tiberius in the enclosure of the temple of Madâmûd. The author indicates their original position and describes the scenes. It appears that apart from Montu a "very great bull" was venerated.

J.J.J.

79638 WILD, Henri, La tombe de Néfer.hotep (I) et Neb.néfer à Deir el-Médîna [No 6] et autres documents les concernant. II, [Le Caire], Publications de l'Institut français d'Archéologie orientale, [1979] (27.5 x 36 cm; [IV p.], 35 pl. [30 folding]) = Mémoires publiés par les membres de l'Institut français d'Archéologie orientale du Caire, 103/2.

The present, first published volume contains drawings of the scenes so far as still visible in Theban Tomb No. 6, which belonged to the chief workman Neferhotep I and his son and successor Nebnufer. Where possible the author has completed the scenes and text with dotted lines.
The volume contains also drawings of some related objects: the pyramidions of tomb 6 (pls 27 and 29) and tomb 216, of Neferhotep II (pls. 28 and 30); offering tables of all three people (pl. 31); a basin of Nebnufer and Neferhotep (II?) (pl. 32); remains of a *snt*-board of Neferhotep I and Nebnufer (?) [=Pusch, our number 79762, p. 295-296] and a shabti of the latter (pl. 33); a fragmentary stela for Reshef of Nebnufer (pl. 34); various fragmentary inscriptions mentioning these persons.
The text to this volume will be published as volume 103/1 of the series.

J.J.J.

79639 WINTER, Erich, Das Kalabsha-Tor in Berlin, *Jahrbuch Preussischer Kulturbesitz*, Berlin 14 (1979), 59-71, with 1 plan and 4 ill.

In this lecture delivered on account of the official inauguration of the Kalâbsha Gate rebuilt in the Berlin Museum the author relates the recent history of the monument that was discovered as filling blocks of the sanctuary of the temple. He also describes its architecture and, particularly, some of the inscriptions, in which Augustus is called "the god."

J.J.J.

79640 ZIVIE, Alain-Pierre, La tombe de Pached à Deir el-Médineh [No 3], Le Caire, Publications de l'Institut français d'Archéologie orientale, [1979] (27.5 x 35.5 cm; [IV +]144 p., 1 folded plan, 2 folded fig., 35 pl., colour frontispiece) = Mémoires publiés par les Membres de l'Institut français d'Archéologie orientale du Caire, 99.

Publication of Theban Tomb No. 3, that of Pashed, which is one of the most famous in Deir el-Medîna.
The author has divided his study into an introduction and six chapters. Chapter 1 deals with the discovery of the tomb and early studies of it, particularly the unpublished copies of the wall-scenes by Hay. Chapter 2 presents an architectural description of the tomb. Chapter 3 is devoted to the decoration of the innermost or funerary chamber. After introductory remarks i.a. about the (rapid but beautiful) decoration in general and the epigraphy the scenes are described with some somments. They are mostly of a religious character, i.a. B.D. chapters 78, 180 and 181, but there is also a scene with 16 persons in three registers.
In chapter 4 the author studies the fragments of the limestone sarcophagus, also inscribed with chapters of the B.D., e.g. chapters 1, 17 and the second part of chapter 125 (the "Declaration of Innocence"). Chapter 5 deals with some objects seen or found in the tomb and others which perhaps may come from it.
In chapter 6 the author presents his study on Pashed himself and his tomb; the name Pashed; his family (with general remarks on the terms expressing family relations); the problem of Theban Tomb No. 326, generally ascribed to the same Pashed, but without sufficient proof; Pashed's career (with remarks on the recruitment of the workmen) and the date of the tomb (probably Ramses II).
Index on p. 135-138. On the plates photographs of the tomb and its decoration as well as reproductions of Hay's copies of texts and scenes and photographs of the sarcophagus fragments and a shabti.
J.J.J.

CEDAE

For reasons of completeness we add the following information concerning the Collection scientifique of the CEDAE.
In the series of the graffiti there appeared so far:
E. Bresciani, Graffiti démotiques du Dodécaschoene (AEB 69087; Pr. LE 4.50)
Graffiti de la montagne thébaine:
I, 1 (AEB 70116; Pr. LE 14.25); I, 2 (AEB 71119; Pr. LE 5.25); I, 3 (AEB 73156; Pr. LE 4.50); I, 4 (AEB 73157; Pr. LE 6); I, 5 (in preparation).
II, 1 (AEB 70186; Pr. LE 4.50); II, 2 (AEB 71040; Pr. LE 3); II, 3 (AEB 73422; Pr. LE 2.25); II, 4 (AEB 73423; Pr. LE 3.375); II, 5 and 6 see our numbers 79246 and 79247.
III, 1 (AEB 70118; Pr. LE 4.50); III, 2 (AEB 70118; Pr. LE 6); III, 3 (AEB 71121; Pr. LE 4); III, 4 (AEB 73628; Pr. LE 4.50); III, 5 (AEB 73629; Pr. LE 4.50); III, 6 (AEB 74629; Pr. LE 4.50); III, 7 see our number 79257.

IV, 1 (AEB 70117; Pr. LE 3.75); IV, 2 (AEB 71122; Pr. LE 2.50);
IV, 3 (AEB 73626; Pr. LE 1.50); IV, 4 (AEB 73627; Pr. LE 1.50);
IV, 5 (AEB 74628; Pr. LE 0.75); IV, 6 in preparation.
In the series of the Theban temples:
Ch. Kuentz, La face sud du massif est du pylone de Ramsès II à Louqsor (AEB 71340; Pr. LE 3.75).
Ramesseum I (AEB 73274; Pr. LE 7.50); IV see below; VI (AEB 74259; Pr. LE 5.25); IX, 1-2 in the press; X see below; XI in the press.
In the series of the Nubian temples:
Grand Temple d'Abou Simbel I, 1 in the press; I, 2 in preparation; II see below; III, 1-2 see below; IV in the press.
Amada I (AEB 68006; Pr. LE 3.75); II (AEB 68059; Pr. LE 6); III (AEB 68060; Pr. LE 2.25); IV (AEB 68021; Pr. LE 6); V (AEB 68118) out of print.
Dandour I (AEB 73006; Pr. LE 7.50); II see below; III see below.
Derr I in the press.
el-Lessiya (AEB 68167) out of print; II (AEB 68005; Pr. LE 3).
Gerf-Hussein I (AEB 78390; Pr. LE 16); II (AEB 74727; Pr. LE 4.50); III see below; IV in the press.
Kalabscha: Daumas, Ouabet (AEB 70145; Pr. LE 1.50); de Meulenaere-Dewachter, La chapelle ptolémaïque, fasc. 1-2 (AEB 70386; Pr. LE 4.50).
In the series Theban Tombs, Valley of the Queens:
Hassanein-Nelson, Tombe du Prince Amon-(her)-khepchef (No. 55): see below.
The publications of the tombs of prince Khaemouaset (No. 44) and the tomb of Ta-nedjemy (No. 33) are in preparation, as well as one of the tombs of the nobles: Sennefer (T.T. No. 96).
All publications of the CEDAE which have so far appeared are listed in their catalogue No. 2 (December 1981), which also lists their forthcoming publications (a price-list is added). The publications can be ordered directly from or exchanged through M. Christian Leblanc, chargé des Publications, Centre d'études et de documentation sur l'ancienne Egypte, 3, Avenue El-Adel Abou Bakr, Carrefour El-Malek el-Afdah, Zamalek, Le Caire (Adresse télégraphique: Arcocentre).

79641 ALY, M., F.-A. HAMID et Ch. LEBLANC, avec la collaboration de S. AUFRÈRE et de A. CHERIF, Le temple de Dandour. II. Dessins, Le Caire, Centre d'études et de documentation sur l'ancienne Egypte, 1979 (21 x 27 cm; portfolio containing V + 16 p., 81 pl. comprising 1 map, 1 plan, 1 ill. and fig. [many folding]); at head of title: Collection scientifique.

The volume contains the drawings of the temple of Dendûr, now in the Metropolitan Museum of Art, New York.
After a preface by Ch. Desroches Noblecourt and Chehata Adam Mohamed the drawings of the various parts of the temple are presented: B. the monumental gate; C. the facade of the pronaos;

D. the South exterior wall of the temple proper; F. the gate of
the facade of the pronaos and G. the pronaos; H. the gate in the
South wall of the pronaos; J. the gate of the antechamber; L.
the gate of the sanctuary; and M. the sanctuary. At the end a
table of concordances between the references on the key-plan,
the drawings in this volume and the photographs in volume III
(our number 79646).

79642   DESROCHES NOBLECOURT, Ch., S. DONADONI, E. EDEL, avec la collaboration de Ch. NIMS, P. CLÈRE, A. BADIE, M. FATHY, FOUAD, M.
NELSON et S. TENAND ULMANN, Grand Temple d'Abou Simbel. [II.]
La Bataille de Qadech. Description et inscriptions. Dessins et
photographies, Le Caire, Centre de documentation et d'études sur
l'ancienne Égypte, 1971 (21 x 27 cm; portfolio containing VI +
65 p., frontispiece = map, 41 pl. [many folding, 5 in colour]
comprising plan, ill. and fig.); at head of title: Collection
scientifique.

After a preface by Gamal Eddine Moukhtar and Ch. Desroches
Noblecourt follows the extensive description of the depiction
of the Battle of Kadesh on the North Wall of the first interior
hall of the Great Temple of Abu Simbel, by Sergio Donadoni,
revised after the photographs of Louis A. Christophe: introduction; general composition; the lower register comprising the
scenes of the camp, the war deliberations, the arrival of the
auxiliaries, and the battle between the Egyptian and Hittite
chariotry; the upper register containing scenes of the Hittite
camp and the fortified city of Kadesh, the fighting king, the
messengers sent out to ask for help, and the booty; the rules
of the composition.
Then S. Donadoni presents the hieroglyphic inscriptions of the
Battle of Kadesh, revised and compared with the edition of
Kuentz by E. Edel. A list of the numbers of the photographs
utilised and preserved at the Centre is added.

79643   DESROCHES NOBLECOURT, Ch., G. MOUKHTAR, Ch. ADAM, Ch. LEBLANC,
M. NELSON, H. el-ACHIRIE, B. FONQUERNIE, G. THOREL, J.-Cl. GOYON,
F. HASSANEIN, M. NELSON, A. SAYED YOUSSEF and R. SCHUMANN-
ANTELME, Le Ramesseum. X. Les annexes nord-ouest (I'''), Le
Caire, Centre d'études et de documentation sur l'ancienne Egypte,
1976 (21 x 27 cm; portfolio containing text part: 273 p., fig.,
plans; plate part: frontispiece, 71 pl. [some folding] comprising
plans, fig. and ill., 8 p.); at head of title: Collection scientifique [No. 35].

In the first part of this study of the North-West annexe rooms
complex of the Ramesseum (siglum I''') is devoted to the architecture. In the first chapter H. el-Achirie and B. Fonquernie
point out the various phases of the construction of the North-
West annexes and devote particular attention to the architectonic
description and the construction technique of the columned room
situated in the middle of the group of annexes. In chapter 2
G. Thorel presents a study of the vaulted rooms of the group of
annexes and the staircase, which is illustrated by drawings of

In the archaeological part of the book, chapter 3, by R. Schumann Antelme, is concerned with the archaeological description of the various parts of the North-West annexe complex, after remarks on its composition of pre-, post- and contemporary Ramesside elements in general: the South gallery-court with portico and its entrance; the columned room and its entrance; the 12 magazines adjacent to the columned room and their staircase. Remarks on i.a. the measurements of the bricks and on the stamped bricks follow. Chapter 4, by F. Hassanein and M. Nelson, describes two funerary pits and the objects there found, and chapter 5, by R. Schumann Antelme and A. Sayed Youssef, a tomb and its contents found in the chapel in the court with portico.
Then follows the part containing the commentary by J.-Cl. Goyon. In chapter 6 he summarizes the problems of the study of the annexe complex (the history of the Ramesside construction; the original situation in the time of Ramses II and modifications in later periods). In chapter 7 he studies the role of the dependencies in general in the organisation of the temple and the North-West annexe complex in particular and deals with problems of their possible function as House of Life ($pr-\mathit{c}nh$) as scriptorium or chancery, and as a dependency of the temple treasury ($pr-h\underline{d}$).
In an additional chapter 8, also by J.-Cl. Goyon, a catalogue of the objects found scattered on the surface of the site is prepared. The volume is concluded by various indexes: general, names of places, persons, deities and modern authors, and Egyptian words in transcription.

79644 DONADONI, S., H. el-ACHIRIE, Ch. LEBLANC et F. ABDEL-HAMID, avec la collaboration de J. CERNÝ et F. GHATTAS, Grand Temple d'Abou Simbel. III. Les salles du trésor sud (fascicules I-II), Le Caire, Centre d'études et de documentation sur l'ancienne Égypte, 1975 (21 x 27 cm; portfolio, fasc. I: 91 p., frontispiece, 64 pl. *[many folding]* comprising plans, fig. and ill.; fasc. II: 7 p., 37 pl. *[many folding]* containing fig.); at head of title: Collection scientifique.

The first of the two fascicules devoted to the South Treasury Rooms of the Great Temple of Abu Simbel was composed by S. Donadoni. H. el-Achirie and Ch. Leblanc, with the collaboration of J. Černý and F. Ghattas. After the presentation of the architecture of the three rooms (sigla N-O-P) follows the archaeological description of the scenes showing Ramses making offerings or in adoration before the gods or in their company, and the legends to the scenes. The fascicule ends with a table listing the colours used in the scenes, an index of divinities and tables of crowns and hair-dresses, royal as well as divine.
The second fascicule by Fouad Abdel-Hamid, with the collaboration of S. Donadoni and Ch. Leblanc, contains drawings of the complete scenes. A table of concordances with the archaeological, epigraphic and photographic documentation in the first fascicule concludes this fascicule.

79645   HASSANEIN, F. et M. NELSON, La Tombe du Prince Amon-(her)-
        khepchef, Le Caire, Centre d'études et de documentation sur
        l'ancienne Égypte, 1976 (21 x 27 cm; portfolio containing X +
        122 p., frontispiece, 46 pl. [some folding; 3 in colour] com-
        prising plans, fig. and ill.); at head of title: Collection
        scientifique: Vallée des Reines.

        In the preface Ch. Desroches Noblecourt and Chehata Adam Mohammed
        introduce this new series of publications of tombs in the Valley
        of the Queens in the Collection scientifique, of which the pre-
        sent publication is the first one. They relate the program to
        be carried out and present general information on the valley and
        its tombs.
        After an introduction on the tomb proper (Valley of the Queens
        No. 55), its occupant, and the possible reasons for his untimely
        death and a bibliography, the authors describe the plan of the
        tomb; orientation; themes; technique; composition; followed by
        the description of the costumes, crowns, hairdresses and jewels
        worn by the divinities, the king and the prince. Short notes are
        devoted to i.a. the sceptres and emblems, hieroglyphs and the style.
        Then the authors present a minute archaeological description of
        the various parts of the tomb, followed by the hieroglyphic
        texts.
        Concordance tables at the end.

79646   IBRAHIM, F. et Ch. LEBLANC, Le Temple de Dandour. III. Planches
        photographiques et indices, Le Caire, Centre d'études et de
        documentation sur l'ancienne Égypte, 1975 (21 x 27 cm; portfolio
        containing 25 p., frontispiece, 87 pl. [many folding] comprising
        1 map, 1 plan, fig. and ill.); at head of title: Collection
        scientifique.

        The volume contains the photographic plates, accompanied by key-
        plans, of the various parts of the temple of Dendûr. The sigla
        referring to the various parts on the key plan correspond to
        those in our number 79641.
        At the end of the volume a table of concordances between the
        present edition and that of Blackman (1911), and a list of the
        principal scenes.
        The volume is provisionally published without preface, for
        which see the leaflet included in the volume.

79647   el-TANBOULI, M.A.L., Ch. KUENTZ et A.A. SADEK, avec la collabo-
        ration de H. de MEULENAERE, Gerf Hussein. III. La grande salle
        (E). Mur est - piliers et colosses, Le Caire, Centre d'études et
        de documentation sur l'ancienne Égypte, 1975 (21 x 27 cm; port-
        folio containing 87 p., frontispiece, 47 pl. [many folding]
        comprising 1 plan, 7 key-plans, fig. and ill.); at head of title:
        Collection scientifique.

        The volume presents the archaeological description of the East
        wall and the North and South rows of columns with Osiriac statues

of Ramses II in the Great Hypostyle Hall (siglum E) of the rock temple of Gerf Hussein.
The scenes show Ramses II offering before various deities or in their company. The hieroglyphic inscriptions of the pertinent scenes are included in a separate section.
Concordance tables at the end.

79648   YOUSSEF, A.A.-H., Ch. LEBLANC et M. MAHER, Le Ramesseum. IV. Les Batailles de Tunip et de Dapour, Le Caire, Centre d'études et de documentation sur l'ancienne Égypte, 1977 (21 x 27 cm; portfolio containing p. numbered A-M, I-XLIV and 1-28, frontispiece, 7 maps, 35 pl. [many folding, 2 in colour] comprising map, fig. and ill); at head of title: Collection scientifique.

After a preface containing a general introduction by Shehata Adam and Ch. Desroches Noblecourt there follows a historical introduction on the cities of Tunip and Dapur which were both situated in the region of Amurru, a zone of Egyptian, Mitanni and Hittite influence during the N.K. The authors enumerate the references to the cities in N.K. sources (the spellings of the names and the text sources in which they appear are given in separate tables), attempt to localize them and sketch the role of Tunip and Dapur in the Egyptian N.K. politics. In the archaeological description the authors first deal with the battle of Tunip, only represented in the Ramesseum by an inscription, and then with the scene of the battle of Dapur and its text: the pursuit of the chariotry of the enemy and their destruction; the siege of the fortified city and its surrender; the capitulation of the enemy, the killing of the rebellious chiefs and the presentation of the tribute to the king, who was accompanied in this battle by some princes.

e. Architecture

See also our numbers 79100; 79127; 79139; 79499; 79500; 79506; 79518; 79519; 79523; 79525; 79536; 79561; 79565; 79612; 79786 and 79959.

79649   ARNOLD, Dieter, Das Labyrinth und seine Vorbilder, *MDAIK* 35 (1979), 1-9, with 4 fig. including plans.

The author argues that the pyramid complexes of Sesostris III and that of Amenemhat III at Hawâra, instead of following the Memphite tradition as those of their predecessors did, corresponds in many respects with the scheme of the Djoser complex. In this study both XIIth Dynasty complexes are discussed in detail.   J.J.J.

79650   BADAWY, Alexandre, Une hypothèse concernant la construction des pyramides, *in*: *Acts 1st ICE*, 73-77, with 2 fig.

For an enlarged version of this paper, see *JEA* 63 (our number 77059).

79651 BRINKS, Jürgen, Die Entwicklung der königlichen Grabanlagen des
Alten Reiches. Eine strukturelle und historische Analyse altägyptischer Architektur, Hildesheim, Gerstenberg Verlag, 1979
(17 x 23.8 cm; 189 p., 2 maps, 1 fig., 4 tables, 38 plans, 20
loose folding pl. with plans) = Hildesheimer Ägyptologische
Beiträge, 10. Pr. DM 29

The study of the basic structure of the royal funerary complex
in the O.K. is divided, apart from a brief introduction, into
three parts: an extensive study of the funerary complex of Djoser
and its elements; a discussion of all later O.K. funerary complexes that have been preserved; and an attempt to interpret
these complexes as spatial expression of a ritual function.
The first part, on the Djoser complex, consists of two chapters.
In the first, the building history is analysed. The plan has
been altered twice: in phase 2 the model of the Sed-festival
complex at the eastern side and the adoration-cult complex at
the SE corner of the pyramid have been added, in phase 3 the sun
cult complex at the southern side. In the execution of the phases several stages are distinguished.
Then Brinks extensively discusses the elements and their development from the Pre- or Early Dynastic Period onwards. They are:
the offering-cult complex, the elements of which correspond to
those of a house: living quarter, reception-place, court and
entrance hall; the Sed-festival complex and the model of the
Sed-festival, both consisting of six elements; the adoration-
cult complex, which corresponds with the Khentamenti temple in
Abydos (dated by the author to the Ist Dynasty), and the sun-
cult complex (for the first time present in the funerary complex
of Djoser).
Analysing the later history of the royal tombs, from Sekhemkhet
to Pepy II, the same elements appear to be present, although in
some instances superposed one upon another. A summary of the
discussion on p. 147-156.
In a short chapter at the end (157-162) the author explains the
elements as transpositions for the eternity of the major institutions and functions for the king's physical health, the per-
manence of his reign, and his relations with the divinities. The
complex represents the royal dogma.
Bibliography and indexes at the end. J.J.J.

79652 KINK, H.A., Древнеегипетский храм, Moscow, Издательство "Наука",
1979 (11 x 20 cm; 199 p., 7 fig.); at head of title: Академия
Наук СССР. Институт востоковедения. Pr. 1 Р. 10 коп.

'The Ancient Egyptian Temple'.
A study of the temple from a technical viewpoint, based on data
provided by egyptological literature. This is cited from a list
(p. 186-198) of 324 titles, the first 36 of which are in Russian.
After a brief Introduction (3-8), the author deals with the following subject matter under 20 §§: 1. by way of general illustration: a description of the Karnak temple complex (9-32), followed 2. by one of Medinet Habu (32-44). Then, 3. rock temples

follow (mainly that of Abu Simbel - 44-48). Then the building aspects are treated: 4. the stone material itself (48-51), dealing with limestone, quartzite, sandstone, granite and alabaster. 5. Quarrying is described and the ways to process the material, for instance the work on an obelisk (51-62). 6. Levelling and laying foundations (63-75), followed by 7. the erection methods of walls and dovetailing stone building material (75-81). 8. Pylons and staircases (82-88), 9. encircling walls (88-92), 10. various kinds of columns, 11. roofing and vaulting procedures (100-105), 12. drainage systems (105-109), 13. floors and the plastering of them (109-112), 14. doors and windows (112-120), 15. canals, the sacred lake and wells (120-124), 16. decoration of the stone material (124-135) and 17. that of metal elements (135-146). 18. Several constructional aids and appliances, such as slopes and ramps (146-153), 19. the use of wood as construction material (154-156), 20. transport methods and the erection of pillars, obelisks, statues, and the like (156-167). After a conclusion (168-176) an appendix follows (177-184) discussing the role of obelisk inscriptions in the decipherment of hieroglyphs, such as the translation of such a text by Hermapion.

J.F. Borghouts

79653 KITCHEN, Kenneth A., Memphite Tomb-Chapels in the New Kingdom and Later, in: *Festschrift Elmar Edel*, 272-284, with 15 plans and 2 fig.

Study of the typical Memphite tomb chapel from the N.K. to the Late Period on account of the scanty evidence at present known. After briefly discussing the plan, the material construction and the decoration the author presents a condensed summary of seven examples (i.a. Mose, Horemheb, Apuia, Maya, Pa-Aten-em-hab and Nes-Thuty, the latter from the Late Period). A characteristic of the Memphite tomb is the representation on the pillars of the djed-pillar adored or supported by the tomb-owner. The type seems to have undergone practically no evolution during the ages, although from the later periods other types are known too. *J.J.J.*

79654 LAUER, Jean-Philippe, Le développement des complexes funéraires royaux en Égypte depuis les temps prédynastiques jusqu'à la fin de l'Ancien Empire, *BIFAO* 79 (1979), 355-394, with 12 fig., 7 plans and 4 pl.

The author presents his view on the development of the royal funerary complex, from the late Predynastic Period (Hierakonpolis) to Pepi II. A large number of disputed points pass the review, e.g.: the tomb of Horus Adjib at Saqqâra (No. 3038) is not a precursor of the Step Pyramid; the tomb of Horus Qaä with the funerary temple on its north side is indeed a royal tomb; the tombs at Umm el-Qaäb are indeed cenotaphs, while the storehouses in the North Cemetery of Abydos were used for the provisions for Khontamenti (against Kemp, our number 66346); all kings of the IInd Dynasty have had tombs at Saqqâra, though only

two of them have been found; the initial mastaba M1-M2 of the
Step Pyramid was the tomb of Sanakht, Djoser's predecessor; in
the Step Pyramid complex the two elements until then combined,
the facade imitating the great gate and the tomb proper, have
been detached from each other; the south tomb of this complex
is a parallel of the older cenotaphs at Abydos; etc.
The pyramids from the IVth to the VIth Dynasties are all described with their characteristic details showing the development through the ages. J.J.J.

79655 LAUER, J.-Ph., Le triangle sacré dans les monuments de l'Ancien
Empire, in: Acts 1st ICE, 423-424.

Abstract of a paper. For the complete text see our number 77458.

79656 SPENCER, A.J., Brick Architecture in Ancient Egypt, Warminster,
Aris & Phillips Ltd, [1979] (20.8 x 29.7 cm; VI + 159 p., 25
pl., 94 fig., including plans).

The author describes the aim of this book as "to give a detailed
account of the brick architecture of Ancient Egypt and to examine
the constructional techniques which were employed to overcome
individual architectural problems." He concentrates on the Pharaonic Period, omitting Coptic evidence and, mostly, also that
from Nubia.
After the introduction there follows part one dealing with three
general points: the technique of brick manufacture; the earliest
use of brick in Egypt; the bonding corpus (see the plates).
Part two discusses the surviving brick monuments of Egypt, with
special reference to technical and structural problems. In five
chapters the author deals with funerary architecture, religious
architecture, administrative and office buildings, domestic architecture, and fortresses and defensive town walls (in this
chapter also Nubian evidence). In the chapters the buildings
are arranged in a chronological order, with summarizing tables
at the end of each chapter or section. Numerous buildings pass
the review, while all kinds of details are discussed and illustrated by drawings.
Part three is devoted to the systematic discussion of constructional elements: walls of various types; floors and foundations;
arches, vaults and suchlike; solid brick constructions (mastabas
and pyramids); supplementary building materials (wood, stone,
mortar and plaster, etc.); bonding; special bricks (e.g. bricks
of special shapes and exceptional sizes; bricks with stamps);
brick sizes that are of particular value for dating purposes.
An appendix on the metrology of brickwork (p. 149-150) is followed by the indexes.
On the plates the corpus of brick bonds, copies of official
brick stamps, forms of frieze bricks and examples of their inscriptions, examples of private stamps, plans of some buildings,
graphs of brick sizes, and photographs. J.J.J.

79657 SPENCER, A.J., The Brick Foundations of Late-Period Peripteral Temples and their Mythological Origin, in: *Glimpses of Ancient Egypt*, 132-137, with 5 plans.

In contrast to most Egyptian buildings certain Late Period peripteral temples stood on a strong foundation of brick-work. In many cases this platform is even all that has remained of the building. The author suggests that the reason for the elaborate foundation was mythological rather than structural, the sanctuary being placed on the primaeval mound. The same explanation is given for the brick-lined and sand-filled pit found under several, perhaps under all larger Late Period temples. *J.J.J.*

79658 THOMAS, Elizabeth, The ḳ3y of Queen Inḥapy, *JARCE* 16 (1979), 85-92, with 2 fig.

An inquiry into the topography of Theban tomb 320, originally destined to the 18th Dynasty queen Inḥapy and later to Istemkheb, well known for its use as the *cache* for coffins of royal persons. The description is studded with details quoted from the discovery reports by Brugsch and Maspero, and from the later exhibition accounts. The term ḳ3y, 'elevated place', would point to a hall mid-way in the tomb. Four dockets on mummies are ascribed to king Siamun for support in the reconstruction of the order of the burials. *J.F. Borghouts*

f. Sculpture

See also our numbers 79031; 79042; 79126; 79138; 79487; 79512; 79519; 79536; 79537; 79561; 79575; 79586; 79588; 79599; 79601; 79603; 79606; 79607; 79608; 79612; 79621; 79622; 79734; 79746; 79786; 79787; 79788; 79790; 79817; 79841; 79845; 79864; 79868; 79900; 79902; 79904; 79906; 79910 and 79924.

79659 ABITZ, Friedrich, Statuetten in Schreinen als Grabbeigaben in den ägyptischen Königsgräbern der 18. und 19. Dynastie, Wiesbaden, Otto Harrassowitz, 1979 (21 x 29.5 cm; 131 p., 22 fig., 2 folding pl.) = Ägyptologische Abhandlungen, 35.

The subject of this study are the statuettes in shrines and their representations in the royal tombs from the XVIIIth and XIXth Dynasties, which have not been studied before and are scarcely published.
After an introduction the material is presented in chapter 2. First the representations in the "Schlachtraum" (Hall D) and the "Sarkophagkammer" (Hall E) of the tomb of Sethi II; the actual statuettes and shrines from the tomb of Tutankhamon; and at the end those from other royal tombs. In the first two sections the statuettes and their representations are described within the context in which they occur.

Chapter 3 contains the analysis of the material, the more necessary since their context is far from clear. The author also uses the evidence from the representations in the tomb of Rekhmire. In the last section an attempt to describe the arrangement of the statuettes, which appear to consist of five groups (see diagram on p. 60).
Chapter 4 is devoted to their religious meaning - they evidently play a part in the burial rites and are connected with the ascension and resurrection of the dead. The author successively studies the figures of "living" gods and of mummy-shaped divinities, while a short section is devoted particularly to the room of the sarcophagus in Sethi's tomb. In the second part of this chapter the author discusses particular figures: the goddess Menkeret and the boy with the sistrum; royal figures and their suite of standards; the animal figures: a goose, a cow-head and a snake. In order to detect their meaning the author studies several texts from the funerary literature.
A short last chapter deals with similar statuettes represented in private tombs and in friezes of objects on coffins.
Summary on p. 120-125. J.J.J.

79660 Anonymous, The Ernest Brummer Collection. Art Objects from Ancient Egypt to the Renaissance, *The Connoisseur*, London 202, No. 812 (October 1979), 79-85, with 26 ill. (25 in colour).

The upper part of a basalt statue of a male, in the academic Saite style, is depicted. See our number 79581.

79661 CARDON, Patrick D., Amenmesse: An Egyptian Royal Head of the Nineteenth Dynasty in the Metropolitan Museum, *Metropolitan Museum Journal*, New York 14 (1979), 5-14, with 9 ill.

The article is devoted to the art-historical discussion of a N.K. royal head in the Metropolitan Museum of Art (Rogers Fund, Inv. No. 34.2.2.). The material is painted quartzite, the height 48 cm. After preliminary remarks on the problem of usurpation and emulation in statuary the author carefully describes the head representing a king wearing the *khepresh*-crown, paying particular attention to the phenomenon of rough parts of the surface connected with the application of ochre. He was able to match it with a headless staff-bearing statue in the Hypostyle Hall at Karnak, which was usurped by Seti II. The composition of the features of the head, some early and others late XIXth Dynasty, apart from some individualistic traits, makes it difficult to attribute the head to a particular period or reign. These conflicting elements were resolved by the study in our number 79686.

79662 DESROCHES-NOBLECOURT, Christiane, Un couple de seigneurs du palais sous Aménophis II, *La Revue du Louvre et des Musées de France*, Paris 29 (1979), 280-290, with 1 map, 1 plan and 20 fig. and ill.

The author publishes the upper part of a group statue (of the man only the head is left), which was recently acquired by the Louvre (Inv. No. E 27.161). She extensively describes the particularly fine statue group which preserved its full colours, and translates the lines on the back of the seat of the couple. The piece is attributed to the Overseer of the Chambers of the Palace Senynefer and his wife Hatshepsut, who is known from cenotaph no. 11 at Gebel Silsila and lived in the time of Amenophis II. He was the brother of Wesersatet, viceroy of Kush.
Remarks on the orientation of statue groups at the end of the article.

79663 DOETSCH-AMBERGER, Ellen, Eine Löwenstatuette der Mert-Hapi, *GM* Heft 31 (1979), 19-26, with 2 pl.

Der beschriebene Löwe befindet sich in Kölner Privatbesitz. Der Fundort ist unbekannt; er wurde im Handel erworben. Der Löwe aus hellem Sandstein liegt auf einer bestossenen Bodenplatte. Zwischen den vorgestreckten Vorderpranken greift der Löwe einen Sockel, der auf einer Platte liegt, die gut geglättet ist und einem flachen Bassin gleicht. Auf den Aussenflächen der Platte befindet sich ein Hieroglyphenband mit zwei Opferformeln, die dem Ka der Königsschwester Mert-Hapi gelten. Sie ist die Schwester Nektanebos I. Der liegende Löwe mit einer Opferplatte scheint singulär zu sein; er könnte symbolisch als "Opfergebender" verstanden werden.
Inge Hofmann

79664 GRAEFE, Erhart, Noch einmal Osiris-Lunus, *JEA* 65 (1979), 171-173, with 1 pl.

Describes a bronze statuette in the Musée des Beaux-Arts Lyon, H1712, and the significance of the part played by this lunar form of the deity.
E.P. Uphill

79665 GRIFFITHS, J. Gwyn, The Striding Bronze Figure of Osiris-Iʿaḥ at Lyon, *JEA* 65 (1979), 174-175.

Forms a series of comments on our previous number by Graefe, and suggests the abandonment of the term "Osiris-Lunus" due to its imprecision.
E.P. Uphill

79666 INSLEY, Christine, A Bronze Statuette of Unnūfer, Choachyte of King Ḥarsiēse, in the Fitzwilliam Museum, *JEA* 65 (1979), 167-169, with 2 pl.

Describes this statuette, gives inscription, and suggests a date of seventh century B.C.
E.P. Uphill

79667 KISS, Zsolt, Une étape mal connu de l'art égyptien d'époque romaine. Les portraits de Caracalla, *in*: *Acts 1st ICE*, 377-381, with 4 pl.

Discussion of some portraits of Caracalla as representations of a stage in the development of Roman art in Egypt. J.J.J.

79668 McNAUGHT, Lewis, New Light on an Ancient Face, *The Illustrated London News*, London 267, No. 6969 (April 1979), 81, with 2 ill.

The author briefly discusses the possibility of a new identification of a colossal head in the British Museum, thought to represent Tuthmosis III, to Ramses II.

79669 MICHALOWSKI, Kazimierz, Égypte, [Paris], Hachette Réalités, [1978] (21 x 28 cm; 191 p., colour frontispiece, colour ill. on cover, 158 ill. [32 in colour], 3 fig., 1 map); series: Histoire mondiale de la sculpture.

The author first introduces the principles of ancient Egyptian art. After a note on colours and a short chapter on sculptors in society he presents a selection of masterpieces in illustrations and captions. At the end of the book general documentation on ancient Egypt, and an index.
We did not see the original Italian-Japanese edition: Egitto, Mondadori-Shogakukan, 1978 = Storia della Scultura nel Mondo, 2. There is also an English edition: Great Sculpture of Ancient Egypt, New York, Reynal & Company, in association with William Morrow and Company, Inc., 1978 = Reynal's World History of Great Sculpture ($ 25).

79670 MILLS, A.J., Two Sekhmet Statues at Trewithen in Cornwall, *JEA* 65 (1979), 166, with 1 pl.

Describes the upper part of two statues of black granite probably to be associated with the Mut temple at Karnak.
 E.P. *Uphill*

79671 MÜLLER, Maya, Zum Bildnistypus Thutmosis' I, *GM* Heft 32 (1979), 27-38, with 6 ill. on 5 pl.

Das Gesicht Thutmosis' I. ist nur von der Sitzstatue Turin 1374 und von der Osirispfeilerstatue von Karnak (Kairo CG 42051) inschriftlich gesichert bekannt. Beide Köpfe werden ausführlich beschrieben und sodann zwei weitere Köpfe demselben Herrscher zugeschrieben. Es handelt sich um den Kopf London BM 1238, der 1906 beim Südende des Suezkanals gefunden wurde und um den Kopf im Nationalmuseum Stockholm (EG 68). *Inge Hofmann*

79672 PETERSON, Bengt, Ein kuschitischer Osiris, *Orientalia Suecana*, Uppsala 27-28 (1978-1979), 28-30, with 3 ill.

Publication of a bronze Osiris statuette in the Medelhavsmuseet Inv. Nr. MME 1974:155), that on account of its stylistic characteristics is ascribed to the XXVth Dynasty. J.J.J.

79673 PETERSON, Bengt, Sobek - der Krokodilgott. Eine Skulptur in Stockholm, *Medelhavsmuseet Bulletin*, Stockholm 14 (1979), 3-8, with 5 ill.

Publication of a limestone figure of a crocodile on a base (MME 1977:1). The inscription mentions the overseer of the cattle of the Ramesseum Panefer. The piece is dated to the XXth Dynasty and may perhaps be connected with an (as yet) unknown sanctuary of Sobk in Thebes. The author also mentions a steatite statuette of a crocodile of an unknown date (MM 19257).   J.J.J.

79674 RAVEN, Maarten J., Papyrus-Sheaths and Ptah-Sokar-Osiris Statues, *OMRO* 59-60 (1978-1979), 251-296, with 4 fig. and 3 pl.

The author presents an extensive study of the form, function and symbolic meaning of the so-called papyrus-sheaths and Ptah-Sokar-Osiris statues, based on instances in museums and on excavation reports.
After a definition of the type of mummiform statue and a survey of their treatment in the egyptological literature a section is devoted to their origins: a particular type of wooden shawabtis, figures placed in one of the niches of the burial chamber, and some others.
Then the author deals with the typology, dividing the statues into four main types, in a more or less chronological order, while stressing that numerous miscellaneous classes exist.
Turning to function and meaning, the author devotes a section to the inscriptions and the next one to the hymn occurring on some statues, which is given in hieroglyphs (several actual texts in parallel columns), transliteration, and translation with notes. Next the colour symbolism, the crowns, clothing and attributes of the figures, the contents of the cavities, and the symbolic aspect of the base are dealt with. A summary of the results on p. 290-291.
In an appendix a list of Egyptian sites from which the statues are known to have come. Bibliography on p. 293-296.   J.J.J.

79675 REEVES, C.N., A New Statue Fragment for Mersuʿankh, *GM* Heft 35 (1979), 47-49, with 2 ill. on 1 pl. and 1 fig.

Das Fragment, das aus der Basis und den Unterschenkeln eines ausschreitenden Beamten besteht, gehörte zu einer Statue des Mersuʿankh vom Ende der 5. Dynastie. Es wurde im Kunsthandel erworben und befindet sich im Besitz des Verfassers.
Inge Hofmann

79676 SATZINGER, Helmut, Votivstatuen mit Emblemstäben, *in*: Acts 1st *ICE*, 565-567.

The author discusses staff-bearing statuary, royal as well as private, from the Ramesside Period.

79677 SCHOTT, Erika, Eine Antef Statuette, *in*: *Festschrift Elmar Edel*, 390-396, with 1 pl.

Publication of a limestone statuette of a kneeling man with *nw*-vessels in his hands, from a private collection in Basel. It bears the name '*Intf*. The author draws up a list of 25 statues in this position, all except two representing royal persons, and suggests that the present piece represents one of the Antefs of the XIth Dynasty. On stylistical and other reasons she thinks it was Antef II. It may have come from his tomb in el-Tarif.
J.J.J.

79678 SIMPSON, William Kelly, Egyptian Statuary of Courtiers in Dynasty 18, *Bulletin of the Museum of Fine Arts*, Boston 77 (1979), 36-49.

The author publishes several pieces of XVIIIth Dynasty statuary, the recent acquisition of which filled a gap in the collection of the Museum of Fine Arts.
They are: an upper part of an archaizing statue from the early reign of Hatshepsut or somewhat earlier (W.E. Nickerson Fund No. 2.1972.396); the upper part of the male figure of a seated pair of Ahmose called Pa-tjenna, son of the viceroy of Kush Ahmose Turo, probably from the reign of Tuthmosis III (E.J. and M.S. Holmes Fund No. 1972.359), with two inscribed fragments of the seat of this pair statue; a seated statue of an official called Wesi (Acc. No. 09.525), from the reign of Tuthmosis III; a seated statue of the Overseer of the Workshops Tju-tju, in the archaizing style from the time of Hatshepsut (Acc. No. 1979.38); the upper part of the statuette of a seated scribe, probably from the time of Amenophis II (Acc. No. 1979.205); the wooden statuette of In-pehwy-sen, reign of Tuthmosis III or IV (Acc. No. 11.1497); the right and complementary left side of the head of a statue, from the reign of Amenophis III (Acc. No. 44.28 + 1979.42); the upper part of a statuette, probably reign of Amenophis III (Acc. No. 1972.360); a battered head of red quartzite, reign of Amenophis III (M.E. Evans Fund No. 29.729); a superior head of a seated scribe, from the time of Horemheb or slightly later (Acc.No. 42.467); and lastly, a fine late Amarna head (Acc. No. 1976.602).

79679 SIST, L.C.M., A Statue of Bakenkhons in the University Museum of Rome, *in*: *Acts 1st ICE*, 583-585.

Short report on the discovery of a fragmentary statue of the high priest Bakenkhons son of Amenemopet in the Museum of the Istituto di Studi del Vicino Oriente of the University of Rome.

79680 TEFNIN, Roland, La statuaire d'Hatshepsout. Portrait royal et politique sous la 18e Dynastie, Bruxelles, Fondation Égyptologique Reine Élisabeth, 1979 (21.7 x 28.5 cm; XII + 196 p., 5 tables, 35 pl., 9 fig.) = Monumenta aegyptiaca, 4.

In the introduction the author stresses the great value of the well-documented Hatshepsut statuary for a study in depth.
The first part of the book is devoted to the analysis of the statues, the various types of which are studied in eight chapters. In chapter 1 he describes her seated statues, all from Deir el-Bahri and now in the Metropolitan Museum of Art, New York and from a comparison he draws the conclusion that they grew less feminine in course of time. A separate section is devoted to the feminine and feminizing statues of Hatshepsut which do not come from the series recovered by the excavations at Deir el-Bahri. Chapter 2 is concerned with the Osiris statues of the queen in the various parts of her funerary temple. After a presentation of the individual pieces and a general description of the features of the type he establishes a relative chronology of the three stages discernible in the Osiris statues. In the following chapters the author follows more or less the same system: presentation of the individual pieces with their data, a general description of the type, and their place in the chronology. First he deals in the chapters 3-5 with respectively the large and the small kneeling statues and the few standing ones. Then he studies in chapters 6-8 respectively the granite sphinxes, the sandstone ones (divided into those of the lower court and of the avenue) and the type having a mane. Then follows in part 2 the synthesis of the study of the material. The first two chapters are devoted to the criteria for the establishment of a relative chronology of Hatshepsut's statuary, a chronological tabulation and the coherence of this evaluation. In chapter 3 the author distinguishes three types (with slight variations) of the physiognomy of the queen and draws up a list of the 10 most important statues wrongly attributed to Hatshepsut, two problematical pieces in this respect, and three works to be attributed to her. In the last chapter 4, dealing with the place of Hatshepsut's statuary in the sculptural evolution during the XVIIIth Dynasty, the author makes remarks on the religious and political aspects of Hatshepsut's statuary, apart from those on the artistic development, the style of sculpture and the portrait problem.
Bibliography and indexes at the end of the book.

79681   VACHALA, Břetislav, Ein weiterer Beleg fur die Königin Repewetnebu?, ZÄS 106 (1979), 176, with 2 ill.

Veröffentlichung der Fragmente C 663 + 796 + 952 und G 171, vom Tschechoslowakischen Ägyptologischen Institut der Karlsuniversität in der Mastaba des Ptahshepses in Abusir gefunden. Es handelt sich um Alabasterstatuetten mit den Titeln einer Königin. Wahrscheinlich war sie Repewetnebu, die Hauptfrau des Königs Neuserre, bisher nur vom Fragment Berlin 17438 bekannt.
M. Heerma v. Voss

79682 VANDERSLEYEN, C., Sur quelques statues usurpées par Ramsès II (British Museum 61 et Louvre A 20), *in*: *Acts 1st ICE*, 665-669.

The author attempts to demonstrate that the statue B.M. Inv. No. 61, amongst others usurped by Ramses II, is to be attributed to Amenophis II, and the statue Louvre Inv. No. A 20 to Amenophis III.

79683 VARGA, Edith, Une tête de bois peint d'Égypte, *Bulletin du Musée Hongrois des Beaux-Arts*, Budapest 53 (1979), 5-16, with 9 ill. and a Hungarian version on p. 225-230.

The author studies a painted wooden head in the Budapest museum (Inv. No. 58.2-E), of unknown provenance and after its stylistic qualities to be dated to the early Ramesside Period. She suggests it to belong to the so-called "bustes de laraires" whose function is still uncertain. In this connection she publishes a curious wooden object from a private collection in Budapest, consisting of a shoulderless painted bust (probably of a woman) and two painted wooden feathers fixed on a common wooden base. The rather primitive execution suggests a local artisan to be its maker, while the Osiris feathers point at a funerary context.
J.J.J.

79684 WILLIAMS, Ellen Reeder, A Bronze Statuette of Isis-Aphrodite, *JARCE* 16 (1979), 93-101, with 3 pl.

This statuette (Johns Hopkins Archaeol. Coll., h. 30 cm) to which 15 parallel pieces are listed, is an egyptianizing representation of Isis-Aphrodite as a standing nude woman holding in one hand the stem of a lotus on whose blossom Harpocrates is sitting. On account of the hairstyle, this group may be dated to the Roman era (1st-3rd centuries). This piece was cast in one, although the mould itself was apparently constructed from separately made wax parts. The statuette (probably from a household shrine) goes typologically back to the Hellenistic period and testifies to a syncretism of Isis-Hathor and Aphrodite (the latter being inspired on the ideology of the Ptolemaic queens as a fertility goddess), witness a sometimes worn amulet in the form of a crescent moon. This type of statuette is related to the nude terracotta female figurines called 'brides of death' of the Hellenistic and later periods which were likewise primarily meant for the living.   J.F. Borghouts

79685 YURCO, Frank J., Amenhotep III and Ramesses II: The Standing Colossi at Luxor, *in*: *Acts 1st ICE*, 687-690.

Abstract of a paper.
The full version of the study will be published in a forthcoming issue of *SAK*, together with a study by Mrs. Christine Strauss, discussing the art-historical evidence from the colossi at Luxor.

79686 YURCO, Frank J., Amenmesse: Six Statues at Karnak, *Metropolitan Museum Journal*, New York 14 (1979), 15-31, with 15 ill. and fig.

The author discusses three related statues in the central part of the Hypostyle Hall, to one of which the head published in our number 79661 belongs, and three others, also related, of which two are before the porch of the Second Pylon at Karnak and the third in the Festival Hall. They are all of reddish quartzite and were all usurped by Sethi II. Of each of the six statues he presents the inscriptions, a short description, a discussion and a bibliography. Preserved traces of the original inscriptions on two of them revealed that they were dedicated by king Amenmesse, as all the group were, in view of their close relation. Then the author devotes his attention to their original location which probably was the transverse axis of the Hypostyle Hall. Evidence from one of the statues is helping greatly to identify Amenmesse's mother with queen Takhat (statue Cairo CG 1198), a daughter of, most likely, Ramses II. The author puts forward the hypothesis that queen Takhat was at some time the chief queen of Ramses II or Merenptah, since this suits the evidence. The implication that Amenmesse was of royal ancestry clarifies the stress he placed upon his relationship to Ramses II and Sethi I and the presence of his monuments on a processional axis of the Hypostyle Hall so closely connected with their names. A reconstructed pedigree of Amenmesse is added.

g. Relief and painting

See also our numbers 79042; 79075; 79085; 79108; 79242; 79258; 79259; 79260; 79261; 79322; 79445; 79448; 79490; 79507; 79519; 79523; 79528; 79544; 79546; 79571; 79599; 79601; 79606; 79607; 79612; 79616; 79618; 79619; 79620; 79627; 79638; 79734; 79746; 79786; 79788; 79791; 79805; 79822; 79831; 79841; 79900; 79929; 79940; 79953 and 79955.

79687 BRUNNER, Hellmut, Illustrierte Bücher im alten Ägypten, *in*: *Wort und Bild*. Symposion des Fachbereichs Altertums- und Kulturwissenschaften zum 500jährigen Jubiläum der Eberhard-Karls-Universität Tübingen 1977. Herausgegeben von Hellmut Brunner, Richard Kannicht, Klaus Schwager, München, Wilhelm Fink Verlag, 1979, 201-218, with 7 fig. and 3 pl.

The author discusses the relations between text and representation, either on papyri or on tomb and temple walls. Various possibilities pass the review: pure illustration (mathematical texts), illustration that can gradually become independent (e.g. the mythological papyri that evolved from the B.D.), illustrations that were meant as a help to the performer of a ritual (the Dramatic Ramesseum Papyrus), illustrations that actually relate a different matter (the scenes of the Divine Birth of the King that contain an ancient story), pictures that inform us about the essentials to which the texts add those elements that cannot be depicted (the M.K. coffins), pictures that constitute a complement to the texts (the scenes of the Kadesh battle, in which the pictures relate the facts, the texts mainly the emotions). J.J.J.

79688 BRUNNER-TRAUT, Emma, Egyptian Artists' Sketches. Figured Ostraka from the Gayer-Anderson Collection in the Fitzwilliam Museum, Cambridge, Istanbul, Nederlands Historisch-Archaeologisch Instituut, 1979 (19.5 x 26.6 cm; X + 89 p., 7 fig., 40 pl., ill. on cover) = Uitgaven van het Nederlands Historisch-Archaeologisch Instituut te Istanbul, 45; rev. *BiOr* 37 (1980), 162-163 (Lise Manniche).

This is the publication of the 46 figured ostraca (fifteen of them with representations on both sides) that came to the Fitzwilliam Museum from the Gayer-Anderson Collection in 1949. For the other part of this collection, preserved in Stockholm, see our number 73554.
Since the present book is also intended to serve as a guidebook for visitors of the collection a general introduction to figured ostraca and to animal stories (by chance only one instance, no. 26, occurs in this collection) precede the catalogue proper. On p. 19-20 general remarks as to the collection.
The catalogue arranges the ostraca according to the subjects. One, unique, instance represents a temple doorway with a human figure, a head and a hieroglyphic text; six present gods, goddesses and demi-gods; six royal persons; six men and two women; the others various animals, except no. 49 which is a lump of limestone with miscellaneous designs in relief. That the total number is 49 (for 46 pieces) finds its explanation in the separation in a few instances of the recto and the verso, where the subjects belong to different categories.
Each ostracon is minutely described and full technical data are given, including bibliography (if available) and references to parallels. The few texts on the ostraca are presented in facsimile and translation. All representations are depicted by a photograph, a few by a drawing too.
On p. 81 a brief conclusion. Concordances on p. 84-87. J.J.J.

79689 BRUNNER, Emma, Die grüne Sonne, *in*: *Festschrift Elmar Edel*, 54-59.

The author explains the instances in which the colour of the sun is $mfk3t$ (turquoise) or $hsbd$ (lapis lazuli) from the optic-physiological phenomenon of the successive contrast: the red/yellow sun was seen in "after-sight" as green/blue. J.J.J.

79690 Corpus antiquitatum aegyptiacarum. Lose-Blatt-Katalog ägyptischer Altertümer. Pelizaeus-Museum. Lieferung 7 = Karl MARTIN, Reliefs des Alten Reiches. Teil 2, Mainz/Rhein, Verlag Philipp von Zabern, 1979 (21 x 30 cm; portfolio containing [IV] + 104 loose p., 71 loose pl.). Pr. DM 68

Although the 7th fascicle of the C.A.A. in the Pelizaeus Museum, Hildesheim, being the second part of the publication of the O.K. relief (fragments), has already been published as a sequel to fascicle 3 (our number 78179), fascicles 5 and 6 have not yet appeared. The second part of the O.K. reliefs will be followed by a third. It contains mostly acquisitions from Junker's excavations after the First World War and those earlier, not yet dealt with in the previous part. The 34 generally larger and coherent parts comprise (fragments of) offering tables, wall reliefs, false doors and architraves, and various parts of the mastabas of *Mny* and notably *Sšm-nfr* IV. The pieces mainly date from the VIth Dynasty.

79691 FARAG, Sami, Gamal WAHBA, Adel FARID, Inscribed Blocks of the Ramesside Period and of King Taharqa, found at Philae (Notizie da File, III), *Oriens Antiquus* 18 (1979), 281-289, with 14 fig. and 3 pl.

The authors publish some blocks previous to the Ptolemaic Period which have come to light during the dismantling operations at Philae. They are blocks from the Ramesside Period bearing the names of Sethos I, Ramses III and Ramses XI suggesting the possibility of N.K. shrines on the island, and inscribed fragments from probably one building of king Taharqa, presumably pulled down when Nectanebo erected his own monuments.

79692 FARID, Adel, Blocks from a Temple of Tuthmosis III at Dakka, *CdE* LIV, No. 107 (1979), 1-7, with 4 fig.

L'auteur mentionne quelques blocs découverts dans le dromos du temple de Dakka qui rappellent le style d'Amada. Il est parvenu à reconstituer huit scènes, dont il se contente de publier quatre en épures.   *Ph. Derchain*

79693 FARID, Adel, New Ptolemaic Blocks from Rubᶜ-el-Maganin-Armant, *MDAIK* 35 (1979), 59-74, with 2 fig. and 4 pl.

In a collapsed fortification wall near the gate of Antoninus Pius in Armant a number of blocks from a Ptolemaic temple have been discovered in 1935-37 (see Porter-Moss V, 158). Recent excavations led to the rediscovery of some of them amd the finding of some new ones. They are here published, the scenes in photograph and description, the inscriptions also in hand-copies with translation. In view of the incompleteness of the material an interpretation of the original architectural content is still impossible.   *J.J.J.*

79694 KARKOWSKI, J., The Question of the Beautiful Feast of the Valley Representations in Hatshepsut's Temple at Deir el-Bahari, *in*: *Acts 1st ICE*, 359-364, with 1 fig.

Partly on account of new fragments added to the walls of the Upper Court of the Hatshepsut temple the author studies the decoration on its E. and N. walls. He argues that on the former the scenes on the S. wing refer to the Opet festival, on the N. wing to the Festival of the Valley, which is continued on the N. wall. The representation of these festivals may symbolise through chosen episodes the major Theban festivals in general, as texts seem to indicate, thus interlinking the Queen's cult with that of Amon. J.J.J.

79695 KEMP, Barry J., Wall Paintings from the Workmen's Village at el-ʿAmarna, *JEA* 65 (1979), 47-53, with 2 pl and 3 fig.

These murals were discovered in 1921-22 during the clearance of the village and were in the front rooms of House 3 Main Street and House 10 Long Wall Street. The photographs and line drawings made from them are published here. The first covered the full width of the north wall being 2m 80 wide by *c*. 1m high, and consisted of a group of dancing Bes-figures and the goddess Thoueris. The other was around 1m 80 wide and depicted a line of three female figures with two small girls. Traces of the feet of a fourth adult survive. Comparisons are made with tomb paintings and those at Deir el-Medîna and the connection with childbirth noted. E.P.Uphill

79696 KOZLOFF, A.P., A Study of the Painters of the Tomb of Menna, No. 69, *in*: *Acts 1st ICE*, 395-402, with 16 pl.

Proceeding from Černý's statement that in the royal tombs the two "sides" of the workmen's gang each decorated one side, and suggesting (without any proof) that the same men decorated the private tombs, the author attempts to distinguish different hands on both sides of the tomb of Menna (No. 69). It appears that, apart from the Menna Master, no painter worked on both sides. The same organisation of the work can be established in the tomb of Pairi (No. 139). The hand of the Menna Master the author also recognises in the scenes from the so-called tomb of Nebamun in the British Museum. J.J.J.

79697 KRUG, Antje, Die Sahure-Reliefs, [Frankfurt am Main, Liebieghaus, 1978] (20 x 21 cm; 44 p., ill. on cover, 13 plans, ill. and fig., 11 pl.) = Liebieghaus Monographie, 3.

After the presentation of a relevant episode from the Pap. Westcar, and remarks on the position of the Vth Dynasty, the background of the O.K. and the monuments of the IVth and Vth Dynasties, the author describes the temple and pyramid complex of king Sahure at Abusir with special attention to the reliefs at present in the possession of the Liebieghaus. Brief notes on the temple of the complex of Niuserre and a pedigree of the IVth and Vth Dynasties follow.
The booklet is concluded by a catalogue of the reliefs and the fragments, giving data, description and bibliography.

79698   KURTH, D., Die Dekoration der Säulen im Pronaos des Tempels von Edfu, *in*: *Acts 1st ICE*, 413-417, with 2 fig.

The author demonstrates that the decoration of the 12 columns of the pronaos of the Edfu temple, bands as well as scenes, follows a strict composition scheme and a unity of form amd content. In it the claim of the leading position of Horus of Edfu among all gods of Egypt is expressed.

79699   MANNICHE, Lise, The Complexion of Queen Ahmosi Nefertere, *Acta Orientalia*, Copenhagen 40 (1979), 11-19, with 4 pl.

The author deals with the reason why in several posthumous representations queen Ahmose Nofertari is represented with a black skin. She argues that the black complexion has to do with a stage in the transformation of the deceased king. Queen Ahmose Nofertari, as the mother not only of Amenophis I but of the dynastic line, was the perfect embodiment of the idea of regeneration: the black fertile ḫprw out of which the living red ḫprw was to emerge.   J.J.J.

79700   MARTIN, Geoffrey T., A Block from the Memphite Tomb of Ḥoremḥeb in Chicago, *JNES* 38 (1979), 33-35, with 1 ill.

This limestone fragment measuring 47 cm wide by 35 cm high, Inv. No. 10591, was purchased in Cairo in 1920. It forms part of the right side of a scene in raised relief showing a king at a Window of Appearances with foreign captives before it, and can be located as having belonged to a scene on the south wall of the Great Court of the tomb. The king shown was probably Tutankhamūn or Ay.   *E.P. Uphill*

79701   MELTZER, Edmund S., Akhenaten's Lost Temples, *Fate Magazine*, January 1979, 40-50, with 5 ill., 1 fig. and 1 map.

Article for the general reader about the Akhenaten Temple Project.

79702   MYŚLIWIEC, Karol, Un relief de la fin du Moyen Empire, *BIFAO* 79 (1979), 141-154, with 2 fig. and 1 pl.

Publication of a rhyodazite relief block representing a king offering two *nw*-vessels (Cairo No. Temp. 18/11/14/22). On account of its stylistic qualities it is dated to the M.K., probably Amenemhat III or, less likely, one of his immediate successors. From comparison with a similar representation of Sebekemsaf I from Madâmûd and a relief head of Sesostris I from el-Lisht its provenance is argued to be the latter site. J.J.J.

79703   PECK, William H., Materialien und Zweck altägyptischer Zeichnungen, *Antike Welt*, Feldmeilen 10, Heft 1 (1979), 16-26, with 10 ill.

The article consists of one chapter from the German edition of
our number 78612: Ägyptische Zeichnungen aus drei Jahrtausenden,
Bergisch-Gladbach, Gustav-Lübbe Verlag, 1979 (Pr. DM 58).

79704 TAWFIK, Sayed, Aton Studies. 5. Cult Objects on Blocks from the
Aton Temple(s) at Thebes, *MDAIK* 35 (1979), 335-344, with 10 fig.
and 3 pl.

Sequel to our number 76766.
This part of the series is devoted to the *nmst* jars that appear
in many scenes of the Aton temple(s) at Thebes. It is a flat-
bottomed vessel with rounded shoulders and a mouth with or
without a spout. The author discusses the material of which it
was made (gold, silver, faience, granite), its contents and
functions. It was used in temple rituals, probably also in the
heb-sed procession, but whether in the rite of "Opening the
Mouth" or the funerary rituals of the Amarna Period is uncertain.
                                                              J.J.J.

79705 THOMAS, Angela P., Two Monuments from Abydos in Bolton Museum,
in: *Glimpses of Ancient Egypt*, 20-25, with 6 ill.

The two monuments in the Bolton Museum here thoroughly studied
are: 1. two blocks of a lintel (No. 53.02.6) from the M.K. tomb
of a high steward Nebankh of whom four other monuments are known
(ANOC 46); 2. five adjoining relief fragments (No. 53.06.7) from
the Osiris temple area, representing i.a. the head of king
Amenophis III.   J.J.J.

79706 TRIGGER, Bruce G., The Narmer Palette in Cross-Cultural Per-
spective, *in*: *Festschrift Elmar Edel*, 409-419, with 2 fig.

The author studies the scene on the verso of the Narmer Palette
which depicts the king brandishing his mace over a supine enemy.
Parallels from other civilisations make us aware of a wide range
of possible explanations. Nakedness of an enemy, for instance,
is also found in Mesopotamia and Mexico, indicating that he is
humiliated. Representing a combat in the form of a duel reflects
an early phase in the organisational development; actual battle
scenes appear only later.   J.J.J.

79707 VACHALA, Břetislav, Počítač a tajemství staroegyptského
panovníka, *Lide a země*, Praha 28, No. 1 (1979), 21-26.

"Der Computer und das Geheimnis eines altägyptischen Herrschers."
Verfasser macht mit den Rekonstruktionsarbeiten des Echnaton-
tempels bekannt ("Akhenaten Temple Project").   *B. Vachala*

79708 VANDERSLEYEN, Claude, De l'usage du relief dans le creux à l'époque ramesside, *BSFE* No. 86 (octobre 1979), 16-38, with 12 ill.

L'Ancien Empire réservait le relief dans le creux aux parois exposées au soleil, que ce soit réellement ou en théorie. Dans les tombes amarniennes, Aton rayonne parmi des reliefs techniquement apparentés à ce procédé. Les bords du creux, jusque là réguliers, Amarna les rompt pour nuancer la rondeur des corps et la profondeur de l'espace. L'avantage fondamental du relief dans le creux aurait été de traduire plus librement les variétés d'épaisseur. L'inspiration nouvelle pouvait utiliser un modelé ténu, presque réduit au dessin du contour. Ce tendre maniérisme, Ramsès II en a recueilli le fruit pour son répertoire militaire, expressioniste. Chez lui, le relief dans un creux accusé prédomine, la ligne a priorité sur la profondeur, mais les batailles détachent le roi seul d'un grouillement "pictural". Donadoni voit l'originalité esthétique du règne dans l'aptitude impressioniste. Il dut y avoir choix délibéré, selon l'élan romantique du temps. Dans ces compositions fougueuses sans registre, la douleur des victimes provoque une sorte de sympathie. La splendide chasse au taureau sauvage, de Ramsès III, garde encore quelque chose des plans multiples de l'art amarnien.
J. Custers

79709 WERNER, Edward K., Identification of Nefertiti in *Talatat* Reliefs Previously Published as Akhenaten, *Orientalia* 48 (1979), 324-331, with 4 pl.

Deux critères iconographiques combinés permettraient de reconnaître indubitablement Néfertiti sur les reliefs de Karnak: une perruque particulière et le double uraeus. La coiffure est celle des beaux canopes de Merytaton (MMA 30.8.54). Réunissant les termes d'Aldred et de J. Samson, Werner la nomme "perruque nubienne pointue". Elle comprend jusqu'à cinq couches de tresses ou de rouleaux. Akhenaton ne la montre jamais à Karnak; en sa compagnie, la reine arbore nécessairement une couronne à plumes. Pour porter la perruque nubienne, elle doit être seule ou accompagnée de sa fille. L'uraeus double, ornement royal sous la dynastie "koushite", apparaît auparavant, en particulier chez Tiyi, Néfertary et Néfertiti. Celle-ci le présente au debut du règne sur diverses coiffures. L'auteur restitue à Néfertiti les "talatates" J.207 à 209 du Musée de Louqsor, ainsi que le no. 64.199.2 de Brooklyn, comparé à Cleveland CMA 76.4. Ce dernier "portrait" montre un bandeau, comme le bloc J.208 (nouveau numéro: 2805-12). La perruque pointue à bandeau, rare chez Néfertiti, est fréquente pour les particuliers à la "Late Period" d'Amarna. Sur la même Zipfel-Stufen-Perücke (Roeder), voir *JEA* 1980, K. Bosse-Griffiths, p. 79.
J. Custers

79710 WORSHAM, Charles E., A Reinterpretation of the So-called Bread Loaves in Egyptian Offerings Scenes, *JARCE* 16 (1979), 7-10, with 2 pl.

Loaves on offering tables before which the deceased is shown
sitting may show a typical reed-like form (𓇑) in M.K. representations. In other instances these elongated standing objects show characteristics of both the offering loaves and the
flowering reeds. Although perhaps due to stylistic variation,
the new imagery obtains a firm footing by the XIth Dynasty and
then may evoke the Field Of Offerings (sḫ.t ḥtp.w) where, according to religious texts, the deceased receives his food
supply.
Cfr our number 73520, unquoted here.   J.F. Borghouts

79711 ZIVIE, Alain-Pierre, Une tombe d'époque amarnienne à Saqqarah,
       BSFE No. 84 (mars 1979), 21-32, with 3 ill.

A Saqqarah, non loin de la maison de Lauer, une tombe rupestre
quasi ensablée a attiré l'attention de l'auteur. Celui-ci a pu
y reconnaître au moins quatre pieces; la facade a disparu. Le
nom du propriétaire, le vizir ꜥpr-i3, figure au dictionnaire de
Ranke, qui le lit Aper-El, le considérant comme cananéen. Petrie
a encore copié les éléments r/l (bouche et trait); ses notes ont
gardé des signes presque effacés, tel le groupe "l'Aton vivant",
capital pour la datation. L'épouse du vizir s'appelait Ouriai
(ou Ourya). Les parois latérales des première et troisième
salles, à plafond cintré, s'ornaient d'une corniche à gorge, de
"pilastres" et de panneaux. L'un de ces panneaux aurait porté
une scène de funérailles; le panneau principal, dont les personnages martelés étaient d'un style excellent, portait une
scène de lustration . Le texte énumère les titres et épithètes
honorifiques de ce vizir (du Nord?) inconnu jusqu'ici, du moins
sous ce nom. L'une des trois tombes voisines, presque inacces-
sibles, appartenait à un officier au nom de consonance étrangère,
presque contemporain de Thoutmosis IV ou d'Aménophis III: voir
notre no. 79266.   J. Custers

h. Tomb equipment, furniture and cult objects

See also our numbers 79049; 79073; 79126; 79133; 79208; 79326; 79446;
79448; 79510; 79512; 79523; 79525; 79536; 79540; 79560; 79561; 79565;
79570; 79571; 79573; 79589; 79600; 79601; 79606; 79608; 79614; 79620;
79638; 79640; 79643; 79659; 79674; 79683; 79704; 79748; 79770; 79805;
79901; 79904; 79906; 79940 and 791008.

79712 AUBERT, Jacques-F., Chaoubtis, chabtis et ouchebtis, CdE LIV,
       No. 107 (1979), 57-72.

Article de recension consacré au livre de Hans D. Schneider,
Shabtis (notre no. 77685).
L'auteur, qui a également écrit sur les ouchebtis (notre no.
74044) se préoccupe de montrer les différences de conception
entre son ouvrage et celui de Schneider, beaucoup plus systéma-
tique et comprenant un catalogue très copieux. Ce dernier

ouvrage est examiné en détail et parfois enrichi de citations nouvelles. Dans l'ensemble pourtant, il ressort que les thèses d'Aubert, qui n'est pas égyptologue, restent moins précises que celles du savant hollandais.   *Ph. Derchain*

79713 BECKER-COLONNA, A.L., Myths and Symbols in a Cartonnage Coffin of the XXIst Dynasty from the Sutro Collection at San Francisco State University, *in*: *Acts 1st ICE*, 95-101, with 1 pl.

The author discusses the cartonnage lid of a coffin, which belonged to *Ns-pr-n-nwb*, a doorkeeper of the temple of Amon from the XXIst Dynasty. The piece, the black coating of which has recently been removed, is richly decorated. The author deals extensively with the figures and scenes. At the end remarks on the provenance (Lower Egypt?) and quality of the piece. It hardly looks possible that its owner was a simple doorkeeper.
J.J.J.

79714 BRESCIANI, Edda, Un usciabti del generale Psamtek-sa-Neit nel Museo "L. Pogliaghi" a Varese, *Egitto e Vicino Oriente* 2 (1979), 49-55, with 2 pl. and 3 fig.

Les collections du Musée Lodovico Pogliaghi, près de Varèse, contiennent plusieurs objets égyptiens, non numérotés, dont 4 oushebtis de faience; l'auteur publie l'un de ceux-ci. Le défunt momiforme à barbe tressée, perruque lisse et grandes oreilles, tient des outils agricoles. Le pilier dorsal porte deux colonnes d'un texte qui couvre la base et se développe en dix lignes horizontales sur la statuette: c'est le chapitre VI du Livre des Morts, sans variantes ni erreurs particulières. La typologie comme le nom du personnage indiquent la XXVIe dynastie: il s'agit du général Psamétik-sa-Neith, fils du général Psamétik-aoui-Neith et de la dame Neith-emhat. Sept autres oushebtis à son nom sont déjà connus, mais celui-ci porte la seule mention du patronyme, absent également des canopes, conservés au Musée du Louvre. Aucun cartouche n'entoure dans l'exemplaire de Varèse le nom royal, partie du nom des deux généraux. La datation probable serait le règne d'Amasis plutôt que celui de Psamétik II.   *J. Custers*

79715 BRUNNER, Hellmut, Sokar im Totentempel Amenophis' III., *in*: *Festschrift Elmar Edel*, 60-65, with 5 fig. and 1 pl.

Recently the Egyptological Institute at Tübingen acquired a small object (*c.* 4.5 x 5 cm) which is clearly the roof of a chapel (Inv. No. 1728). It bears a text with the names of Amenophis III and the words *Skr m t3 ḥwt Nb-m3ʿt-Rʿ*, and belonged to a sanctuary of Sokaris in the mortuary temple of Amenophis III. Discussing what type of statue could have been standing in it, Brunner points at an ithyphallic golden figure of a bird with a Ptah-head (see our number 4357, 4, note 1), now in a private Swiss collection. From the direction of the writing on the roof it can be concluded that the statuette represented a king.   *J.J.J.*

79716 DANERI de RODRIGO, Alicia, Las piezas egipcias del Museo de Ciencias Naturales de la Plata (Primera Parte). I. Ushebti, *Revista del Instituto de Historia Antigua Oriental*, Buenos Aires 4 (1978), 129-134.

Publication of a series of nine shabtis in the Museo de Ciencias Naturales de la Plata, Buenos Aires province (MLP No. 23-31), all dated to the Saite-Persian Periods.   *J.R. Ogdon*

79717 DESROCHES-NOBLECOURT, Christiane, Quatre objets protodynastiques provenant d'un "trésor funéraire, *La Revue du Louvre et des Musées de France*, Paris 29 (1979), 108-117, with 26 fig. and ill.

The author publishes four predynastic vessels in the form of or bearing the representation of animals (Inv. Nos. E 27.200-27.203). A longer study devoted to these acquisitions of the Louvre Museum has appeared in the Livre du Centenaire. Mélanges préparés par l'Institut français d'Archéologie orientale, 1980 (= MIFAO, 104).

79718 DOLZANI, C., Problemi sul significato religioso e cultuale dei vasi canopi, *in*: *Acts 1st ICE*, 163-174.

Five different problems concerning the canopic vessels are briefly dealt with: their Egyptian name as well as the origin of their modern appellation; their earliest instances and origin; the early texts to the identity and functions of the sons of Horus; the evolution of the shape of the canopic vessel; the evolution of the concept "sons of Horus" as protectors of the deceased.   *J.J.J.*

79719 van DIJK, Jac., Egyptian Antiquities in the Bijbels Museum Amsterdam (I), *GM* Heft 36 (1979), 7-14, with 3 fig. and 4 ill. on 2 pl.

In den folgenden Nummern dieser Zeitschrift sollen die etwa 60 ägyptischen Stücke aus dem Biblischen Museum in Amsterdam vorgestellt werden, die aus der Sammlung des holländischen Predigers L. Schouten (1828-1905) stammen. Zunächst wird ein anthropoider Sarkophag vorgestellt (Inv.-Nr. 2): er ist 194 cm lang, besteht aus bemalten Holz und stammt vermutlich aus dem Fayyum. Erworben wurde er 1906 vom "Director of the Cairo Museum" durch einen Missionar. Der Sarkophag stammt aus der frühen Ptolemäerzeit. Der Text wird in Faksimile gebracht und kommentiert.
                                                        Inge Hofmann

79720 EVRARD-DERRIKS, Claire et Jan QUAEGEBEUR, La situle décorée de Nesnakhtiou au Musée Royal de Mariemont, *CdE* LIV, No. 107 (1979), 26-56, with 2 ill. and 2 fig.

Publication d'une situle d'origine thébaine datable de 350-150 a.C. (probablement même 300-250). Photographies, fac-similé des scènes, transcription des textes ainsi qu'un commentaire exhaustif de l'ensemble de l'objet sont accompagnés d'une suite de recherches onomastiques étendues. *Ph. Derchain*

79721 FINKENSTAEDT, Elisabeth, Egyptian Ivory Tusks and Tubes, ZÄS 106 (1979), 51-59, with 4 ill.

The author discards the virtually exclusively Amratian date proposed for worked hippopotamus tusks and tubes in predynastic Egyptian graves. Naqada, Mahasna and Badari offer Gerzean evidence.
We may postulate chronological and typological synchronisms between Egypt and Syria at the end of the Gerzean Period, i.a. before the Syrian imports from Egypt in historic times. Tubes and anchors in Anatolia, Greece and the Cyclades are later than the Egyptian and Syrian examples and raise a separate and still unsolved problem in derivation. *M. Heerma v. Voss*

79722 GOUT-MINAULT, Anne, Deux fonctionnaires de la XIXe Dynastie en poste au Soudan (Saï- inventaire 1126, 1147-1150 et 1153), *in*: *Hommages Sauneron* I, 33-41, with 3 pl.

Discussion of three shawabtis and two heart scarabs from tomb No. 2 at Sai. They belong, with a few other objects, to a secretary (sš šʿt; the author adduces material for this function) Horemheb and a wʿb-priest Ky-iry. The type of the shawabtis suggests a XIXth Dynasty date, so that Sai may have belonged to the few still occupied places of that period. *J.J.J.*

79723 MÁLEK, Jaromír, An ointment-slab of Sekhemptaḥ, *GM* Heft 33 (1979), 35-40, with 1 fig.

Es wird eine weitere Salbpalette vorgestellt, die von C.M. Firth wahrscheinlich bei der Pyramide des Teti in Saqqara gefunden wurde und von der sich eine Zeichnung sowie Bemerkungen zum Material und den Massen in den Papieren von Battiscombe Gunn (MSS. R.2.4 und Notebook 12, No. 109) im Griffith-Institut von Oxford fand. Die beschriftete Palette wird kommentiert und eine Liste von 34 beschrifteten Salbpaletten aus der 5. und 6. Dynastie angeführt. *Inge Hofmann*

79724 MÁLEK, Jaromír, A Shawabti of the Draughtsman Pay of Deir el-Medîna, *RdE* 31 (1979), 153-156, with 1 ill. and 1 fig.

Publication d'un chaouabti provenant d'une collection privée au nom d'un sš-kd m st Mꜣʿt Pay, portant la formule usuelle des chouabtis de Deir el-Medina. L'auteur cherche à identifier ce Pay à l'un de ceux qui auraient pu vivre entre le règne de Horemheb et le début de celui de Ramsès II. *Ph. Derchain*

79725 RABINOVITCH, Abraham, Découverte de sarcophages de style égyptien dans la bande de Gaza, *Le Monde de la Bible*, Paris No. 11 (Novembre-Décembre 1979), 52-54, with 4 ill.

On the discovery of anthropoid clay coffins at Deir el-Balah by Trude Dothan.

79726 SHORE, A.F., Votive Objects from Dendera of the Graeco-Roman Period, in: *Glimpses of Ancient Egypt*, 138-160, with 7 ill. and 3 fig.

The author deals with a number of metal objects which from the style of their Demotic dedicatory inscription formed part of the ritual furniture of the Dendera temple. Of the objects listed a few are published here, namely, a silver dish (MMA 26.2.46), a silver bowl (Kelsey Museum 3727) and the foot of an offering table or incense stand (BM 59571). To the hoard also belong two bronze tablets (BM 57371 and 57372), one with a Demotic text, the other with a Demotic inscription on one side and a hieroglyphic on the other. The texts are presented in facsimile, transliteration and translation with comments. They record lists of titles, benefactions to the temple and benefits accruing to the benefactor. Although badly legible it seems probable that they both had identical contents. They constitute so far the only surviving examples of the use of metal tablets for inscribing texts, a practice mentioned already in the N.K.   J.J.J.

79727 van WALSEM, R., The *pss̆-kf*. An Investigation of an Ancient Egyptian Funerary Instrument, *OMRO* 59-60 (1978-1979), 193-249, with 1 pl., 13 fig., 8 tables and a summary in Dutch on p. 244-245.

The author studies the *pss̆-kf* instrument that is mentioned in the Opening of the Mouth ritual and of which a fairly large number of instances, some from model sets, have been preserved. He first deals with the scarce actual data about the function of the instrument and with the traditional theories about its meaning. Then he minutely discusses its occurrences in the texts; the variant writings; the components of the word (*kf*, "flint"; *ps̆s̆* perhaps due to its bifurcated shape); its place in the funerary practices; its development during the ages. At the end a section on the prehistoric *pss̆-kf*.
The author defends the theory that its original function was to support the chin of the deceased. This was soon forgotten, however; hence the wide range of writings and shapes.   J.J.J.

79228 WINTER, Erich, Der ägyptische Sarg des Landesmuseums Trier, *Landeskundliche Vierteljahrsblätter*, Trier 25, Heft 4 (1979), 163-164.

Brief remarks to a lecture with slides. The coffin concerned belonged to a lady *P3̆.s̆-t̆3w-(m)-ʿ.wy-rw* and dates from about the XXVIth Dynasty.

79729 ZIEGLER, Christiane, A propos du rite des quatre boules, *BIFAO* 79 (1979), 437-439, with 1 pl.

The balls of resin found in the Graeco-Roman necropolis of Tihna and preserved in the Louvre Museum (Nos. E 12196-12199; 12202-3 and 12205), inscribed with the names of the goddesses Wadjet, Sekhemtet, Bastet and Sakhmet and connected with lion heads of clay that serve the same function, belong to a ritual recently studied by Goyon (see our number 75280).   J.J.J.

79730 ZIVIE, Alain-Pierre, Nouveaux aperçus sur les "coudées votives". L'apport original de deux fragments provenant de Basse Égypte, in: Hommages Sauneron I, 319-343, with 7 fig. and 2 pl.

By publishing two fragments of votive cubit rods the author once more adduces material to the study of this type of object (cfr our numbers 72808 and 77841). The pieces belong to a private collection in Paris and may come from Ḥurbeit. One explicitly mentions Nectanebo I, the other may be of the same period. The texts contain several new elements.   J.J.J.

i. Minor arts, small objects, utensils, pottery, dress

See also our numbers 79034; 79112; 79133; 79431; 79482; 79508; 79512; 79518; 79523; 79525; 79526; 79528; 79536; 79541; 79545; 79560; 79561; 79571; 79588; 79592; 79599; 79601; 79603; 79606; 79607; 79612; 79624; 79644; 79645; 79674; 79709; 79786; 79791; 79817; 79818; 79893; 79894; 79900; 79912; 79913; 79914 and 79915.

79731 AMIRAN, Ruth and Jonathan GLASS, An Archaeological-Petrographical Study of 15 W-Ware Pots in the Ashmolean Museum, *Tel Aviv*, Tel Aviv 6 (1979), 54-59, with 2 fig. and 1 table.

The authors study 15 Predynastic Wavy-handle pottery vessels (Petrie's classification: W-Ware) which is of Canaanite character, all at present in the Ashmolean Museum, Oxford. After a classification in descending order according to the archaeological evaluation of their degree of similarity to an original Canaanite prototype (3 possible imports; 3 possible early copies; 6 standard W-pots; 3 later W-pots), follows the petrographical analysis. In all approaches Naqada jar No. 1895.521 compares best with an Early Bronze I jar from Arad.

79732 BERGER, Catherine, Audran LABROUSSE et Jean LECLANT, Présentation préliminaire de la céramique recueillie par la MAFS au temple haut et à la pyramide de Pépi Ier, Saqqarah. Campagnes 1970-1971 et 1978-1979, Paris, 1979 (21 x 29.5 cm; 27 p., 1 pl., 11 fig. [= pl. 1-11]) = Publications de l'U.R.A. No. 4. Cahiers No. 2.

Sequel to our number 78076.
This second fascicle is devoted to the pottery found in the storerooms and in the pyramid itself. The majority date from the N.K. (pl. 2-10), a few instances from the O.K. (pl. 1), all alabaster vessels, or from the Islamic Period (pl. 11).   J.J.J.

79733 BERLEV, O.D., and S.I. KHODZHASH, Наконечник колья фараона яхмеса I из государственного музея нзобразительных искусств имени A.S. Пушкина, ВДИ 1 (147), 1979, 82-83, with 1 ill. and an English summary on p. 83.

"A Spearhead of the Pharaoh Ahmose in the Pushkin Museum."
The object's inscription testifies to the liberation from the Hyksos.

79734 BIANCHI, Robert S., Ex-votos of Dynasty XXVI, *MDAIK* 35 (1979), 15-22, with 7 pl.

This is an attempt to bring some order in the so-called Ptolemaic Sculptor's models by identifying some of them which can be dated to the XXVIth Dynasty and defining their characteristics. The objects studied are: Brooklyn Acc. No. 5380, with on the recto the cartouche of Psammetichus I and on the verso a representation of Mut; Museum Narodowe, Warsaw, No. 14276 (from Edfu), with on both sides a king, once with the cartouche of Amasis; Walters Art Gallery, Baltimore, No. WAG 341 = 22.294, with a king on the recto and part of the scene of a lion trampling a foe on the verso. On account of these and other evidence Bianchi concludes that in the Saite Period a new type of ex-voto was introduced, frequently preserving its grid and often mistakenly called unfinished.
J.J.J.

79735 BRISSAUD, Philippe, Le céramique égyptienne du règne d'Amenophis II à la fin de l'époque ramesside, *in*: *Hommages Sauneron* I, 11-32, with 2 pl.

The author presents a broad introduction to the study of ceramics dating from the period of the reign of Amenophis II to the end of the N.K., their material, forms, decoration, contents and use. He gives a survey of the little that is known about the subject, makes remarks on production techniques of vases, and discusses vases with a painted and those with a relief decoration.
J.J.J.

79736 Bulletin de liaison du Groupe International d'Étude de la Céramique égyptienne, [Le Caire] 4 (1979).

Sequel to our number 78136.
Again the bulletin first lists notes to pottery from various sites, presented by several authors and arranged in a geographical order from the North to Meroe. In the second chapter various communications on current matters. After an index to chapters 1 and 2 and a list of recent publications on pottery chapter 5 contains summaries of 15 of the 17 papers read during the Second International Congress of Egyptologists in Grenoble, September 1979.
J.J.J.

79737 CLOSE, Angela E., The Identification of Style in Lithic Artefacts from North East Africa, [Cairo], Institut d'Égypte, 1977 (17 x 24 cm; VIII + 314 p., 20 fig., 82 tables) = Mémoires de l'Institut d'Égypte, 61.

This volume is the fourth in a series of reports on research related to the Combined Prehistoric Expedition. It is concerned with the identification of stylistic variability in, and the definition of social groupings from, the archaeological record of the Late and Epipalaeolithic of North Africa.
After a mainly theoretical introductory chapter, the author in chapter 2 briefly discusses previous work on the period. In chapter 3 she presents her methods of analysis, and in chapter 4 her material: twenty-four assemblages, including eleven from the Nile Valley (Nubia and the Esna area). The next three chapters are each devoted to variability of a single attribute of backed bladelets. In chapter 8 a tentative grouping of the material, based on Cluster Analysis, is proposed, and conclusions are presented.
A bibliography on p. 258-263 is followed by two statistical Appendices. *J. v. d. Vliet*

79738 DAVID, A.R., Toys and Games from Kahun in the Manchester Museum Collection, in: *Glimpses of Ancient Egypt*, 12-15, with 6 ill.

Description of some toys (dolls, balls, etc.) and gaming boards and pieces found by Petrie in the M.K. town of Kahun and at present preserved in the Manchester Museum. A few more important objects are illustrated by photographs. *J.J.J.*

79739 DEWACHTER, Michel, Le type No. 2 du *Corpus* des cônes funéraires, *RdE* 31 (1979), 152-153.

Quelques observations et hypothèses à propos de deux fragments. *Ph. Derchain*

79740 EATON-KRAUSS, M., The Khat Headdress to the End of the Amarna Period, in: *Acts 1st ICE*, 188-192.

Abridged version of the article that has been published in our number 77207.

79741 FROST, Honor, Egypt and Stone Anchors: Some Recent Discoveries, *The Mariner's Mirror*, London 65 (1979), 137-161, with 13 ill. and fig.

After introductory remarks on the motives for the study of anchors and the significance of the discovery of sea-going anchors in ancient Egypt the author deals with the question of sea-going ships in ancient Egypt. She then extensively describes and discusses the anchors found in Egypt, the earliest of which are the anchors and pierced stones found in O.K. contexts.

She devotes particular attention to the anchor shrine and a
monument associated with anchors at Wadi Gawâsîs, which are
datable to the XIIth Dynasty. In this connection she studies
the question of shipyards on the banks of the Nile, the possible
dismantling for transport, the size of the ships, their use for
the voyage to Punt, and the votive context of the anchors.
After remarks on the Cypriote-type anchor found in the Amon
temple at Karnak and on two atypical specimens coming from the
temple of Isidorus by the Canopic branch of the Nile the crucial
importance of the discoveries at Wadi Gawâsîs is stressed in the
conclusion.
Compare our number 79761.

79742 GINTER, Bolesław, Janusz K. KOZŁOWSKI und Barbara DROBNIEWICZ,
Silexindustrien von El Tarîf. Ein Beitrag zur Entwicklung der
Prädynastischen Kulturen in Ober-Ägypten. Mit einem Beitrag von
Wiesław Heflik, Mainz am Rhein, Verlag Philipp von Zabern, [1979]
(27 x 35.5 cm; 78 p., 26 fig. including 1 map and 1 plan, 18
tables, 88 pl.) = Archäologische Veröffentlichungen. Deutsches
Archäologisches Institut Abteilung Kairo, 26; rev. *BiOr* 38
(1981), 33-34 (Pierre M. Vermeersch). Pr. DM 135

The authors present the analysis of the vast collection of Predynastic lithic material which was found during the German
excavations in the necropolis of el-Tarîf (see also our number
76033).
After a discussion in the first chapter of the topography and
stratigraphy of the site including the geomorphological characteristics and a palaeoclimatological interpretation, they deal
in the second chapter with the Palaeolithic material, which is
described and the cultural position of which is discussed. In
chapters 3 and 4 the material is divided respectively after that
of a silex-industry labelled Series-A and the artefacts of a
Series-B, the various types of stones and tools of which are
extensively described. The industry of Series-A is discussed
in the light of the pre-Neolithic and Neolithic cultures in the
Nile Valley in chapter 3, while a traseological analysis of some
selected silex artefacts of the Series-B is presented in chapter
4. Chapter 5 contains the comparison between the two series,
including a discussion of the material of the Series-B in the
light of the Neolithic silex industries in the Nile Valley and
the origin of some of its typological elements.
The last chapter 6 is devoted to the silex and stone artefacts
from the Dynastic Period.
Bibliography at the end of the book.

79743 GOLDSTEIN, Sidney M., A Unique Royal Head, *Journal of Glass
Studies*, Corning, New York 21 (1979), 8-16, with 11 ill.

The author publishes a miniature royal head, recently acquired
by the Corning Museum of Glass (Inv. No. 79.1.4). It is made of
a bright and lustrous medium blue glass, not easily recognisable

as such. After having described the object he discusses its manufacturing technique. It was probably cast by the lost wax technique, retouched and polished with a wheel and some type of non-rotary hand tools. The author dates the head to the reign of Amenhotep II on stylistic grounds.
For a colour ill., although having not exactly the blue colour mentioned above, see the front cover and the frontispiece of the same periodical 22 (1980).

79744 HENNESSY, John Basil, Ancient Near Eastern Pottery, [Tokyo], Kodansha, [1979] (25.5 x 37 cm; 304 p., 120 colour pl. [= p. 29-219], 104 ill. on 13 pl. [= p. 221-248], 2 maps, 2 tables; cased) = Masterpieces of Western and Near Eastern Ceramics, 1.

The main interest of this book which is written in Japanese and English lies in its splendid photographs.
After an introduction on ancient Near Eastern Pottery the author presents first in colour 120 pottery objects with captions including data, from the entire ancient Near East. Then follows in monochrome another series of 101 objects, equally comprising unglazed earthenware, terracotta and faience. This part of the catalogue is preceded by an index which is arranged after country of provenance. The book concludes with more extensive descriptions, again with data, of the objects illustrated on the colour pl.
A synchronising chronological table is added.

79745 HOPE, Colin A., Dakhleh Oasis Project. Report on the Study of the Pottery and Kilns, *JSSEA* 9 (1978-1979), 187-201, with 4 pl.

The attempts to date the pottery found during the first season were based on comparison with material from the Nile Valley and on finds of coins, Demotic and Greek ostraca and Coptic papyrus. For the classification of locally made pottery the find of kilns with unfired vessels was of importance.
The author presents a provisional classification of the wares found during the season and a description of the eight kilns of various periods that have been discovered.   J.J.J.

79746 HOSTENS-DELEU, Ria, Beeldhouwers-modellen in de egyptische afdeling van de Koninklijke Musea voor Kunst en Geschiedenis, *Bulletin des Musées Royaux d'Art et d'Histoire/Bulletin van de Koninklijke Musea van Kunst en Geschiedenis*, Bruxelles 49 (1977), 1979, 5-66, with 40 ill. on 16 pl. and a French summary on p. 49.

"Sculptors' Models in the Egyptian Department of the Royal Museums of Art and History."
In the introduction the author first surveys the various opinions on the functions of the so-called "sculptors' models." From the widespread places of provenance she concludes that the pieces were indeed models for the apprentices. Although the models are usually dated to the Late Period she argues that they were used

already since the O.K., but more systematically in the Late
Period, probably in order to create a regulated national art as
opposed to foreign influences. Then follows the catalogue proper
of 74 pieces, the provenance of which is only seldom known.
They are arranged after the two main divisions of sculpture, in
the round and reliefs, each subdivided into: kings and queens,
private persons, animals, hieroglyphs, architectural elements,
and linear studies. After inventory number, description, bibliography and parallels there are given the technical data such
as dimensions, material, provenance, date and state of preservation. Index to inventory nos. at the end.

79747 KÁKOSY, Ladislas, Amulette avec représentations de décans au
Musée des Beaux-Arts, *Bulletin du Musée Hongrois des Beaux-Arts*,
Budapest 52 (1979), 3-10, with 11 ill. and a Hungarian version
on p. 109-113.

Publication of a small Sakhmet statuette from the collection of
the museum in Budapest (Inv. No. 51 2329), the most important
detail of which is the figures on the side of the throne of
grotesque snakes with legs and arms, representing the decans.
Two other fragmentary pieces from the same collection are briefly
mentioned. They are ascribed to the 1st millennium B.C. and may
be presents given at the New Year.
In this connection the author discusses the history of the concept of the decans and their representations.   *J.J.J.*

79748 KENDALL, Timothy, Passing through the Netherworld. The Meaning
and Play of *Senet*, an Ancient Egyptian Funerary Game, Boston,
Museum of Fine Arts. Department of Egyptian and Ancient Near
Eastern Art, 1978 (14 x 21.5 cm; 67 + 7 additional unnumbered
p., 38 + 4 fig. and ill. *[3 on cover]*; added set of board, 14
playing pieces, 4 dice sticks, and leaflet containing the rules
of the play).   Pr. set £8

Produced and distributed by the Kirk Game Company Inc., POB 478,
Belmont, Mass. 02178.
Apart from the game the complete set also includes a booklet
meant for the scholar. After introductory remarks on the game
of *senet* in chapter 1 the author in chapter 2 traces its history
from the Predynastic Period to the N.K. on account of archaeological and pictorial evidence. In chapter 3 the author discusses the connections between the game and the Egyptian beliefs
concerning death and afterlife. In chapter 4 follows the later
history of *senet* from the T.I.P. to the Christian era, while
special attention is paid to the pertinent episode in the Demotic
story of Senet. Chapter 5 is devoted to the names and meanings
of the squares on the board of the funerary *senet* game. Chapter
6 is concerned with the religious and funerary texts relating to
the game of *senet*, which are primarily quotations from B.D. Ch.
17 and the tomb of Tjanefer (Theban Tomb No. 158). The last
chapter 7 deals with the rules for playing *senet*, the funerary

setting implicit in the game, and the equipment and the actual playing of the game.
Corrections, with additional notes and comments are added in a separate leaflet.
Compare also our number 79762.

79749 KURTH, Dieter, Ein Grabkegel vom Grab des Suti und Hor, *GM* Heft 31 (1979), 63-66, with 3 fig.

Es wird ein bisher unbekannter Grabkegel des Hor vorgestellt, der 1978 in Medinet Habu erworben wurde und sich jetzt in Kölner Privatbesitz befindet. Er stimmt vollkommen mit einem der beiden bisher bekannten Grabkegel des Hor überein. Die nunmehr bekannten drei Grabkegel sind aus gewichtigen Gründen, die der Verfasser erläutert, den Stelen der Zwillingsbrüder Suti und Hor, zweier Oberbaumeister unter Amenophis III., zuzuordnen.
Inge Hofmann

79750 LANDI, Sheila and Rosalind M. HALL, The Discovery and Conservation of an Ancient Egyptian Linen Tunic, *Studies in Conservation*, London 24 (1979), 141-152, with 2 fig. and 9 ill.

In 1977 a sleeved linen tunic was discovered in University College London (U.C. 28614B') that came from Petrie's excavations at Tarkhan. It was dated to the 1st Dynasty, a date first confirmed by a radiocarbon test, but a later one pointed to the Vth Dynasty.
The garment is carefully described (for a photograph, see also *JEA* 67 (1981), pl. XX, 2), comparative evidence is adduced, and the later date is rejected. The last section extensively discusses the conservation techniques. *J.J.J.*

79751 LILYQUIST, Christine, Ancient Egyptian Mirrors from the Earliest Times through the Middle Kingdom, München - Berlin, Deutscher Kunstverlag, 1979 (21 x 29.7 cm; XIV + 170 p., numerous fig., 69 pl.) = Münchner Ägyptologische Studien, 27.   Pr. DM 110

This work contains the first part of a thesis on mirrors and has been completed, according to the preface, in 1971. It covers the period from the beginning of Egyptian history to the end of the M.K., and includes material from Nubia (also from Kerma) and Byblos.
The introduction explains the scope of the study and the means to date the mirrors and their representations. Section I (p. 1-48) presents the corpus of dated mirrors. It is divided after periods in a chronological order, each subdivided after sites and ending with objects of unknown context. The mirrors and representations are briefly indicated within the context in which they have been found and which suggests their date. An extensive analysis of the methods of dating at selected sites of two periods, late O.K. - early M.K. and M.K. - late M.K. is given in the Appendix (102-144). Here the work of several excavators at various sites is extensively discussed.

Section II (49-95) contains the analysis of the subject: physical characteristics of the mirror (the reflective surface, the handles and the containers); nomenclature; types of contexts in which they are found (graves, temples, houses, etc.); provenance; the owners (sex, titles, names); iconography of reflective surface and handles. Throughout representations and actual objects are taken together.
In section III (96-99) conclusions as regards Egypt's history and its social and religious life are presented. There follows (100-101) a table indicating the results of chemical analyses of some mirrors.
At the end of the book a bibliography (145-153) and indexes to museum numbers, representations of mirrors and burials yielding these objects, and the features for dating. On the plates drawings and photographs of some pieces and of containers as well as of representations on tomb walls, stelae, false doors and coffins.
For mirrors, see also our number 76238. *J.J.J.*

79752 LITTAUER, Mary A., and J. CROUWEL, An Egyptian Wheel in Brooklyn, *JEA* 65 (1979), 107-120, with 3 pl. and 2 fig.

This wheel (Acc. No. 37.1700) was purchased by H. Abbott between 1832 and 1843. It is c. 0.96m. in diameter with six spokes, and is said to have come from a tomb near the pyramids of Dahshur. It appears to belong to a Late Period chariot possibly of a type influenced by Asiatic types, and many examples are used for comparison in order to establish that this was Persian. *E.P. Uphill*

79753 LUNSINGH SCHEURLEER, R.A., La faience de Mît Rahîneh, *in*: *Acts 1st ICE*, 441-442.

Paper on the faience of Mit Rahineh from the Hellenistic Period, also called "Naucratis Pottery."

79754 McNAUGHT, Lewis, A Small Inscribed Vessel of Senenmut, *JEA* 65 (1979), 163-164, with 1 fig.

Describes this vase, BM 29333, and comments on the title "Overseer of the Cows of Amun" inscribed on it. *E.P. Uphill*

79755 MATTHIAE, Gabriella Scandone, Un oggetto faraonico della XIII dinastia dalla "Tomba del Signore dei Capridi", *Studi Eblaiti*, Roma 1, 7-8 (1979), with 3 pl.

The author publishes four fragments of a stick, possibly a club, made of bone and sheathed with metal bands, which was found in a tomb near palace Q at Ebla, from the Middle Bronze Age II. She describes and discusses the fragments, particularly the one bearing a representation of two baboons adoring a royal name which reads $\underline{H}tp-ib-r^c$. She argues that the object is of Egyptian origin, the reversed htp-sign and the absence of the complementary p being due to a later restoration by an artisan not familiar with Egyptian. The king may be identified with $Ḥtp-ỉb-rˁ$ $Ḥr-nḏ-ḥr-ỉt.f$ of the XIIIth Dynasty. The possibility of a reading $Sḥtp-ỉb-rˁ$, the prenomen of Amenemhat I, is excluded. In the light of other documents and monuments of this king, among which a statue fragment from Tell ed-Dabˁa and two scarabs from Jericho, as well as other evidence concerning the XIIIth Dynasty kings in Syria-Palestine the author discusses the position of the XIIIth Dynasty and its contacts with Syria-Palestine.

79756   MATTHIAE, Gabriella Scandone, Vasi iscritti di Chefren e Pepi I dal Palazzo Reale G di Ebla, *Studi Eblaiti*, Roma 1, 3-4 (1979), 33-43, with 3 pl.

Fragments of a diorite vessel bearing the name of Chefren and of an alabaster one bearing the name of Pepi I were found in the Royal Palace G at Tell Mardikh, dating from the Early Bronze IVa.
The objects are described and their historical importance is discussed in the light of many Egyptian finds from the O.K. at Byblos. Although they may have entered Ebla through contacts with Byblos, whether hostile or not, the author does not exclude the possibility of a direct contact between Egypt and this northernmost city of importance in Syria.

79757   MOZEL, Ilana, A Male Partner for the Gilat Woman?, *Tel Aviv*, Tel Aviv 6 (1979), 26-27, with 1 fig.

A vessel found by Petrie at Ballas portraying a seated male with barrel-shaped body whose sexual organs are stressed and a vessel of a female found at Gilat are indicative of the strong cultural links that existed between Chalcolithic Canaan and Predynastic Egypt.

79758   MÜLLER, Hans-Wolfgang, Goldschmuck und ein Faiencekelch aus dem Grabe des Herihor (?), *Pantheon*, München 38 (1979), 237-246, with 4 fig. and 17 ill. (2 in colour) and summaries in English and French on p. 294.

Publication of a golden bracelet with a large turquoise, two simpler golden bracelets and a faience relief chalice, all in a private collection. The large bracelet is inscribed with the name of the first prophet of Amon Herihor. The objects are minutely described, particularly the representations on the chalice (cfr Tait's article, our number 63493). On account of stylistic arguments the author ascribes them to the same period. He suggests that they may come from the unknown tomb of Herihor.
                                                                J.J.J.

79759 NEEDLER, Winifred, Three Pieces of Unpatterned Linen from Ancient Egypt in the Royal Ontario Museum, in: *Studies in Textile History*. In Memory of Harold B. Burnham, Edited by Veronica Servers, Toronto, Royal Ontario Museum, [1979], 238-251, with 5 ill.

After some preliminary remarks on patterned and unpatterned linen before and in the M.K. and on the history of textiles in ancient Egypt the author publishes and discusses three pieces of linen in the Royal Ontario Museum: Acc. No. 910.85.223; O.K. (Late IIIrd or early IVth Dynasty); provenance Maidum; very small and threadbare; fine weave.
Acc. No. 907.18.20; M.K.; linen cloth in fine herringbone pleating; probably from the tomb of king Mentuhotep Neb-hepet-Re at Deir el-Bahri.
Acc. No. 906.18.41; M.K. from a royal XIth Dynasty tomb in the mortuary temple of king Mentuhotep Neb-hepet-Re at Deir el-Bahri; rectangular garment with selvage fringe on one long side.
Summary of the discussions at the end of the article.

79760 NIBBI, Alessandra, A Fifth Dynasty Anchor from Abusir, *GM* Heft 32 (1979), 39-46, with 4 ill. on 2 pl.

Der im Kestner-Museum in Hannover befindliche Anker wird beschrieben; er stammt aus Abusir aus dem Grab des Kahotep und gehört in die 5. Dynastie. Die religiöse Bedeutung eines Ankers wird betont und auf weitere Ankerfunde in Ägypten hingewiesen.
Inge Hofmann

79761 NIBBI, Alessandra, A Further Note on the Fifth Dynasty Anchor from Abusir, *GM* Heft 33 (1979), 41-46, with 1 ill.

Vgl. die vorhergehende Nr. Es wird die Frage diskutiert, ob der als Anker identifizierte Block von einer Scheintür stammen kann. Da der Anker keinen praktischen Zweck erfüllt haben konnte, wird er als Votivgabe und symbolisch verstanden. Sie setzt sich mit der Arbeit von H. Frost (vgl. unsere Nr. 79741) über Anker in Ägypten auseinander, wobei die Hauptprobleme die ägyptischen Seeschiffe, Punt und die Herkunft von Bauholz sind.
Inge Hofmann

79762 PUSCH, Edgar B., Das Senet-Brettspiel im alten Ägypten. Teil 1. Das inschriftliche und archäologische Material. Textband [und] Tafelband, München-Berlin, Deutscher Kunstverlag, 1979 (21 x 29.7 cm; [Teil 1.1:] X + 421 p.; [Teil 1.2:] 106 pl.) = Münchner Ägyptologische Studien, 38; rev. *BiOr* 38 (1981), 48-49 (Alain-Pierre Zivie); *Stadion* 5 (1979), 278-281 (Wolfgang Decker).
Pr. DM 140

These volumes contain the first part of the study on the *snt* board game presenting the textual and archaeological material; discussion of the material will follow in part 2.
The text volume consists of three chapters: a catalogue of representations (p. 1-147), a catalogue of the actual objects

(149-383), and the extant copies of the "large board-game text" (385-400).
In the first chapter 43 representations are listed in a chronological order, from the O.K. to the Late Period. Excluded are mostly the vignettes to B.D. chapter 17 since because of their small size they hardly allow to identify details; only two of them (from the B.D. of Any and Hunefer) are listed as examples (nos. 36-37). For each representation full technical data are given (name of the owner, date, provenance, technique and bibliography), followed by a description which particularly pays attention to the number of players; place and form of the game board; number, form and place of the playing pieces; inscriptions, if any (given in facsimile with transliteration and translation) and the context of the scene.
Chapter 2, the catalogue of actual game boards, consists of 84 numbers, including some of a doubtful character (e.g. no. 17). They are again presented in a chronological order, from the only Predynastic item that is known to some from the Late Period. For each the technical data, a description and eventually the text are given. For an explanation of the terms used, see p. 151-153.
Chapter 3 deals with the N.K. text that uses the *snt* game for a description of the journey through the Netherworld (cfr our number 74576). The three known copies (Pap. Cairo 58037, Pap. Turin 1775 and a text on the wall of Theban Tomb No. 359) are described and the text itself is presented in hieroglyphs, the parallel readings of the three variants under each other. The plate volume contains of almost every representation and actual object a drawing, in several instances also a photograph; of the text the copies from Theban Tomb No. 359 and Pap. Cairo 58037 are given in photograph, that of the Turin Papyrus in facsimile.
Compare our number 79748.
J.J.J.

79763   RAMOND, Pierre, Un socle pour une statuette de Thot (Collection Pierre Ramond no. 70-146), *JEA* 65 (1979), 169-171, with 1 pl. and 1 fig.

Gives dimensions, inscription, translation and notes relating to this faience base.   *E.P. Uphill*

79764   RUSSMANN, Edna R., Some Reflections on the Regalia of the Kushite Kings of Egypt, *in*: *Africa in Antiquity*, 49-53, with 4 ill. on 4 pl.

Obgleich die kuschitischen Könige ausser der blauen Krone alle anderen ägyptischen Kronen getragen zu haben scheinen, so sind sie jedoch meist mit einem so völlig unägyptischen Kopfputz geschmückt, dass sonst nicht zu identifizierende Köpfe ihrer Dynastie zugerechnet werden können. Es ist dies eine eng anliegende Kappe und gewöhnlich ein breites Diadem, von den zwei lange Bandenden auf den Rücken herabfallen. Vorn ist der doppelte Uräus angebracht. Um einen Aufbau von 4 Federn zu halten, ist gelegentlich auf dem Kopf ein kleiner Modius angebracht. Es stellt sich die Frage, ob das Diadem um die Kappe oder nicht vielmehr um den unbedeckten Kopf gelegt wurde; es scheint so zu sein, dass die Kuschitenherrscher keine Kappe trugen, wohl aber die ägyptischen Könige, die sie sonst getreulich nachahmten. Der Symbolgehalt des Doppeluräus als Repräsentation von Ober und Unterägypten wird diskutiert. *Inge Hofmann*

79765 SEEFRIED, Monique, Glass Core Pendants Found in the Mediterranean Area, *Journal of Glass Studies*, Corning, New York 21 (1979), 17-26, with 1 fig., 1 map and 22 ill.

The types of glass core pendants found in Egypt, which are only few, are mentioned on p. 22.

79766 WATSON, Adrienne, Four Objects from the Liverpool School of Archaeology and Oriental Studies, *in*: *Glimpses of Ancient Egypt*, 16-19, with 4 ill. and 1 fig.

The objects here described are: an inscribed copper mirror (E1510), possibly from the late O.K.; a glazed steatite private-name scarab (E1074), from the S.I.P.; a rim sherd of a chalice in green faience (E 215), with the representation of a king on his chariot (partly broken off), not unlike those published by Tait in our number 63493; a model sistrum in blue faience (E 202), from the Late Period. *J.J.J.*

79767 WESSETZKY, Guillaume, Cônes funéraires du Musée des Beaux-Arts, *Bulletin du Musée Hongrois des Beaux-Arts*, Budapest 53 (1979), 17-20, with 6 ill. and a Hungarian version on p. 231-233.

After general remarks on the meaning of the funerary cones the author publishes three of the instances preserved in the Budapest Museum: one of corpus No. 504, another of No. 186, and a fragmentary one of No. 170. *J.J.J.*

79768 ZIEGLER, Christiane Les bijoux au temps des pharaons, *Dossiers de l'archéologie*, Paris No. 40 (décembre 1979-janvier 1980), 28-43, with 1 fig., 24 ill. and 8 colour ill.

Article for the general reader about Egyptian jewellery, dealing with the materials (gold, silver, precious stones), the jewellers and their techniques, the types of jewels and the motifs. *J.J.J.*

79769 ZIEGLER, Christiane, Catalogue des instruments de musique égyptiens, Paris, Éditions de la Réunion des Musées Nationaux, 1979 (21 x 27 cm; 135 p., 1 map, 2 fig., 20 + 130 ill., coloured frontispiece); at head of title: Musée du Louvre. Département des antiquités égyptiennes.

After Lise Manniche's study on Egyptian musical instruments (our number 75484) and Anderson's catalogue of these objects in the British Museum (our number 76017) this is the third recent book on the subject, publishing the 130 musical instruments or parts of them that are preserved in the Louvre Museum.

After a preface by Chr. Desroches-Noblecourt and a short introduction the catalogue proper consists of three parts: percussion, wind and stringed instruments, each divided into some chapters that deal with one or two related instruments. The chapters are headed by the pertinent Egyptian words, where known, and a detailed and important discussion of the instrument, dealing i.a. with its typology. Then follows the description of the objects, with full technical data and a photograph.

The following instruments are here published: clappers (nos. 1-18) and a pair of castanets (no. 19); sistra of various materials and shapes, by far the largest group (nos. 20-84); cymbals (85-91) and crotals (92-99); a drum (100) and a tambourine (101); an oblique flute or nay (102), a multiple flute (103), a double clarinet (104), oboes (105-114), reed pipes (115-116) and a trumpet (117); harps (118-125), lyres (126-128) and lutes (129-130).

A table with the data of chemical analyses on p. 127, followed by a bibliography and a table of concordances.   J.J.J.

79770   ZIEGLER, Christiane, Deux étoffes funéraires égyptiennes, *Revue du Louvre et des Musées de France*, Paris 29 (1979), 251-257, with 10 ill.

On account of an exhibition "Tissages et vêtements de l'Égypte ancienne" in the Musée d'Art et d'Essai the author presents some remarks about funerary tissues in general and deals particularly with two instances. They are: 1. the shroud of a chantress of Amon Djedmut (XXIst Dynasty) with a representation of the lady in front of the deified Amenophis I (Louvre E 10301); 2. bandages of the mummy of the Ptah-priest Wennefer (late Ptolemaic or early Roman Period) inscribed with the first fifteen chapters of the B.D. accompanied by vignettes showing the stages of the funeral.
                                                                J.J.J.

j. Scarabs and seals

See also our numbers 79508; 79519; 79560; 79563; 79564; 79606; 79722; 79766; 79805; 79912; 79914 and 79915.

79771   BAQUÉS, L., The Foundation Date of Ibiza from the Egyptian Scarabs Found There, *in*: *Acts 1st ICE*, 87-94, with 2 pl.

Puig des Molins, a ridge W. of the present city of Ibiza, was the cemetery of the Punic settlement there. The author here discusses a representative choice from the scarabs from the tombs (see also our number 76649) and discusses their chronology. Definitive conclusions as regards the foundation date of the Punic city could not be achieved.   J.J.J.

79772 BENEDUM, Jost, Herzskarabäus, *Medizinhistorisches Journal*, Stuttgart 14 (1979), 135-136, with 1 ill.

Note on the heart scarab.

79773 Corpus antiquitatum aegyptiacarum. Lose-Blatt-Katalog ägyptischer Altertümer. Kestner-Museum Hannover. Lieferung 2 = Irmtraut BESTE, Skarabäen. Teil 2, Mainz/Rhein, Verlag Philipp von Zabern, 1979 (21 x 30 cm; portfolio containing [II] + 188 p. including 91 groups of ill.).   Pr. DM 68

This second in a series of three fascicles is a sequel to our number 78176, in the preface of which particulars are given on the scarab collection. The 187 scarabs, described after the CAA model, range from the S.I.P. to the Late Period.

79774 Corpus antiquitatum aegyptiacarum. Lose-Blatt-Katalog ägyptischer Altertümer. Kestner-Museum Hannover, Lieferung 3 = Irmtraut BESTE, Skarabäen. Teil 3, Mainz/Rhein, Verlag Philipp von Zabern, 1979 (21 x 30 cm; portfolio containing [II] + 169 loose p. including 77 groups of ill.).   Pr. DM 68

The third fascicle on the scarab collection of the Kestner Museum (see our preceding number and 78176) contains descriptions of 70 scarabs. They can be divided into two groups: Nos. 1976.3-57, all from art dealers, mostly dating from the S.I.P. and fewer dating from the N.K., and Nos. 1976,83-106, nearly all from the collection of the Duke of Northumberland, Alnwick Castle, mainly dating from the M.K. to the S.I.P. and only a few from the early N.K. Hornung-Staehelin, Skarabäen aus Basler Sammlungen (our number 76387) could be included now.

79775 DAUMAS, François, Sur un scarabée portant une inscription curieuse, *in*: *Hommages Sauneron* I, 155-166, with 1 pl.

Publication of a green jasper scarab in a private collection, that bears an unusual inscription. The author ascribes the piece on account of its hieroglyphs to the Saite Period, discusses its material and its possible meaning, and deals with the inscription: "My ka endures while you exist", suggesting that it means that a woman gave the scarab to a man.   J.J.J.

79776 DOTHAN, M. et D. CONRAD, Akko (1978), *Revue Biblique*, Paris 86 (1979), 441-444, with 1 plan.

From the levels dating from 1400-1300 came a scarab with the name of Ramses II, which corroborates the evidence on the Karnak war reliefs of a victory of Ramses II over the city of Akko.

79777 HODJACHE, S.I., Principes fondamentaux dans l'étude des scarabées égyptiens ornementées, *in*: *Acts 1st ICE*, 297-305, with 2 pl.

Survey of the ornaments inscribed on the bases of scarabs, illustrated on pieces from the Pushkin Museum of Arts, Moscow.
J.J.J.

79778 HODJASH, Swetlana, Ein Skaraboid mit einer weiblichen Sphinx aus dem Staatlichen Pushkin Museum, Moskau, *ZÄS* 106 (1979), 132-137, with 1 ill. and 1 fig.

Veröffentlichungen eines Stückes aus der Sammlung Golenischeff; hellgrünes Glas; 1 7 x 1.2 x 0.8 cm. Die Darstellung zeigt eine stehende weibliche Sphinx mit Flügeln und Doppelkrone, eine Sonnenscheibe und eine Schlange (oben); eine Sonnenscheibe und einen Skarabäus, beide geflügelt (unten). Verfasserin schliesst auf eine phönikische Herkunft und eine Datierung in das 1. Viertel des 1. Jahrtausends v.u.Z.
M. *Heerma v. Voss*

79779 HÖLBL, Günther, Typologische Arbeit bei der Interpretation von nicht klar lesbaren Skarabäenflachseiten, *SAK* 7 (1979), 89-102, with 1 fig.

After discussing earlier attempts to interpret illegible signs on scarabs as symbols for the dead (Grenfell) or as cryptography (Drioton), and stating that the latter principle could hardly occur on scarabs of an original foreign provenance, the author argues that a formal typological study offers various advantages for solving the problems. He illustrates this with two examples. In a table he presents a system of related types characterised by a goose in central position.
J.J.J.

79780 HORN, Siegfried H., An Egyptian Scarab in Early Roman Tomb F. 31, *Andrews University Seminary Studies*, Berrien Springs 16 (1978), 223-224, with 1 ill. on a pl.

A scarab from the N.K. was found in an early Roman tomb during the excavations at Tell Ḥesbân, Transjordan.

79781 JONES, M., The Royal Lion-Hunt Scarab of Amenophis III in the Grosvenor Museum, Chester (Chester 429.E/1930), *JEA* 65 (1979), 165-166, with 1 pl.

Describes a lion hunt scarab of unknown provenance and gives its dimensions and colour.
E.P. Uphill

79782 KEMP, Barry J., An Early Heart-Scarab Plate in Gold from Abydos, *in*: Glimpses of Ancient Egypt, 26-29, with 2 ill. and 4 fig.

The object here published came from Garstang's 1907 excavations in the North Cemetery at Abydos and is preserved in the School of Archaeology and Oriental Studies in Liverpool (E 944). It consists of a thin sheet of gold with a separate band, bent to an oval shape, fixed on the back to provide a mount for a scarab. Nine lines of incised hieroglyphs contain the text of B.D. chapter 30 B, here translated with some comments. The date of the tomb from which the object came is uncertain, but it may be from the N.K.   J.J.J.

79783   MARTIN, Geoffrey T., Private-Name Seals in the Alnwick Castle Collection, *MDAIK* 35 (1979), 215-226, with 3 fig.

On the occasion of the sale of scarabs and seals from the Alnwick Castle Collection (Spring 1975) the author has been allowed to examine the objects and to publish the private-name seals. The publication constitutes an addition to his study of name-seals (our number 71390).
Eighty-seven of them are briefly described, with the pertinent data and a drawing of the bottom. They are all earlier than the N.K., except the last one which may date from the Late Period.
At the end an index of the personal names and titles.   J.J.J.

79784   VERGA, Silvana, Scarabei e scaraboidi nel Museo Nazionale Pepoli di Trapani, *Sicilia Archaeologica*, Trapani 12, No. 40 (1979), 27-36, with 1 ill.

The author publishes 15 scarabs and scaraboids from the Museo Nazionale Pepoli at Trapani, Sicily. Data and a description of each piece are given.

79785   VODOZ, Irene, Catalogue raisonné des scarabées gravés du Musée d'art et d'histoire de Genève, Genève, [Musée d'art et d'histoire], 1979 (20 x 26 cm; 176 p., numerous fig., 37 pl., 3 ill. on cover).

Museum edition with a slightly different title and on a different scale (only less margin) of our number 78831.

k. General and varia

See also our numbers 79458; 79561; 79582; 79606; 79643 and 79669.

79786   ALDRED, Cyril, Paul BARGUET, Christiane DESROCHES-NOBLECOURT, Jean LECLANT, Hans-Wolfgang MÜLLER, L'Empire des Conquérants. L'Égypte au Nouvel Empire (1560-1070), Paris, Gallimard, [1978] (21 x 28 cm; [VIII +] 345 p., 431 ill. [including 1 colour frontispiece; many in colour], fig., plans and maps) = Le monde égyptien. Les pharaons, [2] = L'Univers des formes, [27]; rev. *BiOr* 38 (1981), 71 (anonymous).

Sequel to our number 78013.
Including the short introduction and conclusion by J. Leclant this book follows the same order as the previous one, and is concerned with the N.K.
In the first part the main subjects of art and architecture are

dealt with. P. Barguet discusses in the first chapter on architecture first the cult temples, and then the funerary temples and royal tombs, while a short section is devoted to civil and urban architecture. In one chapter H.W. Müller discusses in a chronological order relief and painting (including that of the Amarna Period) which by its nature is mainly concerned with private tombs. The same procedure is followed by C. Aldred in the chapter on statuary, in which most attention is paid to the royal statuary. The last chapter, by C. Desroches-Noblecourt, is devoted to the minor arts and arranged after the various handicrafts and themes.
In the second part follows in illustrations an integrated arrangement of the above subjects after periods, while the third part contains the general documentation, of which that on plans, etc. is presented with commentary by P. Barguet. Then follows a chronological table listing i.a. the main achievements, and extensive bibliography and index. Maps at the end.
The German edition of our number 78013 called Ägypten. Erster Band. Das Alte und das Mittlere Reich. Von der Vorgeschichte bis zum Ende der Hyksoszeit (1560 v. Chr.) and that of the present volume, Ägypten. Zweiter Band. Das Grossreich. 1560-1070 v. Chr. were published in 1979 and 1980 by the Verlag C.H. Beck, München in their series Universum der Kunst, Band 26 and 27 (Pr. each DM 168).

79787   BERLANDINI, Jocelyne, Petits monuments royaux de la XXIe à la XXVe dynastie, *in*: *Hommages Sauneron* I, 89-114, with 4 pl.

Publication of some small royal documents from the T.I.P. preserved in the IFAO. They are: a vase and a broken plaquette of a Psusennes, probably the first; the socle of a dyad of Takeloth III (the author gives a list of the various writings of this name) and his wife $Bt3t$ (?), with in an appendix (p. 98-109) a study on an aegis (Louvre E 7167) bearing the names of Osorkon IV and Queen Tadibastet, called $mwt\ ntr$ (the title is extensively discussed), probably his mother; the counterpoise of a menat of Piye; a faience bead and an alabaster fragment with the name of Shabaka.
                                                                                                J.J.J.

79788   BRESCIANI, Edda, Un edificio di Kha-anekh-Ra Sobek-hotep ad Abido (MSS Acerbi, Biblioteca Comunale di Mantova), *Egitto e Vicino Oriente* 2 (1979), 1-20, with 7 ill., 5 fig. and 1 plan.

Le Mantouan Giuseppe Acerbi, consul d'Autriche à Alexandrie de 1826 à 1835, laissa trois relations illustrées de voyages en Égypte. Les deux premières sont consacrées aux années 1828/29, au cours desquelles il vit Gebel Silsileh et Thèbes en compagnie de Champollion et de Rosellini; la troisième décrit le Fayoum de 1829/30. Mme Bresciani compte publier ces relations de voyage. Cet article signale l'existence en mars 1829, entre les temples abydéniens de Sethi Ier et de Ramsès II, d'une "chambrette" de calcaire, d'un beau travail mais à demi ruinée. Acerbi y a copié les cartouches de Khâ-ankh-Rê Sobekhotep, protégés par un vautour et par un faucon; il signale en facade quatre figures du roi accueilli chez les dieux: ces indications permettent de reconstituer l'ensemble. Du même souverain, le Louvre a conservé cinq fragments de relief (B 3-5; 9, 10), le Musée de Leiden un autel de granit (C 13) et la collection Amherst un fragment de base de statuette: le tout provient d'Abydos. Les deux groupes du Louvre, dont le second ornait une autre paroi, ont pu être emportés avant le passage d'Acerbi, mais appartiennent probablement à la même chapelle-cénotaphe.   *J. Custers*

79789 DEWACHTER, Michel, A propos de quelques édifices méconnus de Karnak-Nord, *CdE* LIV, No. 107 (1979), 8-25.

L'auteur cherche à retrouver quelques édifices mentionnés dans la littérature égyptologique du 19e siècle mais dont l'existence reste souvent difficile à définir. Ce sont le Temple F de Lepsius, la chapelle d'Osiris Pamérès, le monument à colonnes de Nitocris, les chapelles d'Osiris-Padedânkh et d'Osiris-Nebdjet et la soi-disant chapelle souterraine d'Hatchepsout. Certains pourraient même ne jamais avoir existé.   *Ph. Derchain*

79790 HABACHI, L., New Light on Objects of Unknown Provenance (3). A Head of Queen Tcuy and a Block of Shabaka now Kept in Museums Abroad, *GM* Heft 31 (1979), 47-57, with 1 fig. and 1 pl.

Das erste Objekt, das sich noch vor einigen Jahren in Ägypten befand und kürzlich als Erwerb des Louvre 1973 veröffentlicht wurde, ist eine Büste der Königin Touy, der Frau Sethos I. und Mutter Ramses II. Das zweite Objekt, gleichfalls vor einiger Zeit noch in Ägypten, ist ein Block Shabakas, der sich gemäss dem Katalog von 1967 im West-Berliner Ägyptischen Museum befindet (Inv. Nr. 39/66). Beide Objekte werden vorgestellt; der Shabaka-Block war in der Kapelle Sethos I. deponiert, zusammen mit einem Blockfragment Taharqas, das gleichfalls verschwunden ist.
   Inge Hofmann

79791 HARI, Robert, Faux et usage de faux ou: le commerce des dieux égyptiens, *Bulletin Société d'Égyptologie*, Genève No. 1 (Mai 1979), 27-35, with 3 pl.

After an introduction of the, in many instances "mystical", admiration for ancient Egypt the author deals with the manufacture of forgeries that resulted from it, discussing three instances: a funerary cone and a Ramesside relief in his own collection, and a relief in the Boston Museum. He indicates the "mistakes" in the inscription on the latter.
In a postscript more forgeries are mentioned, among which the bowl with the inscription from year 16 of Horemheb (see our number 73596).   *J.J.J.*

79792 HOOD, Sinclair, The Arts in Prehistoric Greece, *[Harmondsworth]*, Penguin Books, *[1978]* (14.5 x 21.5 cm; 311 p., frontispiece, 237 fig. and ill., 2 maps, 2 plans, 1 chart) = The Pelican History of Art; rev. *AJA* 84 (1980), 538-539 (James C. Wright).

As is apparent from the epilogue stating that the art of the Aegean Bronze Age belonged to the oriental world of its time and the conclusion in which the author draws many parallels with Egypt, ancient Egyptian art is mentioned throughout in the various chapters. These chapters are concerned with pottery; painting; sculpture; wood, shell, bone, ivory, faience, glass; stone and metal vases; arms; jewellery; seals and gems, all kinds of objects mainly dating from the Bronze Age.

79793 KAMEL, Ibrahim, Studies for Discussion about King Ahmose's Tomb, *ASAE* 63 (1979), 115-130, with 3 pl.

The author argues along various lines that very likely the tomb of Ahmose, like those of his forebears, has to be sought in Draʿ Abû el-Nagaʿ, probably at its southern end, and that it may be untouched since the mummy was removed to the cachette. In this connection he mentions the discovery of a tomb called Bab ibn Soleiman which has never been excavated. *J.J.J.*

79794 LIPIŃSKA, Jadwiga, Ramses II - patron sztuki, *Meander*, Warszawa 33, 6 (1978), 295-299, with a Latin summary on p. 299.

"Ramses II, patron of the arts."

79795 LLEWELLYN, Briony, Egyptian Antiquities on the Art Market, *The Connoisseur*, London 202, No. 811 (September 1979), 56-57, with 9 ill.

Various objects are depicted.

79796 PARLASCA, K., Persische Elemente in der frühptolemäischen Kunst, *in*: *Akten des VII. Internationalen Kongresses für Iranische Kunst und Archäologie*. München, 7.-10. September 1976, Berlin, Dietrich Reimer Verlag, 1979 (= Archäologische Mitteilungen aus Iran. Ergänzungsband, 6), 317-323, with 9 ill.

The conspicuous Achaemenid elements in early Ptolemaic art object can hardly be a continuation of the influences from the time of the first Persian domination (XXVIIth Dynasty), but may be dependent on a new influx of Persian artists and artisans after the fall of Persepolis and of the art objects originating from the booty of the expeditions of Alexander the Great.

79797 POMERANTSEVA, N.A., К вопросу о традициях и каноне в искусстве Амарны, *in*: Шампольон и дешифровка, 88-105, with 5 ill. and 6 fig.

"On the Problem of the Traditions and the Canon in the Art of Amarna."
The author argues that the Amarna art, reliefs and statues, shows the application of the traditional canon of proportions, together with new iconographic traits. Since these reflected the ideas of the period they have not been developed afterwards.   *J.J.J.*

79798   ROSTRON, P.R., Glass from the Nile of Pharaohs' Pomade, *Glass*, Redhill, Surrey 55, No. 5 (May 1978), 252-255, with 2 ill.

The author relates some stories concerned with glass in ancient Egypt.

79799   SHILOH, Yigal, The Proto-Aeolic Capital and Israelite Ashlar Masonry, Jerusalem, Israel Exploration Society, 1979 (19 x 28 cm; X + 95 p., 91 fig., 36 pl.) = Qedem. Monographs of the Institute of Archaeology, 11.

In this study of the proto-Aeolic capital the author devotes in chapter 3, on the Proto-Aeolic capital in Palestine and in neighbouring cultures, a section to the problem of Egyptian influence upon the proto-Aeolic capital (p. 42-43).

79800   VACHALA, Břetislav, "Nová" svatyně na Elefantině, *Lidé a země*, Praha 28, No. 7 (1979), 322-324.

"Ein 'neues' Heiligtum auf Elefantine."
Beschreibung der 1974/75 erfolgten Wiederaufbauarbeiten eines Heiligtums eines ehemaligen Ptolemäertempels in Kalabscha auf dem Südzipfel der Insel Elephantine.   *B. Vachala*

VI. RELIGION

a. Gods, mythology, cosmology, syncretism, symbolism

See also our numbers 79112; 79120; 79126; 79130; 79131; 79133; 79134; 79137; 79157; 79244; 79228; 79237; 79241; 79259; 79280; 79305; 79306; 79385; 79413; 79448; 79451; 79470; 79519; 79524; 79546; 79617; 79626; 79632; 79637; 79657; 79659; 79664; 79665; 79673; 79684; 79695; 79698; 79713; 79718; 79747; 79840; 79847; 79854; 79895; 79920; 79973; 79975 and 79981.

79801   BONGRANI FANFONI, Luisa, Il nome di Osiride: una proposta interpretative, *Vicino Oriente*, Roma 2 (1979), 19-22.

Conceiving Osiris as a hypostasis of the dead king the author recognises in the P.T. the first stage of the later Osiris myth in which Osiris and the king are already separated. In this connection she explains the name of Osiris as meaning "place of the action" ("luogo del fare"), interpreting *iri* as "performing a ritual." The logical subject of the action was Horus, its aim the continuation of kingship. J.J.J.

79802 BRIEND, J., La création de l'homme dans les textes égyptiens, *Le Monde de la Bible*, Paris No. 9 (Mai-Juin-Juillet 1979), 28-29, with 2 ill. and 1 fig.

Brief note on the Egyptian conception of the creation of man and the world.

79803 BRIEND, J., Hathor, *Le Monde de la Bible*, Paris No. 10 (Août-Septembre 1979), 29, with 2 ill.

Brief note on the goddess Hathor.

79804 DERCHAIN-URTEL, Maria Theresia, Synkretismus in ägyptischer Ikonographie. Die Göttin Tjenenet, Wiesbaden, Otto Harrassowitz, 1979 (17 x 24 cm; [XII] + 86 p., 7 pl.) = Göttinger Orientforschungen. Veröffentlichungen des Sonderforschungsbereiches Orientalistik and der Georg-August Universität Göttingen. IV. Reihe: Ägypten, 8 = Synkretistische Erscheinungen in der ägyptischen Religion, 4; rev. *CdE* LV, No. 109-110 (1980), 125-127 (Bengt Birkstam); *Oriens Antiquus* 19 (1980), 315-317 (Luisa Bongrani Fanfoni). Pr. DM 20

After introductory remarks on the study of syncretistic phenomena based on textual evidence the author points out why she chose the goddess Tjenenet and her attributes as an example of an iconographical study of syncretism.
The first part of the study is devoted to her characteristic attribute, the ⚱ -sign (uterus; F45) which she only shares with Meskhenet. Although she being the wife of Month rarely appears outside Tôd, Armant, Karnak and Medamûd she occurs more often in the more widely spread Theban Ennead, often extended with five gods from the Theban region, in which case it is headed by Month and closed by his wife Tjenenet (Iunit). The couple being split is explained from the fact that the gods are grouped concentrically around the sungod, Re, who is not represented, but implicitly centrally present. On account of the Greco-Roman temple texts she points out that the occurrence of the Theban Ennead is connected with sunrise, moonrise and coronation, they forming a context of birth and rebirth. She also discusses the association of the coronation, the justification of Horus son of Isis and birth of god and king.
Then she turns to Meskhenet having the same attribute. The goddess occurs either as an individual or as a concept name common to the four goddesses of the Ennead. This phenomenon and her role connected with birth are exemplified through passages from the Greco-Roman temple texts. Confronting the two goddesses in the summary she concludes that the common attribute connects the two in analogous activities having birth (in a wide sense including rebirth of the King at his coronation) as the

central theme. Meskhenet has a limited range bound by situation, space and time, while Tjenenet has a wider, cosmic orientation. They have complementary functions, the common feature of which is expressed through the 𝕐-sign.
The second part of the study deals with the other attributes of Tjenenet. 1. Tjenenet wearing the vulture headdress, the attribute of Nekhbet, together with Month in a coronation scene at Tôd. Transfer of function through adoption of attribute. 2. The same is the case with an incense offering scene at Edfu, where Tjenenet-Iunit is wearing the uraeus on her forehead, associating her with the goddess Wadjet. 3. Examples from Armant of Tjenenet wearing the Mut crown, one time in a scene from the mammisi of Armant, where Amun plays a role in the company of Rattaui on account of his important position in the legend of the divine birth of Pharaoh. Adoption of attribute, but no transfer of function. 4. The tendency of adaptation to the basic conception of a scene is distinguishable in an astral-oriented scene from Dendera, where Tjenenet is wearing the sun disk.
In many cases of syncretistic iconography there are only ad hoc connections involved, which did not develop a life of their own. The author notices that the attribute 𝕐 is never transferred to another goddess.
An excursus is concerned with the possibility of Tjenenet in animal shape, and the meaning of her name and references to her birth. Index of names and sources at the end of the book.

79805 GOFF, Beatrice L., Symbols of Ancient Egypt in the Late Period. The Twenty-first Dynasty, The Hague-Paris-New York, Mouton Publishers, [1979] (16 x 24 cm; XXVI + 309 p., 87 pl. with 159 fig. and ill.) = Religion and Society, 13.   Pr. DM 156

This book is not only of importance because of its subject, the XXIst Dynasty and the religious symbols of that period, but also since the author renders account of the theoretical presuppositions it is based on.
In the introduction the author sets forth that the book is "an attempt to make comprehensible the dominant religious ideas that were expressed in Egyptian symbols at the beginning of the first millennium B.C." She argues why she applies the "horizontal" (synchronic) way of approach and formulates five guiding principles: to determine the dominant forms, to investigate their relationships, to emphasise the forms that became a popular style, to examine the ways in which they distort the reality, and to utilise the greatest circumspection in drawing inferences about early periods from knowledge about later ones (p. 7).
In the first chapter, on methods, particularly the last principle is elaborated. Mrs Goff stresses that, in accordance with the Egyptian view, egyptologists tend to overvalue the stability of Egyptian religious thought. She discusses a number of changes, e.g. in the role of the king and in cosmic beliefs. They are in accordance with the "pre-logical" mentality; a new approach to a problem, no matter how inconsistent, was found when the old one

was likely to be inefficient. Since the conditions determined
the cultural and religious attitude, the traditions in classical
authors cannot be used to explain these attitudes during Pharaonic times.
Chapter 2 is devoted to the political history of the XXIst Dynasty, discussing each of the rulers, in the North as well as in
the South. This chapter has been written before the author read
Kitchen's 'The Third Intermediate Period' (our number 73405);
see p. 270, note 239.
Chapter 3 discusses the material and the artistic trends it shows.
First, in order to demonstrate that more traditional than new
forms occurred, the retention of earlier monuments in Thebes is
dealt with. There follow discussions of the sarcophagi from the
period, with a detailed study of their posts such as headdresses,
collars, symbols on various parts of the body; ornaments accompanying them, both in and outside the sarcophagus; canopic vases,
shawabtis, papyri, and wall decorations in tombs, houses and
temples.
The next three chapters are devoted to the "significance" of the
symbols: the three levels in their use (already published in
1968, see our number 68239), their complexity and their values.
The distinction of symbol and sign is discussed, the wide scope
of a symbol's applicability, objective and subjective attitudes
toward symbols, the contradictory emotions that can be expressed
by them, and symbols of aggression. In the chapter on values
various concepts pass the review: stability, truth, life, personal dignity. There are also sections on the mystery in Egyptian religion and the role of mythology, about which Mrs. Goff
states that mythical allusions were focussed on meeting a need
of a particular moment in the life of an individual; 'no mythical
pattern was so crystalized that it could not be utilized as the
artist desired' (p. 205).
The last four chapters each deal with one of the major symbols
used during the XXIst Dynasty: the scarab, the falcon, the vulture and the winged solar disk. In each its varied forms, its
cosmic significance, its other values, particularly that of a
symbol of power, are discussed. Together these chapters constitute the chosen examples illustrating the author's view as
explained systematically in the preceding chapters.
The illustrations and figures on the plates constitute an integrated part of the argument. Notes on p. 257-299; indexes
p. 301-309.
The book is distributed by Walter de Gruyter & Co., Berlin.

J.J.J.

79806   GOURLAY, Yvon J.-L., Les seigneurs et les *baou* vivants à
        Chedenou, *in*: *Hommages Sauneron* I, 363-380, with 2 fig.

The author collects and studies five documents concerning the
$b3w$ of Shedenu (Hurbeit). He i.a. discusses the emblem of the
city, its lords, and the gods and $b3w$ living in it. His conclusion is that the lords of Shedenu are the representation of

local divinities, while the gods and $b3w$ personify the power to act at a large distance, the destructive power of the fighting Horus, that is, Hormerty.　　　　　　　　　　　　　　　　J.J.J.

79807　GRIFFITHS, J. Gwyn, Egyptian Nationalism in the Edfu Temple Texts, in: *Glimpses of Ancient Egypt*, 174-179.

Proceeding from a passage in Fairman's "The Triumph of Horus" (our number 74187) the author, stressing the enduring force of the national Horus-religion, discusses the duplicity of attitude that resulted from the conception of Seth as well as Horus as identical with the foreign rulers. In the texts of Edfu there is no clear instance that the official cult rejected the doctrine that the Pharaoh was Horus.　　　　　　　　　　　　　　J.J.J.

79808　GRIMM, Alfred, $Dwn-h3t$ und $Rs-hr$ als Namen eines Torwächters in der Unterwelt. Zu zwei Beinamen des Sobek und zur Bezeichnung krokodilköpfiger Gottheiten, *GM* Heft 31 (1979), 27-34.

In dem zur Spruchsammlung des "Zweiwegebuches" gehörenden Spruch 1100 aus dem Corpus der Sargtexte wird ein unterweltlicher Dämon genannt, dessen Namen bisher verschieden übersetzt wurde. Der in Frage stehende Torwächter hat zwei Namen, die sich beide auf sein Gesicht beziehen: "Der vorstreckt die Stirn" und "Der mit wachsamen Gesicht." Hinzugezogene andere Sprüche zeigen, dass beide Bezeichnungen dem Krokodil und davon abgeleitet dem Gott Sobek galten. Daher wird der in Spruch 1100 genannte Torwächter in seiner Erscheinungsform ebenfalls krokodilgestaltig oder zumindest krokodilsköpfig vorzustellen sein.　　　*Inge Hofmann*

79809　GUGLIELMI, W., Die *Mr.tj*, ägyptische Vorläufer der Sirenen?, in: *Acts 1st ICE*, 255-264.

The female demons called $mr(r)ty$, occurring i.a. in C.T., Spell 439-450, were conceived as birds. The author discusses textual and iconographical evidence for them and argues that they are similar to the Sirens of the classical antiquity.　　　　　　　J.J.J.

79810　GUTBUB, Adolphe, La tortue animal cosmique bénéfique à l'époque ptolémaïque et romaine, in: *Hommages Sauneron* I, 391-435, with 2 fig.

Proceeding from representations of the turtle in the temples of Esna and Kôm Ombo the author extensively discusses its role and representations, before the Late Period as well as in some Ptolemaic texts. Not protected by the possession of a sanctuary it passed into the magical sphere (magical staves) being compared with the hippopotamus that was ritually killed and almost assimilated with Apophis, the enemy of Re. It also played, however, a beneficient part on vessels holding water and became a mythical representation of the sources of the Nile. Assimilated with Geb, the reservoir of the Nile water, it is also used to represent the universe.　　　　　　　　　　　　　　　　　　　　　　J.J.J.

79811 IBRAHIM, Mohiy el-Din, The God of the Great Temple of Edfu, *in*: *Glimpses of Ancient Egypt*, 170-173.

The author deals with an inscription on the exterior W. wall of the Edfu temple in which the god is presented as one of the Mythical Ancestors. The text is given in hieroglyphs, transliteration and translation.
J.J.J.

79812 JUNGE, Friedrich, Isis und die ägyptischen Mysterien, *in*: *Aspekte der spätägyptischen Religion*, 93-115.

The author argues that the Hellenistic-Roman Isis and her mystery religion in their development from 400 B.C. to A.D. 400 were in essence not of Graeco-Roman character with Egyptian shades, but of genuine Egyptian nature in Hellenistic guise. However, the Egyptian appearance of the goddess in the Roman imperial period does not originate from direct Egyptian influence, but was the effect of nostalgia on the part of the Roman culture.
In order to demonstrate this the author discusses: 1. The basic elements of the Isis cult in Hellenism: the Isis mysteries and Isis as a cosmic and saviour goddess in the Greek religious world. 2. Isis in Egyptian religion of the Late Period, which is dominated by the rise of a transcendent supreme god, who is at the same time a saviour god, and the victory of Osiris. These two characteristic developments of religious conceptions melt together in the Late Period, particularly in the figure of Isis. 3. Cult and mystery: the basic elements of the Isis mysteries after Apuleius, Metamorphoses Book XI and their background. They are the mystical event as performed in the main ritual in the sanctuary; the admission to participate in the cult through initiation, which shows also elements of the funerary cult; and the Isis mystery communities, which are identical with the Egyptian cult societies of the Late Period (see already our number 72132).

79813 KUHLMANN, K.P., Zur angeblichen Lokalgöttin *Jin-Ins-Mḥj.t*, GM Heft 31 (1979), 57-62.

In den spätzeitlichen Inschriften des von Eje angelegten Felstempels nordöstlich von Achmim ist eine Passage enthalten, aus der Kees die Existenz einer sonst nicht nachweisbaren Göttin namens *Ijn-ins* bzw. *Ijn-ins-Mḥjt* ableiten zu können glaubte. Verfasser zeigt jedoch auf, dass die fragliche Stelle folgendermassen zu übersetzen ist: "Priester der Uto, die zu dem kommt, der sie anruft, die im Norden von Achmim haust" und dass die Göttin aus dem ägyptischen Pantheon zu streichen ist. Compare our number 79626.
Inge Hofmann

79814 LURKER, Manfred, Das Tier als Symbol im alten Ägypten, *Natur und Museum*, Frankfurt 109, 4 (1979), 97-111, with 21 ill. and fig.

The author sketches some aspects of the animal in ancient Egypt:

its role in mythology, the animal shape of gods, the relation between king and animal, and the animal in funerary belief.

79815 MYŚLIWIEC, Karol, Beziehungen zwischen Atum und Osiris nach dem Mittleren Reich, *MDAIK* 35 (1979), 195-213, with 10 fig. and 7 pl.

Within the framework of his Atum studies (see our numbers 78572 and 78817) the author here discusses the development in the relations between Atum and Osiris, from the time just before the Amarna Period onwards. In this connection he first deals with three stelae, one of an Amenhotep (Turin Cat. 1523), dating from before Akhnaton, and two from Theban Tomb No. 41, of Amenemope, from the early XIXth Dynasty. On both Atum and Osiris are represented, but the latter two clearly Osiris in a more favourable position (a full offering table, whereas before Atum only a vessel).
The author then discusses the way in which Atum is represented during and after the N.K., his insignia and epithets. The syncretistic form with Osiris appears to be a form only.   J.J.J.

79816 MYŚLIWIEC, K., Les problèmes des recherches sur l'iconographie du dieu Atoum, *in*: *Acts 1st ICE*, 489-491.

Introduction of the author's studies on the god Atum. As the first volume appeared our number 78572 (on the sacred animals) and as the second volume, on the name, epithets and iconography of Atum, appeared our number 79817.

79817 MYŚLIWIEC, Karol, Studien zum Gott Atum. Band II. Name - Epitheta - Ikonographie, Hildesheim, Gerstenberg Verlag, 1979 (17 x 23.8 cm; XVI + 295 p., 18 fig., 17 pl.) = Hildesheimer Ägyptologische Beiträge, 8.   Pr. DM 45

Sequel to our number 78572.
The present volume discusses in three parts the names, epithets and iconography of Atum. In the first part all variants of the writing of his name are listed and discussed: with and without i, uncommon writings with a beetle, monkey, snake, etc. Summary on p. 72-77, followed by a survey of the attempts to explain the name.
The second part devoted to the epithets of the god, begins with a chapter on Atum's name used in connection with a toponym or a temple's name. First of all Heliopolis (in Lower as well as in Upper Egypt), then a large number of other places and temples throughout both parts of the country. A second chapter deals with the mythological topography: primeval waters, heaven, sun-disk, horizon, netherworld, the bark; but also Atum in relation to other gods, e.g. the Ennead, as creator-god, as lord of various phenomena: the Truth, elements of nature or abstract concepts, etc. The last paragraph discusses qualities of Atum: "great", "good", "divine", "with the beautiful face", etc. Summary of this part on p. 203-206.

In the third part, on the iconography, first a chapter on the anthropomorphic representations of Atum and his earliest occurrences in reliefs (from the M.K.). Other chapters discuss his headdress, his insignia and the colours of his body, while at the end some uncommon representations are mentioned.
There follows a catalogue of 25 numbers, in which unpublished texts and representations of various kinds (scenes on temple and tomb walls, on coffins, and two statues) are discussed, with drawings and photographs. They date from the N.K. and afterwards, and are chosen either because they show rare or as yet unknown traits or are particularly illustrative of "classical" forms.
Indexes on p. 272-290.
J.J.J.

79818 SCHULMAN, Alan R., The Winged Reshep, *JARCE* 16 (1979), 69-84.

Criteria are given to pinpoint Reshep iconographically and to distinguish him from other Asiatic gods such as Ḳeserty, Mikal and Baʿal Saphon, or Seth shown in Asiatic guise. Apart from certain ornamental details (such as the conical crown, collar, tasselled kilt, amlets, armor; gazelle head) the attitude is decisive: R. when occurring alone usually brandishes a weapon but as member of a triad the arm is hanging down, although the weapon is still present. This fits e.g. the MMA statuette published by Simpson (our number 2575) but the identity of the winged Asiatic deity on a scarab in the Cassirer collection (our number 59120) and its immediate parallels is less certain. A detailed list of 42 ascertained Reshep representations follows, amplifying the documentation given by Fulco (our number 76263).
J.F. Borghouts

79819 el-TANBOULI, M.A.L., Some Remarks on the Temple of Gerf Hussein, *in*: *Acts 1st ICE*, 635-640.

The author makes some remarks on the decoration of the rock temple of Gerf Hussein: the local Nubian gods, Horus of Buhen (Halfa) and of Baki (Kubbân) instead of Amon-Re and Re-Harakhti in the scene representing the king smiting the enemies.

79820 TAWFIK, Sayed, Was Aton - The God of Akhenaten - only a Manifestation of the God Re?, *in*: *Acts 1st ICE*, 641-643.

The author attempts to prove that Aton was only a name of Re. The complete text was published in our number 76766.

79821 VERNUS, Pascal, Amon $p3$-ʿḏr: de la piété "populaire" à la spéculation théologique, *in*: *Hommages Sauneron* I, 463-476.

After presenting a list of 17 references to Amon $p3$-ʿḏr, dating from the reign of Osorkon II to the Ptolemaic Period, as well as a list of writings of ʿḏr (Hebr. עזר), "to help", the author argues that this object of personal piety in the N.K. became integrated into the Theban theology. The cult of the divinity was spread to Edfu and Dendera, perhaps even to Tanis. J.J.J.

79822   WESTENDORF, Wolfhart, Vom Sonnentier zum Sonnenboot, *in*: *Festschrift Elmar Edel*, 432-445, with 5 fig.

The animals occurring as bearers of the sun in pre- and early historical representations have been replaced by the sun-bark. The author studies the various ways in which old and new elements are connected, e.g. animals towing the sun-bark or a mixed figure of animals and bark. In an excursus the sledge as a cultic vessel is discussed. The author also deals with combinations of vessel and animal in rock-drawings and the catalogue of parts of ships in C.T. and B.D. J.J.J.

b. Theology, religious attitude, ethics and world view

See also our numbers 79056; 79069; 79075; 79307 and 79823.

79823   ASSMANN, Jan, Primat und Transzendenz. Struktur und Genese der ägyptischen Vorstellung eines "Höchsten Wesens", *in*: *Aspekte der spätägyptischen Religion*, 7-42.

The study consists of three parts. 1. Proceeding from the late Hellenistic-Roman pantheistic conception of a great god of the world whose body is the cosmos, the author recognises this element's model as present in the Egyptian Late Period religion, side by side with the conception of god being a trinity of *ba*, image and body. In his opinion this conception of a pantheistic great cosmic god is already present in the elements model (air, Nile, light) and the personal model of the Theban theology of Amun-Re as supreme god in the Ramesside Period.
2. The author demonstrates that the conception of the supreme god is a very old religious institution, which is defined by two "constellations", one the relation with kingship and the other the position within the divine world, the extremes of which can be characterised as supremacy and transcendence. He explains the concept "constellation" as based, on the one hand, on the idea of a person as a number of constituents and, on the other hand, as a part of a superordinated whole, from which a person derives his status. In the light of this last definition the author studies the father-son constellation of king and god and that of the god's position in the divine constellation. The god's status as supreme god in the divine world is indissolubly connected with the god-kingship constellation. The revolutionary religious reform of the Amarna Period in which the god Aton is impersonal and exclusively unique abandoned the traditional polytheistic conception of the world and paved the way for a wider horizon.
3. On account of a variety of religious texts the author demonstrates how in the Ramesside Period the concept of a supreme god

who created the world was transformed by the Theban theologians into one in which god represents the world. This resulted in the transcendence of one great cosmic deity in a pantheistic sense who is timeless and all pervading, but hidden.

79824 ASSMANN, Jan, Weisheit, Loyalismus und Frömmigkeit, *in*: *Studien zu altägyptischen Lebenslehren*, 11-72.

In the introduction the author makes basic remarks about the relation between God, Maat and act-and-effect.
Proceeding from the texts on personal piety he then demonstrates that they in some aspects belong to a tradition which goes back to the wisdom literature. In order to define the concept of personal piety he investigates the words, expressions and formulas in mainly N.K. documents concerning the characteristic mutual God-man relation. This resulted in the discovery of two basic structures of the formulas: the mutuality formula expressing the beneficiality of God for the one attached to him; and the makarismos (Seligpreisung) stating that the person who is attached to God is happy, mostly with an apodosis mentioning the concrete realisation in benefactions. The first type occurs mainly in hymns, the second in the texts of personal piety. The underlying idea of human need and God's helping hand is amply discussed.
Concerned with the question of the origin of the formulas, discussed in the second section, the author traces back their form-historical connections through the Amarna texts to the Loyalistic Instructions of the M.K.: they function there as an appeal for the decision when a fundamental choice has to be made. This loyalism forms the missing link between wisdom and personal piety. As for the Amarna religion, the author argues that this negative experience caused the break-through of the personal piety.
The article is concluded by an enumeration of the quotations and the sources for the mutuality formula and the makarismos.

79825 BERGMAN, Jan, Discours d'adieu - testament - discours posthume. Testaments juifs et enseignements égyptiens, *in*: *Sagesse et religion*. Colloque de Strasbourg (octobre 1976), Paris, Presses Universitaires de France, [1979] (at head of title: Bibliothèque des Centres d'Études Supérieures spécialisés. Travaux du Centre d'Études Supérieures spécialisé d'Histoire des Religions de Strasbourg), 21-50.

Proceeding from a group of "testaments" composed in Israel in the beginning of the Christian Era the author studies first the close connections between farewell sermon, testament and posthumous sermon, together forming the testamentary genre which is distinguishable in the Jewish sapiental literature during the last ages B.C. He characterises the genre as a spiritual or ethical testament and analyses its features on account of the Jewish sources. He then turns to the ancient Egyptian wisdom literature in which the genre is also clearly present. In this

connection he discusses the prologue and the epilogue of the
Instruction of Ptahhotep, as well as the minor O.K. wisdom texts
(Kagemni, Hardjedef and Imhotep), the M.K. Instruction for Merikare and that of Amenemhat I, the Antef Song of the Harper, and
the encomium of the sages in Pap. Ch. Beatty IV, vso 2,5-3,11.
He points out that the persistence of the names of authors of
wisdom literature in the tradition is understandable through the
function of wisdom texts as a spiritual testament, one without
the name of the testator being without value. This clarifies
also the relation between instruction and autobiography in the
funerary context of the tomb.
The last pages are devoted to a comparison of the texts from the
two cultural contexts and to some remarks on the Isis aretalogies
with respect to the testamentary genre.

79826   BERGMAN, Jan, Gedanken zum Thema "Lehre-Testament-Grab-Name", *in*:
        Studien zu altägyptischen Lebenslehren, 73-104.

        The author discusses the connections between the words instruct-
        ion, name, testament and tomb, stressing that much of it is
        rather hypothetical. Most of his thoughts are devoted to the
        background of the older Instructions of Imhotep and Hordjedef,
        Kagemni and Ptahhotep, while the last one is utilised as main
        source. First he deals with the relation instruction-testament
        (to be understood as ethical will) by exemplifying the charac-
        teristics of a testament (double time perspective, close con-
        nection between testator and heir, guarantee of continuity) on
        account of quotations from Ptahhotep. The connection instruction-
        tomb may be indicated e.g. by certain parts of the Wisdom of
        Ptahhotep. Studying the connection instruction-name-tomb the
        author amply dwells on the Antef Harper's Song and the "Encomium
        of the Ancient Sages" (Pap. Ch. Beatty IV, vso 2,5-3,11). In
        his final remarks he attempts to integrate the connotations and
        associations of the formative words on account of Imhotep.

79827   BONNARD, P.-E., De la Sagesse personnifiée dans l'Ancien Testa-
        ment à la Sagesse en personne dans le Nouveau, *in*: *La Sagesse de
        l'Ancien Testament* par M. Gilbert, Gembloux, Éditions J. Duculot
        S.A./Leuven, University Press, [1979] (= Bibliotheca Ephemeridum
        Theologicarum Lovaniensium, 51), 117-149.

        In a section in which the author deals with the origin and in-
        fluence of the personification of the Divine Wisdom in the O.T.
        he discusses the possible role of the goddess Maat in this re-
        spect, excluding, however, a direct literary influence by Egypt.

79828   BRUNNER-TRAUT, Emma, Weiterleben der ägyptischen Lebenslehren in
        den koptischen Apophtegmata am Beispiel des Schweigens, *in*:
        Studien zu altägyptischen Lebenslehren, 173-216.

        The author investigates how far the rules concerning silence of
        the early Coptic eremites were influenced by the Egyptian atti-

tude. For this purpose she divides silence into ten characteristic types and examines their motifs. Quoting a large number of citations she discusses first the Coptic evidence and next explores the ancient Egyptian sources as regards comparable contents.

Silence as a general rule ordered by the cult, as expression of courtesy, as gesture of meekness and means of self-control are all well-attested in the Egyptian texts. The sections 5 and 6 of the Coptic evidence, dealing with responsibility and the avoidance of verbal sin, are discussed in combination as regards the Egyptian sources. Mystical, contemplative silence as a preparation for the divine word and self-renunciation (mortificatio) are almost absent in the Egyptian world, but the ninth type, obligatory silence on account of the secrets of the mysteries, is well-attested. The last type is called relative silence and deals with the relation between being silent and uttering relevant speech at due time.

In her conclusion the author argues that given the many parallels, the central role of silence in ancient Egyptian thought and other similarities, adoption by the Coptic monks is probable.

79829 DAUMAS, François, L'âme égyptienne à la veille de la fondation d'Alexandrie, *Le Monde de la Bible*, Paris No. 8 (Mars-Avril 1979), 28.

Brief note on the spirit of the texts in the tomb of Petosiris. See also our number 79108.

79830 DERCHAIN, Philippe, Der ägyptische Gott als Person und Funktion, *in*: *Aspekte der spätägyptischen Religion*, 43-45.

The author briefly defines the Egyptian divinity on account of two pairs of interconnected qualities: the god is conceived as a person who is present in the cult statue of the temple and in heaven, and whose power is manifest in the phenomena of nature, which are expressed in the myth.

79831 GAMER-WALLERT, Ingrid, Bilder des Alltags oder mehr? Beischriften als wertvolle Interpretationshilfen altägyptischer Darstellungen, *in*: *Wort und Bild*. Symposion des Fachbereichs Altertums- und Kulturwissenschaften zum 500-jährigen Jubiläum der Eberhard-Karls-Universität Tübingen 1977. Herausgegeben von Hellmut Brunner, Richard Kannicht, Klaus Schwager, München, Wilhelm Fink Verlag, 1979, 170-180, with 2 fig. and 3 pl.

After remarks on the close relation between word and representation, their polyinterpretability and hidden meaning, the interpretation of which often remains purely hypothetical, the author considers two examples offering more appropriate links. First the chess-game: the vicinity of the harp-player on the walls of the strongly religiously oriented wall scenes in Ramesside times alludes to mortality and death; there is a clear connection with

B.D. ch. 17 concerned with glorification. The game with its 30 squares symbolises the various dangers and stations in the struggle in between death and glorification which has to be won by the deceased. The second example is the scene of the tomb owner and his wife drinking water from a pond in the shadow of palm trees, which is connected with B.D. ch. 62-63. Apart from the more obvious connotations of shadow and the danger of thirst, the dead persons want to change into the palm tree, which is a holy tree of Min, the fertility god; the scene may be concerned with the man's virility.

79832 GRIESHAMMER, Reinhard, Gott und das Negative nach Quellen der ägyptischen Spätzeit, *in: Aspekte der spätägyptischen Religion*, 79-92.

After general remarks on the negative forces, evil, which endanger the cosmic order, Maʿat, and their role in the realm of the gods, the hereafter and the present world, for the individual as well as for the society, the author studies one aspect, i.e. the attitude and activity of god as regards evil in the texts of the Greco-Roman temples.
This is best exemplified by the very frequently occurring scenes of the "presentation of Maʿat" by the king to a god (or vice versa), which also deals with the fate of evil (*isft*) and its personification in the evil ones (*isftyw*). Conspicuous in almost all legends to the ritual scene is the divine (sometimes royal) judicial activity of separating Maʿat from evil. Isfet appears as the general conception of evil, as opposed to Maʿat.
The author also devotes some attention to the conceptions of evil in the profane sphere, but references to evil (here also as general conception, not as sin) are of a rare occurrence.
He argues that the other word for evil, *grg*, which is generally translated "lie, falsehood" has a wider semantic range: "intrigue, threat to world order."

79833 HAAG, Herbert, Das Bild als Gefahr für den Glauben, *in: Wort und Bild*. Symposion des Fachbereichs Altertums- und Kulturwissenschaften zum 500-jährigen Jubiläum der Eberhard-Karls-Universität Tübingen 1977. Herausgegeben von Hellmut Brunner, Richard Kannicht, Klaus Schwager, München, Wilhelm Fink Verlag, 1979, 151-165, with 2 fig.

In this article on the incompatibility of representation and monotheism the author devotes some remarks to Akhnaton's religious reform.

79834 KÁKOSY, L., Some Problems of Late-Egyptian Religion, *in: Acts 1st ICE*, 347-352.

Stressing that in the Late Period profound changes transformed the Egyptian religion and that traditional beliefs ceased to dominate in large areas, the author argues that classical authors correctly recorded phenomena of the living religion, with few elements of priestly wisdom. He presents some examples of the changed belief in the sphere of the funerary cults (e.g. renewed interest in the astral afterlife), religion (the symbolic character of animal worship) and iconography. J.J.J.

79835 van de WALLE, B., Les textes d'Amarna se réfèrent-ils à une doctrine morale ?, in: *Studien zu altägyptischen Lebenslehren*, 353-362.

The author studies the question whether Akhnaton wanted to introduce a new elaborate doctrine in which the norms of life and the destination of the afterlife were in accordance with his theological system. He concludes that the conceptions concerning the human ideal and the norms of moral life, and concerning the afterlife, which were present in the new doctrine, were, although in line with the traditional morals, adapted to the spirit and the conditions of life in the Amarna Period. This resulted in a choice of prescriptions which reflected the ideal of life and theology of the king.

c. Funerary belief and funerary cult

See also our numbers 79069; 79123; 79224 79354; 79356; 79420; 79598; 79600; 79614; 79651; 79654; 79659; 79710; 79718; 79727; 79748; 79762; 79812; 79814 and 79835.

79836 BLEEKER, C.J., Het oord van stilte. Dood en eeuwigheid naar oud-Egyptisch geloofsbesef, Katwijk, Servire, *[1979]* (15 x 23.5 cm; 127 p., 16 pl. *[6 in colour]*). Pr. fl. 48

"The place of silence. Death and eternity after ancient Egyptian belief."
In the foreword the author points out that the ancient Egyptian attitude towards death is sharply distinct from that of other ancient peoples. After remarks on the attitude towards death in general he presents various information and points of discussion concerning the B.D. and its spells which he utilised as the basic source of his study. In the next chapter he sketches the character of the ancient Egyptian religion.
Then, dealing with the mythological and ritual preconceptions of the immortality belief, he discusses the magical power of the deceased being based on knowledge, particularly the significance of knowing secret matters; the mythical geography of the realm of the dead; and the funerary ritual. Life after death is the subject of the next chapter. In this connection the author points out that the Egyptian conception of man as consisting of components such as *ach*, *ba* and *ka*; the ambivalent position of the dead in the netherworld; the relation of the deceased to the gods; his justification in the judgement of the dead; and his

resurrection. The last chapter is devoted to the role of the gods in guaranteeing the happiness of the deceased after death. For this purpose he divides them in a functional arrangement: the sun god and his circle; the Osiris configuration; and some other gods. A brief postface concludes the book, which is amply provided with passages from the B.D.
Notes at the end of each chapter.
It is to be noticed that the diacritical marks in the transliteration of Egyptian words are in general absent.

79837 HUNTINGTON, Richard and Peter METCALF, Celebrations of Death. The Anthropology of Mortuary Ritual, Cambridge University Press, [1979] (15.3 x 22.7 cm; XVI + 230 p., 2 maps, 2 plans, 2 fig., 3 diagrams, 9 ill.).

Within the context of an anthropological study of mortuary rituals in various parts of the world, particularly in Indonesia and Madagascar, in the third part (on the dead king and immortal kingship), the authors devote a section to "Pyramid Building in the Context of Early Egypt." In the steady elaboration of tomb architecture culminating in the IVth Dynasty pyramids - which they conceive to be cenotaphs - the authors see reflected an ecological crisis leading to increasing social stratification. The reason for building pyramids was the need for a corporate project that focussed upon the person of the king.
Although the other sections do not refer to Egypt they contain material that could be compared with profit with the Egyptian evidence.   J.J.J

79838 WRIGHT, G.R.H., The Egyptian Sparagmos, *MDAIK* 35 (1979), 345-358.

The author first discusses the occurrence reported by Petrie of mutilated burials from the Prehistoric Period, these mutilations being previous to the burial itself. After summarising opinions of several scholars he discusses successively the archaeological facts at issue (which he accepts as correct in several cases), their interpretation, and references to the custom in later religious literature. He explains the custom as a means to promote resurrectio sub specie renovatio by way of sympathetic magic, practised only on a few "elect" members of the community.
Perhaps the concept of mummification (conservation) and sparagmos (renovation) intermingled in the early stage of mummification, a situation reflected in funerary texts.   J.J.J.

d. Temple, priests, cult and ritual

See also our numbers 79056; 79112; 79133; 79255; 79273; 79356; 79449; 79470; 79546; 79573; 79575; 79576; 79624; 79626; 79632; 79633; 79643; 79651; 79657; 79694; 79704; 79729; 79741; 79760; 79761; 79812; 79854; 79888; 79895 and 79896.

79839 BEINLICH, Horst, Die spezifischen Opfer des oberägyptischen Gaue, *SAK* 7 (1979), 11-22.

Proceeding from Derchain's study of the specific rites for the nome deities in the Edfu temple (see our number 62138) the author draws up a list of the offerings occurring in the nome processions. Whereas the former show large variations, the latter are fairly uniform, each nome with its own specific offering. This presents evidence for the cults, but also for the economic position of each nome.
A table with the specific offerings and rites of the Upper Egyptian nomes on p. 20-21.   J.J.J.

79840 DORESSE, Marianne, Le dieu voilé dans sa châsse et la fête du début de la décade, *RdE* 31 (1979), 36-65, with 1 fig.

L'auteur rassemble cette fois les documents d'un quatrième chapitre de son étude de l'Amon "aniconique" (voir nos Nos. 71165 et 73203), consacrés à la fête mentionnée dans le titre. Elle les classe chronologiquement de la XVIIIe dyn. jusqu'à l'époque romaine.
Le chapitre V est consacré au culte d'Amenemipet à Djémé, puis à l'énumération des stations de son culte situées en dehors des parcours de sa procession, puis enfin au trajet de la procession décadaire sur le rive ouest.
Malgré une pagination continue des trois articles, il n'est pas toujours facile de retrouver les documents utilisés dans cette dernière partie et publiés précédemment.   *Ph. Derchain*

79841 GITTON, Michel, Le clergé féminin au Nouvel Empire, *in*: *Acts 1st ICE*, 225-228.

The author deals with the donation stela of Ahmose-Nefertari, some blocks of the "Red Chapel" of Hatshepsut, and the unpublished statue BM 1280, all three presenting material for the study of the office of the Divine Consort in the early XVIIIth Dynasty.   J.J.J.

79842 GRAEFE, Erhart, König und Gott als Garanten der Zukunft (Notwendiger Ritualvollzug neben göttlicher Selbstbildung) nach Inschriften der griechisch-römischen Tempel. Mit einem Anhang: Eine Hypothese zur Erklärung der sogenannten Pektoralopferszenen und dem Verhältnis zwischen Ritualgeschehen und bildlicher Darstellung in den späten Tempeln, *in*: *Aspekte der spätägyptischen Religion*, 47-78, with 1 fig.

The study is divided into two parts, each dealing with one of two related conceptions. The first part is concerned with the obligation of the king to present offerings and to perform the ritual in order to demand the gods to maintain the cosmic order. This duty is expressed by $tp\ b3(t)$, the dutiful act which the gods in their turn have already set in the heart of the king.

The author lists 12 texts in the Greco-Roman temples (Edfu, Dendara, Kom Ombo) in which the expression occurs, thereby mentioning the cult object presented in the accompanying scene (i.a. maʿat-figure, pectoral, collar). The 13th example of the expression is from the Late Period statue Cairo CG 688. He discusses the two constituent elements of the expression: tp which expresses some kind of superlative, "maximum" and which is also used to form compound abstracts; and $bȝ(t)$, which is probably identical with the older Egyptian word $bȝ(ȝ)t$, "(good) character." In the second part the author attempts to demonstrate that the demiurge guarantees the endurance of the world, although the king's repeated performance of the cultic acts is necessary. In his opinion this guarantee is expressed in the epithet $sr\ iyt$, "the one who announces the future." He extensively discusses the 21 texts taken from various monuments (numbered 14-34; 7 of them already collected in our number 64371) in which the epithet occurs. Using a wide variety of examples he argues that the epithet denotes "knowledge in advance, the announcement of things to happen" not "prophecy", and that it is probably not connected with oracles.

In the appendix the author presents his hypothesis for the understanding of the scenes of the offering of pectorals and for the relation between ritual act and representation. From the examination of 50 scenes of the presentation of pectorals it is clear that in the titles of the accompanying spells the word $wḏȝ$ is written as the normal word for "amulet", but also with the pectoral-sign as phonogram or determinative, and that in some cases representation and text show a discrepancy, since the text mentions another pectoral. This may be explained from the phenomenon that after the selection of the text passages the priests had to find vignettes for the various spells. Since the word $wḏȝ$, "amulet" could also be written with the pectoral-sign they chose for a spell with the general title of the presentation of an amulet a scene with that of a pectoral, the vignette being rather a determinative to the text than showing a cult act performed in reality.

79843   HANDOUSSA, Tohfa, A propos de l'offrande $šbt$, *SAK* 7 (1979), 65-74, with 1 fig.

Study on the offering called $šbt$, which occurs not too frequently on the walls of temples from the Pharaonic Period. The author lists 26 instances until the reign of Nectanebo, and discusses the writings of $šbt$ and the divinities to which it is offered, which appear to be all leontocephalic. He concludes, i.a. on account of a clepsydra of Amenophis III, that $šbt$ is the symbol of the regular return of organised time, the restoration of the cosmic order.   J.J.J.

79844   HEERMA VAN VOSS, M.S.H.G., The Cista Mystica in the Cult and Mysteries of Isis, *in: Studies in Hellenistic Religions*. Edited by M.J. Vermaseren, Leiden, E.J. Brill, 1979 (= Études préliminaires aux religions orientales dans l'Empire romain, 78), 23-27.

The author investigates iconographic and other details concerning the *cista mystica* and its context. The object is of Egyptian origin. Its predecessor was the "mystery chest" of our numbers 69245 and 71259.

M. Heerma van Voss

79845 HOLM-RASMUSSEN, Torben, On the Statue Cult of Nectanebos II, *Acta Orientalia*, Copenhagen 40 (1979), 21-25, with 1 pl.

There is a general tendency to conclude that evidence of a statue cult of Nectanebo II, whether in the form of a falcon statue or through priestly titles, is an indication of the king's building activity. Referring to the "Priesterdekrete" of the Ptolemaic Period which state the introduction of special cults with statues, priests and festivals for the king, and summarising what we know about Nectanebo's activities, the author suggests that the latter's statue cult had a similar justification, namely recognition of his deeds in general.
A few words are added on the falcon statues of Nectanebo.

J.J.J.

79846 IBRAHIM, Mohiy Eldin, An Oblation Offered to Reigning King and Queen, *in*: Acts 1st ICE, 319-325, with 1 fig.

The author deals with a scene on the N. wall of the Hall of Offerings in the Edfu temple in which Hapy brings an offering to the royal pair. He presents the accompanying texts in hieroglyphs, transliteration and translation, and suggests that ceremonies for the Royal Ancestors as here represented took place daily in all temples immediately after the conclusion of the daily ritual for the chief god.

J.J.J.

79847 LASKOWSKA-KUSZTAL, Ewa, Remarques sur le sanctuaire ptolémaïque à Deir el-Bahari, *in*: Acts 1st ICE, 419-421.

The importance of the Ptolemaic sanctuary on the area of the Hatshepsut temple at Deir el-Bâhri lies in the fact that its cult was exclusively devoted to the deified Imhotep and Amenhotep son of Hapu.

79848 STADELMANN, Rainer, Totentempel und Millionenjahrhaus in Theben, *MDAIK* 35 (1979), 303-321, with 3 fig. containing plans.

Proceeding his studies on the royal mortuary temples of Thebes (see our number 78762) the author argues that the "House of Millions of Years" was also a procession temple. He studies in detail the development of the plan, from the temples of Hatshepsut and Tuthmosis III to that of Sethi I. Two fundamental concepts rule the overall scheme: the offering to the dead king before a false door, and the cult of the bark, while other concepts are included from the O.K. pyramid temples, such as the *pr-wrw* and the court of the statues. By the appearance of a number of other divinities besides the Amon triad the mortuary temple became a real god's temple.

J.J.J.

79849   ZIVIE, Christiane M., Les rites d'érection de l'obélisque et du pilier Ioun, *in*: *Hommages Sauneron* I, 477-498, with 1 pl.

The author studies the scenes of the rite of erecting obelisks from the Ptolemaic and Roman Periods, mentioning an unpublished instance from Deir el-Shelwît. She deals with the solar aspects of the rite and points out its close connections with the rite of erecting the pillar *iwn*, discussing particularly the instances from the N.K. and the T.I.P.   J.J.J.

e. Kingship

See also our numbers 79071; 79204; 79224; 79255; 79280; 79317; 79449; 79651; 79694; 79699; 79706; 79764; 79801; 79804; 79805; 79807; 79814; 79837; 79842; 79867 and 79920.

79850   BLUMENTHAL, Elke, Darstellung und Selbstdarstellung des ägyptischen Königtums. Untersuchungen zur schriftlichen Überlieferung des Mittleren Reiches, *Ethnographisch-Archäologische Zeitschrift*, Berlin 20 (1979), 79-94.

Summary of the author's Habilitationsschrift. See already our number 77095.

79851   BLUMENTHAL, Elke, Darstellung und Selbstdarstellung des ägyptischen Königtums. Untersuchungen zur schriftlichen Überlieferung des Mittleren Reiches, *Wissenschaftliche Zeitschrift der Karl-Marx-Universität*. Gesellschafts- und Sprachwissenschaftliche Reihe, Leipzig 28 (1979), 153.

See our preceding number.

79852   GERMOND, Philippe, Le roi et le retour de l'inondation, *Bulletin Société d'Égyptologie*, Genève No. 1 (Mai 1979), 5-12.

From some texts, not only from Edfu but already from the N.K., it appears that the Egyptians held the king responsible for the annual return of the inundation, whether he acted himself or implored the gods who were connected with the inundation, particularly Hathor-Sakhmet.   J.J.J.

79853   LORTON, David, Towards a Constitutional Approach to Ancient Egyptian Kingship, *JAOS* 99 (1979), 460-465.

A review article of our number 75042.

79854   STRICKER, B.H., Jezus' koningsschap, Amsterdam, Oxford, New York, B.V. Noord-Hollandsche Uitgeversmaatschappij, 1979 (16 x 24 cm; 28 p., 1 fig.) = Mededelingen der Koninklijke Nederlandse Akademie van Wetenschappen, Afd. Letterkunde. Nieuwe Reeks, Deel 42, No. 6, 183-210.

The author studies three aspects of the kingship of Jesus. First the anointment, with reference to that of the king by Horus and Thoth and of private persons (cones on their heads in N.K. banquet scenes). Secondly, the alliance by which the prominent of the state transferred their power to the pretender and which was sealed by the oath and the joint eating of the offering. In this respect he refers to the murder of Osiris by Seth who cut his body in 26 pieces which were presented to his accomplices. Thirdly, the last supper: the cleaning of the feet is compared with that of the feet of pharaoh during the *sed*-festival.

f. Magic and popular religion

See also our numbers 79259; 79261; 79470; 79524; 79821 and 79834.

79855 OGDON, Jorge R., Las manipulaciones mágicas en el antiguo Egipto, Asunción-Buenos Aires, 1979 (53 p., 8 fig., 13 pl.) = Estudios Egiptológicos, 1.

In the introduction the author defines a magical act as comprising two fundamental aspects: the recitative and the gesture. In the first part of the book the author puts forward a new sense for the hand-gestures made by the herdsmen while crossing a ford with their cattle, a current scene in O.K. mastabas. By analysing *Hirtengesch.*, a love poem, the texts attached to the above mentioned scenes, and some minor texts and representations from the O. and M.K., he suggests that the so-called "water-spell" has the ultimate purpose of protecting and preserving the life of the endangered beings, which may be humans, animals, or vegetables (the latter in farming scenes where the gestures are directed towards the crop-grains). The repulsing of the malignant beings (crocodiles, hippopotami or lions) is only a secondary effect of the application of the magical act in question, as clearly demonstrated by *Hirtengesch.* and the love poem, where the personage says that the spell is made for him and not against the dangerous being. A minor text in an O.K. mastaba seems to reassure this sense, since there the protection is made for the being "who is in the water". As the hand-gestures can be made outside the scope of the herdsmen scenes, it seems obvious that "water-spell" is the title applied to the charm exclusively in such scenes or where crossing water is involved. In the other cases no title at all is given to the magical act. On the other hand, the magician in charge of performing the magical act differs in the scenes. While in the herdsmen scenes he always is a $hwḏw$ (var. $hwḏw$) - a special class of the $wḥ^ꜥ$ workmen - in a hunting scene from the mastaba of Ptahhotpe he is a $ḥm-kꜣ$. The attributes of the $hwḏw$, nonetheless, are consistent in the herdsmen scenes: a special kind of garment with a projection in the front, and a round-pointed stick.

In the second part, the author studies the application on certain postures during the funerary ceremonies, such as the recep-

tion of the coffin in the necropolis by the *Muw*-dancers or the
"Two Kites" (i.e., priestesses personifying Isis and Nephthys),
concluding that the same are protective attitudes directed to
the coffin or the way it should pass over. Other series of
gestures are defined by the author as "imitative gestures",
being those made by the Nine Companions. He says that the same
are related to the different operations performed during the
rites of Opening of the Mouth and the Eyes, since the postures
are always related to a part of the head, and which will enable
the dead to restore his vital functions.
In the Conclusions, the author offers an explanation on the
origin of the magical hand-gestures destined to protect the life,
since the same was applied during the Archaic Period to the
person of the king himself. He concludes that the theory of the
protection of life is of popular origin. He notes that the
application of this spell to the dead is the result of the mon-
istic viewpoint which postulates an afterlife and the eternal
well being of the honoured defuncts.
The book closes with General and Egyptian indexes.   *J.R. Ogdon*

79856 SMELIK, K.A.D., The Cult of the Ibis in the Graeco-Roman Period.
With Special Attention to the Data from the Papyri, *in*: *Studies in Hellenistic Religion*. Edited by M.J. Vermaseren, Leiden, E.J.
Brill, 1979 (= Études préliminaires aux religions orientales dans
l'empire romain, 78), 225-243, with 1 map.

The author studies the cult of the ibis in the Greco-Roman Period,
mainly on account of the Greek papyri mostly dating from the 2nd
century B.C., but also the Demotic archive of Hor. Several aspects are dealt with: the temple cult, the feeding and breeding,
and mummification and burial of the ibises in the cult centres;
the economical aspects of the temple and its priesthood; the
organisation of the cult; the sharing of the facilities as regards the cult of the ibis and that of the falcon; and the spread
of the cult over the whole country.

79857 SMELIK, K.A.D., De ibiscultus in Grieks-Romeins Egypte, *Spiegel Historiael*, Haarlem 14 (1979), 392-398, with 9 ill. and 1 fig.

After a discussion of the Egyptian animal worship in general and
its growing importance in later ages the author deals with the
ibis cult, particularly in the Greco-Roman Period. The article
is illustrated by photographs of some objects in the Allard
Pierson Museum, Amsterdam.   *J.J J.*

79858 TADEMA-SPORRY, B., Profylactische en genezende stenen beelden
uit Egypte, *Organorama*, Oss 16, No. 1 (1979), 13-16, with 6
colour ill.

"Prophylactic and healing stone statues from Egypt".
Popular article, dealing with i.a. the statue of Djed-Hor-le-
Sauveur, the god Bes, Horus cippi, and royal statues with pro-
phylactic and curing power.

g. General and varia

See also our numbers 79117; 79449; 79455; 79883; 79919; 79920 and 791001.

79859   GÖRG, Manfred, Zum Namen der Punischen Göttin Tinnit, *Ugarit-Forschungen* 11 (1979), 303-306.

Since the character and iconography of the Punic goddess *Tnt* show a close affinity to the Egyptian goddesses Isis and Hathor, the first of whom often bears the epithet *nṯr.t*, "the Divine", Coptic ⲚⲈⲈⲦⲈ. This late pronunciation preceded by *t ꜣ* may have led to the Punic name *Tnt*.

79860   QUAEGEBEUR, Jan, Pour un inventaire raisonné des données relatives à la religion égyptienne d'après les sources documentaires grecques, *in*: Acts 1st ICE, 533-542.

The author draws attention to the importance of Greek sources for knowledge about the Egyptian religion. The case is exemplified by several instances. Extensive notes are added.

79861   RINGGREN, Helmer, Die Religionen des Alten Orients, Göttingen, Vandenhoeck & Ruprecht, 1979 (16.2 x 24.3 cm; 255 p.); series: Grundrisse zum Alten Testament. Das Alte Testament Deutsch. Ergänzungsreihe. Sonderband.

The first chapter is devoted to the Egyptian religion. After a short discussion of divinity in general the author presents a general survey comprising mythology, cosmogonies as well as mythological stories, aspects of the cult such as temple, priest, daily ritual, feasts, oracles, magic and witchcraft, and further, kingship, the god-man relation, and lastly funerary beliefs.
We did not see the original Swedish edition Främre Orientens Religioner i Gammal Tid, Stockholm, Svenska Bokförlaget/Bonniers, 1967.

79862   SZOLC, Piotr, Analyse des archäologischen Materials in Bezug auf seine religiösen Inhalte, *in*: Acts 1st ICE, 629-634.

The author stresses the value of semiotics which allows us to classify and codify the ways religion expresses itself in objects.

VII. SOCIETY AND CULTURE

a. Civil organisation, titles and functions, military organisation

See also our numbers 79044; 79100; 79254; 79256; 79306; 79429; 79430; 79432; 79439; 79449; 79466; 79494; 79561; 79706; 79722; 79787; 79837; 79885; 79890; 79916; 79922 and 79936.

79863 BOGOSLOVSKIY, E.S., Должностное владение в древнем Египте и дата реорганизации службы царского некрополя, in: Письменные памятники и проблемы истории культуры народов востока. XIV годичная сессия ло ив АН СССР (Доклады и сообщения). Декабрь 1978 г. Часть I, Moscow, [Издательство "Наука". Главная редакция восточной литературы], 1979, 21-27.

'Official property in Ancient Egypt and materials on the re-organisation of duties in the royal necropolis'.
Not seen.

79864 BOGOSLOVSKY, E.S., "Слуги" фараонов, богов и частных лиц (к социальной истории Египта XVI-XIV вв до н.э.), Москва, Издательство "Наука". Главная редакция восточной литературы, 1979 (14.5 x 21.7 cm; 236 p., 32 pl. [= p. 205-236], ill. on cover; an English summary on p. 195-202); at head of title: Академия Наук СССР. Институт востоковедения. Pr. 1р. 50к.

" 'Servants' of Pharaohs, Gods and Private Persons (on the Social History of Egypt XVI-XIVth Century B.C.)."
The author studies the position of the people called $sdm-^{c}\check{s}$ in the XVIIIth Dynasty, on account of published and many unpublished sources (cfr the Avtoreferat of his thesis, our number 68083). Chapter I deals with the history of the problem In chapter II the material of the study is discussed as well as the combinations in which $sdm-^{c}\check{s}$ occurs. Chapter III is devoted to the iconography: the way in which the "listeners to the call" are depicted, e.g. offering to his deceased master or to a god or receiving offerings himself. Attention is paid to the changes in the iconography at the end of the 14th century B.C. and to statues of a $sdm-^{c}\check{s}$.
The core of the book, chapters IV to VI, is devoted to these people in the service of high officials and priests, of the king, and of the temples. Several sections deal with special subjects, such as, for instance: the private personnel of Senenmut; the $sdm-^{c}\check{s}$ as kinsman of his master; high officials and courtiers as $sdm-^{c}\check{s}$ of the king; the necropolis workmen; the application of the term $sdm-^{c}\check{s}$ to the inhabitants of neighbouring countries; the personnel of the "White Houses" in the temples; the "salaries" of the servants. A summary on p. 142-147, roughly similar to the English summary, which, however, is provided with many notes referring to sources and literature.

The main conclusion of the author is that $sḏm-ꜥš$ indicates a kind of servant, from slave and toiling workman on an estate to its manager, from high official to workman in the service of the king or the temple. It thus refers not to a class, but to a relation of its bearer to his master; it is not a socio-economic but a social term. In households of officials it is restricted to those who literally could hear their master, peasants in the field being excluded; in the royal estates and the temples a more figurative meaning was used.
Bibliography on p. 180-190; indexes p. 191-194. The plates bear photographs and line drawings of part of the material.   J.J.J.

79865   BRYAN, Betsy M., The Title "Foster Brother of the King", *JSSEA* 9 (1978-1979), 117-123.

The author argues that the title $sn\ n\ mn\ꜥ(t)\ nswt$, which is found, with variants, with Kenamun, Senmut, and others, actually means "brother of the nurse/tutor of the king".   J.J.J.

79866   FATTOVICH, R., Trends in the Study of Predynastic Social Structures, *in*: *Acts 1st ICE*, 215-220.

The author, discussing the possibilities of reconstructing the Badarian and Naqadan societies, deals in five short sections with cemeteries, settlements, kinship terminology, oral traditions, and prehistoric survivals in historical times, indicating the conclusions we draw from each of the subjects for the Predynastic society.   J.J.J.

79867   GARCIA PELAYO, M., Las Formas Políticas en el Antiguo Oriente, Caracas, Monte Avila Editores, 1979 (233 p.).

On p. 113-191 the author analyses the political structures of the Pharaonic state, beginning with a brief introduction about the influence of the physical characteristics of the country, the Egyptian concept of 'historical' time, and a schematic outline of Egyptian history down to the Late Period, with emphasis on historical and political changes. Then he proceeds by describing the functioning of the theocratic character of royalty, the administrative organisation, and concludes with a brief commentary on the social aspects of Egyptian culture and the impact of the political idea upon the structure of the society.
   J.R. Ogdon

79868   GILLAM, Robyn A., An instance of the title $jmy-r\ šwt\ nšmt$ on a statuette in a private collection, *GM* Heft 36 (1979), 15-28, with 2 fig. on 1 pl.

Die Inschrift auf dem Fragment einer Statuette nennt einen Horus $mꜣꜥ\ ḫrw$. Die Statuette gehört ins Mittlere Reich und soll aus Saqqara stammen, wo zumindest im Neuen Reich dieser Gott zusammen mit anderen Gottheiten verehrt wurde. Der Inhaber trägt den

Titel eines *i̓my-r šwt nšmt*, der sich wohl aus dem eines *i̓my-r sš(wy)* entwickelt hat. In beiden scheint der religiöse Aspekt zu überwiegen; der Titel wird mehr bedeuten, als dass sein Träger lediglich Aufseher der Jagd und Fischerei bzw. der königlichen Vergnügungen war. In einer Tabelle werden alle bekannten Träger des Titels aufgeführt.

Inge Hofmann

79869 HOFFMAN, Michael A., Egypt Before the Pharaohs. The Prehistoric Foundations of Egyptian Civilization, New York, Alfred A. Knopf, 1979 (15.5 x 24 cm; XXI + 391 p., 78 fig. and ill., 5 maps, 1 plan, 12 tables). Pr. $ 16

This is an up-to-date survey of the Egyptian pre- and proto-history ranging from the Palaeolithic origins to the IInd Dynasty, written in a lively style and intended both for laymen and scholars. On some pages the evidence, tombs, pottery or flint artifacts, is discussed as in a scholarly study, while on others the author relates the history of excavators, with characteristics of their personalities and techniques. In general the artifacts are treated as means to reconstruct the social history.
In the first chapter of the introduction (part I) the author sets forth his aims and methods, stating i.a. that by relating the discoveries, mistakes and breakthroughs of many scholars he also describes the history of prehistoric research in Egypt. Chapters 2 and 3 deal with chronological problems and the ecological background.
Then follow five parts, each divided into some chapters, successively devoted to: the Palaeolithic Age, the Predynastic cultures of Upper Egypt, those of Lower Egypt, the civilizations in the desert around the Nile Valley and in Nubia, and the transition from Prehistory to the Dynastic Period.
One of the major themes of Hoffman is that in the Neolithic Period a fundamental difference can be established between the social structures of Upper and Lower Egypt, which is demonstrated i.a. from the sites of Hierakonpolis and Badari as against that of Maadi; the latter a trade-oriented, the former a status-oriented culture.
A second theme is how the traits of Upper Egyptian society became preponderant in the emerging pharaonic state, and along which ways the latter came into existence. In a postscript (chapter 21) the time of Khasekhemui is briefly discussed as a symbol of this transition from the old regime to a new order.
The study bristles with stimulating remarks on a large number of subjects and applies recent archaeological and anthropological theories. As examples we mention Colin Renfrew's theory of the multiplier effect (p. 303 ff) and the results of the comparative study on burial rituals by Metcalf and Huntington (p. 326 ff.).
Illustrations, figures and tables constitute an essential part of the argument.
The English edition has been published by Routledge & Kegan Paul, London, 1980 (£10.50).

J.J.J.

79870   KEMP, B.J., The City of el-Amarna as a Source for the Study of Urban Society in Egypt, *in*: *Acts 1st ICE*, 369-370.

Short version of our number 77408.

79871   KRUCHTEN, J.-M., L'évolution de la gestion domaniale sous le Nouvel Empire égyptien, *in*: *State and Temple Economy in the Ancient Near East*. II, 517-525.

The author studies the function of the $rw\underline{d}w$ in the N.K. In a general sense they are "representatives" of a higher authority, and this meaning was retained throughout the period, but they were particularly agents concerned with the management of the domains on two levels: directly under the intendant responsible for the management of the entire domain, and also on a local level. The latter function disappears from the texts after the XXth Dynasty, which is explained by the gradual disappearance of direct exploitation of the domains due to increasing shortage of personnel.   J.J.J.

79872   KRZYŻANIAK, Lech, Trends in the Socio-Economic Development of Egyptian Predynastic Societies, *in*: *Acts 1st ICE*, 407-412.

On account of a hypothesis posited in our number 77443 the author attempts to show how settlement and burial ground relationships in the Middle Egyptian Predynastic sites of Qau-Badari, Mostagedda and Matmar reflect the changing economic patterns of predynastic social groups. The consequences of the population growth (controlled irrigation and new settlements in the Nile-flooded zone) explain the rapid diminishing of settlement sites in the lower desert.

79873   MALAISE, Michel, Les monuments privés du Moyen Empire, leur classement, un corpus, une histoire des institutions, *in*: *Acts 1st ICE*, 449-452.

The author discusses the procedures necessary to result in a history of the institutions of the M.K.

79874   MARTIN, G.T., The New Kingdom Necropolis at Saqqâra, *in*: *Acts 1st ICE*, 457-463.

After having pointed out that only few of the high administrative officials were buried in Thebes in the period of Amenophis III to Horemheb which was scrutinised by him, the author expresses his view that whereas Thebes was principally a sacerdotal capital, the administrative capital was Memphis. The possible N.K. necropolis south of the Unas complex at Saqqara will perhaps yield rich information and finds, e.g. concerning the administration.

79875   MENU, Bernadette, Les rapports de dépendance en Égypte à l'époque saïte et perse, *in*: *Acts 1st ICE*, 477-482.

On account of some 15 documents from the Saite and Persian Periods the author discusses the words $ḥm$ and $bȝk$, generally translated "slave". She concludes that private slavery did not exist in the Late Period and that the "sales of slaves" are in fact only concerned with the servitude of a person.

79876 PEREMANS, W., Notes sur l'administration civile et financière de l'Égypte sous les Lagides, *Ancient Society*, Leuven 10 (1979), 139-149.

The author investigates the presence of Egyptians in the Ptolemaic administration.

79877 ROBINS, Gay, The Relationships Specified by Egyptian Kinship Terms of the Middle and New Kingdoms, *CdE* LIV, No. 108 (1979), 197-207, with 13 fig.

L'auteur tente de préciser les conceptions égyptiennes concernant les relations de parenté en analysant les expressions dans lesquelles entrent en composition (au génitif d'ordinaire) les termes it, mwt, $sȝ$, $sȝt$, sn, snt et $ḥmt$. Partant de quelques exemples concrets, elle trace à la fin de son article plusieurs tableaux qui rendent abstraitement la nomenclature des liens de parenté en égyptien. *Ph. Derchain*

79878 RÖMER, Malte, Zum Problem von Titulatur und Herkunft bei den ägyptischen "Königssohnen" des Alten Reiches, [Berlin, Höpfner GmbH, Dissertationsdruck, 1977] (14.5 x 20.5 cm; X + 231 p.).

In the first part of this dissertation of the Freie Universität Berlin the author collects the evidence concerning the titulary of the King's sons ($sȝ-nswt$) to the end of the Old Kingdom, in a chronological order which is differentiated after places such as Saqqâra, Gîza, Meidum, Dashur, Abusir and Abu Roash. In the second part he discusses the role of the King's sons within the Egyptian government. He investigates their position with respect to the king and the $iry-ḫt-nswt$. In his discussion of the King's sons as bearers of official titles the theory of Helck (our number 3358) passes the review, as well as the structure of the titularies borne by the King's sons among which occur groups containing the titles $iri-pʿt$, $ḥȝty-ʿ$, $smr wʿty$. It is apparent from the study that the title $sȝ-nswt$ does not belong to any of the coherent groups, although the title occurs among them.
At the end a list of the distribution of the titles over the various officials discussed and an index to the private names.

79879 RUSZCZYC, Barbara, Dziecko w starożytnym Egipcie, *Meander*, Warszawa 34, No. 5-6 (1979), 229-235, with 5 ill.

"The Child in Ancient Egypt."

79880 VACHALA, Břetislav, Ein neuer Beleg der Polygamie für das Alte Reich ?, *ZÄS* 106 (1979), 87-88.

Vgl. unsere Nummer 76424.
Verfasser führt einen weiteren möglichen Beleg an. Es handelt sich um den Besitzer des Grabes Giza Nr. 5150 aus dem Beginn der 5. Dyn.
M. Heerma v. Voss

79881 VACHALA, Břetislav, Výrobci základních materiálních hodnot v egyptské Staré říši, *Nový Orient*, Praha 34, No. 1 (1979), 27-28.

"Die Produzenten der materiellen Werte im ägyptischen A.R." Verfasser behandelt die Kategorien *mrt*, *ḥm*, *bȝk*, *ḏt* und *ỉ sww*, die im A.R. zur Bezeichnung der Produzenten der materiellen Werte dienen. Im Terminus *mrt* sieht er die zahlreich vertretene und monolithe Masse der ausgebeuteten Bevölkerung und ausländischer Sklaven.
B. Vachala

b. Economy and law; economic activities

See also our numbers 79053; 79069; 79161; 79201; 79279; 79307; 79430; 79464; 79494; 79498; 79616; 79669; 79741; 79752; 79761; 79872; 79912; 79916; 79917; 79942 and 79995.

79882 ALLAM, S., Altägyptisches Recht (Forschungsstand - Perspektiven), *in*: *Acts 1st ICE*, 61-65.

The author makes general remarks about our knowledge of Egyptian law, the sources for its study, its social background, etc.
J.J.J.

79883 ALLAM, Schafik, Die Rolle der Gottheit im Recht, *Das Altertum*, Berlin 25 (1979), 103-112, with 7 ill.

The author first briefly discusses the relation between justice and religion and the position of God in this respect in the ancient Israelite, Babylonian and Islamic cultures. More attention is paid to ancient Egyptian aspects. After remarks on the principle of Maat and funerary foundations he devotes his attention to juridical procedure in Deir el-Medîna, particularly the oracle.

79884 BOGAERT, R., Synthèse finale, *in*: *State and Temple Economy in the Ancient Near East*. II, 745-762.

Synthesis of the papers of the symposium. Ancient Egypt is dealt with on p. 754-756.

79885 BOGOSLOVSKY, E.S., Собственность и должностное владение в древнем Египте (по материалам из Дёр эль-Медина), ВДИ 1 (147), 1979, 3-23, with an English summary on p. 23.

"Property and Ex-Officio Possessions in Ancient Egypt (Based on Material from Deir el-Medîna)."
On account of a number of ostraca the author argues that the necropolis workmen received from the state (the king) an ex-officio possession consisting of a house (pr), an ʿt, a ḫnw and a tomb (mʿḥʿt), in some instances also a storehouse (wḏꜣ). These possessions could not be divided or transmitted by inheritance. If a workman built a house by his own hands, with his own tools and on "no man's land", it became his property and could be sold by him. The workmen also possessed "slaves" and cattle.
The rights of the smdt as regards private property were restricted. They had no official holdings and were exploited by the workmen.
The craftsmen were not "free" in the antique sense. In case of a reorganisation they could be transferred to the status of the smdt. Not all their children were included in the gang, some being reduced to smdt-people.   J.J.J.

79886 ENDESFELDER, E., Zur Frage des Bewasserung in pharaonischen Ägypten, in: Acts 1st ICE, 203-208.

Abridged version of our next number.

79887 ENDESFELDER, Erika, Zur Frage der Bewässerung im pharaonischen Ägypten, ZÄS 106 (1979), 37-51.

Verfasserin erörtert:
a) die physischen Bedingungen des Landes, die Aufgaben und die sich aus ihnen ergebenden Methoden der Bewässerung;
b) den Zeitpunkt der Einführung organisierter Methoden der Bewässerung (Kanäle seit dem Ende des Alten Reiches; Anfang des Bassinbewässerung in der 1. Zwischenzeit);
c) die Rolle, die die Bewässerung als Machtfaktor für die Herausbildung und Existenz des pharaonischen Staates gespielt hat (keine).
Vgl. unsere Nummer 78713.   M. Heerma v. Voss

79888 GOEDICKE, Hans, Cult-Temple and 'State' during the Old Kingdom in Egypt, in: State and Temple Economy in the Ancient Near East. I, 113-131.

While no information is available about the existence of organised religious cults in prehistoric Egypt, local cults can be traced from the very beginning of Egyptian history, though they had hardly any economic significance. The Horus cult, however, closely connected with kingship, is early known from Hierakonpolis and expanded over the entire country. To it came, as the decree of Mycerinus proves, the Hathor cult at Tehne, that received allocations, though it does not seem to have had an endowment in agricultural land. Under the Vth Dynasty we learn about donations to what seem to be "divine collectives" (nṯrw, *bȝw*), explained by the author as being the veterans of the state's service. The turning point came with Neferirkare, who exempted the priests of Abydos - not the cult - from taxation, so that the "priests", that is, the holders of god's land, became a privileged group. In the VIth Dynasty follows the transformation of this social distinction to the removal of cults from the royal supervision.

J.J.J.

79889 GRUNERT, Stefan, Untersuchungen zum Haus- und Grundeigentum im ptolemäischen Ägypten anhand der demotischen Kaufverträge aus Theben, *Ethnographisch-Archäologische Zeitschrift*, Berlin 20 (1979), 95-103.

Summary of the author's dissertation, which is planned to be published in the series "Schriften zur Geschichte und Kultur des alten Orients" of the Zentralinstitut für alte Geschichte und Archäologie, Berlin.

79890 HANDOUSSA, Tohfa, Remarks on ꜥq ḥbs, *GM* Heft 36 (1979), 29-30.

In den Eheverträgen spielt die Regelung des Unterhaltes der Frau eine wichtige Rolle. Es handelt sich dabei um die ꜥq ḥbs-Klausel, die möglicherweise bis in das Neue Reich zurückdatiert werden kann, wenn sie auch erst seit 315 v. Chr. belegt ist.

Inge Hofmann

79891 JANSSEN, Jac. J., The Role of the Temple in the Egyptian Economy During the New Kingdom, *in*: *State and Temple Economy in the Ancient Near East*. II, 505-515.

After a short general sketch of the problem of the study of the economic history of ancient Egypt the author stresses the necessity of both investigation of specific subjects and the construction of a hypothetical framework. He sets forth his ideas on a local subsistence economy at the basic level and a redistribution economy at state level. Among the state organisations engaged in collecting and redistributing taxes were the temples, the economic function of which is pointed out. In this connection he discusses their landed property on account of the Wilbour Papyrus and the Great Papyrus Harris. He answers the questions of what the temples did with the revenues from their domains and with the offerings , partly functioning as a means of redistribution, particularly the daily offerings but also those on special occasions such as feasts and festivals, for the temple personnel proper, the people under their command, as well as common people. The figures are compared with those of Deir el Medîna.

79892 JORDAN, R., Ein Beitrag zur Geldwirtschaft im Pharaonenreich, *Geldgeschichtliche Nachrichten* 69 (1979), 7-9, with 2 ill.

Article for the general reader on monetary aspects of the Egyptian culture.

79893   KELLEY, A.L., The Production of Pottery in Ancient Egypt, *in*: *Acts 1st ICE*, 365-368.

Proceeding from a potter's scene in the tomb of Ti the author draws up some hypotheses concerning the theme "pottery and society" in Egypt.   J.J.J.

79894   MERRILLEES, R.S., Opium Again in Antiquity, *Levant*, London 11 (1979), 167-171, with 1 ill. on a pl.

Proceeding from two gold pins whose heads resemble opium poppy capsules, in the Norbert Schimmel collection, the author offers a rapid survey of our knowledge about opium in the ancient Near East including Egypt.

79895   NIBBI, Alessandra, Some Remarks on the Assumption of Ancient Egyptian Sea-Going, *The Mariner's Mirror*, London 65 (1979), 201-208, with 1 map.

The author defends the thesis that the ancient Egyptians never went to sea in sea-going ships. This thesis is posited on account of the following reasons: the Egyptians knew no god of the sea; the inconclusive evidence as regards the boats represented on the Punt reliefs of the Deir el-Bahri temple; the absence of harbours in ancient Egypt; the insuitability of the coast line of the Delta in the pharaonic period for travel by large vessels; the total absence of the characteristics of a port at Wâdi Gawâsîs, which, moreover, was no part of the Egyptian culture at all; the impossibility of the claim that ancient Egypt imported wood from the Lebanon; the doubt that the geographical name *kbn/kpny*, always written in the Egyptian texts with the hill-side determinative, can be equated with the present Byblos; the inconclusive evidence as regards anchors, among which the anchor altar found at Wâdi Gawâsîs.

79896   QUAEGEBEUR, J., Documents égyptiens et rôle économique du clergé en Égypte hellénistique, *in*: *State and Temple Economy in the Ancient Near East*. II, 707-729.

At present Demotic and hieroglyphic sources play only a minor role in the studies of the economy of Ptolemaic Egypt while the texts, so far as published, are not easily accessible for non-specialists and their economic implications neglected by their editors. In this paper the author indicates the possibilities that study of these sources can offer. He discusses some aspects of the economic role of the clergy, e.g. that it was mainly the temples themselves that paid for their building program; that the priest occupied a privileged position in the country; that they, being the intellectuals, constituted the bureaucracy of the royal administration. Quaegebeur then attempts to show what the Demotic and hieroglyphic texts may add to our knowledge and he presents a survey of the economic activities of the priests and the temples, stressing that we have to take into account historical developments. J.J.J.

79897 REINEKE, Walter F., Waren die šwtyw wirklich Kaufleute ?, *Altorientalische Forschungen*, Berlin 6 (1979), 5-14.

Within a picture of the Egyptian economy during the N.K. the author discusses the position of the šwtyw. He argues that there was no room for "free merchants", the šwtyw being merely agents of institutions and temples. Only gradually, from the XXIst Dynasty onwards, the economic conditions were fulfilled for the development of a class of independent traders working for their own profit. J.J.J.

79898 VLEEMING, Sven P., Some Notes on the Artabe in Pathyris, *Enchoria* 9 (1979), 93-100.

The author discusses the writings of *it*, *sw*, *bd.t* and *ˤq* in the texts from Pathyris and closes his study with some remarks on the artabe used there. He comes to the conclusion that they used at least two different artabae: ± 60 hin and ± 48 hin.
W. Brunsch

79899 WENDORF, Fred, Romuald SCHILD, Nabil el-HADIDI, Angela E. CLOSE, Michael KOBUSIEWICZ, Hanna WIECKOWSKA, Bahay ISAAWI, Herbert HAAS, Use of Barley in the Egyptian Late Palaeolithic, *Science*, Washington D.C. 205, No. 4413 (28 September 1979), 1341-1347, with 1 map, 1 ill., and 2 fig.

Several grains of barley have been recovered from Late Palaeolithic sites at Wadi Kubbaniya near Aswân. They possibly record an initial stage of food production.

c. Prosopography, genealogies

See also our numbers 79142; 79235; 79236; 79237; 79238; 79244; 79248; 79256; 79265; 79446; 79449; 79507; 79640; 79662 and 79711.

79900 BERLANDINI, Jocelyne, Varia memphitica III, *BIFAO* 79 (1979), 249-265, with 4 pl.

Sequel to our number 77080.
The present article in the series on persons from the N.K. buried in the Memphite necropolis is devoted to the steward of the Ramesseum, general Ramessesnakht, from the first half of the reign of Ramses II. Three monuments are discussed: a wall fragment (Brussels E 5183) representing his head and presenting his titles and name as well as those of his wife Tuy, a support of a vase (?) dedicated to Isis (Turin N. 22052), and a statuette of his mother Nasha (Louvre E 11523). Each piece is minutely described, the texts given in hieroglyphs and translation with

comments. At the end the author discusses the functions of
Ramessesnakht, mentioning i.a. other stewards of the Ramesseum
from the reign of Ramses II buried in Saqqâra, other persons of
the same name, and his genealogy. Perhaps Ramessesnakht was a
foreigner by birth. J.J.J.

79901 BIERBRIER, M.L., More Light on the Family of Montemhat, in:
Glimpses of Ancient Egypt, 116-118, with 1 chart.

The author makes use of Vassali's copies of parts of some coffins,
since disappeared, from the cache of the Montu priests which he
made in 1862. From this material he is able to add some names
to the family tree of Montemhat (for the results, see chart I).
J.J.J.

79902 CLÈRE, Jacques Jean, Le problème des personnes mentionnées sur
une statue d'époque tardive ("naophore" Vatican No. 97), in:
Hommages Sauneron I, 347-362.

The "naophorous" statue Vatican No. 97, from the beginning of the
Ptolemaic Period or slightly earlier, belongs to the group of
statues dedicated by one person on behalf of another. In this
case it was a Djedhor who made it for his grandfather Herro.
The author studies the inscriptions and argues that the father
bears a name containing the name of Sobk (the following signs
are lost). The words $mnh-ib$, usually conceived to be his name,
actually means "devoted" and qualify the preceding word "son".
J.J.J.

79903 GRAEFE, Erhart, Bemerkungen zu Ramose, dem Besitzer von TT 46,
GM Heft 33 (1979), 13-15.

Der Titel des Besitzers des Grabes Nr. 46 lautet "Gelobter der
Gottesgemahlin Ahmose-Nofretere". Zugleich war er Hohepriester
des Amun im Tempel von $Mn-st$, dem Totentempel der Ahmose-Nofretere und "Vorsteher der Pferde des Herrn der Beiden Länder".
Nur eine Untersuchung des Grabes kann Klarheit darüber verschaffen, welchem König Ramose gedient hat. *Inge Hofmann*

79904 HABACHI, Labib, Unknown or Little-known Monuments of Tutankhamun
and of his Viziers, in: Glimpses of Ancient Egypt, 32-41, with
4 fig. and 5 ill.

The author publishes or re-publishes some monuments of Tutankhamun and his viziers, namely: the upper part of a doorway, probably from Memphis (preserved in the Egyptian Museum in East
Berlin; see v. Bissing, Sitzb. K. Bayer. Akad. der Wiss., Phil.-
hist. Kl., Jahrg. 1914, Abh. 3) and a door-lintel, also from
Memphis and found re-used in the tomb of Prince Sheshonq (see
Badawi, our number 4384). Discussing the viziers of this period
he argues that Eye was never vizier, but Penthu and Usermontu
were. For the latter he quotes a stelophorous statue (not a

stela!) now Cairo Museum TN 22/6/37/1 (see *Urk.* IV, 2080-2083), a fragment of a statue seen with an antiquities dealer (cfr Newberry, *PSBA* 27 (1905)) and part of a sarcophagus discovered in a deserted monastery N. of Gurna. On account of these and other evidence Habachi draws up the family tree of Usermontu.

J.J.J.

79905 KITCHEN, K.A., Some Ramesside Friends of Mine, *JSSEA* 9 (1978-1979), 13-20.

Four brief notes on various subjects, namely: 1. on the fact that of Vizier Paser no wife is mentioned anywhere in his numerous monuments and that he appears to have strived to revive the glories and tradition of Egypt; 2. On the family of Urhiya, perhaps a Hurrian, who was a general under Sethos I and Ramses II, particularly on the careers of his sons and grandsons; 3. On the vizier(s) Prehotep (rejecting Altenmüller's suggestions in our number 75009); 4. On sandals and scandals connected with the first jubilee of Ramses II (referring to O. Dem 446 and O. Ashm. Mus. 1945.37+33 + O. Michael. 90).

J.J.J.

79906 RUFFLE, John and K.A. KITCHEN, The Family of Urhiya and Yupa, High Stewards of the Ramesseum, *in*: *Glimpses of Ancient Egypt*, 55-74, with 5 fig. and 12 ill.

In part 1 the first author discusses the monuments of Urhiya and his son Yupa; particularly the recently acquired stela of Nebnehehabsu, also a son of Urhiya, in the Birmingham City Museum (No. 134'72), but also 4 other stelae (Musée des Beaux-Arts, Lyon, No. 84; Turin No. 1465; Louvre E 3143; Musée Calvet, Avignon, A4), two sarcophagus lids of Yupa (Cairo TR 28/11/24/5 and Musées Royaux, Brussels, E 5189) and a statue of him (Krannert Art Museum, Illinois, 67-3-3), all with photographs. Moreover, 8 more documents are briefly mentioned.
The second author deals in part 2 with the family history, reconstructing the genealogy and discussing the careers. Urhiya began his career as military commander under Seti I, while Yupa, who also was a military man in his youth, is known from year 5 to year 54 of Ramses II. Both became managers of the Ramesseum's endowments. Other members of the family, particularly Yupa's son Hatiay, are also discussed.

J.J.J.

79907 Van SICLEN, Charles C., The Identity of a Figure in the Tomb of Kenamun, *Sarapis* 5, No. 1 (1979), 17-20, with 1 pl.

In the tomb of Kenamun (Theban Tomb No. 93) the figure was depicted of a mayor of This and overseer of the prophets of Onuris, whose name was hacked out. The author suggests that it may have been Amenhotep, perhaps the owner of the lost Theban Tomb No. A19 and known from funerary cone 482, the shawabti Cairo CG 46537, the small block statue Leiden D 59, and a statue of a seated scribe in the Brooklyn Museum (No. 37.29E). On the latter

he is called the son of Nebiry. Whether he was Kenamun's brother is uncertain.
For an abstract of this article, see our number 75690. J.J.J.

79908 VITTMANN, Günther, Zum Eigentümer des thebanischen Grabes 243, *GM* Heft 31 (1979), 77.

Mit grosser Wahrscheinlichkeit ist der Inhaber von TT 243 *P3-mjw*, der Sohn des *Ḥr-s3-3śt*, Sohnes des *P3j f-t3w*, der im 14. Jahr Psametichs I. eine Anfrage an Amun-Re richtet. *Inge Hofmann*

d. Cultural interrelations

See also our numbers 79009; 79139; 79431; 79469; 79498; 79560; 79721; 79725; 79757; 79771; 79778; 79780; 79792; 79796; 79799; 791014 and 791017.

79909 ANDREU, Guillemette, Les égyptiens au Sinaï, *Le Monde de la Bible*, Paris No. 10 (Août-Septembre 1979), 26-28, with 4 ill. and 1 fig.

On the centres of Egyptian activities in the Sinai.

79910 de CONTENSON, H., Rās Šamra - Ugarit (Ausgrabungen und Forschungsreisen, Ausgrabungstätigkeit in Syrien. Zusammengestellt von Hartmut Kühne), *AfO* 26 (1978/1979), 162-165, with 2 pl.

A steatite statuette of Egyptian origin, datable to the XIXth Dynasty was found in the so-called Maison aux Albâtres, one of the great houses at Ugarit. The object is depicted.

79911 DAVIS, Whitney M., Ancient Naukratis and the Cypriotes in Egypt, *GM* Heft 35 (1979), 13-23.

Obgleich Naukratis eine ostgriechische Gründung ist, muss der zypriotische Anteil am Handel während der Saitenzeit und möglicherweise auch später höher veranschlagt werden als bisher getan wurde. Die wichtigsten zypriotischen Fundobjekte aus Naukratis werden kurz besprochen. Sie zeigen alle kaum ägyptischen Einfluss, während auf Zypern selbst Kunstwerke aus der gleichen Zeit ägyptisierende Charakteristika aufweisen. Die ägyptisch-zypriotischen Beziehungen waren mehr oder weniger auf Naukratis beschränkt, in der eben nicht nur Festlands- und Inselgriechen lebten, sondern die wesentlich mehr international war.
Inge Hofmann

79912 HELCK, Wolfgang, Die Beziehungen Ägyptens und Vorderasiens zur Ägäis bis ins 7. Jahrhundert v. Chr., Darmstadt, Wissenschaftliche Buchgesellschaft, 1979 (12.7 x 20 cm; XIV + 355 p., 56 fig., 4 tables) = Erträge der Forschung, 120; rev. *BiOr* 37 (1980), 321-324 (Anthony J. Spalinger); *Ugarit-Forschungen* 12 (1980), 481 (O. Loretz). Pr. DM 44

This comprehensive study of the relations between ancient Egypt
and the Near East on the one hand and the Aegean world on the
other the author deals with a large number of subjects, many of
which belong to the field of Egyptology.
In chapter A, on archaeological evidence for most ancient relations, there are sections on Aegean material found in O. and
M.K. Egypt, particularly the Treasure of Tôd, on early Egyptian
influence on Crete, and on the origin of the spiral motif on
Egyptian seals; for the latter the author, against Ward (see our
number 71608), suggests influence from the North.
Chapter B discusses written documents, mostly Egyptian, that
mention Cretan places (e.g. the "Ortsnamenliste" of Amenophis
III) and the geographical problems connected with them. Chapter
C deals with trade routes to the Aegean world. The author considers direct connections between Egypt and Crete not impossible,
although there is as yet no evidence for them.
Chapter D is devoted to three chronological problems: the Kamares
vessels found in Egypt (all of uncertain date) and the beginning
of MM II (argued to be contemporary with the S.I.P.); the lid of
the Khayan vessel and the beginning of MM III (c. 1610 B.C.); the
beginning of LM II (dated on account of the changes in the dress
of the foreigners in Rekhmire's tomb c. 1445 B.C., while the destruction of the Cretan palaces is dated to c. 1400 B.C.).
In chapter E various aspects of Cretan-Egyptian relations during
the N.K. pass the review: weapons with Cretan motifs; representations of "Cretans" in Egyptian tombs; objects connected with
the Aegean civilisation; "Cretan" motifs in Egypt; LM and Myc.
vessels in Egypt (with a catalogue); aegyptiaca from the S.I.P.
and the N.K. found in the Aegean world; traces of the Cretan
language in Egyptian texts.
Chapter G deals with the Sea Peoples, their origin and nature,
and the chronology of the end of the Mycenaean era. The author
could for this subject not yet have seen Sandars' study (our
number 78701).
The other chapters (F and H-L) mainly deal with the mutual relations between the Aegean world and the Near East, although here
too references to Egypt occur occasionally.
Conclusions on p. 253-255, followed by the notes (257-330) and
indexes (333-355).   J.J.J.

79913   HELCK, W., Einige Betrachtungen zu den frühesten Beziehungen
        zwischen Ägypten und Vorderasien, *Ugarit-Forschungen* 11 (1979),
        357-363.

        Stressing that Menes is only a point on a line of development and
        that writing was hardly a sudden invention independent of the
        Sumerians the author attacks the hypothesis of the dependence of
        Egypt's Dynastic beginnings upon Djemdet-Nasr stimulation. He
        discusses the basic concepts of the theory such as that of the
        city and the Sumerian, or better Elamite influence. He argues
        that, as for the city, the Sumerian culture differed essentially
        from the Egyptian and that the presumed influence cannot be est-

ablished on the basis of the presence of certain motifs from that culture. The problem whether the foreign ceramics elements in Egypt are to be attributed to trade or to cultural influence is discussed in some detail.

79914 HÖLBL, Günther, Beziehungen der ägyptischen Kultur zu Altitalien. I: Textteil. II: Katalog, Leiden, E.J. Brill, 1979 (15.5 x 24.5 cm; Teil I: XXIV + 394 p., colour frontispiece, 16 fig.; Teil II: VI + 287 p., 5 folding maps, 8 colour pl., 182 pl.) = Études préliminaires aux religions orientales dans l'empire romain, 62, I-II; rev. *Acta Archaeologica Academiae Scientiarum Hungaricae* 32 (1980), 476-477 (L. Castiglione); *BiOr* 38 (1981), 68-71 (Gabriella Scandone Matthiae). Pr. set fl. 480

In the introduction the author points out his aim to elucidate the connections between and the influence of Egypt on Italy, directly and indirectly, on account of the objects and motifs of Egyptian origin found on mainland Italy in the period from circa 800-300 B.C. Also remarks are made as to the role of the Etruscans, Greeks and Phoenicians in this respect. The introduction is followed by an excursus on the question whether the *Tr̆s* of the Egyptian sources about the Sea Peoples are to be equated with, or at least belong to, the same ethnic group as the Tursenoi-Etruscans.
In the first part of the first volume, which deals with the Egyptian and Egyptianising objects, the author begins with a survey of the Egyptian faience production technique. In the second chapter he describes the various types of vessels manufactured in Egyptian faience or glazed pottery technique and he summarises the discussion. The third chapter is devoted to figured amulets, and scarabs and scaraboids. The various finds of groups of scarabs (and scaraboids) and their chronology are discussed, as well as the undersides of the scarabs. The problem of the provenance of the Egyptianising and Egyptian amulets and scarabs is discussed in a separate section. He then deals with some particular types of objects: lyre player seals; glass, amber and hard stone scarabs and scaraboids. The chapter is concluded by some suggestions as to the significance of the amulets in Italy.
After a short chapter on stone alabastra chapter 5 is concerned with finds of glass objects in prehellenistic times and deals with the various areas of production, the types of objects such as vessels and pearls, and connections.
The last chapter of the first part is devoted to other Egyptian and Egyptianising objects from Italy.
In the second part of the first volume the author studies the Egyptian motifs on objects which were found in Italy in three chapters: Egyptian motifs on Phoenician metal bowls (and related vessels) and on ivory objects from Etruria; spread motifs such as the sphinx, the griffon and the lotus.
In a long summary on the contents of the first volume the connections and influences pass the review.
The second volume contains the catalogue of the objects arranged

after regions and places, illustrated by maps, and two indexes, one general and the other comprising the Museum inventory nos. in concordance with the nos. of the present catalogue.

79915 HÖLBL, G., Zeugnisse ägyptischer Kultur im vorrömischen Italien, in: *Acts 1st ICE*, 313-318, with 2 pl.

The author lists first a few single pieces, i.e. a (lost) *'Imsti-* vessel of Psammetichus I from Viterbo and a vessel of the $ḥry\ mš^c$ $n\ ḥ3w-nbw\ B3k-n-rn.f$ called $^cnḫ-Nfr-ib-R^c$ (middle sixth century B.C.). He then deals with three groups of objects: faience vessels (among them the famous vase of Bocchoris), figurative amulets and scarabs and scaraboids (divided into four groups, of which one genuine Egyptian).
J.J.J.

79916 HOFMANN, Inge, Der Sudan als ägyptische Kolonie im Altertum, Wien, 1979 (14.5 x 20.5 cm; 53 p., 1 map) = Beiträge zur Ägyptologie, 2 = Veröffentlichungen der Institute für Afrikanistik und Ägyptologie der Universität Wien, 5.

Das Büchlein ist eine populärwissenschaftliche Darstellung des Sudan als ägyptische Kolonie. Nach einer geschichtlichen Einführung wird die Stellung und der Aufgabenbereich des Vizekönigs, seine Mitarbeiter sowie die Nubier und ihre Stellung im Kolonialgebiet untersucht. Ein dritter Teil befasst sich mit den Abgaben an Gold, Sklaven, Nutzvieh, Wildtieren und ihren Produkten, Elfenbein, Holz und Holzprodukten, den vegetabilischen und mineralischen Stoffen. Abschliessend werden die Folgen der Kolonisation für Nubien dargelegt.
Inge Hofmann

79917 KLENGEL, Horst, Handel und Händler im alten Orient, Wien-Köln-Graz, Hermann Böhlaus Nachf., 1979 (17 x 24.5 cm; 247 p., 6 maps, 2 plans, 12 fig., 35 pl. [3 in colour], 1 folding p. containing a map and a fig.).
Pr. ÖS 298

In the section on Byblos (p. 64-70) Egypt is referred to constantly. Egypt's lack in certain raw materials in general, but, more specifically, timber and the role of Byblos in this respect, is discussed. The author stresses that the delivery took place in the Western Delta.
The trade in the Bronze Age - N.K. is dealt with on p. 132-195: the role of Ugarit and Byblos; the N.K. expansion; the Amarna Letters and the reciprocal gifts as a means of diplomacy; the unsafe trade routes overland; the sea trade; the Syrian-Egyptian trade contacts, as exemplified by the paintings in the Theban tomb of Kenamun; cultural exchange; the trip of Wenamun to Byblos against the background of the international political situation.

79918 LANG, Bernhard, Schule und Unterricht im alten Israel, in: *La Sagesse de l'Ancien Testament*, par M. Gilbert, Gembloux, Éditions J. Duculot S.A./Leuven, University Press, [1979] (= Bibliotheca Ephemeridum Theologicarum Lovaniensium, 51), 186-201.

The author i.a. compares the various stages of education in ancient Israel and ancient Egypt, which run parallel.

79919 LOULLOUPIS, M.C., Evidence of Egyptian Cults in Cyprus, *in*: *Acts 1st ICE*, 431-439.

The Egyptian cults in Cyprus, introduced during the N.K., went through three stages: personal, communal and state cult. The archaeological evidence is discussed.
Extensive footnotes.

79920 NOGUERA, Anthony, How African was Egypt? A Comparative Study of Ancient Egyptian and Black African Cultures, New York/Washington/Atlanta/Hollywood, Vantage Press, [1976] (13.5 x 21 cm; [V] + 217 p., 134 fig., 7 maps).   Pr. $ 7

In this book without notes the author argues that from the simultaneous study of ancient Egypt and black African cultures it becomes apparent that ancient Egypt was a product of African cultures welded together by Semitic invaders.
After preliminary remarks in chapter 1 and the presentation of historical and cultural information about primarily the predynastic cultures of ancient Egypt in chapter 2 he deals in chapters 3 and 4 with the climate and the peoples of the Sahara, which plays a basic role in his argument: it began to get more humid about 7000 B.C. and started to dry up around 2000 B.C., thus allowing much more life there and cultural contacts between the South Sahara and ancient Egypt than so far assumed. In chapter 5 he sketches the history of the Nubian area. Chapter 6 is devoted to the movements of and similarities between the Hamitic and Negro racial groups. In chapter 7 he draws comparisons between the ancient Egyptian and other African agricultural deities, while chapter 8 is concerned with the hunter-gatherers of the African continent, whose culture was similar to early Egyptian hunter-gatherer culture, and with whom ancient Egypt at least enjoyed contact in historic times. The chapters 9-10 are devoted to the importance of totemism and phallicism in the African culture.
Chapters 11-18 deal with divine kingship: first in general and then in various African cultural areas, chapter 12 being exclusively devoted to the Egyptian - Nubian region, although comparisons with Egypt are made in the other chapters.
In the summary and conclusion the author remarks that emphasis has been placed on non-material similarities, material culture being an uncertain factor, and that it is not possible to explain pre-Islamic Egyptian and black African similarities by claiming a common outside Semitic or other influence. A selected bibliography arranged after regions, and an index at the end.

79921 PADRO, J., A propos des trouvailles égyptiennes dans la Péninsule Ibérique: Considérations sur les relations de l'Égypte avec l'Occident de l'Europe à la Basse Epoque, *in*: *Acts 1st ICE*, 507-514.

The author offers a short survey of the Egyptian finds on the Iberian peninsula and devotes remarks to their transmission. Extensive notes.

79922 SHINNIE, P.L., Urbanism in the Ancient Sudan, *in*: *Glimpses of Ancient Egypt*, 123-126.

Towns in Nubia were in the main an exotic feature introduced from the north, with in earlier times little influence on the life of the rural population. The author presents a brief survey of the towns in Nubia, Egyptian such as Buhen in the O.K. and Aniba, Buhen, Amara West and Senbi in the N.K., as well as their successors (Kerma perhaps being the oldest indigenous town) in the South. Town dwelling may have been, in the Meroitic Period, exotic in inspiration, but it seems to have gained a certain importance and continued to preserve that in later ages.

J.J.J.

79923 STRANGE, John, The Aegean Foreigners in Rekhmire's Tomb and the Keftiu-Problem, *in*: *Acts 1st ICE*, 605-608.

The author first argues that the caption referring to the tribute of the West in the text concerning the foreign lands in the tomb of Rekhmire should be translated: "Coming in peace by the chiefs of Keftiu *and* the Islands in the midst of the sea. . ." On account of the accompanying representation in the tomb of Rekhmire being a palimpsest and older examples from other tombs the author concludes that the Aegean foreigners in the tomb come from the Islands in the midst of the Sea, not from Keftiu. Thus the painting is irrelevant for the discussion of the Keftiu problem. See now J. Strange, Caphtor/Keftiu. A New Investigation, Leiden, E.J. Brill, 1980 (= Acta Theologica Danica, 14).

79924 TROLLE, Steffen, An Egyptian Head from Camirus, Rhodes, *Acta Archaeologica*, København 49 (1978), 1979, 139-150, with 8 ill.

The author extensively describes and compares a head from the XXVth-XXVIth Dynasties, which was found in Camirus, Rhodes, and is the only documented piece from that period found by excavation in Greece. He argues that it arrived there in the 7th century B.C. and that the local impact of the Egyptian statuette on Rhodian art of the 7th century B.C. can be traced.

79925 TUTUNDŽIĆ, S.P., Ways of Relations between Upper Egypt and Palestine during the Late Chalcolithic Period, *in*: *Acts 1st ICE*, 651-659.

The author argues that the direct Red Sea route was used as an important way of communication between Gerzean Egypt and Late Chalcolithic Palestine.

79926 VERCOUTTER, Jean, L'Image du Noir dans l'Égypte Ancienne (dès Origines à la XXVe dyn.), *in*: *Africa in Antiquity*, 19-22.

Es wird davon ausgegangen, dass die ägyptische Ikonographie uns eine Vorstellung vom physischen Aspekt der schwarzen Bevölkerung geben kann, die die Ägypter nach Thutmosis III. kennenlernten. Das Pygmäen-Problem wird erneut aufgerollt und dafür plädiert, dass die Ägypter bereits sehr früh Kontakte zu Gebieten hatten, in denen Neger lebten und die sie in der 2. Hälfte des 3. vorchristlichen Jahrtausends darstellten. Doch erst im Verlaufe der 18. Dynastie erscheinen sie in grosser Anzahl auf den Abbildungen. Die Schlussfolgerung, die südlichen Nachbarn Ägyptens seien Neger, kann aber nicht gezogen werden, denn sie widerspräche dem anthropologischen Befund. Verfasser hält die aufgeworfenen Probleme für noch nicht gelöst. *Inge Hofmann*

e. General and varia

See also our numbers 79086; 79334; 79575; 79751; 79937 and 791008.

79927 DECKER, Wolfgang, Das sogenannte Agonale und der altägyptische Sport, *in*: *Festschrift Elmar Edel*, 90-104.

The author argues that the agonal character of the Greek civilisation is not so exceptional as has been suggested; in Egypt matches and competition have also played an important role. He adduces several examples; i.a. from the Stories of Sinuhe and Horus and Seth and the bride-agon of the Doomed Prince, although it is not certain that the latter reflects indeed an Egyptian custom. On the other hand, Herodotus' record of the agon in Chemnis probably reflects a genuine Egyptian custom. Royal sportive actions are not quite an agon since Pharaoh by his very nature always wins; only the shooting of Amenophis II (inscription of Medamût) may have contained real competition. *J.J.J.*

79928 DECKER, Wolfgang, Zum Stand der Erforschung der altägyptischen Sportgeschichte, *in*: *Acts 1st ICE*, 149-153.

Survey of the present position of the history of ancient Egyptian sport, indicating also the requirements for further study.
  J.J.J.

79929 GUGLIELMI, Waltraud, Humor in Wort und Bild auf altägyptischen Grabdarstellungen, *in*: *Wort und Bild*. Symposion des Fachbereichs Altertums- und Kulturwissenschaften zum 500-jährigen Jubiläum der Eberhard-Karls-Universität Tübingen 1977. Herausgegeben von Hellmut Brunner, Richard Kannicht, Klaus Schwager, München, Wilhelm Fink Verlag, 1979, 181-200, with 8 fig.

As the main motive for the expression of humour in representation and accompanying word the author names the ancient Egyptian joy

in life and laughter. Although the selection of and artistic expression in scenes had to be approved and accepted by the owner the artist's pleasure in reproducing daily life on earth on the tomb walls is evident. This can be characterised as a shift from the objective-sacral to the subjective-psychological.
Then the author devotes her attention to the various expressions of humour in scenes and accompanying texts from the O.K. to the N.K.: comic aspects of creatures in behaviour, appearance, words or situation; exaggeration; vulgarity, rarely obscenity and scolding; comic situations on account of the tension between regulations, morals and human weakness; the arrogant and the "poseur" as victims of humorous expression; parody; idiomatic expressions with double intention; and caricatures, particularly types from the lower levels of society.
Some concluding words on the stimulating exchange between word and representation.

79930 GUGLIELMI, Waltraud, Probleme bei der Anwendung der Begriffe "Komik", "Ironie" und "Humor" auf die altägyptische Literatur, *GM* Heft 36 (1979), 69-85.

"Humor" in der Literatur wird zunächst als ein Verfahren definiert, das Wirklichkeitselemente so anleuchtet, dass sie entstellt werden. Das zentrale Problem dabei ist, ob der Humorbegriff - als subjektive Beleuchtung einer objektiven Begebenheit, die als solche keinerlei komische Qualität haben muss -, der ein gehöriges Mass an Selbstdistanz voraussetzt und der im poetischen Realismus mit der Freisetzung des Individuums und der Auflösung der Form eng verbunden ist, in Ägypten vorhanden war oder nicht. Zum Ironiebegriff wird gerechnet und durch ägyptische Beispiele belegt: Übertreibung in der Affirmation, Widerholung, Emphase, Abweichungsstilistik.
Inge Hofmann

79931 MONTET, Pierre, Egipat u doba Ramzesa, Zagreb, Naprijed, 1979 (13.5 x 20.5 cm; 315 p.); series: Biblioteka svakodnevni život.

Serbo-Croatian version of: La vie quotidienne en Égypte au temps des Ramsès, Paris, Hachette, 1946.

79932 SCHOTT, E., Bücher und Bibliotheken im alten Ägypten, *in*: *Acts 1st ICE*, 579.

Short progress report on the preparation of a monograph on books and libraries in ancient Egypt.
See already our number 72646.

VIII. SCIENCE AND TECHNOLOGY

a. Science and medicine

See also our numbers 79098; 79209; 79212 and 79423.

79933   GIACARDI, Livia and Silvia Clara ROERO, La matematica delle civiltà archaiche. Egitto, Mesopotamia, Grecia. Prefazione e Introduzione di Tullio Viola, [Torino, Edizione Stampatori, 1979] (11.2 x 18.1 cm; 321 p., 106 fig. including maps, 16 pl.); series: Stampatori di dattica, 13.   Pr. L. 6500

This pocket book is one in a series of didactic works and is devoted to the history of mathematics. Ancient Egypt is dealt with in chapter 2 (p. 57-110). After an introduction about land and civilisation, history, religion, art and technics there follows a discussion about mathematics: the sources of our knowledge, arithmetic and geometry; illustrated by several figures. Some chosen problems are explained, and a few technical notes with references to scientific works, also recent ones, are added. At the end a select bibliography.   J.J.J.

79934   HOFFMANN-AXTHELM, Walter, Is the Practice of Dentistry in Ancient Egypt an Archaeological Fact ?, *Bulletin of the History of Dentistry*, New York 27, No. 2 (October, 1979), 71-78, with 3 fig. and 4 ill.

After a survey of opinions pro and contra the existence of dental surgery in ancient Egypt the author reconsiders the evidence from Egyptian designations of professions and particularly wire-bound teeth among which a recent find at el-Qatta (see our numbers 71199, 72422 and 76339). He concludes that in spite of the occurrence of some dental restorations the existence of a dental profession is not proved.

79935   ISKANDER, Zaky, James HARRIS and Shafik FARID, Further Evidence of Dental Prosthesis in Ancient Egypt, *ASAE* 63 (1979), 103-113, with 10 pl. (5 in colour).

The authors first describe three specimens of dental prosthesis previously found in Egypt (one from the O.K., the other two from the Late and Ptolemaic Periods) and two specimens found near Sidon but supposed to be Egyptian (5th and 4th centuries B.C.). They then discuss more extensively the gold bridge found in 1952 in a burial from the IVth Dynasty at el-Qatta. They conclude against the opinion of Leek (see our number 67369) that indeed the Egyptians practised dentistry in its true sense as far back as the O.K.   J.J.J.

79936 KOLTA, Kamal Sabri, "swnw ○ ḯ "-Arzt und Hersteller von Heil-
mitteln im alten Ägypten, *Beiträge zur Geschichte der Pharmazie*,
Stuttgart 31 (1979), 9-12, with 2 ill.

The author discusses the position of the physician (*swnw*) in
Egypt, dealing with various aspects of his profession, general
physician, surgeon, etc., and particularly his activities as
apothecary in composing medical drugs.   J.J.J.

79937 REINEKE, W.F., Mathematik und Gesellschaft im Alten Ägypten, *in*:
Acts 1st ICE, 543-551.

The author characterises Egyptian mathematics and draws the conclusion that it is the result of a long chain of tradition, to
which nothing new was added after the N.K. and that complicated
problems were solved by simple and long methods. Then he turns
to the question when basic knowledge of Egyptian mathematics was
collected and when higher levels were attained. This is discussed in the light of the needs of a developing culture.

79938 SCHWARTZ, Jean-Claude, Le médecine dentaire dans l'Égypte pharaonique, *Bulletin Société d'Égyptologie*, Genève No. 2 (Novembre
1979), 37-43, with 2 fig.

The author, studying ancient Egyptian dentures and their knowledge about affections of the teeth concludes that there did not
exist a dentistry in the modern sense.   J.J.J.

79939 STROUHAL, E., Maternity of Ancient Egypt, *in*: *Anthropology of
Maternity*. Anthropologia maternitatis. Proceedings of the Con-
ference held in Prague, November 26-29, 1975. Edited by Antonius
Doležal - Jaroslav Gutvirth, [Praha], Universitatis Carolina
Pragensis, 1977, 287-292, with 3 ill.

The author briefly surveys some aspects of maternity in Ancient
Egypt, such as ancient Egyptian anatomical and medical knowledge
concerning the vulva and the uterus, pregnancy, delivery, puer-
peral and suckling periods, and palaeopathology.

b. Technology

See also our numbers 79592; 79652; 79684; 79743; 79752; 79768 and
79914.

79940 BASCH, Lucien, Roman Triremes and the Outriggerless Phoenician
Trireme, *The Mariner's Mirror*, London 65 (1979), 289-326.

In this article on the trireme (for other studies cfr our numbers
72447, 75549 and 79945) the author devotes attention to a scene
from the naval battle of Ramses III against the Sea Peoples on
the walls of the Medinet Habu temple, on p. 302-305. A boat

model from Armant playing a role in the dispute is examined on p. 312 ff.

79941 DAVEY, C.J., Some Ancient Near Eastern Pot Bellows, *Levant*, London 11 (1979), 101-111, with 4 fig. and 1 map.

In this article on pot bellows in the Ancient Near East the meagre Egyptian evidence is also discussed. They are first depicted in the tomb of Rekhmire. In spite of the large scale Egyptian mining and smelting activities at Timna, Sinai, no bellows have come to light.

79942 LITTAUER, M.A. and J.H. CROUWEL, Wheeled Vehicles and Ridden Animals in the Ancient Near East. Drawings by J. Morel, Leiden/Köln, E.J. Brill, 1979 (19.5 x 24.7 cm; X + 185 p., 85 fig. on 39 pl.) = Handbuch der Orientalistik. Siebente Abteilung: Kunst und Archäologie. Erster Band: Der Alte Vordere Orient. Zweiter Abschnitt: Die Denkmäler. B-Vorderasien. Lieferung 1; rev. *AJA* 85 (1981), 227-228 (Trudy S. Kawami); *ZDMG* 131 (1981), 207 (W[olfgang] R[öllig]).

It is only in chapter 8, on the later second millennium B.C. (c. 1600-1000 B.C.) that Egyptian evidence on wheeled vehicles and ridden animals plays a substantial role. Hittite four-wheelers are depicted in the Battle of Kadesh scenes of Ramses II. Egyptian baggage-carts in the Kadesh reliefs, although very small, have six-spoked wheels and look like chariots from which the screens have been removed. The reliefs of the battle against the Sea Peoples by Ramses III shows the carts in which the Sea Peoples travelled. The chariot, however, is very well documented in Egypt, actual as well as depicted. Its parts are described in detail: box, axle, wheels (almost always six-spoked), draught pole. As for draught animals, the authors state that chariot teams were almost exclusively composed of horses. Next follows the description of harnessing and the parts of the bridle: the various types of bits, reins and bridle accessories such as blinkers. The chariot was used primarily for military purposes, but also for hunting, and even more peaceful purposes. There is little evidence for Egyptians riding on horseback.
The chapter is concluded by a summary. Very extensive bibliography at the end of the book.
The subject is summarised in J.H. Crouwel, Aegean Bronze Age Chariots and Their Near Eastern Background, *Bulletin. Institute of Classical Studies*, London 25 (1978), 174-175.

79943 LLOYD, Alan B., Herodotus 2.96.1-2, *Classical Quarterly*, Oxford 29 (1979), 45-48.

The traditional interpretation of i.a. the word ζυγά, "thwarts" in Herodotus 2.96.1-2 provides a perfect description of a style of Nilotic boat-building from the M.K. onwards, the construction principles of which differ from those of the Cheops boats.

79944 MASSCHELEIN-KLEINER, L. and L. MAES, Ancient Dyeing Techniques in Eastern Mediterranean Regions, *in*: *ICOM Committee for Conservation*. 5th Triennial Meeting, Zagreb, 1-8 October 1978. Preprints, No. 78/9/3, 10 p.

Comparison of the craft of dyeing in Ancient Egypt, Nubia and Palestine by the analysis of textiles which are mostly dated to A.D. 1-600.

79945 MORRISON, J.S., The First Triremes, *The Mariner's Mirror*, London 65 (1979), 53-63.

The article is a reconsideration of the origin of the trireme, which subject was i.a. discussed previously in our numbers 72447, 75549 and 77068. See also our number 79940.

79946 NICHOLSON, Eric D., The Ancient Craft of Gold Beating, *Gold Bulletin*, Marshalltown 12, No. 4 (October 1979), 161-166, with 1 fig. and 4 ill. (3 in colour).

In this article on gold beating some attention is paid to ancient Egypt.

79947 WERTIME, Theodore A., Pyrotechnology: Man's Fire-Using Crafts, *in*: *Early Technologies*. Edited by Denise Schmandt-Besserat, Malibu, Undena Publications, 1979 (= Invited Lectures on the Middle East at the University of Texas at Austin, 3), 17-25.

A short note is devoted to the sudden eruption of cored glass vessels in Mesopotamia and Egypt toward 1400 B.C. (p. 20).

IX. THE COUNTRY AND NEIGHBOURING AREAS

a. Natural environment

See also our numbers 79494; 79505; 79540; 79561; 79601; 79616; 79867; 79920; 791000; 791001 and 791008.

79948 ALPIN, Pierre, Histoire Naturelle de l'Égypte. 1581-1584. Traduit du Latin, et présenté par R. de Fenoyl. Annotation de R. de Fenoyl et S. Sauneron. Index de Marcelle Desdames, 2 vols, *[Le Caire, Institut français d'Archéologie orientale, 1979]* (16.5 x 19.6 cm; XXXII + 583 p., 24 pl. *[1 folding]*, fig. on cover) = Collection des voyageurs occidentaux en Égypte, 20.

Prospero Alpini, born near Venice in 1553, studied medicine in Padua and stayed in Egypt from 1580-1584, mostly in Cairo. His "Rerum Aegyptiarum Libri IV", as he himself called the book, has been published for the first time long after his death (1617) in Leiden in 1735. During his life, however, studies on special subjects, e.g. medicine and plants in Egypt, had already appeared, subjects which recur in the present book (Alpin's book on medicine has now appeared as vol. 21 [1980] in the same series, that on plants as vol. 22 [1980]). The introduction deals with the author's life and works and with the publication of the present book which was translated from Latin. It consists of four "books" and a preface. Book I deals with the country, the cities and manners and customs of their inhabitants; chapter IV describes the pyramids and the sphinx, chapter V discusses mummies and tombs. Book II is devoted to religion and medicine; book III to soils and plants; book IV to animals.
Extensive indexes (p. 475-582) to several subjects enable the scholar to consult this study, which has been highly valued e.g. by botanists.
J.J.J.

79949 BRIER, B. and BENNETT, M.V.L., Autopsies on Fish Mummies. Possible identification of the Classical Phagrus, *JEA* 65 (1979), 128-133, with 7 pl. and 1 fig.

A 25.4 cm. long mummified fish was X-rayed, then unwrapped and autopsied. The wrappings indicated a Ptolemaic date and radio carbon dating gave 275 A.D. ± 340 years. Other fish also examined appear to belong to the same species *Bagrus Bayad* and this supports Thompson's identification of it with the Phagrus.
E.P. Uphill

79950 CLUTTON-BROCK, J. and R. BURLEIGH, Notes on the Osteology of the Arab Horse with Reference to the Skeleton Collected in Egypt by Sir F. Petrie, *Bulletin of the British Museum of Natural History*, London, 1979, p.

A horse skeleton from Egypt donated by Petrie to the British Museum of Natural History (no provenance known) which was previously assumed to be ancient turned out to be only a few hundred years old on account of radiocarbon dating. Some other valuable material collected by Petrie is briefly discussed.

79951 DEBONO, Fernand, A propos de la curieuse représentation d'une girafe dans l'ouvrage de Belon du Mans, *in*: Hommages Sauneron II, 417-458, with 1 fig. and 2 pl.

Proceeding from the picture of a giraffe in the Voyage en Égypte by Belon du Mans (our number 70053) the author discusses the role of the animal in the entire Egyptian history. He i.a. deals with the use of its tail and skin in Pharaonic times, its representations with horizontal neck, its names in Arabic and Egyptian, representations in which it wears a halter, its capture, etc.
J.J.J.

79952   EDWARDS, I.E.S., Zoomorphic Anomalies in Tutankhamun's Treasures, *AJA* 83 (1979), 205-206.

Reply to our number 78670, defending in three of the four instances the author's earlier suggestions.   J.J.J.

79953   HOULIHAN, Patrick F. and Steven M. GOODMAN, Comments on the Identification of Birds Depicted on Tutankhamun's Embossed Gold Fan, *JSSEA* 9 (1978-1979), 219-224, with 1 pl.

The authors do not agree with Reed and Osborn (see our number 78670) that the birds depicted on Tutankhamun's fan are bustards. Although admitting that Egyptian artists did not intend exact realism to be the focus of their efforts they argue that the birds show characteristics of immature juvenile ostriches (under four months old), or, less probably, their extinct relatives.
    J.J.J.

79954   NIBBI, Alessandra, Some Remarks on Ass and Horse in Ancient Egypt and the Absence of the Mule, *ZÄS* 106 (1979), 148-168, with 15 fig. and 1 pl.

A survey and a discussion of the scanty archaeological and zoological information available.
I. The Ass in Ancient Egypt: p. 148-155.
II. The Wild Ass: p. 156-159.
III. The Horse in the Egyptian Context: p. 160-166. The second half of this section is devoted to the Przewalski horse.
IV. The Absence of the Mule: p. 166-168. There is no evidence that the ancient Egyptians ever used mules.   *M. Heerma v. Voss*

79955   NIBBI, Alessandra, The "Trees and Towns" Palette, *ASAE* 63 (1979), 143-154, with 2 fig. and 1 pl.

After stating that, whatever recent attempts to improve the position, our environmental information on the Prehistoric and Dynastic Periods is still small, the author studies the "trees and towns" palette in the Cairo Museum. She argues that on the bottom of one side an acacia wood is represented situated East of the Delta. The harnessed donkeys or onagers point to the same direction. Presence of woods in that area is in accordance with our growing knowledge about climate and vegetation in predynastic times.   J.J.J.

79956   STOL, M., On Trees, Mountains, and Millstones in the Ancient Near East. With a Chapter by K. van Lerberghe, Leiden, Ex Oriente Lux, 1979 (19.5 x 26.7 cm; XII + 104 p., 1 map) = Mededelingen en Verhandelingen van het Vooraziatisch-Egyptisch Genootschap "Ex Oriente Lux", 21.

Although written by an Assyriologist and mainly dealing with Near Eastern materials the author devoted a few sections to Egyptian evidence.

On p. 20-21 he discusses *sntr*, identifying it after Loret as
"resin of the terebinth." Compare also p. 54-55, on the Greek
word ρητυνη, which is perhaps the Coptic ⲔⲞⲚⲦⲈ (= *sntr*).
On p. 42-44 the Egyptian evidence for ebony is briefly dealt
with, its use in handicraft and medicine and the application of
ebony gum (*kmyt*) in the embalmment process.   J.J.J.

79957   THOMAS, Elizabeth, *Papio Hamadryas* and the Rising Sun, BES 1
(1979), 91-94, with 1 pl.

The author studies the possible physiological reason for the
hands-on-knees gesture at sunrise of the baboon (*papio hamadryas*),
which activity is known as "sunning" or "welcoming" the sun disk.
The explanation may be that the baboons huddle together in cool
cloudy mornings and are grateful for the sun's rays, whether or
not this heat is required for the proper functioning of their
bodies.

b. Topography, toponymy, maps

See also our numbers 79100; 79147; 79221; 79228; 79246; 79247; 79277;
79310; 79335; 79390; 79420; 79451; 79455; 79461; 79470; 79473; 79474;
79478; 79485; 79487; 79494; 79515; 79608; 79648; 79839; 79895; 79912;
79914; 79923 and 791037.

79958   AHARONI, Yohanan and Michael AVI-YONAH, The Modern Bible Atlas.
Revised Edition, Prepared by Carta, Ltd, London-Boston-Sydney,
George Allen & Unwin, [1979] (22.5 x 29.5 cm; 184 p., 264 maps,
numerous ill. and fig.).   Pr. £10

Apart from a foreword by Magnus Magnusson, the book consists of
maps accompanied by captions and pertinent illustrations or figures. A large number of maps, especially in the part on the
Canaanite Period, is concerned with the events in the history of
the connections between ancient Egypt and Syria-Palestine.
At the end of the book a key to maps according to books of the
Bible, chronological tables, and an index.

79959   Anonymous, The Berkeley Map of the Theban Necropolis. Report of
the Second Season, 1979, *Newsletter ARCE* No. 109 (Summer 1979),
separately numbered [II] + 20 p., with 2 maps, 3 plans, 3 fig.,
1 ill. and a summary on p. 1.

Sequel to our number 78033.
After remarks on the topographical surveying (completion of
survey control, standards of accuracy, and aerial photography)
there is a summary of the progress in mapping the royal tombs.
To provide an idea of the type of information the work of the
project in the tombs of Ramses IV and VI, and Sethi I is briefly
discussed. Particular attention is paid to the comparison of
the Berkeley, the Carter and the Pap. Turin measurements for the
tombs of Ramses IV and VI.

79960 ASTOUR, Michael C., Yahveh in Egyptian Topographical Lists, *in*: *Festschrift Elmar Edel*, 17-34, with 1 map.

The list of Asiatic toponyms in the temple of ʿAmâra West, copied from Amenophis III's temple at Soleb, contains six names preceded by *t3 š3sw*, one of which is *ya-h-wa*, usually conceived to be the oldest occurrence of the tetragrammaton YHWH and assigned to an area in Edom. Astour, however, argues on account of other topographical lists, particularly that from Medînet Habu, that the Shasu districts are to be localised in the Bîgâʿ in Syria (see map on p. 34).   J.J.J.

79961 BONNEAU, Danielle, Niloupolis du Fayoum, *in*: *Actes du XVe Congrès International de Papyrologie. Quatrième partie. Papyrologie documentaire, [Bruxelles - Louvain 29 août - 3 septembre 1977. Édités par Jean Bingen et Georges Nachtergael]*, Bruxelles, Fondation Égyptologique Reine Élisabeth, 1979 (= Papyrologica Bruxellensia, 19), 258-273.

On account of information from the names of plots of land, those of waters, and the cult of the Nile/Hâpi the author attempts to localise Niloupolis of the Fayoum. She thinks that the town was situated at Tell el-Rusâs.

79962 BRIEND, J., Une expedition dans le Sinai en 1978, *Le Monde de la Bible*, Paris No. 10 (Août-Septembre 1979), 5-17, with 22 ill. and 2 maps.

The author deals i.a. with the following subjects: Serabit el-Khadim, the Hathor temple there, the copper mines at Bir Nasb, the turquoise mines at Wadi Maghara, the Wadi Kharij, the Wadi Baba and the Wadi Mukatteb.

79963 DUMAS, François, Les textes géographiques du trésor D' du temple de Dendara, *in*: *State and Temple Economy in the Ancient Near East*. II, 689-705.

The author studies the texts in the Treasury of the Dendera temple (room D' = IV) accompanying geographical figures, comparing them with others from room Q (= VII) and from Edfu. He lists 15 toponyms, discussing their position and the minerals and precious stones said to come from them. Apart from *Tfrr* from which lapis lazuli was procured all regions are situated in Egypt, Sinai or Nubia and Sudan, which reflects the actual economic position. On the other hand, the old theory that all countries deliver their products needed by the gods still governs the texts.
                                                                         J.J.J.

79964 DEROY, Louis, Autour du nom d'Éléphantine, *in*: *Berichte des XII. Internationalen Kongresses für Namenforschung*. Bern, 25.-29. August 1975. Band II, herausgegeben von Henri Draye, Leuven,

International Centre of Onomastics, in Kommission bei dem Verlag Peeters, 1977, 196-200.

On some words in various languages deriving from the word $3bw$, meaning "ivory", "elephant" and the island of Elephantine.

79965 EDEL, Elmar, Zwei ägyptische Ortsbezeichnungen, *Orientalia* 48 (1979), 82-90, with 2 fig.

Le "Bulletin de la bataille de Qadesh à Louqsor indique parmi les alliés des Hittites le chef de *'ns3*. Une région bien connue des textes hittites et assyriens correspond à ce toponyme: Alše (lire Alsé) entre le Haut Euphrate et le Tigre; le nom peut apparaître sous d'autres aspects: Alzi(ya), plus tard Enzi(te). L'auteur replace, à Karnak, un bloc attestant une graphie identique, au dessus du "Poème" près duquel il gît; deux formes différentes apparaissent au Ramesseum. Le nom mentionné n'implique aucune alliance historique réelle. Un second bloc de Karnak porte: "Troupes de Masa, combattants des Lyciens".
La grande liste asiatique de Thoutmosis III cite un *Twrbnt*, à comprendre comme Turbanda, attesté avec Tounip en KBo VIII 38. Ce toponyme revient, écrit *Dwrb3n3*, sous Ramsès III à Médinet Habou. Nous aurions donc la voyelle a notée *3* dans *s3* (Aa 18) du premier nom, et la même valeur ici dans *b3* (G 29), après le signe du "poussin" (notant u). Helck ne serait pas fondé à rejeter l'assimilation de *B3-bi-r* à Babylone, mentionnée après sa région *Sngr*, dans la liste d'Aménophis II; enfin *P3-b3-ḫ* n'équivaudrait pas à Bambykè mais à Pabaḫḫi, fréquemment mentionné.

J. Custers

79966 GIVEON, Raphael, Remarks on some Egyptian Toponym Lists Concerning Canaan, *in*: *Festschrift Elmar Edel*, 135-141.

The author deals with four subjects: 1. the boustrophedon order of toponyms in the Sheshonq list; 2. some orthographs in the same list; 3. the toponym *twl3r* in the list of Amâra West, perhaps a mistake for *rw-el*; 4. Hekalim (*Hk3lm*) occurring in the list of Tuthmosis III and of Amenophis III and on scarabs.

J.J.J

79967 GÖRG, Manfred, Identifikation von Fremdnamen. Das methodische Problem am Beispiel einer Palimpsestschreibung aus dem Totentempel Amenophis III., *in*: *Festschrift Elmar Edel*, 152-173, with 1 pl.

The topographical lists pose two problems: the correspondence in sound between the Egyptian and indigenous names, and the arrangements of the toponyms, either notional, topographical or territorial. As an example the author discusses the palimpsest name *ʿ3-rw-ḏ3-n3* from the list B_N of Edel's "Ortsnamenliste" (see our number 66181), arguing that in an earlier phase perhaps *ʿ3-rw-w(?)-n(i?)* = *ʿrn* had been written, the later inclusion of

$ḏ₃-₃$ possibly being a "Verschlimmbesserung". Possibly ḫalumni was meant, probably situated near the Jarmuk.
J.J.J.

79968 GÖRG, Manfred, Mitanni in Gruppenschreibung, GM Heft 32 (1979), 17-19, with 2 ill. on 1 pl.

Es wird die in unserer Nr. 78301 diskutierte originelle Wiedergabe des Landesnamens Mitanni im Vergleich mit den sonstigen Belegen in hieroglyphischer Fassung betrachtet und der Frage der Gruppenschreibung nachgegangen. In einer wohl Amenophis II. zuzuweisenden Nordländerliste erscheint der Name an einer Stelle (Position IV,8) in einer Gruppenschreibung mit der Auslautschreibung n₃.
Inge Hofmann

79969 GÖRG, Manfred, Namenstudien IV: Asiatische Ortsnamen in ptolemäischen Listen, *Biblische Notizen*, Bamberg Heft 10 (1979), 16-21, with 2 ill.

The author discusses: 5 geographical Asiatic names on two blocks originating from Xois; the geographical name $wrš$ in the name list from the Esna temple (cfr our numbers 71172 and 71204, p. 188); and the name of the island of Cyprus in the Decree of Canopus.

79970 GÖRG, Manfred, Das Ratespiel um $Mw-ḳd$, GM Heft 32 (1979), 21-22.

Bei der Diskussion des Problems, ob mit $p₃ jm ʿ₃ n mw-ḳd$ der Euphrat oder das Rote Meer gemeint sei, macht der Verfasser darauf aufmerksam, dass es sich um hieroglyphische Entsprechungen gleichlautender akkadischer Bildungen handeln kann: *mu-gādi* "Wasser(gegend) des Euphrat". Daher sei die Ansicht, das Rote Meer könne schon in der ägyptischen Perspektive der 19. und 20. Dynastie ebenso wie der Persische Golf als Teil des "Grossen Meeres der Euphratregion" gegolten haben, noch nicht endgültig widerlegt.
Inge Hofmann

79971 GOHARY, J.D., Nefertiti at Karnak, *in*: *Glimpses of Ancient Egypt*, 30-31.

The author draws attention to the name of an Aton building in Karnak that is called $gm(t)-p₃-ʾItn$, in some instances with, in others without t, and suggests that they are two different buildings. The names are to be translated as "He/she who found the Aton". The building $gmt-p₃-ʾItn$ seems to be particularly connected with Nefertiti.
J.J.J.

79972 GOYON, Georges, Est-ce enfin Sakhebou?, *in*: *Hommages Sauneron* I, 43-50, with 1 map and 1 pl.

The author, referring to earlier studies, suggests that the canal along the border of the W. desert (see our number 71214) and the orientation of the pyramids (see our numbers 70220 and

74254) both add to the plausibility that Zât el Kôm is indeed Sakhebu, as Sauneron has suggested. There is here a transversal canal to the Nile which may be the Canal of the Two Fishes. In this connection the author suggests a slightly altered translation of the answer of Djedi from the Pap. Westcar. J.J.J.

79973 GRENIER, Jean-Claude, Djédem 𓂞𓈗 dans les textes du temple de Tôd, in: *Hommages Sauneron* I, 381-389.

The author, publishing 13 new references to the toponym Djedem, is able to confirm Sauneron's suggestions (see our number 74641, 5-7; see also our number 77845), adding a few data. Djedem, the place where Montu defeated Apophis on the first day of the year, is situated very near the temple of Tôd. J.J.J.

79974 GRZYBEK, Erhard, Der Name der Insel Zypern im Dekret von Kanopus, *Bulletin Société d'Egyptologie*, Genève No. 1 (Mai 1979), 17-22.

The author argues that the name for Cyprus in the Decree of Canopus, usually read as $iw\ Sbyn$, actually means $iw\ Slmyn$, "the island of Salamis". The following words $nty\ m\ hr(y)-ib\ w\underline{3}d-wr$ he explains as "which also is that-in-the-heart-of-the-Great-Green", that is, Cyprus in its old name. J.J.J.

79975 el-KORDY, Zeinab, Les noms de la ville de Dendera inscrits dans la Crypte des Archives, in: *Acts 1st ICE*, 391-394.

In crypt no. 9 = West Crypt 3 (Porter-Moss VI, 90-91), called by Daumas the Crypt of the Archives, is inscribed a list of names of the city (or, rather, the temple complex and its parts). They are here discussed, particularly the divinities which occur in them. J.J.J.

79976 KRUCHTEN, Jean-Marie, Le terme topographique "Mesherou", *Annuaire de l'Institut de Philologie et d'Histoire Orientales et Slaves*, Bruxelles 22 (1978), 23-28.

Studying the toponym $mšrw$ that occurs a dozen times in the Pap. Wilbour and also once in the Gurob fragments where it is written with the determinatives of water and canal, the author connects the word with $išrw$, "moonshaped lake" (see our number 64428, VI = 74641, VI). The writing with or without the prefix m may be due to dialectal differences. In Pap. Wilbour A94, 7 and in other texts $mšrw$ is connected with Sobk. It may be that $mšrw$ in C.T. Spell 160 (Hathor $nbt\ mšrw$) originally had the same meaning and was re-interpreted by the scribe as "twilight", as the determinative shows. Perhaps both meanings "twilight" and "lake" have a common origin, since it is to the lake where the animals go to drink in the evening. J.J.J.

79977 LECLANT, Jean, Le nom de Chypre dans les textes hiéroglyphiques, in: *Salamine de Chypre. Histoire et Archéologie* (= Colloques

Internationaux du Centre National de la Recherche Scientifique, No. 578, Lyon, 13-17 mars 1978), 131-135.

The author discusses two toponyms which both may indicate Alasia (=Cyprus), namely ʾIrs(ȝ) and ʾIsy, the latter also in the form ʾIsby (𓇋 > 𓇌 > 𓇋𓏭).
                       J.J.J.

79978 NORTH, Robert, A History of Biblical Map Making, Wiesbaden, Dr. Ludwig Reichert Verlag, 1979 (16 x 24 cm; XI + 177 p., 20 fig., plans and maps, 3 colour pl. [1 folding]) = Beihefte zum Tübinger Atlas des Vorderen Orients. Reihe B (Geisteswissenschaften), 32.

In chapter 2 concerned with the earliest Biblical area maps a section is devoted to ancient Egyptian field-maps and expedition records.

79979 OGDON, Jorge Roberto, The Old Kingdom Name for the Canopic Branch of the Nile Delta, *JSSEA* 9 (1978-1979), 65-73, with 5 fig.

The author lists five instances from O.K. tombs of the words *mr ỉmntt (-nfrt)*, "Canal of the Beautiful (Goddess)-of-the-West." He suggests that it is the earlier name of *ỉtrw ʾImntt*, the Canopic Branch of the Nile.   J.J.J.

79980 OSING, Jürgen, Zu einer Fremdvölkerliste Ramses' II. in Karnak, *GM* Heft 36 (1979), 37-38.

Die grosse Fremdvölkerliste Ramses' II. in Karnak ist im wesentlichen nach der Vorlage der beiden entsprechenden Listen Sethos' I. zusammengestellt. Sie ist ebenso und grundsätzlich mit der gleichen Abfolge von Namen angelegt wie diese, nur verkürzt um eine Anzahl afrikanischer und asiatischer Namen. Sie beginnt von oben her mit dem Neun-Bogen-Namen *Tȝ šmꜥw*, dann eine Anzahl afrikanischer Namen und dann sieben weitere Neun-Bogen-Namen (*Ṯḥnw – Jwntjw Ztj – Tȝ mḥw – [Ḥȝw nbwt] – Šȝt – Šḥt jȝm – Pḏtjw šwt*). *Mntjw nw Stt* findet sich allerdings nicht am Anfang der Reihe 5, sondern in Reihe 6, und dann springt die Fortsetzung der Namen wieder zurück in Reihe 5. Wenn daher die beiden Gruppen asiatischer Namen in den Reihen 5 und 6 miteinander vertauscht sind, so beruht das auf einem Fehler, der bei der Redaktion der Vorlage oder erst beim Anbringen der Vorzeichnung auf der Wand entstanden ist.   *Inge Hofmann*

79981 PLUMLEY, J. Martin, Gods and Pharaohs at Qasr Ibrim, *in*: *Glimpses of Ancient Egypt*, 127-131.

For Pharaonic activities at Qasr Ibrîm before the N.K. no evidence has been found, but in that time it came to be regarded as a place of special religious importance, being associated with Horus of Miꜥam. The author discusses the various monuments from the N.K., from a stela of Amenophis I to a slab with the cartouches of either Ramses IV or VI, as well as those from the

Kushite to the Meroitic Period. It was probably in the latter that Ibrîm became a fortress. J.J.J.

79982 RAINEY, Anson F., Toponymic Problems, *Tel Aviv*, Tel Aviv 6 (1979), 158-162.

The author proposes to identify the Akkadian toponym Rāḫiṣum/ Rûḫiṣu with Rôg'iṣu which occurs in the topographical list of Tuthmosis III (No. 79). The place is somewhere in the vicinity of Qatna, but yet within the Egyptian province of Canaan.

79983 SCHENKEL, Wolfgang, Atlantis: die "namenlose" Insel, *GM* Heft 36 (1979), 57-60.

Der Name "Atlantis" lässt sich "ägyptisch" etymologisieren: at-lant=s "die Namenlose (Insel)". *Inge Hofmann*

79984 SEEBASS, Horst, Der israelische Name der Bucht von *Bēsān* und der Name Beth Schean, *Zeitschrift des Deutschen Palästina-Vereins*, Wiesbaden 95 (1979), 166-172.

The Egyptian evidence for the toponym Beth S(h)an makes a Semitic transcription $b(j)t$ $š^ʾl$ probable. The author proposes to connect the element $š^ʾl$ with Tell eṣ-Ṣarim (Rehob) in the middle of the bend of Beth S(h)an.

79985 SPALINGER, Anthony J., Some Notes on the Libyans of the Old Kingdom and the Later Historical Reflexes, *JSSEA* 9 (1978-1979), 125-162, with 3 maps.

The author summarises our knowledge about the names $Tḫnw$ and $Tmḥ$, discussing at length some details such as the relief of Sahure, which has been much copied by later rulers down to Taharqa and may itself perhaps go back to a historical relief of Snofru, and the expedition to Yam of Harkhuf, with particular attention to 19th century travellers' accounts of the desert routes through the region West of Nubia. His main results are: $Tmḥw$ originally indicated a people in the W.Delta, and was early extended to include all of Egypt's Western neighbours, ultimately becoming an archaic word; $Tmḥ$, in the O.K. indicating a people W. of the Dongola Reach (Yam), also expanded to include all lands W. of Egypt, but remained during the M.K. an up-to-date appellation for this area. By the N.K. both words had lost any specific sense. J.J.J.

79986 STÖRK, Lothar, Beginn und Ende einer Reise nach Punt: das Wadi Tumilat, *GM* Heft 35 (1979), 93-98.

Trotz einer Reihe ungelöster Probleme und offener Fragen werden die verschiedenen Untersuchungen von A. Nibbi akzeptiert, die ergaben, dass mit $w3ḏ-wr$ das Wadi Tumilat gemeint sei, zu dem Punt als ein Teil gehöre. Punt kann allerdings auch auf dem Wasserwege erreicht werden. *Inge Hofmann*

79987   WEEKS, K.R., An Archaeological Map of the Theban Necropolis, *in*: *Acts 1st ICE*, 677-678.

For more detailed reports see now our numbers 78033 and 79959, and K.R. Weeks, *Newsletter ARCE* No. 113 (Winter 1980), [p. 27-50].

79988   ZIBELIUS, Karola, Function of Ancient Egyptian Place Names, *in*: *Acts 1st ICE*, 693-698.

From the immediate relationship of the ancient Egyptian with his place names expressed through i.a. the multiple nomenclature for a place the basic function and significance can be investigated. Various aspects of toponymy are discussed.

79989   ZIBELIUS, Karola, Zu Form und Inhalt der Ortsnamen des Alten Reiches, *in*: *Festschrift Elmar Edel*, 456-477.

Analysis of the toponyms from the O.K. based on the material presented in our number 78891. As regards the grammatical structure the author points out the preponderance of names composed of nouns over those consisting of a sentence; the latter almost exclusively occur for domains and pyramids. Mrs Zibelius also argues against Lefebvre (our number 184) that pyramid names may very well be genitive constructions. In the last part of the article she presents examples of toponyms derived from various concepts: types of land, plants and animals, kings and man, etc.
                                                                                                J.J.J.

c. Physical anthropology and mummies

See also our numbers 79523; 79560; 79601; 79606; 79612; 79926 and 79939.

79990   DYSON, Stephen L., The Mummy of Middletown, *Archaeology* 32, No. 5 (September/October 1979), 57-59, with 5 ill.

Short report on the unwrapping of a mummy in the Natural History Museum of the Wesleyan University at Middletown, Connecticut.

79991   DZIERŻYKRAY-ROGALSKI, Tadeusz, Les ossements du gouverneur du Mastaba V de Balat, *BIFAO* 79 (1979), 479-482, with 2 pl.

Under the remains of the sarcophagus in mastaba V at Balât the incomplete and badly preserved bones of the governor were found, which are here studied. He was a man of 50-55 years old and of a racial type common in Egypt.   J.J.J.

79992   DZIERŻYKRAY-ROGALSKI, Tadeusz, Paléopathologie des habitants de l'oasis de Dakhleh à l'époque ptolémaïque, *BIFAO* 79 (1979), 63-69, with 2 pl.

Analysis of skeletal remains from the el-Dakhla Oasis, dating from the Ptolemaic Period. Particular attention is paid to four cases of lepra, which perhaps may suggest that victims of that disease were sent to the Oasis in that period. J.J.J.

79993 DZIERŻYKRAY-ROGALSKI, Tadeusz, Recherches anthropologiques menées dans l'oasis de Dakhleh au cours de la IIIe campagne de fouilles à Balat, *BIFAO* 79 (1979), 71-76, with 1 pl.

Analysis of part of the skeletal material from mastaba II, found in the superstructure and dating from later periods than the tomb itself. The relatively high age points to the prosperity of these people. In mastaba V the remains of the owner (the governor) were found (see our number 79991). No more cases of lepra were discovered (see our preceding number). J.J.J.

79994 FALKE, T.H.M., Onderzoek van een Egyptische mummie met behulp van nieuwe röntgentechnieken, *Nederlands Tijdschrift voor Geneeskunde*, Amsterdam 123, No. 19 (1979), 802-806, with 7 ill.

"Investigation of an Egyptian Mummy with the Help of New X-ray Techniques".
After a brief historical survey of the investigation of mummies the author presents the results of the investigation of a mummy in the Biblical Museum in Amsterdam. The mummy probably dates from the N.K.

79995 GRILLETTO, R.R., Comparaison entre les Égyptiens dynastiques d'Asiut et de Gebelen au niveau de la carie et de l'usure des dents, *in*: *Acts 1st ICE*, 249-273, with 1 fig.

Comparison of the dentures of 296 dynastic skulls from Asyût and 217 from Gebelein as regards caries and dental attrition leads to the conclusion that in the former city the standard of living was higher but the rate of caries too. J.J.J.

79996 GRILLETTO, Renato, La stature des anciens Égyptiens d'Asiut et de Gebelen (Haut Égypte), *L'Anthropologie*, Paris 83 (1979), 455-459, with 6 tables and French and English summaries.

The author compares the stature of ancient Egyptian people from the cemeteries of Asyût and Gebelein. There is no notable difference in stature between them.

79997 HARRIS, James E., Edward F. WENTE et alii, The Identification of the Mummy of the "Elder Lady" in the Tomb of Amenhotep II as Queen Tiye, *Delaware Medical Journal*, Wilmington, Delaware 51, No. 2 (February, 1979), 39-93, with 6 ill. and fig.

Compare already our number 78347.

79998   HARRISON, R.G., R.C. CONNOLLY, Soheir AHMED, A.B. ABDALLA and
         M. el GHAWABY, A Mummified Foetus from the Tomb of Tutankhamun,
         Antiquity 53 (1979), 19-21, with 1 pl.

   The authors investigate one of the two still-born foetuses from
   the tomb of Tutankhamun, at present in the Department of Anatomy,
   University of Cairo. After a general, a radiographic and a
   serological examination, they state that the possible relationship of the foetus, which displays Sprengel's deformity, to
   other individuals is unresolved, but several possibilities are
   briefly discussed.

79999   LLAGOSTERA, E., Radiological Aspects of the Egyptian Mummies of
         the Museo Arqueologico Nacional of Madrid, *in*: *Acts 1st ICE*,
         427-429.

   Short description of five mummies in the National Archaeological
   Museum in Madrid.

791000 Manchester Museum Mummy Project. Multidisciplinary Research on
          Ancient Egyptian Mummified Remains. Edited by A. Rosalie David,
          Manchester, Published by Manchester Museum, Distributed by Man-
          chester University Press, [1979] (21 x 30.5 cm; VIII + 160 p.,
          167 ill., 14 fig., 25 tables); rev. *BiOr* 37 (1980), 154-155
          (Suzanne Ratié).   Pr. £ 20.25

   Report of the multidisciplinary research on mummies in the
   Manchester Museum.
   Besides the introduction and the conclusion (159-160), A.R.
   David also presents the Catalogue of Egyptian Human and Animal
   Mummified Remains (1-17) arranged after human mummies, human
   parts and animal mummies (Inv. No., date, provenance, length,
   acquisition date, description).
   R. Garner, Experimental Mummification (19-24): experiments
   carried out on animals in order to make a comparison with ancient Egyptian mummification.
   I. Isherwood, H Jarvis and R.A. Fawcett, Radiology of the Manchester Mummies (25-64): the results of the examination of the
   individual mummies are presented (description of the bodies) and
   subjects such as age, sex, embalming and restorations, and disease, are discussed.
   F. Filce Leek, The Dental History of the Manchester Mummies
   (65-77): description of the dental condition of the individual
   mummies and a summarising discussion.
   A. Fletcher, The Fingerprint Examination (79-82): examination
   of the fingerprints of the mummy called Asru.
   E. Tapp, The Unwrapping of a Mummy (83-93); the unwrapping of
   the mummy No. 1770 and remarks on the state of the body. The
   body seems to date from c. 1000 B.C. whilst the bandages were
   some 1300 years later in age.
   E. Tapp, Disease in the Manchester Mummies (95-102): investigation of diseases in the mummies of Nekht-ankh, Asru and No.
   1770, followed by a commentary.

A. Curry, C. Anfield and E. Tapp, Electron Microscopy of the
Manchester Mummies (103-111): introduction to the various methods
of microscopy, results according to these techniques, and evaluation of the techniques.
A. Curry, The Insects, Associated with the Manchester Mummies
(113-117): introduction on insects in ancient Egypt, results
from the mummies, and discussion.
G.G. Benson, S.R. Hemingway and F N. Leach, The Analysis of the
Wrappings of Mummy 1770 (119-131): investigation and discussion
of the bandage fabric, surface deposits on the bandages, and
bandage impregnation of the mummy No. 1770.
J.P. Wild, The Textiles from the Mummy 1770 (133-136): charact-
erisation and discussion of the textiles from the mummy No. 1770.
K.C. Hodge and G.W.A. Newton, Radiocarbon Dating (137-147):
after an extensive explanation on radiocarbon dating and its
relation to Egyptian chronology follows the report of an experiment carried out on the bones and the wrappings of the mummy No.
1770.
R.A.H. Neave, The Reconstruction of the Heads and Faces of three
Ancient Egyptian Mummies (149-157): report on the reconstruction
of the heads of two M.K. brothers on account of their skulls and
that of the female mummy No. 1770.

791001 Mysteries of the Mummies. The Story of the Manchester University
Investigation, Edited by Rosalie David, London, Cassell, [1978]
(17 x 25.5 cm; 192 p., frontispiece, 1 map, numerous fig. and
ill., 10 colour pl., 2 colour ill. on cover).

The following members of the Manchester Mummy Team contributed
to the present book: G.G. Benson, A. Curry, A.R. David, D.M.
Dixon, A. Fletcher, R. Garner, S. Hemingway, I. Isherwood,
H. Jarvis, F.N. Leach, F.F. Leek, R.A.H. Neave, G.W.A. Newton
and E. Tapp. They were primarily concerned with the unwrapping
and the investiagtion of a female mummy (No. 1770), but also
with 17 other human and 22 animal mummies. The basic aims of
the project were to gather as much information as possible for
this group relating to existing knowledge about ancient Egypt
and to the pathology and causes of death of the mummies, and
to develop a methodology for the examination of Egyptian mummies.
While the first part of the book deals with the background:
history and geography, social and religious life, and mummification in ancient Egypt the second part is devoted to the examination proper. Chapter 4 deals with the unwrapping of mummy
No. 1770, while chapter 5 is concerned with the radiological
examination of the whole group of mummies. In chapters 6 and 7
are discussed respectively their pathology and dental conditions.
After chapter 8 on the microfauna of insects found with the
mummies there follows in chapter 9 a description of the complete
reconstruction in wax of the head of Mummy No. 1770 and a comparison of the reconstructed heads of the brothers from the M.K.
Of all mummies the fingerprints were taken.
A short epilogue and an index conclude the book.

The American edition appeared with Charles Scribner's Sons, New York, 1978 ($ 15).

791002 NEAVE, Richard, Mummies waren eens Mensen, *Organorama*, Oss 16, No. 4 (1979), 17-20 with 13 ill. (1 on cover, 12 in colour).

The author tries to reconstruct the lifelike appearance of two brothers, whose mummies are at present in the Egyptian collection of the Manchester Museum.

791003 ŠILAR, Jan, Radiocarbon Dating of Some Mummy and Coffin Samples (= Eugen Strouhal, Multidisciplinary Research on Egyptian Mummies in Czechoslowakia, VIII), *ZÄS* 106 (1979), 82-87, with 1 table and 1 fig.

Sequel to our number 77557.
Three textiles of mummy wrappings and a wooden coffin wedge (fragment) have been dated. Stalks of reed from a zikkurat at Aqar Quf, Iraq, were used as reference samples.
Considerable agreement was reached with the results of Smithsonian, Egyptological, and embalming technical dating.
M. Heerma v. Voss

791004 STROUHAL, Eugen, Anthropologische Funde aus dem Areal der Pyramide des Königs Amenemhet III. in Dahshur, *MDAIK* 35 (1979), 323-333, with 5 pl.

During the campaign of the German Institute at Dahshûr in 1976 human remains have been found, mostly near the entrance of the pyramid. Together they belong to seven persons, three men, three women and a child. The author presents a report on the anthropological analysis of the skeletons. The remains thought to be possibly those of Amenemhat III appeared to be those of a woman.
In an appendix D. Arnold presents details to the position and date of the human remains.
J.J.J.

791005 STROUHAL, Evžen, Československá spolupráce na antropologickém výzkumu starověkého Egypta, *Zprávy Československé společnosti orientalistické při ČSAV*, Praha 16, No. 2 (1979), 29-32.

"Die Mitarbeit der Tschechoslowakei bei der anthropologischen Erforschung Altägyptens".
Bericht über anthropologische Funde aus dem Grabe Haremhabs in Sakkara und der Begräbnisstatte von Mitgliedern einer Mönchsgemeinschaft des 5. und 6. Jh. u. Z. in Nordsakkara sowie Auswertung der Funde. Die Funde stammen aus Grabungskampagnen der Egypt Exploration Society.
B. Vachala

791006 STROUHAL, Eugen, Comments on the Paper of J.J. Castillos, A Late Egyptian Mummy at the National History Museum of Montevideo (*RdE* 28, 48-60), *RdE* 31 (1979), 157.

A propos d'un détail de technique du traitement des momies observable sur une radiographie publiée dans l'article commenté.
Ph. Derchain

791007 STROUHAL, Evžen, Egyptská královna Mútnodžemet ve světle antropologického výzkumu, *Nový Orient*, Praha 34, No. 10 (1979), 309-311.

"Die ägyptische Königin Mutnodjemet im Lichte anthropologischer Forschung."
Verfasser macht mit den Ergebnissen anthropologischer Untersuchungen menschlicher Skelettreste bekannt, die sich in der Pfeilerhalle des Grabes Haremhabs in Sakkara fanden, wohin sie aus der Hauptsargkammer offensichtlich von Grabräubern verbracht worden waren. Den archäologischen Funden zufolge handelt es sich um Überbleibsel der Gattin Haremhebs, der Königin Mutnodjemet, die im Alter von 35-40 Jahren starb. Unter den Überbleibseln der Königin fanden sich die Knochen eines Embryos bzw. Neugeborenen, des möglichen Nachfolgers Haremhebs. Der verzweifelte Versuch, den König trotz fortgeschrittenen Alters und pathologischer Störungen einen Thronfolger zu schenken, kostete Mutnodjemet das Leben. Die eigentliche Todesursache von Mutter und Kind ist jedoch nicht feststellbar. *B. Vachala*

791008 STROUHAL, Eugen and Luboš VYHNANEK, Egyptian Mummies in Czechoslovak Collections = *Sborník Národního Muzea v Praze*, Praha 35B, No. 1-4, 1979, 199 p., 1 map, 1 fig., 141 ill., 13 tables, 2 + 24 pl.

The volume contains a profound study of all mummies, human as well as animal, that are preserved in Czechoslovak collections. The first two chapters present an outline of the history of research on mummies and mummification, and a survey of Egyptian mummification techniques. In chapter 3 a discussion of the research methods applied for the investigation on which the book reports and a list of the material.
The following chapters present extensive discussions of each item, complete human mummies (53 instances) and parts of them, e.g. isolated heads. Each item is carefully discussed: its history so far as known, outer appearance, defects and dislocations, mummification techniques, etc. There are also described the objects connected with the mummies, if any, for instance the coffins and the wrappings.
Then follow chapters on animal mummies, written in cooperation with biologists: J. Hanzák, J. Čihar and V. Manzák. They deal with fish and reptiles, birds, and mammals. A short chapter on five fakes is added. In total no less than 173 items are treated.
The results as regards the human remains are discussed in chapters 12-14, namely: dating and mummification techniques, demographic data, and bone variations and palaeopathology as concluded from radiological examination. In chapter 15 (by

J. Hanzák) the results as regards the mummified fauna.
An extensive bibliography (p. 185-195) and a Czech summary at
the end. J.J.J.

791009 STROUHAL, E. and L. VYHNANEK, Research on Egyptian Mummies in Czechoslovakia, *in*: *Acts 1st ICE*, 615-619.

A report on the examination of Egyptian mummies in Czechoslovakian collections. Compare our numbers 76108, 76143, 76757, 76813-76815, 77324, 77557, 77746, and our preceding number.

791010 de TASSIGNY, C. et M. BROUQUI, Adaptation à la desinfection de la momie de Ramses II du procédé de radio-sterilisation gamma, *in*: *ICOM Committee for Conservation*. 5th Triennial Meeting, Zagreb, 1-8, October 1978. Preprints, No. 78/17/5, 16 p. with abstract, 6 fig. and 1 table.

On a conservation treatment technique applied on the mummy of Ramses II.

791011 ZIMMERMAN, Michael R., Palaeopathologic Diagnosis Based on Experimental Mummification, *American Journal of Physical Anthropology*, Philadelphia 51 (July, August, September, November 1979), 235-243, with 1 table.

Report on experimental mummification which was undertaken to study the changes seen in experimentally mummified and rehydrated tissues, normal as well as pathologic, and of which the results could be compared with those of the normal methods of palaeopathology.

X. NUBIAN STUDIES

See also our numbers 79065; 79139; 79142; 79161; 79264; 79459; 79463; 79495; 79576; 79602; 79609; 79610; 79617; 79736; 79916; 79920; 79926; and 79981.

791012 ABDALLA, Abdelgadir M., Examples of Incremental Repetition in Meroitic Personal Names Containing Verbal Complexes, *in*: *Beiträge zur meroitischen Grammatik*, 155-180.

Verfasser vertritt die Ansicht, dass die Struktur meroitischer Personennamen ihm Einblicke in Strukturphänomene böten. Er isoliert in den Personennamen Verben und Verbalkomplexe unbekannter Bedeutung, die er z.B. in den Benediktionsverben wiederfindet. Verbale Präfixe und Suffixe sollen auch in den Personennamen erkennbar sein (zum Problem der Segmentierung meroitischer Wörter vgl. unsere Nr. 791043, S. 23 f.). Es wird darauf verwiesen, dass gewisse Komplexe in den Namen mehrerer Mitglieder derselben Familie wiederkehren, ein Ergebnis, das bei der Segmentierung zusammengesetzter Personennamen und beim Studium des meroitischen Soziallebens weiterhelfen kann. *Inge Hofmann*

791013 Abdallah Nirqi 1964. The Hungarian Excavation in Egyptian Nubia. Studies by L. Castiglione, L. Barkóczi, Á. Salamon, Gy. Hajnóczi, L. Kákosy, L. Török and V. Pósa = Offprints from the Acta Archaeologica Academiae Scientiarum Hungaricae, Vols. 26 (1974) and 27 (1975), Budapest, 1979.

Zu den zusammengestellten Sonderdrucken über die ungarischen Arbeiten in Abdallah Nirqi vgl. unsere Nummern 74739, 75592, 75729 und 75730. *Inge Hofmann*

791014 ADAMS, William Y., Kush and the Peoples of Northeast Africa, *in*: *Africa in Antiquity*, 9-14.

Es werden die Beziehungen zwischen den alten Kuschiten und die sie umgebenden Völker untersucht: Kuschiten und Beja, Kuschiten und Aksum, Kuschiten und Niloten, Kuschiten und Nubier, Kuschiten und Ägypten, Kuschiten und Römer. Es wurde dabei festgestellt, dass, entgegen der landläufigen Meinung, der Einfluss des kuschitischen Reiches auf die umliegenden Völkerschaften nur gering war, mit Ausnahme der Nubier, die Erben und Nachfolger wurden und diese Erbschaft weitergaben bis hin zur heutigen Demokratischen Republik des Sudan. *Inge Hofmann*

791015 ADAMS, W.Y., R.C. ALLEN, P.M. GARTKIEWICZ, P.G. FRENCH, Elisabeth CROWFOOT and R.D. ANDERSON, Qaṣr Ibrîm 1978, *JEA* 65 (1979), 30-41, with 2 plans and 3 pl.

The mud brick temple of Taharqa is now known to be the centre of an extensive complex of religious buildings, a fairly large stone-built temple being built to the west of it in Napatan or early Meroitic times (Temple 4). This had a hypostyle hall with eight columns but little remained of the sanctuary chambers. Alongside was an 11 m. square stone tower connected by a wall reaching the Podium. The fortifications round the site seem to have been rebuilt following the Roman occupation 23-21 B.C. Fourteen Bosnian houses were excavated and some Late Christian structures one being later used as a stable for animals. Further work on the cathedral and recording of its decorative features was carried out, an inscription possibly indicating bishop Miel as the builder. Many small objects and fragments of textiles were also recovered and a stela of an army commander Neferʿankh (?). *E.P. Uphill*

791016 ALLEN, Roger C., The 1979 Colorado-Kentucky-Expedition to Kulubnarti, Democratic Republic of the Sudan, *Nyame Akuma*, Montreal No. 15 (1979), 51-53.

Es wurden Ausgrabungen auf zwei Friedhöfen der christlichen Epoche mit dem Ziel durchgeführt, menschliche Überreste für die Studien biokultureller Anthropologie zu erhalten. Die Gräber waren solche, die auch für andere nubische Friedhöfe der christlichen Zeit typisch sind. Der Erhaltungszustand der Leichen war wegen des trockenen Klimas sehr gut, auch Textilien - Gewänder und Decken - hatten sich z.T. erhalten. Die Sammlung von Artefakten ist gering. *Inge Hofmann*

791017 BIANCHI, Robert S., Ptolemaic Influences on the Arts of the Late Napatan and Early Meroitic Periods, *in*: *Africa in Antiquity*, 65-69.

Der Artikel beschäftigt sich mit dem Einfluss der einheimisch-ägyptischen Kunst auf die spätnapatanische und frühmeroitische Periode. Es werden freundschaftliche Beziehungen zwischen dem ägyptischen und meroitischen Reich festgestellt, die erst unter den Römern abgebrochen wurden. Kulturelle Beeinflussungen erfolgten auf dem Gebiet der Architektur, dem Titulaturwesen, den Libationstafeln, der Statuenherstellung (z.B. eingelegte Augen, bestimmte Gewänder); die Vergoldung von Privatstelen und Tempelreliefs, die gleichfalls übernommen wurde, bedeutete eine Vergöttlichung des Dargestellten. Die Napatäer und Meroiten übernahmen so ägyptische Themen und Motive, die sie jedoch nach ihren Wünschen und Gegebenheiten umformten. *Inge Hofmann*

791018 BIERWISCH, Manfred, Eine tote Sprache und lebendige Linguisten, *in*: *Beiträge zur meroitischen Grammatik*, 95-112.

Kommentar zu unserer Nr. 791043: es wird der Frage nachgegangen, wie sprachliche Daten und Fakten auf der Grundlage aller erreichbaren Einsichten und Hypothesen über natürliche Sprachen im allgemeinen beschrieben und erklärt werden können. Es wird näher eingegangen auf die phonologische Interpretation des meroitischen Schriftsystems, die Probleme der syntaktischen Strukturebene, besonders der mehrfachen Bedeutung des Morphems -*li* und auf das Affixparadigma der Benediktionsverben.
Inge Hofmann

791019 BIETAK, Manfred, Ceramics of the C-Group Culture, *in*: *Africa in Antiquity*, 107-127, with 12 fig.

Ausgehend von der grossen Bedeutung, die die Töpferei für die Träger der C-Kultur hatte, wird das Rohmaterial und die Produktionstechnik, Form und Funktion der Keramik untersucht und ein Überblick über die typischsten Gefässe der C-Kultur und ihrer Dekoration gegeben. Selbst in der heutigen nubischen Kunst werden Motive verwendet, die sich bereits in der C- und sogar in der A-Kultur nachweisen lassen. *Inge Hofmann*

791020 BONNET, Charles, Remarques sur la ville de Kerma, *in*: *Hommages Sauneron* I, 3-10, with 1 plan and 3 pl.

Making some observations on the site of Kerma on account of recent excavations the author i.a. points out that in the North sanctuaries have been found, one probably from the Ethiopian Period; in this area also the occurrence of bakeries is attested. Near the *deffufa* remains of what may be an enclosure wall were found; it was destroyed by fire, its bricks having been re-employed during the N.K. In the Western section cemeteries of various periods have been found, in which a round structure that may be a tomb of an unknown type. J.J.J.

791021 BOTHMER, Bernard V., Ancient Nubia and the Northern Sudan: A New Field of Art History, *in*: *Africa in Antiquity*, 177-180, with 4 ill. on 4 pl.

Die Kunstgeschichte in Nubien geht bis zum Ende des vierten vorchristlichen Jahrtausends zurück (A-Kultur), es sei denn, die Statuette von El Kadada gehört tätsächlich noch dem Neolithikum an. Zu diesem Typ gehört auch die kopflose Frauenstatuette Brooklyn no. L 78.3. Es werden kurz einige Kulturen des Sudan besprochen und das einheimische Element in ihnen betont. Inge Hofmann

791022 BRAUNER, Siegmund, Die Entwicklung der Afrikanistik an der Universität Leipzig (Zum Wirken von Hans Stumme und August Klingenheben), *Wissenschaftliche Zeitschrift der Karl-Marx-Universität*. Gesellschafts- und Sprachwissenschaftliche Reihe, Leipzig 28 (1979), 131-144.

Survey of the history of the study of African cultures in Leipzig.

791023 BRILLIANT, Richard, Africa and the Arts of Greece and Rome, *in*: *Africa in Antiquity*, 55-64.

Der Artikel befasst sich mit drei Themenkreisen: Repräsentationen von Afrikanern, wobei Schwarze oder Äthiopier an erster Stelle als Afrikanischer galten, weniger Libyer und Berber; Darstellungen von afrikanischen Ortsbeschreibungen und dem Leben seiner Bewohner: dazu gehören vor allem die Themen mit den Kämpfen der Pygmäen gegen grössere Tiere und das Leben am Nil; Abstraktionen und Personifikationen, vor allem symbolisiert durch typisch afrikanische Tiere: so personifizierte die Darstellung einer jungen Frau mit einem Helm aus einem Elefantenschädel und begleitet von einem Löwen oder Tiger Afrika. Abschliessend wird auf griechische und römische Kunst in Afrika verwiesen.
 Inge Hofmann

791024 BURSTEIN, Stanley M., The Nubian Campaigns of C. Petronius and George Reisner's Second Meroitic Kingdom of Napata, *ZÄS* 106 (1979), 95-105.

Classical sources do not support Reisner's theory (1923) of a divided Nubia in the first century. Quite the contrary, all the

texts dealing with the political geography of Hellenistic Nubia reveal a single kingdom, based at Meroe. They do confirm, however, Reisner's important observation of a Napatan revival in that period.
M. Heerma v. Voss

791025 DONADONI, S., Missione Archaeologica nel Sudan dell'Università di Roma, *Nyame Akuma*, Montreal No. 15 (1979), 55-56.

Die Arbeiten am Jebel Barkal wurden weitergeführt. Eine Reihe von Ziegelsteinmauern in der Nähe des Tempels 1300 gehören wohl zu einem grossen "Palast". Einige Feuerstellen konnten identifiziert werden. Gebäude 1500 in der Nähe des Berges enthielt zwei Arten von Säulen, deren Erhaltungszustand und Masse unterschiedlich waren. Der Eingang zu einem grösseren Komplex konnte festgestellt werden.
Inge Hofmann

791026 DESANGES, Jehan et Serge LANCEL, Bibliographie analytique de l'Afrique Antique XI (1975), Paris, E. de Boccard, 1979 (21 x 27 cm; 34 p.).

Hinsichtlich der Arbeiten, der über das nördliche Afrika 1975 erschienen sind, werden vor allem Quellen, Bibliographien, historische Geographie, das punische Afrika, die unabhängigen Königreiche, die römische Periode und das afrikanische Christentum analytisch vorgestellt.
Inge Hofmann

791027 FERNEA, Robert A., Tradition and Change in Egyptian Nubia, *in*: *Africa in Antiquity*, 41-48.

Feldforschungsarbeit über Tradition und Wandel der nubischen Kultur seit der Aussiedlung der Bevölkerung nach Kom Ombo.
Inge Hofmann

791028 GEUS, Francis, Rapport annuel d'activité 1977-1978, Khartoum, Service des Antiquités du Soudan Section Française de Recherche Archéologique - Sudan Antiquities Service French archaeological research unit, 1979 (21 x 27 cm; 42 p., 2 maps, 9 fig. and 14 pl.).

Der Distrikt von Abudiya, südlich des Dal-Kataraktes, wurde erneut untersucht und 16 Stellen gründlicher erforscht, die sich auf vier Gruppen verteilen lassen: Siedlungen aus dem Neolithikum und der Kerma-Kultur sowie Gräber der letztgenannten Epoche, der meroitischen (?) und der christlichen Zeit. Eine Sammlung von Keramik scheint aus napatanischer Zeit zu stammen, bei K 133 dürfte es sich um ein muslimisches Massengrab handeln.
Der Geologe P. Poupet entdeckte intensive Steinbruchsarbeiten entlang dem Tal, die möglicherweise auf Goldgewinnung schliessen lassen.
Inge Hofmann

791029 GEUS, Francis, Rapport annuel d'activité 1978-1979, Université de Lille III, 1979 (20.5 x 27 cm; 37 p., 11 fig., 46 ill. on 15

pl.) = Service des Antiquités du Soudan, Section Française de
Recherche Archéologique - Sudan Antiquities Service, French
Archaeological Research Unit.

Es wird ein Überblick über die Tätigkeit des französisch-
sudanesischen Teams gegeben: die Ausgrabungen in el Kadada
wurden intensiv weitergeführt, wobei drei verschiedene Areale
freigelegt wurden. Die Gräber stammen aus der neolithischen
und meroitischen Zeit. Inzwischen sind 262 Begräbnisstellen
in el Kadada ausgegraben worden. Die neolithischen Überreste
sind von besonderem Interesse, weil sie Vergleichsmaterial zum
Neolithikum des zentralen Sudan und zur A- und Kerma-Kultur
bieten. Bisher wurde allerdings nur eine Scherbe der typischen
esh-Shaheinab-Keramik gefunden. Die endgültige Publikation
der Gräber von el Kadada wird vorbereitet. In der Umgebung von
el Kadada wurden weitere Funde getätigt (Keramik der neolithischen
Zeit, Felsbilder, niedrige Tumuli, die meroitischen Begräbnisse
bedecken können). In der Umgebung von Khartum wurde eine Stelle
entdeckt, deren Keramik ähnlich der von el Kadada ist.

Inge Hofmann

791030 GEUS, Francis and Jacques REINOLD, Fouille de sauvetage à el
Kadada (Soudan): I - La Campagne d'Avril 1976, *CRIPEL* 5 [1979],
7-157, with 4 maps, 34 fig. and 51 pl. comprising fig., ill.
and a folding plan.

Kadada, im Distrikt von Taragma nördlich von Shendi gelegen,
blieb trotz der Nähe meroitischer Fundplätze von der Forschung
unbeachtet, bis die Siedlung 1976 entdeckt wurde. Nach einem
kurzen Überblick über die Forschungsgeschichte folgt der Aus-
grabungsbericht von Kadada, einer neolithischen Siedlung. Das
Material, das dabei zutage gefördert wurde, wird in vier grosse
Gruppen eingeteilt und vorgestellt: 1. Keramik, das umfangreich-
ste Material, 2. die lithische Industrie, 3. Knochengerätschaften,
von denen jedoch nur drei Fragmente erhalten blieben und 4.
Schmuckgegenstände, nämlich Perlen und Nasen- oder Lippen-
pflöcke.

Inge Hofmann

791031 GRATIEN, Brigitte, La grande nécropole Kerma de l'île de Sai,
CRIPEL 5 [1979], 159-182, with 1 fig., 9 ill. and 1 plan.

Während der Grabungskampagne 1976/77 sollte die Nordgrenze der
Nekropole untersucht und die Arbeiten in SKC 3 fortgeführt werden. Die Funde in den Gräbern der Nordgrenze gehören in die
klassische Kerma-Epoche. Fünf neue Gräber wurden in SKC 7 B
entdeckt; in ihnen fanden sich Schafe oder Ziegen. Sie gehören
wohl in die Übergangszeit von der mittleren Kerma-Epoche zur
klassischen. Die Ausgrabungen in SKC 1 wurden weitergeführt
und drei Grabtypen gefunden, die in die Kerma-Epochen mittel,
Übergang, klassisch gehören. Das Mobiliar ist sehr schlecht
erhalten. Zum ältesten Teil der Nekropole von Sai gehört SKC 3;
dort wurden die Ausgrabungen weitergeführt. Geopferte Tiere

fanden sich nicht.   Die Funde werden beschrieben, wobei T. 62
als besonders reich und interessant hervorgehoben wird.
Inge Hofmann

791032   GRZYMSKI, Krzystof, Meroe i świat klasyczny, *Meander*, Warszawa
33, 10 (1978), 473-479, with a Latin summary on p. 479.

"Meroe and the Classical World."

791033   HAALAND, Randi, Report on the 1979 season in the Sudan, *Nyame Akuma*, Calgary No. 14 (May 1979), 62.

Bericht über die Weiterführung der Ausgrabungen in El Shaheinab und Untersuchung des Ostufers bei Kadero und Zakiab, um weitere neolithische Überreste zu eruieren.   Die Ausgrabungen in Shaheinab ergaben für Schicht 7 eine Datierung von 5300 ± 100 B.P. und für Schicht 5 5500 ± 100 B.P.
Inge Hofmann

791034   HAALAND, Randi, Some New C-14 Dates from Central Sudan, *Nyame Akuma*, Montreal No. 15 (1979), 56-57.

The two C-14 dates from Esh Shaheinab site are as follows: Layer I (10 cm deep) 5240 ± 80 (T - 3222, MASCA calibrated to 4100 ± 140 B.C.).   Layer V (47-50 cm deep) 5370 ± 80 B.P. (T - 3223, MASCA calibrated to 4240 ± 140 B.C.). Kadero II is dated to 5360 ± 80 B.P. (T - ± 3260, MASCA calibrated to 4230 ± 130 B.C.).   Umm Direiwa gave the following result: 4950 ± 80 (T - 3261, MASCA calibrated to 3740 ± 60 B.C.).
Inge Hofmann

791035   HAINSWORTH, M.E., L'onomastique méroïtique dans les graffites du Dodécaschène, *in*: *Acts 1st ICE*, 277-283.

The author, attempting to evaluate the importance of the Meroitic presence in the Dodekaschoinos, studied the private names occurring in graffiti from that area.   They are written in Meroitic, but also in Greek and Demotic, while some persons bear Meroitic titles.   The total amounts to 182 occurrences.
J.J.J.

791036   HAKEM, Ahmed M. Ali, University of Khartoum Excavations at Sarurab and Bauda, North of Omdurman, *in*: *Africa in Antiquity*, 151-155.

Die Ausgrabungen von Sarurab und Bauda förderten Siedlungen zutage, die aus dem Neolithikum und der meroitischen Zeit stammen und bis in die mitteralterlich christliche oder islamische Epoche reichen.   Die Periode nach dem Neolithikum und vor dem 9. Jahrhundert v. Chr. ist nicht belegt.   *Inge Hofmann*

791037   HINKEL, Friedrich W., The Archaeological Map of the Sudan. II. The Area of the South Libyan Desert.   With the Co-operation of

Anthony J. Mills and an Introduction by Anthony J. Arkell,
Berlin, Akademie-Verlag, 1979 (21.7 x 30.6 cm; portfolio containing 26 folding maps and a booklet: 21.2 x 29.5 cm; VIII +
160 p., 1 map and 1 fig. on inside covers, 28 fig. and maps);
at head of title: Akademie der Wissenschaften der DDR. Zentralinstitut für alte Geschichte und Archäologie; rev. *BiOr* 38
(1981), 64-67 (Bruce G. Trigger).   Pr. M 78

Der 2. Band der Archaeological Map of the Sudan (AMS) erscheint
zuerst; zu ihrer Benutzung und der Erklärung ihres Aufbaues vgl.
unsere Nr. 77346. Von den 280 Fundplätzen, die aus der Literatur und Fundobjekten in Museen bekannt sind, konnten nicht
alle exakt lokalisiert werden. Nur 215 liegen auf heutigem
sudanesischem Gebiet. Einem kurzen historischen Überblick folgt
die Liste der Fundplätze ausserhalb des Sudan, eine Bibliographie,
sowie ein ausführlicher Katalog zu den auf den "unit maps"
NF-35-I bis -P und NE-35-A bis -P eingetragenen Fundplätzen.
                                                Inge Hofmann

791038 HINKEL, Friedrich W., 3. Tagung der Gesellschaft für Nubische
        Studien, Cambridge, 1978, *Ethnographisch-Archäologische Zeit-
        schrift*, Berlin 20 (1979), 548-550.

Brief report on the 3rd Symposium on Nubian Studies, held at
Cambridge in 1978.

791039 HINKEL, Friedrich W., Die Pyramiden von Meroe und die Restaurie-
        rung von Baudenkmälern in der DR Sudan, *in*: *Archäologische
        Denkmale und Umweltgestaltung*. Herausgegeben von Joachim Herr-
        mann, Berlin, Akademie-Verlag, 1978 (= Veröffentlichungen des
        Zentralinstituts für alte Geschichte und Archäologie der Akademie
        der Wissenschaften der DDR, 9), 131-136, with 1 map, 1 fig. and
        2 pl.

Ein Schwerpunkt in den zukünftigen Aktivitäten der Altertümer-
verwaltung im Sudan bilden die Restaurierungsarbeiten an den
zahlreichen Baudenkmälern. Die Restaurierungs- und Rekonstruktionsarbeiten sollen sich anfangs auf die Nordgruppe der Pyramiden von Meroe konzentrieren. Die Konstruktion der 35 Pyramiden
unterschiedlicher Grösse wird beschrieben; Verfasser nimmt
folgende Aufgaben in Angriff: Registrierung und Aufmass aller
verworfenen Relief- und Architekturblöcke mit dem Ziel der
Verwendung und des Einbaus an ihrer unsprünglichen Stelle während der späteren Rekonstruktionsarbeiten; Inbetriebnahme oder
Wiedereröffnung eines günstig gelegenen Steinbruches zur Gewinnung von Sandsteinblöcken, die als Ersatz fehlender Steine
bei den Rekonstruktionsarbeiten benutzt werden; Beginn der Rekonstruktionsarbeiten an einer noch auszuwählenden Pyramide.
Auf den gewonnenen Erfahrungen aufbauend, sollen die Arbeiten in
den darauffolgenden Jahren fortgeführt werden. *Inge Hofmann*

791040 HINKEL, Friedrich W., Die Rettungsarbeiten an den Tempeln Sudanesisch-Nubiens und deren neuer Standort, *in*: *Archäologische Denkmale und Umweltgestaltung*. Herausgegeben von Joachim Herrmann, Berlin, Akademie-Verlag, 1978 (= Veröffentlichungen des Zentralinstituts für alte Geschichte und Archäologie der Akademie der Wissenschaften der DDR, 9), 125-130, with 2 maps, 1 plan and 3 pl.

Bericht über die Verlegung der durch den Bau des Staudammes Sad el Ali gefährdeten Altertumer auf sudanesischem Gebiet, die nach Khartum gebracht wurden, um die Grundlagen und Möglichkeiten für die Herausbildung eines eigenen Geschichtsbildes und bewusstseins in der Bevölkerung zu schaffen. Es handelt sich da um vier Tempel, ein Felsengrab, mehr als hundert Felsinschrifte und Fundobjekte aus Nubien und dem Museum von Wadi Halfa, die nach Khartum transportiert wurden und im neuen National-Museum in Khartum ausgestellt bzw. in Form eines Freilichtmuseums in dessen Garten aufgestellt wurden. (Vgl. auch unsere Nr. 78362).
Inge Hofmann

791041 HINKEL, Friedrich W., Work at the Northern Group of Pyramids at Begrawiya (Meroe) and at the Historical Buildings of Suakin, 1977/78, *Nyame Akuma*, Calgary No. 14 (May 1979), 56-59.

Die Arbeit an den Pyramiden von Meroe beschäftigte sich hauptsächlich mit der Rekonstruktion der Opferkapellen der letzten meroitischen Königspyramiden: Beg. N 25, die einem König gehörte, Beg. N 26, Beg. N 27, Beg. N 32, Beg. N 19. Ausserdem wurden weitere 250 herabgefallene Relief- und Architekturblöcke von verschiedenen Pyramiden numeriert, gemessen und fotografier um eine spätere Rekonstruktionsarbeit der Szenen zu erleichtern
Inge Hofmann

791042 HINKEL, Friedrich W., Work at the Northern Group of Pyramids at Begrawiya (Meroe) and at the Historical Buildings of Suakin, 1978/79, *Nyame Akuma*, Montreal No. 15 (1979), 60-63.

Die Arbeiten an den Pyramiden der Nordgruppe wurden weitergeführt, wobei auf der Aussenwand der nördlichen Kapellenwand vor Beg. N 8 die erste bekannte Architekturzeichnung für eine Pyramide entdeckt wurde. Sie besteht aus allen Elementen, die für die Konstruktion einer Pyramide notwendig sind und erlaubt in ihrer Exaktheit eine unzweideutige Interpretation. Eine detail lierte Publikation über die Entdeckung und ihre Interpretation ist in Vorbereitung. Des weiteren wurde gearbeit an den Pyramiden Beg. N 19, Beg. N 26, Beg. N 36, Beg. N 40, Beg. N 41, Beg. N 42 und N 43 und Beg. N 57. Die Registrierung der herabgefallenen Reliefs wird fortgeführt.
Inge Hofmann

791043 HINTZE, Fritz, Beitrage zur meroitischen Grammatik, *in*: *Beiträ zur meroitischen Grammatik*, 11-92, with 12 tables.

Nach einer Einleitung, die Stellung nimmt zur phonematischen
Interpretation der meroitischen Schrift und zu theoretischen
Fragen, so zu Methoden der grammatischen Analyse, wird im
Kapitel über die syntaktische Struktur der Deskriptionssätze die
Grundlage für eine Systematisierung der in den Deskriptions-
sätzen vorliegenden syntagmatischen Strukturen erarbeitet und
die Anwendung eines strikten Analyseverfahrens ("IC-Analyse")
aufgezeigt. Nachdem für -*li* drei Funktionen festgestellt wer-
den, konnten mit Hilfe von Reduktionsregeln zwei Typen von
"Kernsätzen" beim Nominalsatz aufgezeigt werden: N-*lo* und N-*l*
+ V-*lo*. Das folgende Kapitel behandelt die Frage nach der
grammatischen Struktur und Funktion dieser Sätze. Das vierte
Kapitel behandelt die Struktur der Benediktionsverben in den
Formeln A und B. Es konnte gezeigt werden, dass die vielen
Präfixe auf nur ein Präfix /pas/- zu reduzieren sind, neben dem
eine präfixlose Form steht, die vor einem vokalisch anlautenden
Verb zu /y/- wird. In ihnen wird ein modales (oder temporales?)
Kennzeichen vermutet, etwa /∅/- für Imperativ, /pas/- für Op-
tativ (oder Futur?). Die neun Suffixe bzw. Suffixkombinationen
lassen sich aufgrund von Assimilationen auf /∅/ das als -/a/
aufzufassen ist, -/ket/ und -/to/ reduzieren. Sie werden als
pronominales Kennzeichen erklärt: 2 sg. -/a/, 2. pl. -/ket/,
3. pl. -/to/. Abschliessend wird die Verwendung der Affixe der
Benediktionsverben in den Textgruppen untersucht.

Inge Hofmann

791044 HINTZE, Fritz, Elemente der meroitischen Kultur, *in*: *Africa in Antiquity*, 101-105.

Es wird ein kurzer Überblick über die verschiedenen Ansichten
im Hinblick auf den Charakter der meroitischen Kultur gegeben:
ein monistisches Modell überbetont entweder die ägyptische oder
aber die afrikanische Komponente; ein dualistisches Modell nimmt
an, dass neben der ägyptischen noch eine weitere einheimische Komponente von Bedeutung ist. Verfasser möchte stattdessen von
einem polysynthetischen Modell ausgehen: neben unbewusst und
bewusst übernommenen ägyptischen Elementen spielen fremde (z.B.
assyrische und persische) und autochthone - diese für uns jedoch
am schwersten zu erkennen - Elemente eine Rolle. "Meroitisch"
ist die Art der Synthese fremder und eigenständiger Kulturen.

Inge Hofmann

791045 HINTZE, Fritz, Stellungnahme zu den Kommentaren, *in*: *Beiträge zur meroitischen Grammatik*, 181-201.

Vgl. unsere Nummern 791012, 791018, 791063, 791067, 791069;
791071 and 791080.
Es wird zu folgenden in den Kommentaren erörterten Fragen
Stellung genommen: Methoden der grammatischen Analyse, die kom-
parative Methode (die Lexikostatistik wie die Glottochronologie
sind für den Nachweis einer Sprachverwandtschaft nicht ausrei-

chend), das Suffix *-lo*, das weiterhin als Kopula, nicht als "grammatisches Subjekt" betrachtet wird, die Suffixe *-qo* und *-qe*, wobei *-qo* auf das pronominale *-qe* zurückgeführt wird, die Funktion des *-li* als "Grenzsignal", die Reduktionsregeln, die zwei Kernsätze erkennen lassen und zu den statistischen Beobachtungen mit dem Ergebnis, dass allgemein der lokale Faktor stärker wirkt als der chronologische. *Inge Hofmann*

791046 HINTZE, Ursula, The Graffiti from the Great Enclosure at Musawwarat es Sufra, *in: Africa in Antiquity*, 135-150, with 52 fig. and 6 ill. on 4 pl.

Von den 700 Graffiti, die von der Grossen Anlage in Musawwarat es Sufra stammen, werden 50 vorgestellt, u.a. Apedemak-Darstellungen, Darstellungen von Königen, Prinzen, Feinden, mythologische Szenen (heilige Hochzeit?), Kriegszenen, Schiffs- und Tierabbildungen - ein reichhaltiges Material für zukünftige Forschungen. *Inge Hofmann*

791047 HOFMANN, Inge, Meroitische Chronologie im Lichte von Kunstgegenständen, *in: Africa in Antiquity*, 71-84, with 45 fig.

Importwaren des römisch-hellenistischen Kulturbereiches, die in Gräbern des Nord- und Westfriedhofes von Begarawiyah sowie in einigen wenigen Pyramiden beim Jebel Barkal gefunden wurden, wurden zusammengestellt und mit gleichen Stücken verglichen, die in Ländern westlich, nördlich und östlich des Mittelmeeres gefunden und mehr oder weniger exakt datiert worden sind. Es wurde so versucht, eine Datierung der Waren aus dem Sudan zu gewinnen, die möglicherweise Anhaltspunkte für eine chronologische Einordnung der jeweiligen Grabstätte liefern kann.
Inge Hofmann

791048 HOFMANN, Inge, Noch einmal Apedemak, *GM* Heft 33 (1979), 31-32.

Stellungnahme zu unserer Nr. 791088: nur eine Löwendarstellung mit *hmhm*-Krone wird als Apedemak akzeptiert. *Inge Hofmann*

791049 HOFMANN, Inge, Sprachkontakte in Nubien zur meroitischen Zeit, *Sprache und Geschichte in Afrika*, Hamburg 1 (1979), 21-35.

In den letzten vorchristlichen Jahrhunderten konnten in dem dünn besiedelten nubischen Niltal an Sprachgruppen das Nubische und kuschitische Sprachen und Dialekte miteinander in Kontakt kommen auf die seit dem 1. nachchristlichen Jahrhundert die Meroiten stiessen. Zwischen den Sprechern des Meroitischen, des Nubischen und einer Kuschitensprache werden Kontakte stattgefunden haben. Diese sicher zu greifen und eindeutig zu beweisen, ist aber bei der heutigen Kenntnis des Meroitischen noch nicht möglich. Es können nur Probleme aufgezeigt und mögliche Lösungen vorgeschlagen werden, mehr nicht, wenn man sich nicht im spekulativen Raum bewegen will. *Inge Hofmann*

791050 HOFMANN, I. und A. VORBICHLER, Der Äthiopenlogos bei Herodot, Wien, 1979 (14.5 x 21 cm; XII + 191 p.) = Beiträge zur Afrikanistik Bd. 3 = Veröffentlichungen der Institute für Afrikanistik und Ägyptologie der Universität Wien, 4.

Eine kritische Untersuchung über die Verwertbarkeit der Angaben Herodots über Äthiopien als Quellen für eine meroitische Kulturgeschichte ergab, dass fast alle äthiopischen Episoden mit dem realen Land Kusch südlich von Ägypten nichts zu tun haben - eine Ausnahme bilden Spuren in II, 29 -, sondern Angaben über ein mythisches Sonnenland im Osten sind. Die Schilderung des angeblichen Kambyses-Feldzuges beinhaltet den Mythos vom Helden im Exil, der in die Heimat zu seinem Vater aufbricht und sich dort als dessen Sohn legitimieren muss. Der Versuch, den dem Mythos mit seinen verschiedenen Varianten zugrundeliegenden Initiationsritus auf die geschichtliche Ebene zu transferieren und mit einem realen königlichen Helden zu verbinden, erforderte Verkürzungen und Verzerrungen, die den Mythos kaum noch klar erkennen lassen. Die Quelle stammt vornehmlich aus dem babylonisch-iranischen Raum; der Mythen-, zum Teil bereits Märchenstoff wurde mit griechischem Material angereichert und von einem Ionier in der Mitte des 5. vorchristlichen Jahrhunderts dargestellt, der die philosophischen Ansichten und den ionischen Rationalismus seiner Zeit mitbrachte.   *Inge Hofmann*

791051 JAKOBIELSKI, Stefan, Dongola 1976, *Études et Travaux* 11 (1979), 229-244, with 18 ill.

Bericht über die Ausgrabungen in Dongola: im sogenannten Sektor Faubourg wurde ein rechteckiges Gebäude A ausgegraben, dessen Konstruktion beschrieben wird. Zimmer 3 ist mit einem Christusbild ausgemalt, des weiteren fand sich eine Darstellung des Heiligen Georg oder des Heiligen Theodor dem Stratelaten, beide aus der nubischen Kunst bekannt. Auch eine weitere bekannte Gestalt, der Heilige Merkurios, der den Kaiser Julian Apostata tötet, fand sich in Zimmer 3. Einige Bilder konnten mit Hilfe der Fragmente, die im Sand des Zimmers lagen, rekonstruiert werden. Die in einer Nische angebrachte Christusgestalt ist auf jeder Seite von einem Tondo begleitet, in denen ein griechischer Evangelentext steht (1. Joh. 1, 1-5 und 21, 25). Das Zimmer muss eine besondere Bedeutung gehabt haben. Die Malereien scheinen in das 9. Jahrhundert zu gehören, in dem wohl das gesamte Gebäude errichtet wurde. In spätchristlicher Zeit wurde es umfunktioniert und in nachchristlicher Zeit nicht mehr benötigt und aufgelassen.   *Inge Hofmann*

791052 KLEINSCHROTH, Adolf, Das Reich Kusch und seine wasserwirtschaftlichen Probleme, *Antike Welt*, Feldmeilen 10, Heft 3 (1979), 23-30, with 14 fig., ill., maps and plans.

Nach einem kurzen geschichtlichen Abriss werden die hydrologischen Verhältnisse des Kernlandes des Reiches Kusch untersucht.

Das Gebiet zerfällt in zwei Regionen, deren Grenze etwa auf der Höhe des 5. Kataraktes liegt. Nördlich davon beträgt die jährliche Niederschlagshöhe weniger als 30 mm, so dass sich hier vollaride Wüsten ausbreiten. Südlich davon liegt die semiaride Wüste; die jährliche Niederschlagshöhe beträgt zwischen 30 und 200 mm. In ältester Zeit dehnte sich Kusch nicht wesentlich über den 4. Katarakt hin aus, der Mensch war ganz auf den Fluss oder einen Brunnen angewiesen. Bei Kawa wurde möglicherweise eine Bassinbewässerung angewendet, im Bereich des 2. Kataraktes scheint man den Versuch gemacht zu haben, den Nil mit Hilfe eines Felsendammes aufzustauen. Das meroitische Reich hatte von Ägypten auch die Techniken zur Nutzung des Wassers übernommen; in der Butana entwickelten sich jedoch Niederlassungen weitab von Flüssen, die mit Hilfe der Hafir-Technik Wasserspeicher schufen, deren Anlagen erklärt werden. Eine entscheidende Verbesserung in der Wasserversorgung des Landes wurde durch die Übernahme der Saqiya erreicht. *Inge Hofmann*

791053 KROMER, K., Austrian Excavations in the District of Sayala Lower Nubia, U.A.R. Report of the Third Campaign 1963/4, *ASAE* 63 (1979), 131-136, with 33 pl. including 1 map, 1 cross-section and 1 plan.

The larger part of this report deals with the Coptic settlement.

791054 KRONENBERG, Andreas, Survival of Nubian Traditions, *in*: *Africa in Antiquity*, 173-176.

Als heute noch existierendes Kulturgut in Nubien, das aus der Vergangenheit stammt, wird aufgezählt: das Tragen des Toten zum Grab auf einem *angareb*, das Bedecken des Grabes mit tausend Steinen, die Bedeutung des Nil und die Reinigung mit Nilwasser, der koptische Kalender, der die bäuerliche Tätigkeit reguliert, Wasserrad und *shaduf*, Wörter wie *angeles* für Engel und *kirage* für Sonntag, die Bedeutung Mariens (was aber durchaus islamisch sein kann!), Verehrung von antiken Stätten, die muslimisch interpretiert werden, nubische Verwandtschaftsterminologie, die matrilineare Züge enthalt. *Inge Hofmann*

791055 KRZYŻANIAK, Lech, Kadero (fourth-sixth season, 1975-1976), *Études et Travaux* 11 (1979), 245-252, with 6 fig., ill. and plans.

Die neolithischen Überreste in Kadero umfassen eine Siedlung und einen Begräbnisplatz. Das Fundmaterial von gezähmten Tieren war erstaunlich gross und umfasste Skelettreste von Rindern (Bos primigenius f. taurus), Schafe und Ziegen (Ovis sp., Capra sp.), und Hunden (Canis sp.). Die meisten Jagdtiere waren Antilopen, Gazellen und Fleischfresser (z.B. Acinonyx jubatus). Die beiden Radiokarbon-Daten weisen auf 4100 v.Chr. und 3800 v.Chr. Damit scheint Kadero später anzusetzen zu sein als Esh Shaheinab. Die Bevölkerung scheint autochthon gewesen zu sein, die gezähmten

Tiere müssen von auswärts eingeführt worden sein, möglicherweise aus der Sahara. Ausserdem wurden 15 Gräber aus der meroitischen Epoche gefunden. An Grabbeigaben fanden sich u.a. ein Daumenschutzring aus Stein und eine Pfeilspitze aus Eisen. Ein Grab gehört anscheinend der christlichen Periode an. Es fanden sich Überreste der Holzbedachung der Grabkammer. *Inge Hofmann*

791056 KRZYZANIAK, Lech, Polish Excavations at Kadero, *Nyame Akuma*, Montreal No. 15 (1979), 67-69.

Es wurden u.a. vier neue Gräber (Nr. 44-47) ausgegraben, die wahrscheinlich in die neolithische Epoche gehören. Die stark zusammengezogenen Skelette von Menschen unterschiedlichen Alters waren nur sehr schlecht erhalten. Ein grosser Anhänger aus poliertem Rhyolit wurde zusammen mit zwei Skeletten gefunden. Für die Siedlung Kadero wurde festgestellt, dass der mittlere Teil offensichtlich nicht besiedelt war, sondern als eine Art Kraal für die Viehherden galt, in dem die Tiere während der Regenzeit gehalten wurden. Das dritte Radiocarbon-Datum für die neolithische Siedlung von Kadero ist 5280 ± 90 vor der gegenwärtigen Zeit.
Inge Hofmann

791057 LECLANT, Jean, An Introduction to the Civilization of Nubia: From the Earliest Times to the New Kingdom, *in*: *Africa in Antiquity*, 15-18.

Abriss der nubischen Geschichte vom Paläolithikum über die neolithischen Kulturen, A-, C- und Kerma-Kulturen mit den jeweiligen Beziehungen zu Ägypten bis hin zum Ende des Neuen Reiches mit der Aufgrabe der sudanischen Kolonie, die dann ihrerseits als 25. Dynastie Ägypten erobern kann. *Inge Hofmann*

791058 LECLANT, Jean, Troisième symposium de la Société des Études Nubiennes, Cambridge, 3-8 Juillet 1978, *Orientalia* 48 (1979), 529-530.

Short note on the symposium mentioned in the title, listing the papers.

791059 el MAHI, A. Tigani, The Influence of Man on the Ecosystem. Case study, El Kadero and El Zakyab sites, Central Sudan, *Nyame Akuma*, Calgary No. 14 (May 1979), 60-62.

Die Einführung von Viehzucht in El Kadero und El Zakyab veränderte das bisherige Wirtschaftssystem, das Verhältnis vom Mensch zu Tier wurde ein anderes. Das Rind wurde vom Menschen abhängig, der die Raubtiere abwehren (es fanden sich zahlreiche Überreste von Fleischfressern) und für die Trockenperiode für genügend Wasser sorgen musste. *Inge Hofmann*

791060 el MAHI, A. Tigani, Preliminary analyses of the osteological remains from 4 sq m, excavated from Shaheinab site, *Nyame Akuma*, Montreal No. 15 (1979), 57-59, with 1 map.

An Landtieren wurde identifiziert: *Bos* sp., *Equus* sp., *Damaliscus Korrigum* tiang., *Gazella* sp., *Python* sp., *Varnus* sp., *Limicolaria flammata*. An Wassertieren wurden identifiziert: *Clarias* sp., *Lates niloticus*, *Pila ovata werrni*, *Etheria elliptica*.
Inge Hofmann

791061 MARTIN, Debra R. and George J. ARMELAGOS, Morphometrics of Compact Bone: An Example from Sudanese Nubia, *American Journal of Physical Anthropology*, Philadelphia 51 (July, August, September, November 1979), 571-577, with 7 ill. and fig. and an abstract on p. 571.

Morphometric analysis of compact femoral tissue, applied to an X-group population of 74 adults from Sudanese Nubia, has shed some light on the problem of cortical bone loss (osteoporosis).

791062 MICHAŁOWSKI, Kazimierz, Faras, Seventeen Years after the Discovery, *in*: *Africa in Antiquity*, 31-39, with 11 ill. on 8 pl.

Die Ausgrabungen von Faras förderten nicht nur Wandmalereien und Inschriften zutage, die grossen historischen Wert für die christliche Epoche besitzen, sondern auch Reliefs und Inschriften aus der 18. und 19. Dynastie, Reliefs aus spätmeroitischer oder der sogenannten X-Epoche sowie Keramik aus den verschiedensten Zeiten. Die wissenschaftliche Auswertung der Funde seit 1964 wird dargelegt. Während der ersten Ausstellung der Funde von Faras in Essen und dem damit verbundenen Symposion ergab sich die Notwendigkeit, die Probleme der Geschichte, Archäologie, Sprache, Kunst und der materiellen Kultur Nubiens in eine eigene wissenschaftliche Disziplin zu integrieren, nämlich der Nubiologie. Das Warschauer Zentrum beschäftigt sich mit den historischen und topographischen Problemen, gibt die entdecken Texte heraus und spezialisierte sich auf die Ikonographie.
Inge Hofmann

791063 MILLET, Nicholas B., [Kommentar], *in*: *Beiträge zur meroitischen Grammatik*, 113-114.

Kommentar zu unserer Nr. 791043: es wird das Problem der mehrfachen Bedeutung des Morphems *-li* aufgegriffen. Von der Bedeutung der Titel her kommt er zu dem Ergebnis, dass es sich dabei mit gewissen Einschränkungen doch um einen "bestimmten Artikel" handelt. Die Analyse der Benediktionsverben erscheint überzeugend.
Inge Hofmann

791064 MÜLLER, C. Detlef G., IV. Nubiologisches Colloquium in Cambridge, *Oriens Antiquus* 63 (1979), 194-197.

Short report on the 4th Nubiological Colloquium held at Cambridge in 1978.

791065 NEGM-EL-DIN, Mohammed Sherif, The Future of Sudanese Archaeology, in: *Africa in Antiquity*, 23-29.

Der Sudan ist ein wichtiges Gebiet zur Erforschung der Archäologie und Geschichte von Schwarzafrika. Nach einem Überblick über die bisherige Geschichte der archäologischen Forschungen im Sudan wird deren Zukunft behandelt und zur Zusammenarbeit aufgerufen. Insgesamt 22 ungelöste Probleme werden aufgezeigt, zu deren Lösung das Sudan Directorate General of Antiquities and National Museums, die Universität von Khartum und ausländische archäologische Institutionen beitragen können. *Inge Hofmann*

791066 ONASCH, Christian, Zum Löwenkult von Meroe, OLZ 74 (1979), 101-105.

Review of our number 75819.

791067 PRIESE, Karl-Heinz, [Kommentar], in: *Beiträge zur meroitischen Grammatik*, 115-134.

Kommentar zu unserer Nr. 791043: es wird Stellung genommen 1. zum Kernsatz. In den Deskriptionssätzen ist das "Subjekt" dem Inhalt nach der Tote, das Nomen (N) ist das "Prädikat", das "grammatische Subjekt", die Bezeichnung für den Toten im Satz selbst, muss in einem Kernsatz N-lo dann -lo sein. Für das fakultative -wi wäre eine Kopulafunktion wahrscheinlich. 2. zur Nominalgruppe. Es wird die Funktion des -li erörtert und seine Bedeutung als Determinationssuffix unterstrichen. 3. zur Verbalgruppe im Kernsatz N-l + V-lo. Die Frage bleibt jedoch offen, ob und wie die Überführung einer Verbalgruppe in den Status eines Nomens grammatikalisiert wird - möglicherweise, indem sie wie ein Nomen behandelt wird. *Inge Hofmann*

791068 PROMIŃSKA, Elżbieta, Human Skeletal Remains from the Church of the Granite Columns and the Cruciform Church at Old Dongola (Sudan), *Études et Travaux* 11 (1979), 152-178, with 1 table.

Die untersuchten 18 Gräber stammen aus der Zeit vom Ende des 7. bis zum 12. Jahrhundert. Die Lage der Gräber wird angegeben und das vorhandene Skelettmaterial ausführlich beschrieben. In den 9 Gräbern, die aus der Kirche der Granitsäulen stammen, konnten 5 Männer, 2 Frauen und 4 Kinder identifiziert werden, in den 9 Gräbern der Kreuzförmigen Kirche wurden 6 männliche und 4 weibliche Individuen festgestellt. Das Durchschnittsalter der Männer war 53, das der Frauen 44. Damit wird aber nur eine Sterblichkeitsrate für die hochgestellte soziale Schicht gewonnen, die in der Kirche bestattet wurde, nicht für die gewöhnliche Bevölkerung. Als Durchschnittsgrösse wurde fur 8 Männer 173.8 cm, für 5 Frauen 165.4 cm geschätzt. Die häufigste Krankheit scheint Arthrose gewesen zu sein. Die Anwesenheit von Frauen und Kinder zeigt, dass nicht nur kirchliche Würdenträger und Priester in der Kirche begraben wurden. Die Indi-

viduen, die in den Kirchen von Dongola bestattet waren, gehörten zu der einheimischen nubischen Bevölkerung, charakterisiert durch ihre langen Schädel, die übrigens häufig Verletzungen aufwiesen, und ihre Grösse.
Inge Hofmann

791069 RUŽIČKA, Rudolf, Neue Philologie durch Strukturanalyse, *in*: *Beiträge zur meroitischen Grammatik*, 135-138.

Kommentar zu unserer Nr. 791043: Verfasser konstatiert mit Bewunderung, dass es gelungen ist, moderne methodologische und theoretische Einsichten und Verfahren für die Lösung eines ungewöhnlich schwierigen "philologischen" Problems, der Dechiffrierung und systematischen grammatischen Beschreibung einer sehr wenig bekannten und fragmentarisch "bezeugten" Sprache wie das Meroitische, in einer ganz neuen Weise nutzbar zu machen
Inge Hofmann

791070 SÄVE-SÖDERBERGH, Torgny, The Scandinavian Joint Expedition to Sudanese Nubia. A.J.C. Jacobsen Memorial Lecture, København, Munksgaard, 1979 (15 x 24 cm; 53 p., 1 map, 2 fig., 18 ill.) = Det Kongelige Danske Videnskabernes Selskap. Historiskfilosofiske Meddedelser 49:3; rev. *GM* Heft 38 (1980), 89-90 (Heike Sternberg); *JSSEA* 10 (1979-1980), 173-174 (A.J. Mills).
Pr. DK 50

The paper on the Scandinavian Joint Expedition to Sudanese Nubia begins with a description of the International Nubia Campaign and its background, followed by an explanation of the organisation of the SJE, its aims and methods, the concession area (on the East bank of the Nile, from the Egyptian border to Gamai on the Second Cataract), the quantitive results, and the publications. The main part of the study (p. 20-51) is devoted to a summary of the results. The author follows a chronological order, apart from the first section on rock drawings from various periods, and deals successively with preceramic sites, the Late Neolithic, the A- and C-groups and the N.K., the Late Nubian Sequence (from the T.I.P. to Christian times). For each period the significant material discovered by the SJE and the conclusions to which it leads are discussed: for instance, the find of an imitation Myc. IIIc stirrup vase of faience in a C-group burial, which suggests that the C-group lived till into the Ramesside Period (p. 84).
On p. 52-53 concluding remarks about the interdisciplinary and international cooperation in the Nubia Campaign.   *J.J.J.*

791071 SCHENKEL, Wolfgang, [Kommentar], *in*: *Beiträge zur meroitischen Grammatik*, 139-144.

Kommentar zu unserer Nr. 791043. Der Verfasser nimmt zu folgenden Problemen Stellung: die Strategie zur Erschliessung des Meroitischen, die aktuelle Materialbasis, der "Artikel" -*li* (es ist möglich, von der funktionellen Einheit aller drei Elemente -*li* auszugehen), die Funktion des Infixes -*qe*-.   *Inge Hofmann*

791072 STROUHAL, E., Contribution to the Archaeology and Anthropology of Egyptian Nubia in IVth-VIth Centuries A.D., *in*: *Acts 1st ICE*, 609-613.

Report on the excavation of two X-group (Ballana Culture) cemeteries at Kalabsha and Wadi Qitna.

791073 STROUHAL, Evžen, Kasr Ibrim - poslední svědek civilizace v Násirově jezeru, *Nový Orient*, Praha 34, No. 8 (1979), 243-245.

"Kasr Ibrim - der letzte Zeuge der Zivilisation im Nasser-See." Verfasser legt die Ergebnisse der neuesten archäologischen Forschungen in Kasr Ibrim dar.   B. Vachala

791074 STROUHAL, Evžen, Staroveká Núbie vypovídá, *Věda a život*, Brno 24 (1979), 93-96.

"Altnubien sagt aus." Verfasser skizziert die Problematik Altnubiens im Lichte neuer Forschungen.   B. Vachala

791075 STROUHAL, Evzen, Symposium o staroveké Núbii v Cambridge, *Zprávy Československé společnosti orientalistické při ČSAV*, Praha 16, No. 2 (1979), 62-68.

Ausführlicher Bericht über das im Julii 1978 in Cambridge abgehaltene Symposion über Altnubien.

791076 STROUHAL, E. and J. JUNGWIRTH, Palaeogenetics of the Late Roman - Early Byzantine Cemeteries at Sayala, Egyptian Nubia, *Journal of Human Evolution*, London - New York - San Francisco 8 (1979), 699-703, with 1 fig.

The isolated position as regards physical features of the population of the burial complexes CI-III at Sayala agrees with the hypothesis that it would represent the Blemmyes, who originated from the Eastern Desert.

791077 THURMAN, Christa C. Mayer and Bruce WILLIAMS, Ancient Textiles from Nubia. Meroitic, X-Group, and Christian Fabrics from Ballana and Qustul. An Exhibition Organized by the Art Institute of Chicago. The University of Chicago Oriental Institute Nubian Expedition Excavations between Abu Simbel and the Sudan Frontier, Keith C. Seele, Director, The Art Institute of Chicago, May 26 - August 5, 1979, [Chicago, The Art Institute of Chicago and the University of Chicago, 1979] (23.2 x 31.8 cm; 148 p., colour frontispiece, 8 colour ill., 20 + 184 ill., 3 tables, 2 maps, 7 fig.).

The book is the catalogue of an exhibition held from May 26 - August 5, 1979, organised by the Art Institute of Chicago. The textiles shown were found between 1962 and 1964 by the Oriental Institute Nubian Expedition at Ballana and Qustul, directed by

the late K.C. Seele, and covering the Meroitic, X-group and
Christian periods. A general introduction about this expedition
is written by Mrs. Seele followed by a chronological table with
notes by Bruce Williams, who also wrote the next chapters. The
first treats the geographical, historical and archaeological
background of ancient Nubia and Northern Sudan (maps). The
second deals with the circumstances of discovery (burial types).
The textiles are described and analysed by Christa C.M. Thurman:
materials, colours, procedures (spinning, weaving), decoration,
(original) uses of textiles and a conclusion. This is followed
by fibre and dye analyses (micro-photos), criteria for dating
and explanatory notes to the catalogue. The catalogue consists
of 188 items, fully illustrated by black-and-white photographs.
The description of each item gives the attribution to a cultural
group, contents of the tomb, and details about the textile itself: material, structure, decoration, dimensions and fibre/dye
analyses (if available). The book is concluded by a list of
discarded textiles. No index.   R. van Walsem

791078 TÖRÖK, László, The Art of the Ballana Culture and its Relation
to Late Antique Art, in: *Africa in Antiquity*, 85-100.

Es wird der Frage nachgegangen, inwieweit die Ballana-Kunst
(etwa von 340-570 n.Chr.) als Spiegel für die Entwicklung der
spätantiken Kunst überhaupt dienen kann. Nach einer Untersuchung der Beziehungen zwischen der spätmeroitischen und gräko-
römischen Kunst werden die architektonischen Überreste besprochen, und es wird festgestellt, dass Ballana keine Provinz
spätantiker Kunst ist. Die Untersuchung der Schmuckstücke,
der Metallwaren und der Keramik der Ballana-Kultur zeitigte als
Ergebnis, dass die Ballana-Kunst offensichtlich bewusst aus-
wählte und einfache Formen bevorzugte.   *Inge Hofmann*

791079 TÖRÖK, L., Economic Offices and Officials in Meroitic Nubia (A
Study in Territorial Administration of the Late Meroitic
Kingdom), Budapest, 1979 (17 x 24 cm; XVIII + 246 p., 14 maps)
= Studia Aegyptiaca, 5 = Études Publiées par les Chaires d'His-
toire Ancienne de l'Université Loránd Eötvös de Budapest 26.

Der Verfasser legt im vorliegenden Band eine umfangreiche Studie
zum Thema der Verwaltung und Wirtschaft vor allem des nördlichen
Teiles des meroitischen Reiches vor. Nachdem im Kapitel A die
Beamten aus demotischen und meroitischen Texten vorgestellt
wurden, die wahrscheinlich mit der Wirtschaftsorganisation zu
tun hatten, werden im Kapitel B Ansichten hinsichtlich der
Struktur der meroitischen Wirtschaft und Verwaltung geäussert.
Im Kapitel C wird die Frage nach den Nomoi und ihren Haupt-
städten in der Zeit vom 7. vorchristlichen bis 5. nachchristlichen Jahrhundert gestellt. Das Kapitel D befasst sich ausführlich mit der Geschichte des Dodekaschoinos zwischen
29 v.Chr. und 298 n.Chr., wobei für den Zeitraum zwischen 240/1
und 248/9 n.Chr. eine meroitische Herrschaft über das Gebiet

postuliert wird. Im Kapitel E werden Bemerkungen zur Regierung der meroitischen Vizekönige zwischen dem 1. und 4. Jahrhundert n.Chr. gemacht, die in einem Appendix (p. 179 f.) zusammengestellt werden. Kapitel F behandelt die Herrschaftsform zwischen dem 2. und 3. Katarakt. Im Kapitel G werden die Quellen, die uns hinsichtlich von Wirtschaft und Verwaltung des meroitischen Kernlandes vorliegen, vorgestellt und ausgewertet. Das Schlusskapitel H macht noch einmal deutlich, dass es sich beim meroitischen Reich um drei Teile handelt, deren wirtschaftlicher Hintergrund, sozialer Aufbau und geschichtlicher Verlauf sehr unterschiedlich sind. Detaillierte Indices schliessen die Arbeit ab.
Inge Hofmann

791080 TRIGGER, Bruce G., General Evaluation, *in*: *Beiträge zur meroitischen Grammatik*, 145-154.

Kommentar zu unserer Nr. 791043. Es wird die Warnung unterstrichen, nicht jedes Phonem als wirkliches oder mögliches Morphem zu betrachten. Zum Problem der Methoden bei der grammatischen Analyse (philologisch, komparativ, strukturanalytisch) wird betont, dass die Semantik, soweit erkennbar, herangezogen werden muss. Als Quellen für semantische Informationen werden bilingue Texte, Lehnwörter und vergleichbare Wörter aus verwandten Sprachen und der Kontext genannt. Strukturanalyse allein reicht nicht aus, selbst die bekannten Totentexte wirklich lesen zu können.
Inge Hofmann

791081 VAN GERVEN, Dennis P., The 1979 Kentucky-Colorado Expedition to Kulubnarti, Democratic Republic of the Sudan: The Implications for Physical Anthropology, *Nyame Akuma*, Montreal No. 15 (1979), 53-55.

Von den 400 Individuen aus der christlichen Epoche, die von zwei Friedhöfen von Kulubnarti stammen, sind z.T. die Haut, die Haare und innere Organe erhalten. Die Untersuchungen ergaben, dass Fälle von Arthritis häufig waren. Eine Anzahl von Fragen stellen sich den physischen Anthropologen, die sie in der Zukunft beantworten zu können hoffen.
Inge Hofmann

791082 VERCOUTTER, Jean, La tombe meroitique SA.S.2.T.1 (1) de Sai, *CRIPEL* 5 [1979], 210-236, with 12 fig., ill., maps and plans.

Die 17 Gräber lassen sich in 4 verschiedene Typen einteilen, die beschrieben werden. Von den aufgefundenen meroitischen Gräbern wird der Inhalt von T.1 vorgestellt: das Grabmobiliar war am Kopfende des Sarges niedergelegt worden. Die Schmucksachen waren auf dem Körper gelassen worden. Zu den Grabbeigaben gehören u.a. Glaswaren, ein Armband (?) aus Widderköpfen, ein Dreifuss aus Bronze und kleine Plaketten aus Knochen oder Elfenbein, die jedoch von der Termiten stark zerstört wurden. Aufgrund der importierten Glasgefässe kann das Grab SA.S.2.T.1 in die Zeit zwischen 250 und 350 n.Chr. datiert werden. Die anderen Beigaben lassen an eine Zeit um 200 n.Chr. denken.
Inge Hofmann

791083 VILA, André, La prospection archéologique de la Vallée du Nil, au Sud de la Cataracte de Dal (Nubie Soudanaise). Fascicule 11. Récapitulations et conclusions. Appendices, Paris, Centre National de la Recherche Scientifique, 1979 (21 x 27 cm; 135 p., 98 fig., ill. and maps, 2 maps = frontispiece, 5 tables); at head of title: Section française de recherches archéologiques/ Sudan Antiquities Service Khartoum National Museum.

The fascicule presents the recapitulation and conclusions concerning the previous fascicles, although there will appear still three more, which are devoted to the necropolis of Abri-Missiminia.
First the author tabulates the geographical spreading of the sites in their respective districts and then the sites after their cultural sequence ranging from the Palaeolithic to the post-Christian Period. The largest part of the recapitulation is devoted to a synthesis of the spreading of the subsequent cultural periods over the sites.
In the conclusion the author evaluates the results, the effectiveness and the procedure of this prospection survey, as well as the perspectives. After a map containing all toponyms, a list mentioning the find and accession nos of the objects which entered the National Museum in Khartum and one of corrigenda et addenda follows first an appendix devoted to a description of the ancient Islamic sites, and then one on the archaeological prospection of an alluvial plain on the right bank of the river Rahad.

791084 WENDORF, Fred, Romuald SCHILD and Herbert HAAS, A New Radiocarbon Chronology for Prehistoric Sites in Nubia, *Journal of Field Archaeology*, Boston 6 (1979), 219-223, with 1 table.

Several new dates indicate the need for a significant revision of the original chronology of the sequence of prehistoric cultural developments in Nubia, as yet considered as one of the best-dated series in North Africa.

791085 WENIG, Steffen, Meroitic Painted Ceramics, *in*: *Africa in Antiquity*, 129-134, with 16 ill. on 8 pl.

Ausgehend von der Feststellung, dass mehrere meroitische Gefässe eine ähnliche Darstellung haben, geht der Verfasser den Fragen nach, ob an bestimmten Keramikzentren Malerschulen existierten und ob es möglich ist, einzelne Maler voneinander zu unterscheiden. Beide Fragen liessen sich positiv beantworten. In der Dekoration der meroitischen Gefässe bestehen Unterschiede zwischen dem südlichen und dem nördlichen Gebiet. Der Beginn der Gefässbemalung scheint im Süden gelegen zu haben und kann für das 3. vorchristliche Jahrhundert angenommen werden, während die Produktion im Norden mit der Besiedlung der Meroiten im 1. Jahrhundert v.Chr. beginnt.   *Inge Hofmann*

791086 WENIG, Steffen, Nochmals zu den Elefantengott-Darstellungen in der meroitischen Kunst, *in*: *Festschrift Elmar Edel*, 420-431, with 1 fig., and 11 ill. on 3 pl.

Besprochen wird die Statuette eines stehenden Mannes, die im Palast von Wad Ban Naqa gefunden wurde und die bisher mehrfach als Darstellung des indischen Elefantengottes Ganeśa interpretiert wurde. Der Verfasser hält die Statuette für ein unvollendet gebliebenes Kunstwerk, wodurch sich der "Rüssel" als Nase und Bart erklären lässt. Sie wird verglichen mit der gleichfalls unvollendeten Mykerinos-Statuette Nr. 28. Es wird vermutet, dass die Statuette ein Bild des Gottes Sebiumeker werden sollte. Das Graffito vom Tempel 300 in der Grossen Anlage von Musawwarat es Sufra wird zu Recht als Darstellung eines Pavians gedeutet.
Inge Hofmann

791087 YELLIN, Janice W., A Suggested Interpretation of the Relief Decoration in the Type B Chapels at Begrawiyah North, *in*: *Africa in Antiquity*, 157-164, with 9 fig.

Ausgehend von der Darstellung der Henu-Barke-Prozession des Sokar auf der Südwand der Kapellen des Typs B in Begarawiyah-Nord und der Überlegung, dass das Sokar-Fest vom Choiak-Fest übernommen worden war, kommt die Verfasserin zu dem Ergebnis, dass auch die übrigen Szenen der Kapellen aus dem Choiak-Fest interpretiert werden können.
Inge Hofmann

791088 ŽABKAR, L.V., Quousque tandem abutere, I.H., *GM* Heft 31 (1979), 79-84.

Kritik an den von Hofmann gegen unsere Nr. 75819 vorgebrachten Kritiken; vgl. auch unsere Nr. 76380 und 77362.
Inge Hofmann

INDEX OF AUTHORS

Abd er-Raziq, Mahmud 79201
Abdalla, Abdelgadir M. 79998; 791012
Abdel-Hamid, F. 79641; 79644
Abdel-Hamid Youssef, Ahmad 79200; 79263
Abitz, Friedrich 79659
Abou-Ghazi, Dia' 79506
el-Achirie, H. 79644
Adam Mohamed, Chehata 79641; 79643; 79645; 79648
Adams, William Y. 791014; 791015
Aharoni, Yohanan 79958
Ahmed, Soheir 79998
Aldred, Cyril 79435; 79575; 79576; 79786
Allam, S. 79882; 79883
Allen, J.P. 79165
Allen, Roger C. 791015; 791016
Almagro, M. 79533
Alpin, Pierre 79948
Altenmüller, Hartwig 79321
Aly, M. 79641
Amendt, G. 79366
Amiran, Ruth 79731
Anderson, R.D. 791015
Andreu, Guillemette 79202; 79909
Anfield, C. 791000
Anonymous 79001; 79002; 79026; 79027; 79034; 79035; 79083; 79577; 79578; 79579; 79660; 79959
Arensburg, B. 79560
Arkell, Anthony J. 791037
Armelagos, George J. 791061
Arnold, Dieter 79536; 79624; 79649; 791004
Arnold, Dorothea 79624
Asaad, Hany 79140
Asfour, M.A.M. 79537
Assmann, Jan 79322; 79823; 79824
Astour, Michael C. 79960
Aubert, Jacques-F. 79712
Aufrère, S. 79641
Avi-Yonah, Michael 79958

Badawy, Alexander 79507; 79650
Badger, Gerry 79008
Badie, A. 79642
Bakhry, Hassan S.K. 79538
Balboush, Motawi 79508
Baques, L. 79771
Bareš, Ladislav 79523
Barguet, Paul 79786

Barkóczi, L. 791013
Barta, Winfried 79203; 79323; 79425; 79426; 79436
Basch, Lucien 79940
Basta, Mounir 79084; 79509; 79510
Bauer, K.G. 79502
Becker-Colonna, A.L. 79713
von Beckerath, J. 79437
Bedini, Elsa 79364
Beinlich, Horst 79106; 79839
Beit-Arieh, I. 79560
Bell, Lanny 79065
Bellet, P. 79391
Bendig, William C. 79139
Benedum, Jost 79772
Bennett, M.V.L. 79949
Bens, Jacques 79141
Benson, G.G. 791000; 791001
Bergman, Jan 79046; 79825; 79826
Berger, Catherine 79732
Berlandini, Jocelyne 79427; 79787; 79900
Berlev, O.D. 79204; 79733
Beste, Irmtraut 79773; 79774
Betrò, Maria Carmela 79365
Bianchi, Robert S. 79139; 79734; 791017
Bierbrier, M.L. 79901
Bierwisch, Manfred 791018
Bietak, Manfred 79028; 79029; 79494; 79587; 791019
Bingen, Jean 79030; 79362; 79373; 79380; 79383; 79403; 79961
Bitrakova-Grozdanova, Vera 79107
Björkman, Gun 79031
Bleeker, C.J. 79836
Blumenthal, Elke 79003; 79032; 79850; 79851
Bogaert, R. 79884
Bogoslowsky, E.S. 79033; 79863; 79864; 79885
Böhlig, Alexander 79166
Bongrani Fanfoni, Luisa 79801
Bonhême, Marie-Ange 79438; 79625; 79628
Bonnard, P.-E. 79827
Bonneau, Danielle 79362; 79961
Bonnet, Charles 791020
Borghouts, Joris F. 79167; 79168; 79169; 79170
Bothmer, Bernard V. 79139; 79607; 791021

du Bourguet, Pierre   79257
Bourriau, J.   79034; 79580
Brack, A. and A.   79422
Brandière, Isabelle   79090
Brandl, B.   79560
Brashler, James   79405
Brauner, Siegmund   791022
Bresciani, Edda   79004; 79363; 79364; 79365; 79406; 79714; 79788
Briend, J.   79802; 79803; 79962
Brier, B.   79949
Brilliant, Richard   791023
Brinks, Jürgen   79651
Brissaud, Philippe   79735
Brodbeck, Andreas   79331; 79624
Brouqui, M.   791010
Browne, Gerald M.   79392; 79393
Brunner, Helmut   79171; 79267; 79687; 79715; 79831; 79833; 79929
Brunner-Traut, Emma   79268; 79688; 79689; 79828
Brunsch, Wolfgang   79366; 79394
Bryan, Betsy M.   79269; 79865
Bryce, Glendon E.   79411
Buitron, Diana   79582
Burkhardt, Adelheid   79032
Burleigh, R.   79561; 79950
Burney, Ethel W.   79097
Burnham, Harold B.   79759
Burri, Carla M.   79035; 79036; 79037
Burrini, Gabriele   79005
Burstein, Stanley M.   791024

Caminos, Ricardo   79058
Canby, Jean Vorys   79582
Cardon, Patrick D.   79661
Castiglione, L.   791013
Castioni, Christiane   79583
Cazelles, H.   79151; 79412; 79460
Čejka, Jiří   79495
de Cenival, Françoise   79205
Černý, J.   79644
Červiček, Pavel   79616
Chace, Arnold Buffum   79423
Chadefaud, Catherine   79108
Chappaz, Jean-Luc   79270
Charvát, Petr   79523
Cherif, A.   79641
Chetverukhin, A.S.   79172
Chevrier, Henri   79628
Christophe, Louis A.   79642
Čihar, J.   791008
Clayton, Peter   79006
Clément, Catherine   79109
Clère, Jacques Jean   79206; 79902
Clère, P.   79642
Close, Angela E.   79737; 79899
Clutton-Brock, J.   79561; 79950

Cody, Aelred   79271
Coetzee, J.A.   79557
Cohen, Rudolph   79461
Connolly, R.C.   79998
Conrad, D.   79776
de Contenson, H.   79910
Coquin, René-Georges   79395
Corteggiani, Jean-Pierre   79234; 79584
Costa, Alvimar   79272
Coulson, William D.E.   79511
Couroyer, B.   79207
Cross, Frank Moore   79152; 79462; 79489; 79491
Crouwel J.H.   79752; 79942
Crowfoot-Payne, J.   79497
Crowfoot, Elisabeth   791015
Cruz-Uribe, Eugene   79173; 79367; 79368
Curry, A.   791000; 791001
Curto, Silvio   79007; 79496

Dabrowska-Smektała, E.   79208
Daneri de Rodrigo, Alicia   79716
Daumas, François   79038; 79039; 79209   79775; 79829; 79963
Davey, C.J.   79941
David, A. Rosalie   79738; 791000; 791001
Davis, Whitney M.   79085; 79110; 79911
Debono, Fernand   79951
Decker, Wolfgang   79086; 79927; 79928
Delia, Robert D.   79428
Dembska, A.   79396
Derchain, Philippe   79218; 79830
Derchain-Urtel, Maria-Theresia   79804
Dérobert, Dominique   79583
Deroy, Louis   79964
Desanges, Jehan   791026
Desdames, Marcel   79948
Desroches-Noblecourt, Christiane   79546; 79585; 79641; 79642; 79643; 79645; 79648; 79662; 79717; 79786
Devaney, Sally G.   79139
Devauchelle, Didier   79210; 79362; 79369
Dewachter, Michel   79142; 79739; 79789
Dion, Paul-E.   79211
Dirkse, Peter A.   79405
Dixon, D.M.   79561; 791001
Dobrovits, A.   79111; 79143
Doetsch-Amberger, Ellen   79663
Doležal, Antonius   79939
Dolzani, C.   79718

Donadoni, Sergio   79539; 79642;
    79644; 791025
Donadoni Roveri, Anna Maria   79586
Dondelinger, Edmund   79339
Doresse, Marianne   79840
Doret, Eric   79174; 79175
Dothan, Moshe   79462; 79776
Dothan, Trude   79560
Drappier, D.   79557
Draye, Henri   79964
Dreisine, M.   79040
Drenkhahn, Rosemarie   79095
Drobniewicz, Barbara   79742
Dunand, Françoise   79112
van Dijk, Jac.   79273; 79719
Dyson, Stephen L.   79990
Dzierżykray-Rogalski, Tadeusz,
    79991; 79992; 79993

Eaton-Krauss, M.   79740
Edel, Elmar   79274; 79275; 79502;
    79540; 79642; 79965
Edwards, I.E.S.   79952
Eggebrecht, Arne   79041; 79612
Eiwanger, Jozef   79512
Elanskaya, A. I.   79176; 79177
Elhitta, Mohammed A.   79608
Emery†, Walter B.   79561
Endesfelder, E.   79886; 79887
Engel, Helmut   79009; 79276
Ertman, E.L.   79042
Evans, Robert K.   79594
Evrard-Derriks, Claire   79720
Eyre, C.J.   79347

Fage, J.D.   79459; 79463
Falke, J.H.M.   79994
Farag, Sami   79691
Farid, Adel   79691; 79692; 79693
Farid, Shafik   79935
Fathy, M.   79642
Fattovich, R.   79866
Faulkner, R.O.   79178; 79324
Fawcett, R.A.   791000
Fazly, Q.   79502
Fazzini, Richard   79139
Fecht, Gerhard   79275; 79277
de Fenoyl, R.   79948
Fernea, Robert A.   791027
Fiala, Vladimír   79523
Finegan, Jack   79144
Finkenstaedt, Elisabeth   79721
Fischer, Henry George   79087; 79153;
    79235
Fleming S.J.   79497
Fletcher, A.   791000; 791001
Fonquernie, B.   79643
Foster, John L.   79325
Fouad,   79642

Frandsen, Paul   79464
French, P.G.   791015
Froidefond, Claude   79113
Frost, Honor   79741
Fuscaldo, Perla   79588; 79589

Gaballa, G.A.   79236; 79237; 79238
Gafurov, B.G.   79010
Gale, N.H.   79503
Gamer-Wallert, Ingrid   79831
Garcia Pelayo M.   79867
Garner, A.   791000; 791001
Gartkiewicz, P.M.   791015
Gascou, Jean   79398; 79562
Gaskins, Leanna   79179
Gaudibert, Pierre   79114
George, Beate   79011; 79326
Georgiou, Hara   79465
Germer, Renate   79212
Germond, Philippe   79327; 79852
Geus, Francis   791028; 791029;
    791030
Ghali, Mirrit Boutros   79404
Ghattas, F.   79644
el Ghawaby, M.   79998
Giacardi, Livia   79933
Giammarusti, Antonio   79590
Giddy, Lisa L.   79563; 79564; 79565
Gilbert, M.   79412; 79827; 79918
Gillam, Robyn A.   79868
Ginter, Bolesław   79541; 79742
Gitton, Michel   79348; 79628; 79841
Giveon, Raphael   79966
Glass, Jonathan   79731
Godwin, Joscelyn   79115
Gödecken, K.B.   79498
Goedicke, Hans   79213; 79278; 79483;
    79888
Goff, Beatrice L.   79805
Gohary, J.O.   79971
Gohary, S.G.   79239
Goldstein, Sidney M.   79592; 79743
Goodman, Steven M.   79953
Görg, Manfred   79043; 79214; 79215;
    79216; 79217; 79413; 79466; 79467;
    79468; 79859; 79967; 79968; 79969;
    79970
Gorenc, Marcel   79593
Gourlay, Yvon J.-L.   79240; 79806
Gout-Minault, Anne   79722
Goyon, Jean-Claude   79632; 79643
Goyon, Georges   79972
Graefe, Erhart   79044; 79180; 79218;
    79241; 79439; 79664; 79842; 79903
Gratien, Brigitte   791031
Green, Alberto R.   79469
Green, Michael A.   79181; 79219;
    79279
Grenier, Jean-Claude   79088; 79973

Grieshammer, Reinhard 79832
Griffiths, J. Gwyn 79665; 79807
Grilletto, R.R. 79995; 79996
Grimal, N.-C. 79563; 79564; 79565
Grimm, Alfred 79099; 79154; 79328; 79808
Grossman, Cissy 79139
Grossmann, Peter 79543; 79562
Grunert, Stefan 79370; 79889
Grzybek, Erhard 79974
Grzymski, Krzystof 791032
Guglielmi, Waltraud 79809; 79929; 79930
Guidotti, Cristina 79242
Gundlach, Rolf 79280; 79281
Gutbub, Adolphe 79810
Gutvirth, Jaroslav 79939
Guzman, Diane 79139
Gijsselings, G. 79557

Haag, Herbert 79833
Haaland, Randi 791033; 791034
Haas, Herbert 79899; 791084
Habachi, Labib 79012; 79045; 79243; 79542; 79790; 79904
el-Hadidi, Nadil 79899
Haekal, Fayza Mohammed Hussein 79329
Haeny, Gerhard 79499
Hainsworth, M.E. 791035
Hajnóczi, Gy. 791013
Hakem, Ahmed M. Ali 791036
el-Halim, N.M.A. 79513
Hall, Rosalind M. 79750
Hamon, Paul 79013
Handoussa, Tohfa 79843; 79890
Hanzák, J. 791008
Hari, Robert 79116; 79440; 79583; 79791
Harris, James E. 79935; 79997
Harrison, Margaret 79514
Harrison, R.G. 79998
Hartmann, B. 79117
Hassan, Ali 79220; 79500
Hassanein, F. 79643; 79645
Hawwass, Zaki A. 79515
Hedrick, Charles W. 79405
Heerma van Voss, M. 79014; 79046; 79844
Heflik, Wiesław 79742
Helck, Wolfgang 79095; 79221; 79429; 79912; 79913
Hellbing, Lennard 79470
Hemingway, S.R. 791000; 791001
Hennessy, John Basil 79744
Herrmann, Joachim 791039; 791040
Hesse, Brian 79594
Hinkel, Friedrich W. 791037; 791038; 791039; 791040; 791041; 791042

Hintze, Fritz 79047; 79264; 791043; 791044; 791045
Hintze, Ursula 791046
Hodge, K.C. 791000
Hodjash, S.I. 79048; 79733; 79777; 79778
Hölbl, Günther 79779; 79914; 79915
Hofmann, Inge 79916; 791047; 791048; 791049; 791050
Hoffmann, Michael A. 79869
Hoffmann-Axthelm, Walter 79934
Holm-Rasmussen, Torben 79845
Holthoer, R. 79049
Honko, Lauri 79046
Hood, Sinclair 79792
Hope, Colin A. 79745
Horn, Siegfried H. 79780
Hornung, Erik 79282; 79330; 79331; 79441
Hostens-Deleu, Ria 79746
Houlihan, Patrick F. 79953
Huard, Paul 79616
Hughes, George R. 79368
Humbert, Jean 79118
Huntington, Richard 79837

Ibrahim, F. 79646
Ibrahim, Mohiy el-Din 79332; 79333; 79811; 79846
Insley, Christine 79666
Isaawi, Bahay 79899
Isherwood, I. 791000; 791001
Iskander, Zaky 79935
Iversen, Erik 79119; 79283; 79334

Jahn, Samia al Azharia 79120
Jakobielski, Stefan 791051
James, T.G.H. 79595; 79596; 79597
Jankuhn, D. 79335
Janssen, Jac. J. 79051; 79350; 79891
Jacquet-Gordon, Helen 79244
Jaritz, Horst 79371
Jarosh, Karl 79471
Jarvis, H. 791000; 791001
Jeffreys, D.G. 79528
Johnson, Janet H. 79065; 79574
Joly, Henri 79121
Jones, M. 79781
Jordan, R. 79892
Jungs, Friedrich 79182; 79183; 79184; 79812
Jungwirth, J. 791076

Kacmarek, Hieronim 79122
Kadish, Gerald E. 79336
Kaiser, Werner 79543
Kákosy, Ladislas 79111; 79143; 79747; 79834; 791013

Kamel, Ibrahim 79793
Kanawati, N. 79430
Kannicht, Richard 79687; 79831; 79833; 79929
Kaplan, Haya Ritter 79431
Kaprálová, Eva 79495
Karig, Joachim Selim 79091
Karkowski, Janusz 79544; 79694
Kasser, Rodolphe 79185; 79222
Katsnelson, I.S. 79015; 79016; 79145
Katzenstein, H. Jacob 79472
Keel, Othmar 79284
Kelley, A.L. 79893
Kemp, Barry J. 79058; 79545; 79695; 79782; 79870
Kendall, Timothy 79748
Khodjache, S.I. 79048; 79733; 79777; 79778
el-Khouli, 'Ali 79058
Kink, H.A. 79652
Kischkewitz, H. 79501
Kiss, Zsolt 79667
Kitchen, K.A. 79223; 79285; 79286; 79287; 79288; 79289; 79290; 79291; 79292; 79293; 79294; 79295; 79296; 79297; 79298; 79299; 79300; 79301; 79414; 79442; 79653; 79905; 79906
Kleinschroth, Adolf 791052
Klakowicz, Beatrix E. 79123
Klemm, Dietrich 79566
Klemm, Rosemarie 79052; 79566
Klengel, Horst 79053; 79917
Knauf, Ernst A. 79302
Kobusiewicz, Michael 79899
Koenig, Yvan 79337; 79351; 79352
Kołodko, Monika 79245
Kolos, Daniel 79140
Kolta, Kamal Sabri 79936
el-Kordy, Zeinab 79975
Korecký, Miroslav 79523
Korostovtsev, M.A. 79017; 79186
Kozloff, Arielle P. 79599; 79696
Kozłowski, Janusz K. 79541; 79742
Krauss, R. 79443
Kromer, K. 791053
Kronenberg, Andreas 791054
Kruchten, Jean-Marie 79155; 79303; 79871; 79976
Krug, Antje 79697
Krzyżaniak, Lech 79872; 791055; 791056
Kuchman, Lisa 79432
Kühne, Hartmut 79910
Kuentz, Ch. 79647
Kueny, Gabrielle 79018; 79600; 79601
Kuhlmann, K.P. 79626; 79627; 79813
Kurth, Dieter 79054; 79698; 79749
Kurz, M. 79246; 79247

Kuschke, Arnulf 79473
Kuspit, Donald B. 79124

Labib, Abdel Masih 79156
Labrousse, Audran 79732
Lacau, Pierre 79628
Laffont, Élisabeth 79304
Lafontaine, Guy 79399; 79400
Lalouette, Claire 79224
Lamourette, Christiane 79125
Lancel, Serge 791026
Landi, Sheila 79750
Landy, Victoria 79139
Lang, Bernhard 79918
Laroche, Emmanuel 79126
Larsen, Mogens Trolle 79464
Laskowska-Kusztal, Ewa 79847
Lattin, Floyd 79139; 79602
Lauer, Jean-Philippe 79516; 79654; 79655
Lauffray, J. 79546
Law, R.C.C. 79459
Layton, Bentley 79401
Leach, F.N. 791000; 791001
Leahy, Anthony 79157; 79158; 79444
Leblanc, Ch. 79641; 79643; 79644; 79646; 79648
Leclant, Jean 79019; 79020; 79055; 79056; 79092; 79093; 79126; 79127; 79338; 79632; 79732; 79517; 79786; 79977; 791057; 791058
Leek, F. Filce 791000; 791001
Lehmann, G.A. 79474
Leonard, Albert Jr. 79511
van Lerberghe, K. 79956
Lesko, Leonard H. 79094
Letellier, Bernadette 79629; 79630
Lhote, Henri 79616
Lichtheim Miriam 79372
Lilyquist, Christine 79433; 79751; 79603
Limme, Luc 79604
Lipińska, Jadwiga 79605; 79794
Lise, Giorgio 79606
Littauer, Mary A. 79752; 79942
Liverani, Mario 79187; 79475
Lizana Salafranca, Joaquín G. 79159
Llagostera, Esteban 79057; 79999
Llewellyn, Briony 79795
Lloyd, Alan B. 79058; 79519; 79943
Lobies, J.-P. 79090
Loring, John 79128
Lorton, David 79631; 79853
Loulloupis, M.C. 79919
Lowle, D.A. 79248
Lubetsky, Meir 79225
Lucchesi, Enzo 79402
Lunsingh-Scheurleer, R.A. 79753
Lurker, Manfred 79814

MacCoull, Leslie S.B.   79403; 79404
Macdonald, John   79226
McLeod, Deborah J.   79139
McNaught, Lewis   79668; 79754
MacRae, George W.   79405
Maehler, Herwig   79371
Maes, L.   79944
Magnusson, Magnus   79958
Maher, M.   79648
el Mahi, A. Tigani   791059; 791060
Majewska, Aleksandra   79059
Malaise, Michel   79873
Malamat, Abraham   79476
Málek, Jaromír   79097; 79249; 79723; 79724
Manniche, Lise   79699
Manning, James   79139
Manzák, V.   791008
Marciniak, Marek   79353
Martin, Debra R.   791061
Martin, Geoffrey T.   79058; 79518; 79519; 79700; 79783; 79874
Martin, Karl   79690
Martinák, Vladimír   79523
Masschelein-Kleiner, L.   79944
Masson, Olivier   79424
Matthiae, Gabriella Scandone   79755; 79756
Mayer-Kuckuk, T.   79502
Meeks, Dimitri   79250; 79354
Meier-Brügger, Michael   79096
Mellaart, James   79477
Meltzer, Edmund S.   79188; 79701
Menu, Bernadette   79355; 79373; 79374; 79375; 79875
Merrillees, R.S.   79894
Meshcherky, N.A.   79129
Messiha, Hishmat   79608
Metcalf, Peter   79837
de Meulenaere, H.   79647
Michałowski, Kazimierz   79060; 79669; 791062
Millard, A.   79561
Millet, Nicholas B.   791063
Mills, Anthony J.   79567; 79568; 79569; 79670; 791037
Miosi, F.T.   79305
Mokhtar, Gamal E.   79061; 79642; 79643
Mommsen, H.   79502
de Montebello, Philippe   79603; 79622
Montet, Pierre   79931
Morrison, J.S.   79945
Moss, Rosalind L.B.   79097
Moussa, Ahmed M.   79251
Mozel, Ilana   79757
Mrsich, Tycho   79146
Müller, C. Detlef G.   791064

Mueller, Dieter   79189
Müller, Hans-Wolfgang   79520; 79758; 79786
Müller, Ingeborg   79032
Müller, Maya   79671
Müller-Mehlis, R.   79521
Muller-Aubert, Jocelyne   79583
Munro, Eleanor   79609
Murdoch, William R.   79405
Murnane, William J.   79445
Mussies, Gerard   79130
Myśliwiec, Karol   79702; 79815; 79816; 79817

Na'aman, Nadav   79478; 79479; 79480
Nachtergael, Georges   79362; 79373; 79380; 79383; 79403; 79961
Nassar, Mahassen   79251
Neave, R.A.H.   791000; 791001; 791002
Needler, Winifred   79759
Negm-el-Din, Mohammed Sherif   791065
Nelson, M.   79642; 79643; 79645
Newton, G.W.A.   791000; 791001
Nibbi, Alessandra   79062; 79063; 79760; 79761; 79895; 79954; 79955
Nicholls, R.V.   79519
Nicholson, Eric D.   79946
Nims, Ch.   79642
Niwinski, Andrzej   79446
Noguera, Anthony   79920
von Nordheim, Eckhard   79415
North, Robert   79978
Nur-el-Din, M.A.   79160; 79376; 79377

Ochsenschlager, E.L.   79522
Ockinga, Boyo G.   79227
O'Connor, David   79021; 79547; 79548
Oden, Robert A., Jr.   79306
Oerter, Wolf B.   79064
Ogdon, Jorge Roberto   79228; 79229; 79855; 79979
Oliver, Andrew   79582
O'Mara, Patrick F.   79307
Onascn, Christian   791066
Osing, Jürgen   79190; 79447; 79980
Otte, M.   79557
Otten, Heinrich   79481

Padró, J.   79921
Paolini, Lucia   79364
Parker, Richard A.   79632
Parlasca, Klaus   79607; 79796
Parrott, Douglas M.   79405
Paulissen, E.   79557
Peck, William H.   79703
Pépin, Jean   79131
Peremans, W.   79876

Perepelkin, Yu. Y.   79448
Pérez Die, Maria Carmen   79613
Pernigotti, Sergio   79365; 79378; 79406
Peterson, Bengt   79011; 79022; 79672; 79673
Pezin, Michel   79362; 79379
Pickavance, K.M.   79023
Plumley, J. Martin   79981
Pomerantseva, N.A.   79797
Porter, Bertha   79097
Pósa, V.   791013
Posener, Georges   79024; 79066; 79308; 79309
Posener-Kriéger, P.   79161; 79356; 79357
Presedo Velo, F.J.   79533; 79549
Preston, R.M.F.   79561
Prickett, Martha   79574
Priese, Karl-Heinz   791067
Promińska, Elżbieta   791068
Pusch, Edgar B.   79762

Quaegebeur, Jan   79380; 79720; 79860; 79896
Quecke, Hans   79407

Rabinovitch, Abraham   79725
Rainey, Anson F.   79982
Ramond, Pierre   79763
Ratié, Suzanne   79449
Raven, Maarten J.   79674
Ray, J.D.   79524
Redford, Donald B.   79067; 79132; 79310; 79311; 79450; 79550
Reeves, C.N.   79312; 79675
Reineke, Walter F.   79032; 79897; 79937
Reinhold, Jacques   791030
Reiser-Haslauer, Elfriede   79587
Ridley, R.T.   79313
Ringgren, Helmer   79861
Robins, Gay   79877
Robinson, James M.   79068; 79397; 79405; 79408
Roccati, Alessandro   79191; 79252; 79340; 79590
Römer, Malte   79878
Roero, Silvia Clara   79933
Rössler-Köhler, Ursula   79341
Rogers, J. Michael   79607
Romano, James F.   79139; 79607
Romer, John   79551
Root, Margaret Cool   79614
Roquet, Gérard   79192
Rosenblatt, Arthur   79615
Rosenvasser, A.   79253; 79451
Rossiter, Evelyn   79342
Rostron, P.R.   79798

Rubinstein, R.I.   79343
Ruffle, John   79416; 79906
Ruprecht, Eberhard   79417
Russmann, Edna R.   79603; 79764
Ruszczyc, Barbara   79879
Ružička, Rudolf   791069

Sachs, J.   79098
Sadek, A.A.   79647
Sadek, Ashraf I.   79344
Salamon, Á.   791013
Saleh, A.   79193
Samson, Julia   79452
Satzinger, Helmut   79194; 79587; 79676
Sauneron, S.   79948
Säve-Söderbergh, Torgny   791070
el-Sawi, Ahmed   79525; 79526
el-Sayed, Abdullah   79552
Sayed, Abdel-Monem A.H.   79570
el-Sayed, Ramadan   79230; 79254; 79255
Sayed Youssef, A.   79643
Schachermeyr, Fritz   79482
Schaden, Otto J.   79553
Schenkel, Wolfgang   79069; 79070; 79195; 79983; 791071
Schild, Romuald   79899; 791084
Schmandt-Besserat, Denise   79947
Schneider, Hans D.   79617
Schoedel, William R.   79405
Schott, Erika   79099; 79677; 79932
Schürkes, P.   79502
Schulman, Alan R.   79231; 79256; 79483; 79484; 79818
Schumann-Antelme, R.   79643
Schwager, Klaus   79687; 79831; 79833; 79929
Schwartz, Jean-Claude   79938
Sée, G.   79100
Seebass, Horst   79984
Seefried, Monique   79765
Seidl, Erwin   79381
Seipel, W.   79453
Selem, Petar   79133
Servers, Veronica   79759
Seton-Williams, M.V.   79633
Seyfried, Karl-Joachim   79101
Shafrawi, Galal   79554
Shea, William H.   79485
Shiloh, Yigal   79799
Shimy, M.   79257
Shinnie, P.L.   79459; 79922
Shirun Grumach, Irene   79314
Shore, A.F.   79409; 79726
Šilar, Jan   791003
Silvano, Flora   79364
Silverman, David   79021

Simpson, William Kelly 79258; 79527; 79634; 79678
Sist, Loredana C. 79259; 79679
Śliwa, Joachim 79260; 79541
Smelik, K.A.D. 79856; 79857
Smith, H.S. 79058; 79147; 79528; 79561
Smith, M. 79382
Smith, Patricia 79560
Smitskamp, Rijk 79025
Solmsen, Friedrich 79134
Spalinger, Anthony 79196; 79454; 79455; 79456; 79457; 79486; 79487; 79488; 79985
Spencer, A.J. 79656, 79657
Spencer, Jeffrey 79529
Spies, Otto 79315
Stadelmann, Rainer 79848
Staehelin, Elisabeth 79331
Stahl-Guinand, Bérengère 79583
Steinmann, Frank 79618
Stewart, H.M. 79619
Stierlin, Henri 79148
Störk, Lothar 79135; 79986
Stol, M. 79956
Stós-Fertner, Z. 79503
Strange, John 79923
Stricker, B.H. 79136; 79854
Strouhal, Eugen 79495; 79523; 79939; 791003; 791004; 791005; 791006; 791007; 791008; 791009; 791072; 791073; 791074; 791075; 791076
Stuart, P. 79620
Szentléleky, T. 79137
Szolc, Piotr 79862

Tadema, Auke A. 79635
Tadema Sporry, Bob 79635; 79858
Tadmor, Hayim 79489
Tait, W.J. 79383
el-Tanbouli, M.A.L. 79647; 79819
Tapp, E. 791000; 791001
de Tassigny, C. 791010
Taylor, Jules 79139
Tawfik, Sayed 79704; 79820
Tefnin, Roland 79504; 79680
Tenand Ulmann, S. 79642
Théodoridès, Aristide 79197; 79232; 79358
Thirion, Michelle 79233
Thissen, Heinz-Josef 79384; 79385
Thomas, Angela P. 79705
Thomas, Elizabeth 79658; 79957
Thorel, G. 79643
Thurman Christa C. Mayer 791077
Török, László 791013; 791078; 791079
Toomer, G.J. 79098

Trad, May 79102
Tran Tam Tinh, [V.] 79138
Traunecker, Claude 79261; 79458
Trigger, Bruce G. 79071; 79706; 791080
Trolle, Steffen, 79924
Troy, Lana 79434
Tutundzič, S.P. 79925

Uherek, Zdeněk 79523
Uphill, E.P. 79103
Urbaneč, Zdenek 79495

Vachala, Břetislav 79316; 79530; 79531; 79681; 79707; 79800; 79880; 79881
Valbelle, Dominique 79555; 79637
Valloggia, Michel 79345; 79571; 79572
Vandersleyen, Claude 79682; 79708
Van Elderen, Bastiaan 79556
Van Gerven, Dennis P. 791081
Van Siclen, Charles C. 79907
Varga, Edith 79683
Vercoutter, Jean 79072; 79073; 79074; 79926; 791082
Verga, Silvana 79784
Vermaseren, M.J. 79130; 79844; 79856
Vermeersch, P.M. 79557
Verner, Miroslav 79264; 79359; 79523; 79532
Vernus, Pascal 79317; 79346; 79573; 79821
Vila, André 791083
Vinogradov, I.V. 79360
Viola, Tullio 79933
Vittmann, G. 79104; 79908
Vleeming, Sven P. 79898
Vodoz, Irene 79785
Vorbichler, A. 791050
Vycichl, Werner 79318
Vyhnánek, Luboš 791008; 791009

Wagner, Guy 79562
Wahba, Gamal 79691
van de Walle, B. 79835
van Walsem, R. 79727
Waltke, Bruce K. 79418
Wångstedt, Sten V. 79386
Ward, William A. 79490
Wassef, Mohga 79241
Watson, Adrienne 79766
Watson, P.J. 79198
Watterson, Barbara 79319
Weber, Manfred 79616
Weeks, Kent R. 79075; 79987
Weidmuller, Wilhelm 79162
Weippert, Manfred 79491

Wendorf, Fred   79899; 791084
Wenig, Steffen   791085; 791086
Wente, Edward F.   79320; 79636; 79997
Werner, Edward K.   79105; 79709
Wertime, Theodore A.   79947
Wessetzky, Vilmos   79076; 79077; 79767
Westendorf, Wolfhart   79095; 79199; 79822
Whitcomb, Donald S.   79065; 79574
Whitley, Charles F.   79419
Wieckowska, Hanna   79899
Wild, Henri   79262; 79638
Wild, J.P.   791000
Wildung, Dietrich   79078; 79505; 79621
Wilkes, J.J.   79519
Wilkinson, Charles K.   79622
Williams, Bruce   79065; 791077
Williams, Ellen Reeder   79684
Williams, Francis E.   79405
Wilson, R. McL.   79405
Winlock, Herbert   79536
Winter, Erich   79639; 79728
Wisse, Frederik   79405; 79410
de Wit, Constant   79163
Witakowski, Witold   79492
Wolff, Hans Julius   79387

Worsham, Charles E.   79710
Wright, G.R.H.   79420; 79838
Wysocki, Zygmunt   79558; 79559

Yamauchi, Edwin M.   79421
Yellin, Janice W.   791087
Yoshimura, Sakuji   79149
Youssef, Ahmad Abdel-Hamid   79200; 79263; 79648
Youssef, Sayed A.   79643
Yoyotte, Jean   79079; 79080; 79601
Yurco, Frank J.   79685; 79686

Žába†, Zbyněk   79264; 79523
Žabkar, L.V.   791088
Zadok, Ran   79493
Zamarovský, Vojtěch   79150
Zauzich, K.-Th.   79081; 79371; 79388; 79389; 79390
Zawadowsky, Y.N.   79164
Zibelius, Karola   79988; 79989
Ziegler, Christiane   79265; 79623; 79729; 79768; 79769; 79770
Zimmerman, Michael R.   791011
van Zinderen-Bakker, E.M.   79557
Zivie, Alan-Pierre   79266; 79640; 79711; 79730; 79849
Zonhoven, L.M.J.   79032; 79361